RADIO WARS

RADIO WARS
Truth, Propaganda and the Struggle for Radio Australia

ERROL HODGE

School of Media and Journalism
Queensland University of Technology

CAMBRIDGE
UNIVERSITY PRESS

Published by the Press Syndicate of the University of Cambridge
The Pitt Building, Trumpington Street, Cambridge CB2 1RP, UK
40 West 20th Street, New York NY 10011–4211, USA
10 Stamford Road, Oakleigh, Melbourne 3166, Australia

Printed in Hong Kong by Colorcraft

National Library of Australia cataloguing-in-publication data

Hodge, Errol.
Radio wars; truth, propaganda and the struggle for Radio
Australia.
Bibliography.
Includes index
1. Radio Australia – History. 2. International
broadcasting – Political aspects. 3. International
broadcasting – Australia. I. Title.
384.5406594

Library of Congress cataloguing-in-publication data

Hodge, Errol, 1936–
Radio wars: truth, propaganda and the struggle for radio
Australia / Errol Hodge.
Includes bibliographical references and index.
1. Radio Australia – History. 2. International broadcasting –
Australia – History. I. Title.
HE8697.45.A8H63   1995   94–35093
384.54'06'594–dc20   CIP

A catalogue record for this book is available from the British Library.

ISBN 0 521 47380 2 Hardback

Contents

Illustrations

---

facing page 224

A Brief Chronology of Radio Australia

1939	Prime Minister Menzies launches shortwave service 'Australia Calling'. His speech translated into French, Spanish, German, Dutch.
1940–5	Worldwide broadcasts in English; for brief periods German, Dutch and French to Europe, Afrikaans, Spanish, Italian; from mid-1940 French to Southeast Asia and New Caledonia; from 1941 Dutch to Indonesia; from 1942 Indonesian, Japanese, Thai; from 1943 Mandarin, Cantonese, occasionally Fukienese; in 1945 New Guinea pidgin. Propaganda programs prepared by Department of Information; music and presentation by ABC.
1942–4	Control passes to ABC, but news and commentary programs directed by Department of External Affairs.
1944	Control reverts to Department of Information.
1945–9	Broadcasts in English, French, Dutch, Indonesian, Thai; German (from 1948). Music and programs designed to attract migrants. No commentaries on international issues or unfavourable to government.

1950 Department of Information abolished by new Menzies government. Radio Australia transferred to ABC. Broadcasts in German and Dutch eliminated. Broadcasts continue in English, Indonesian, French and Thai, Mandarin—later 'Standard Chinese' (from 1956), Japanese (1960-90), Vietnamese (from 1962), Cantonese (from 1964), Simple English for Papua New Guinea (1973–93), Papua New Guinea Pidgin—later 'Tok Pisin' (from 1974), Khmer (from 1992).

1950– Pressure from Department of External Affairs (later
c. 1975 Foreign Affairs) to use Radio Australia as an instrument in Cold War. Struggle between department and defenders of Radio Australia's editorial integrity, notably ABC Chairmen Richard Boyer and James Darling and ABC and Radio Australia journalists Walter Hamilton and John Hall. Pressure abates in early 1970s, and Radio Australia virtually independent of Foreign Affairs by mid-1970s.

1950–72 News commentaries as instrument of Cold War.

1965 External Affairs Minister Paul Hasluck tries to have Radio Australia moved to Canberra and put under his department's control. Move frustrated by department secretary, James Plimsoll.

1970 Booster station near Darwin completed.

1974 Darwin station destroyed by Cyclone Tracy.

1975 Indonesia invades East Timor, which is incorporated into Indonesia 1976.

1979–80 'Thought liberation' in China. Radio Australia receives 183,000 letters from People's Republic. (Record total of 566,000 letters for year also includes 198,000 letters in Indonesian and 123,000 from 'overseas Chinese'.)

1980 ABC correspondent Warwick Beutler expelled from Indonesia.

1991 ABC returns to Indonesia. Dili massacre.

1993 Australia Television launched, broadcasting by satellite to all or part of fifteen countries.

Chief Executives of Radio Australia

Chief executives of Radio Australia have had different titles at different times, including Supervisor of Programs (Overseas), Director Overseas Programs, Director Overseas Services, Director Radio Australia, General Manager Radio Australia and General Manager ABC International Broadcasting.

William Macmahon Ball	1940–4
Geoffrey Sawer	1944–5
Thomas Hoey	1946–50
Robin Wood	1950–6
Peter Homfray	1957–75
Philip Koch	1975–80
Peter Barnett	1980–9
Richard Broinowski	1991–2
Derek White	1992–

Abbreviations

ABC	Australian Broadcasting Commission, *later* Corporation
AFP	Agence France Presse
AIDAB	Australian International Development and Assistance Bureau
ANIB	Australian News and Information Bureau
ANZUS Pact	Security treaty between Australia, New Zealand and the United States of America
ASEAN	Association of South-East Asian Nations
ASIO	Australian Secret Intelligence Organisation
ASIS	Australian Secret Intelligence Service
BBC	British Broadcasting Corporation
DEA	Department of External Affairs
DFA(T)	Department of Foreign Affairs (and Trade)
Fretilin	Revolutionary Front for Independent Timor
NIGIS	Netherlands Indies Government Information Service
OPM	Free Papua Organisation
PKI	Indonesian Communist Party
PMG	Postmaster-General
SEATO	South-East Asia Treaty Organisation
UDT	Timor Democratic Union
VOA	Voice of America

Acknowledgments

My first acknowledgment is to my late father, Harry Hodge, teacher and author, who passed on to me his love of history and politics and his fascination with struggles for power among those with faith in the rightness of their cause. I am also grateful to Dr John Dalton, of Monash University, for his enthusiastic, good-humoured and painstaking oversight of the PhD thesis which was the genesis of this book. Many of those I want to acknowledge are protagonists in the story, in particular the late Sir Hermann Black, Mr Creighton Burns, Mr Peter Homfray, Mr Philip Koch, Professor Emeritus Geoffrey Sawer and Dr Clement Semmler. Thanks are also due to Mr Goenawan Mohamad of Jakarta and Dr Zhang Wei-hong of Beijing for their help with photographs. I am grateful to Ms Liz Nathan and Mr Chris Taylor for their help with my research into documents in the archives of the Department of Foreign Affairs and Trade, many of them declassified at my request, and to Ms Pat Kelly for her help with research into ABC Document Archives. I must also acknowledge the valuable suggestions of Associate Professor Rodney Tiffen, of the University of Sydney, without whose help this book would have been far less interesting.

Errol Hodge

Introduction

Radio has revolutionised international communication. It can flash facts, ideas, and opinions (not to mention slogans and lies) across national boundaries to enormous audiences. Governments have been quick to realise the opportunities and dangers of shortwave broadcasting. It is a relatively cheap means by which one nation can project its outlook to others, even when other efforts may be blocked. 'Long-distance broadcasting cannot be confiscated at a frontier or refused a visa or be burnt in a public square.'[1] Shortwave broadcasting can reach audiences in all sections of society, including the illiterate, and those in remote areas.

The audiences for international broadcasts are highest when the domestic media are perceived as inadequate. For decades, large audiences in developing countries have found international broadcasts more attractive. Under authoritarian governments and during national crises, many people have looked to international broadcasters for more reliable news. In recent years, Radio Australia's audiences have been largest in China during the pro-democracy demonstrations and subsequent massacre in Beijing in 1989, and those in Fiji have been largest at the time of the coups of 1987. As recently as 1991, Mikhail Gorbachev, imprisoned at a *dacha* in the southern USSR, listened to BBC radio to keep in touch with developments in Moscow during the attempted military coup.

The most recent official definition of the role of Radio Australia was adopted by the board of the Australian Broadcasting Corporation and endorsed by the expenditure review committee of cabinet in mid-1990:

• to foster international understanding of Australia and to reflect Australia's perspectives on the world. In particular the service endeavours:
• to reflect the multicultural nature and socio-economic diversity of Australian society;
• to encourage a free exchange of information, ideas and knowledge, acting as a credible and responsible window on the world; and
• to foster an understanding of Australian attitudes and values while acknowledging that other attitudes and values exist.

Cabinet endorsed the view that any satisfactory formulation of Radio Australia's purposes must include:

• projecting Australian perspectives and a range of views;
• editorial independence; and
• the importance of news and information together with a high standard of cultural and entertainment programs.[2]

The international shortwave broadcasting environment, of which Radio Australia is part, is extremely competitive. More than eighty nations operate foreign radio services, and several have more than one.[3] The number of hours broadcast has continued to increase steadily over the past few decades.[4] Radio Australia broadcasts for $45^{1}/_{2}$ hours a day in nine languages: English, Indonesian, Standard Chinese (Mandarin), Cantonese, Tok Pisin (Papua New Guinea Pidgin), Vietnamese, Khmer, Thai and French. With a weekly audience of perhaps 10 million, it ranks about in the middle of major broadcasters. The Voice of America, broadcasting for 138 hours a day in forty-six languages, claimed several years ago that it had a weekly audience of about 127 million listeners (a surprisingly precise figure, which has not been updated). The BBC, which broadcasts for 125 hours a day in thirty-eight languages, claims a weekly audience of 130 million.

For more than fifty years, Radio Australia, broadcasting from Melbourne, has communicated with tens, perhaps hundreds, of millions of people in Asia and the Pacific. It has had the potential to create a favourable image of Australia—an outpost of European civilisation in an alien sea—important to its acceptance by its neighbours. It has had the potential to pave the way for Australia's integration into the region, on which the governments of the 1990s have been placing such emphasis.

But Radio Australia's strongest critics have claimed that at times it has done more harm than good. They say its insistence on the right to wash the dirty linen of the neighbours before an audience of millions of those neighbours has alienated both governments and peoples. Some critics see Radio Australia as part of the imbalance in the flow of information between the developed and the developing world, in short, as an example of cultural imperialism. What right, they ask, does Radio Australia have to preach to developing countries (albeit, in recent years, not overtly) about democracy and human rights. Some, including a former secretary of the Department of Foreign Affairs, Sir Arthur Tange, believe there is an arrogance about 'trying to impose Australian values, and Australia's system of democracy' on other countries.[5] Tange said in 1988 that he was not one of those who believed that Australia should adopt 'a missionary role, teaching other people how to have democracy'. This attitude, he believed, reflected a Eurocentric view towards the virtues of parliamentary systems of which most people had had no experience 'and probably in their best interests never should have'. He said that advocacy of an Australian duty to help other countries run 'democratic' systems and preserve human rights was based on 'an intrinsically superior sense of what we have being good for them'. The Australian democratic process, he believed, was unsuitable for societies such as that of Java. Some critics believe Radio Australia would be of more value to Australia if it simply tried to tell listeners about Australia and Australians, and avoided the minefields of trying to inform them about events in the region, including their own countries.

Many defenders of Radio Australia, on the other hand, say that by trying to present a comprehensive and accurate picture of events and issues in the world and in the region, Radio Australia is providing a valuable service the listeners do not always get from the authorities in their own countries, and is helping them to a more accurate and balanced world view. They argue that in this way it can help build a sounder basis for the relationship between Australia and its neighbours. Defenders of Radio Australia also argue that if it censored reports offensive to governments or peoples of Asian and Pacific countries, its listeners would learn not to trust its broadcasts and it would lose its value to the nation.

Australian scholar of Indonesia Professor Jamie Mackie has a foot in both camps. He says his 'line' on Radio Australia is that 'if it didn't exist you'd be mad to invent it (or at least the vernacular programs), but it does, so we must defend its freedom of speech against both our own government and others'.[6]

Since the 1930s shortwave radio has been a major instrument of information and propaganda during wars and periods of international tension. The propaganda war was particularly intense during World War II, when the military struggle between Germany and its allies, on the one hand, and Britain, the Soviet Union and their allies, on the other, had its counterpart in the propaganda war between the BBC, which established a reputation for accuracy and objectivity, Radio Moscow, with its more blatant propaganda, and the radio propaganda of Nazi Germany. The themes of Germany's broadcasts were much the same as the themes of propaganda within the Thousand-Year Reich: anti-Semitism, anti-communism, the superiority of the Aryan race and the German nation, the wisdom and power of the Führer.[7] During the war, shortwave radio was used by both sides to support the morale of military forces, other expatriates and allies. It had a similar role during the Cold War, when there was a huge increase in the amount of international broadcasting by the Soviet Union and the United States.

A British scholar, Julian Hale, has identified four main models of international broadcasting.[8] They are the Nazi model, the communist model, the 'voices of America' (exemplified mainly by the Voice of America) and the BBC model. He asserts that all four models try to do the same thing—to advance what is perceived as the national interest, although in different ways. He depicts the BBC as 'telling the truth in good times and bad, risking charges of insipidity and hypocrisy in order to establish a reputation for credibility in the long term'.[9] The American model, he says, operates 'on the middle ground of more or less single-minded commitment' to its ideology. In fact, Hale's depiction of the BBC is an idealised one, and the reality is that there have been close links between the Foreign Office and the BBC External Services (now called the World Service).

The BBC began broadcasting internationally in December 1932. An exercise in cultural imperialism in the literal sense of the words, the broadcasts were intended to strengthen the cultural (and hence, by extension, the economic and political) bonds between the motherland and the dominions and colonies. Although its wartime broadcasts established a reputation for credibility by telling the bad news along with the good, it was careful never to tell *all* the bad news.

The American model was the last of the four to begin. The Voice of America, which began broadcasting in February 1942, is part of the United States Information Agency, under the direct control of the State Department. There is little attempt to conceal the fact that it is an instrument of foreign policy.

As ABC Chairman Richard (later Sir Richard) Boyer described it in 1950, 'the tendency of the United States is to become more and more polemic. In their own words, to kill the big lie with the big truth.'[10] Another who saw the American broadcasters in this light was general manager Charles (later Sir Charles) Moses. Commenting in 1956 on Radio Australia's first place in the triennial popularity poll of the International

Shortwave Club, he told the ABC commissioners, 'It is notable that the Voice of America, which is a frankly propaganda service, came sixth in the 1956 poll, with 6.36% of votes, whereas our percentage was 17.47%.'[11]

The Voice of America is not without its admirers in Australia, despite a general tendency to disparage it. Malcolm Booker, a former External Affairs officer who was for many years responsible for briefing Radio Australia, said in 1989 that he believed the VOA largely achieved its objectives, very often in the face of strong anti-American sentiment. In the Philippines, for example, the VOA was a thoroughly professional organ-isation of very skilled propaganda experts: 'They know how to plant disin-formation; they know how to frighten people and play on the fears of people.'[12] Tange said in 1988 that he thought the Voice of America much more effective than Radio Australia. He believed it was largely responsible for the fact that the Philippines still had a pro-American government, despite the fall of Marcos.[13]

The differences between the American and British models have been largely a matter of degree. Although the BBC World Service is an integral part of the BBC, its degree of independence is qualified by the licence and agreement of 1981, which names the Foreign Office, together with the Ministry of Defence and the Board of Trade, as the prescribing depart-ments of government which may state the extent of the activities of the World Service.[14] The most important power of all is control of the purse-strings. Radio Australia is funded by the ABC. Britain's external broadcast-ing is funded entirely from grants-in-aid by the British government, with no funds at all coming from the BBC's budget. The Foreign Office is responsible for recommending to Treasury how much should be granted to the World Service. Even though BBC spokesmen deny that in this case the piper plays the tune of him who pays, financial dependence is obviously a very strong incentive to cooperation.

The differences between BBC practice and that of the Voice of America are partly the BBC's success in creating an *illusion* of objectivity. But a significant difference is that the Voice of America is directly con-trolled by government, whereas the BBC World Service is to an extent insulated from government pressures by a statutory body.

Throughout its history, Radio Australia has inevitably presented a world viewpoint both from an Australian perspective and a Western and developed-world perspective. The international news broadcast by Radio Australia originates either from Radio Australia's own correspondents or from Western news agencies, owned in and directed from the developed world. All its news and current affairs programs, including, until recent years, those broadcast in foreign languages, have been prepared by journalists who are almost entirely Australian. Radio Australia has been perceived, and correctly perceived, as contributing to the imbalance in the flow of information which has led most Third World countries to support calls in the United Nations for a new world information order.

The bias towards Australia, the West and the developed world has affected not only the news and current affairs programs.[15] Almost all of those broadcasting general programs in English have been Australians. Furthermore, the executives in charge of all foreign-language sections have been either Australian citizens or long-term residents.[16] Some of the foreign-language broadcasters working under their direction have been naturalised Australians. Even those not naturalised have tended to be Australian in outlook because they have been living in Australia (most of them for many years) and because they have been conscious of working for an organisation which, in some senses, has been an organ of Australian propaganda.

During World War II, Radio Australia operated on the American model. It was run by the Department of Information, except for two wartime years when it was administered by the ABC. But the most significant news and commentary programs throughout the war were run by the Department of External Affairs as part of the war effort, basically as an organ of war propaganda. After the war, direct government control of Radio Australia continued through the Department of Information. It was only when the department was dismantled by the Menzies government in 1950, and Radio Australia was transferred again to the ABC, that its operation became closer to the BBC model.

Nevertheless, during the Cold War, there were persistent attempts by governments and officers of the Department of External Affairs to push Radio Australia towards the American model. The department, seeing Radio Australia as a weapon of great potential in the Cold War, constantly contested control of the service, and would probably have succeeded had it not been for the resistance of a few champions within the ABC (including Radio Australia itself). As some of these attempts were successful (as, for example, with the news commentaries), it cannot be stated unequivocally that the service during this period was run along the lines of the idealised BBC model, though it may often have been close to the way the BBC External Services operated in practice.

In the more liberal 1970s, 1980s and early 1990s, Radio Australia, increasingly with the support of the Department of Foreign Affairs, conformed more closely to the idealised BBC model of international broadcasting. In some ways Australia's international broadcasters have in recent years operated more independently of governments and the Department of Foreign Affairs (now Foreign Affairs and Trade) than their British counterparts. But this has not meant that they have approached absolute objectivity, even if such a goal could be achieved by human beings. Radio Australia has always been subjected to numerous pressures and influences which ensure that its outlook is inevitably Western, Australian and fairly closely aligned with that of the government of the day. Radio Australia remains, as it has always been, part of the imbalance in the flow of information between developed and developing countries.

This book is called *Radio Wars* because warfare of a kind has raged around Australia's international shortwave service for much of its fifty-five years of existence. At different times there have been conflicts between Radio Australia and foreign governments, between Radio Australia and Australian governments and their departments, especially Foreign Affairs, and between Radio Australia and the ABC. The popularity of shortwave has often been a threat to those governments which seek to control what their citizens hear. The contest between the Indonesian authorities and Radio Australia, with its huge Indonesian audience, became particularly virulent after the invasion of East Timor in 1975. Domestically, Radio Australia's struggle for independence from Foreign Affairs lasted more than twenty years. More recently, Radio Australia has sometimes struggled with its parent organisation, the ABC, which neglected it despite its huge audiences. Decisions affecting Radio Australia have often been made primarily for the benefit of the larger ABC.

Can Radio Australia survive its last battle—to maintain its viability and influence in the age of satellite television? And will Australia Television, which may eventually replace it, attach the same importance to credibility, and fight its own battle for independence?

1   Radio Australia at war, 1939—1949

Radio Australia was hastily created by the first Menzies government within a few months of the outbreak of World War II in Europe. Originally named 'Australia Calling', it was created as an instrument of war to explain Australia's (and Britain's) wartime policies to the peoples of the countries (mainly, in those days, colonies) of Asia and the Pacific. Opening the service in Melbourne on 20 December 1939, Prime Minister Menzies said:

> Our reasons for establishing broadcasts of this kind may be quite simply stated. We have decided that over some of the propaganda stations to which you listen, so many strange things are said, not only about Australia, but about the whole of the British Empire, that the time has come to speak for ourselves ... My purpose is to tell you something about Australia and the war. Something about why it is that although we are twelve thousand miles from Europe we are nevertheless involved in a European war and in full partnership with Great Britain in its conduct.[1]

The opening address was translated into German, French, Dutch and Spanish, and regular broadcasts in these languages began the following year. Italian was introduced, albeit briefly, in 1940 and Japanese in 1942, not long after Japan's entry into the war.

There had been calls for an Australian international shortwave service for some years before the war, and hasty plans to launch it were under way by the time Hitler invaded Poland. But in those early days it was a rudimentary operation run on a shoestring: its initial budget was to be not more than £50 a week (five months later raised to £140 a week). Beginning its life in wartime, Radio Australia was immediately thrust into bureaucratic politics without a tradition to sustain its autonomy.

The ABC had appointed a young New South Wales talks officer, George Ivan Smith (who later rose to the most senior position yet held by an Australian in the United Nations Secretariat, Director of External Relations)[2] to work part-time as officer-in-charge of presentation for the opening broadcasts in Sydney, while continuing in his substantive position. The *International Who's Who* said Smith was 'Director of Australian Short-Wave Services' from 1939 to 1941,[3] but in fact his position (at the age of twenty-three) was far less exalted, and his involvement (until early 1940) far briefer.

The 1969 edition of the Radio Australia publication *The Constant Voice*, issued to mark the thirtieth anniversary of the service, blandly asserted that, in wartime, it 'gave factual and objective news—no matter how bad—about the war'.[4] This statement is demonstrably false. Despite the belief of its first director, William Macmahon Ball, that in theory it was desirable to tell the bad news along with the good, if only to build a reputation for credibility, there were constant compromises. Ball realised that in wartime there was a limit to how much truth could be told on the short-wave service. Not surprisingly, much unpalatable news was glossed over or excluded altogether. Even before Japan entered the war, Ball stated unequivocally, 'Many events that make good news stories in the local press—strikes, industrial troubles, political rivalries, crimes—are excluded from our service.'[5] Aged thirty-eight when the war broke out, William Macmahon Ball had been educated at the University of Melbourne, and during the 1930s had studied political science in Britain, Germany, France and the United States. He was to become Professor of Political Science at Melbourne University in 1949, and Emeritus Professor in 1968.

Interviewed in 1980 for an ABC radio program about Radio Australia's war years, Ball was, understandably, considerably more frank about the propagandist nature of the service than he had been during the war:

A war was on, and however much you may deplore it, we were largely a propaganda service. We were trying to tell the world what a wonderful country Australia was, what a wonderful pride we had in lining up first of all with the United Kingdom, and of course, with the outbreak of the Pacific war, lining up with the United States, how proud we were of our allies, what wonderful allies they were, how they stood for freedom, civilisation and everything else, and how very unpleasant the enemy countries were.

Though conceding that Radio Australia had been 'largely a propaganda service', Ball claimed that the propaganda had rarely been crude.

We tried, and with some success I think, to avoid the crudest types of propaganda—the crudest types that indulged in trying to distinguish between races and speaking of the Japanese as an inferior race. We did everything in our power to avoid that kind of thing, but undoubtedly our news commentaries and our talks were propaganda. They were strongly biased in favour of the allies, against the enemy.[6]

Not only did Ball recognise the realities of wartime broadcasting, but ultimate control of the service lay in the hands of two government departments, the Department of Information and the Department of External Affairs. Even during the two years the service was nominally run by the ABC (July 1942 to April 1944), its news and commentaries were controlled by the Department of External Affairs.

One of the many examples of the glossing over of unpalatable news was the way the service reported (or more often failed to report) the bombing of Darwin between February 1942 and November 1943. The Japanese were making (exaggerated) reports of air-raids on Australian towns in their shortwave broadcasts to Asia and the Pacific, so it was considered politic for the Australian service to concede that some such raids had taken place. The Australian broadcasts, however, gave no indication of the extent or frequency of the raids, and certainly made no admission of the devastation in the first raids on Darwin, on 19 February 1942, or the disgraceful behaviour of Australian and American servicemen in its aftermath. In fact, the extent of the disaster was not revealed to Australians themselves until several months later. In the two initial Japanese attacks on Darwin, about 250 people were killed[7] and about 350 wounded. A force of 242 Zero fighters sank an American destroyer, two American transports, a British tanker and an Australian transport, merchant ship, lugger and coal hulk, and destroyed twenty-three allied aircraft, many of them on the ground. Hundreds of civilians, expecting invasion, fled southward, and some air force units were 'temporarily dispersed'.[8] By far the most shameful aspect was the behaviour of members of the armed forces after the raids. Hundreds of them, both Australians and Americans, systematically looted what had been left behind by the fleeing civilians.[9] The military police joined in with the others. The Minister for Territories, Paul Hasluck, described it as a day of 'national shame'.[10] News of the disaster and its aftermath was so tightly suppressed that, two days afterwards, the *Age* put the death toll at fifteen.[11] It was not surprising that Radio Australia carefully avoided giving the Japanese any clue of the success of the raid, and never fully revealed the truth.

The most overtly counter-propagandist of its programs was given the title, 'The Truth of It Is …'. More than ten months after the first raid on Darwin, its producer, Reginald Drake, mocked the exaggerated claims of

Berlin Radio about Japanese raids on Darwin and other Australian cities. He pointed out that some of the raids reported by the Germans not only had not happened, they had not been reported by the Japanese.[12] But significantly, in that program Drake made no reference at all to the devastating first raids on Darwin, or to the extent of the damage wrought in those or subsequent attacks. The Japanese, of course, would have had some idea through aerial surveillance how many ships had been sunk, how many planes had been destroyed and how widespread had been the damage to buildings. But it would have been bad for the morale of the people in the occupied territories, and for Australia's allies, if Australia's shortwave service had even hinted at the devastation. There were sixty-four air-raids on Darwin between February 1942 and November 1943.[13] Radio Australia never revealed that there had been anything like that number.

In contrast with its coverage of the Japanese air raids on Darwin, Radio Australia's reporting of the Japanese midget submarine attack on Sydney Harbour in 1942 was fairly accurate. Two midget submarines had entered Sydney Harbour on the night of 31 May 1942. One fired torpedoes at the American cruiser USS *Chicago*, and missed, but a torpedo hit an Australian barracks ship, HMAS *Kuttabul*, killing nineteen men. Both submarines were destroyed, and their two-man crews killed.[14] The Japanese were broadcasting exaggerated accounts, claiming that one of the submarines had sunk a warship. It is possible that they believed the attack on the *Chicago* had been successful. Ball's deputy, Geoffrey Sawer, recalled in 1988, 'Our instruction from the military censorship people was to tell the whole story because it was a credible story.' He remembered a feeling in the shortwave service that 'the fact of our reporting it would be a plus'. 'Needless to say,' he added, 'we did not report the hasty removal from Sydney of so many thousands of Sydney residents who came to the conclusion that the country was being occupied, and the general state of alarm which this created: we made no mention of that.'[15]

The explanation for the different treatment by the shortwave service of the Darwin and Sydney raids may well have been that the Darwin raids, particularly the first one, were a military setback with few if any redeeming features, the magnitude of which was not generally known among Australia's allies or in the enemy-occupied territories. On the other hand, the submarine raids on Sydney inflicted only minor damage, and were in any case widely reported in the Australian and overseas media.[16]

A sensitive subject which the propagandists believed would give aid and comfort to the enemy was the widespread tension between American and Australian servicemen.[17] This topic was never touched by Radio Australia. The 'propaganda lines' which guided its writers prescribed that they should foster amity between the allies.[18] In its broadcasts to the United States, the service tried to give news and information about 'the friendly co-operation between them [the American troops] and Australians'[19] A script fed to the shortwave service by the director-general of public relations for the Department of the Army typified the propaganda that was sometimes used. It said, in part:

'Firm comradeship had been formed between American and Australian troops in the forward areas,' said Lieutenant E. Fouracre, of Essendon, Melbourne, Victoria, who recently returned to the mainland after nine months in New Guinea. 'The Americans are good fighters and share with the Australians whatever they have,' he said.[20]

It is scarcely surprising that Radio Australia made no reference to the 'Battle of Brisbane', the mass fighting between thousands of Australian and American soldiers that raged for three hours in Brisbane on 26 November 1942.[21] Even though shots fired by an American military policeman killed one Australian soldier and wounded others, and scores of soldiers were injured, some seriously,[22] the service that supposedly 'gave factual and objective news—no matter how bad' never breathed a word about the riot.[23] If Radio Australia had reported the 'Battle of Brisbane', the Japanese shortwave broadcasters, who were concentrating their attacks on Japan's major enemy, the USA,[24] would no doubt have exploited the news with enthusiasm.

White Australia

Another subject that was prohibited on the shortwave service (and discouraged in the domestic media) was the white Australia policy. The propagandists believed reference to it could alienate some of Australia's allies and help the Japanese to drive a wedge between those allies and Australia. Early in 1943, in a secret directive, Ball told those responsible for transmissions in Mandarin that they must eschew all colour-consciousness. He continued: 'This does not mean denouncing the White Australia policy, but it does mean playing it down … It even means avoiding any contemptuous reference to the Japanese, where the contempt might in any way be associated with colour-consciousness.'[25] Prime Minister Curtin told an off-the-record press briefing later in 1943 that even a mention of the policy could be used by Australia's enemies as the foundation for propaganda designed to promote disunity among the allies.[26]

Victoria's state publicity censor, Crayton Burns (father of Creighton Burns, later a news commentator for Radio Australia) notified Ball that 'no reference may be made to any US soldier's colour. The use of the term "negro", "black" or "coloured" is to be avoided.'[27] It was permissible to refer to the work of black trackers in tracking missing airmen within the continental limits of Australia, but (for some reason) no reference might be made to the employment of 'Australian natives' on similar work in adjacent islands.[28] Thomas Hoey, who succeeded Burns as state publicity censor, and was later to succeed Ball as controller of the shortwave service (see chapter 11), issued a directive that 'Comments on the American racial problem by US Service personnel in the South-West Pacific area must be submitted to censorship and will normally be disallowed.'[29]

The propagandists had to be aware of cultural sensitivities as well as racial ones. In the first month of broadcasting, translators pointed out some pitfalls in a statement by Menzies on 15 January 1940: 'I can see no permanent peace in the world except under the guardianship of the English speaking people.' This, it was pointed out, would be 'unpalatable to all except English [presumably British] and American listeners.' For the French, it would have been better to say 'under the guardianship of democratic people'. For the Germans, it would have been better to leave out any reference to placing the world under the guardianship of any particular people.[30]

References to European colonialism were also handled with care. Before Japan entered the war, references to British colonialism in broadcasts to Asia tended to be somewhat apologetic. Ball issued the following guidance for a talk for Southeast and Northeast Asia on Empire Day (24 May), 1941:

Whatever defects or failures there may have been in British Colonial policy, native races know well the difference between Nazi oppression with the inevitable tyranny that springs from the Nazi racial consciousness, and British imperial rule. It is the policy of the British Empire in dealing with colonial people to help them gradually to achieve a fuller measure of freedom and independence. This is still a fact even though sometimes Britain seems to have been tardy in encouraging this process.[31]

After Japan's occupation of the colonies of Southeast Asia, the apologetic tone was replaced by contrasts between Japanese oppression and the enlightenment of the former regimes.

Throughout the Pacific war, stories of Japanese heroism were generally avoided. In late 1943, the following directive was received from the Allied Political Warfare Committee in Canberra:

That stories playing-up Japanese fighting to the death should be discouraged, and the desertion of Japanese soldiers by their officers given full publicity; and that action should be taken both in Australia and in all other Allied countries with the aim of preventing the publication of stories playing up Japanese heroism, sacrifice and invincibility as individuals; such stories from Allied sources being found most useful by the Japanese as propaganda material to occupied territories.[32]

Later, at the 'request' of allied general headquarters in Brisbane, the self-sacrifice of the kamikaze pilots went unreported.[33]

A related subject touched on with extreme caution was the attempted breakout by Japanese prisoners of war at the Featherston Camp in New Zealand in 1943 in which forty-eight of them were killed. The secretary of the Department of External Affairs, Colonel W. R. Hodgson, told Ball that his minister (Dr H. V. Evatt) was particularly concerned at the possible Japanese reaction to news of the incident, and had directed that a full official account be made available to him to help him to counter enemy broadcasts if necessary.[34] Hodgson told Ball to play up the large numbers of prisoners, to indicate that the Japanese were surrendering freely, and to report that they were well fed, content and happy to be out of the miseries of war.[35] A few days later, a secret, decoded message from the United States Office of War Information said: 'The official British report on the Prison Camp Incident is that it should be treated factually, and comment should be that it is known all over the world that the British [who presumably included the New Zealanders] treat their prisoners well.'[36] Predictably, the Japanese were far from satisfied. Referring to the 'murder' of the prisoners, they warned: 'The Japanese Government regards this incident as a precedent to justify any action it may have to take in similar circumstances.'[37]

Eighteen months later, Australia had a breakout on a much larger scale. On 5 August 1944, more than 1100 Japanese prisoners launched a mass escape attempt at Cowra in central western New South Wales. During the massacre that followed, 231 Japanese and four Australian soldiers were killed.[38] Curtin feared that if any hint of the incident reached the enemy before the official investigation and report by the protecting power (Switzerland), 'the interests of a large number of Australians held prisoner of war might be seriously prejudiced'.[39] Partly because of the fear of reprisals against Australian prisoners, but for other reasons as well, the Department of External Affairs gave direct instructions that the breakout should not be mentioned on the shortwave service. Sawer later explained:

They thought it would be almost impossible to give a credible explanation of this to the Japanese in terms that would do anything else than encourage them. Our advice was that this would be treated as lies. The Japanese wouldn't believe either (a) that they had ever been taken prisoner, or (b) that they should have been so incompetent and cowardly as not to gloriously slaughter enormous quantities of whites before they in turn died. This was exactly what all three of our Japanese advisers said: 'Don't touch it: whichever way you do this it will be counter productive.'[40]

So the bloodiest massacre in Australia's history went unreported by the shortwave service.

The issue of Japanese atrocities was related. In the United States, representatives of the British and American governments had been preparing propaganda about atrocities in the hope of securing better Japanese treatment of prisoners of war. In January 1944, President Roosevelt ordered the American chiefs of staff to release to the Office of War Information all details of Japanese atrocities with a view to their publication. He had been prompted by the impending publication in the *Chicago Tribune* and other papers of unauthorised and unverified stories.[41] The issue was a racial minefield. The Washington Combined Emergencies Propaganda Committee instructed that in propaganda to China and India, 'Japanese atrocities against Americans and Europeans must always be linked with atrocities against Asiatics and never reported alone.' For propaganda to occupied Asia, the instruction was, 'Link atrocities against Occidentals with atrocities against Orientals.'[42]

Evatt added his own instructions to the directive from Washington relayed to Australia's shortwave service. As well as passing on the instruction to link atrocities against 'Americans and Europeans' (including Australians) with those against 'Asiatics', he directed that only officially authorised British accounts of Japanese atrocities, such as a statement by the British Foreign Secretary, Anthony Eden, in the House of Commons, were to be broadcast from Australia. Furthermore, Evatt tried to provide an escape hatch for the Japanese as a whole. He directed Australian propagandists to suggest that irresponsible military personnel in more remote territories had caused Japan to lose prestige: that the effect of atrocities, for which the Japanese military leadership was responsible, was to put Japanese nationals as a whole beyond the pale of civilisation.[43]

Soon stories began to emerge about the infamous Burma railway. The censor issued an instruction that, except for official announcements, no reference was permissible to the conditions under which Australian and other allied prisoners were living and working in Thailand and Burma.[44]

Political warfare

Those working in wartime shortwave were encouraged to accentuate the positive as well as to eliminate the negative. The positive, in this context was any even marginally credible 'line' which would advance the allied cause. Australia's positive propaganda campaign began in earnest with the launching of political warfare against Japan in the second half of 1942.[45] Directives listed in a document entitled 'Guidance for Action on Aim I of the British and American Plan of Political Warfare against Japan', issued in August 1942, included: 'Attempt to shake the faith of the Japanese in their government by showing the faulty and dishonourable nature of Japanese leadership … Harp on the fact that the Japanese are hated by all.' This was followed by the remarkable assertion: 'The Japanese cannot make friends in any circumstances.' The directives continued:

Treatment of good news:

(a)   The facts should be reiterated simply and without exaggeration.

(b)   On no account should a minor or local success be presented as an event likely to win the war …

(c)   Having put across good news accurately and repeatedly, pick upon and ridicule Japanese distortions of the facts.

Treatment of bad news:

(a)   Present reverses factually and with dignity …

(b)   Avoid *obvious* [emphasis added] attempts to distract attention from bad news by calling attention to trivial events.

(c)   Avoid answering back …

Treatment of the war at sea:

… stress the danger of operations conducted at long distances from Japanese bases (e.g. Midway).

Treatment of the war in the air:

Indicate … that the full weight of the Allied air arm will some day be in action against them.

Treatment of the land war:

Until we achieve successes in the land war … concentrate on the training and equipment of our new armies …

Treatment of Shinto:

(a)   … stress its primitive and political aspects …

(b)   State that the rulers of Japan have … whipped up a moribund cult …

(c)   Stress on every occasion the Tribalism theme, pointing out the Japanese conception of themselves as a Herrenvolk makes it impossible for them to rule others with success …

(d)   Stress that under the State Shinto system (as under the Nazi system) higher religions are only tolerated as long as they tow [*sic*] the line …

(e)   Avoid mention of the person of the Emperor …

Treatment of atrocities:

Don't play up atrocities, unless instructed to do so from London.[46]

As for Asians in the occupied territories, a badly written, crudely worded directive issued in July 1942 suggested that:

When we first begin to get active victories in the turn of the tide ... Our first idea should be to get the help and faith of the Asiatics in starting that crumble to get themselves a better standard of living; more wives and rice, so to speak.[47]

Ball, with his belief in moderation, understatement and the voice of reason, must have been uneasy about the crude tone of some of the propaganda broadcast by the Australian service. Some of the most purple passages can be found in scripts of the program 'The Truth of It Is ...', by Reginald Drake, dealing with enemy radio propaganda. One of the most colourful of these scripts gave his impression of listening to enemy radio propaganda:

We have our slumbers disturbed by grotesque nightmares; our minds, while in great need of rest, go reeling down labarinthe [*sic*] ... ways, seeking a path through a jungle of falsehood, contradictions, threats, blandishments and stinking rubbish. First of all, there is the horrid babble of tongues: the smug, sneering tones of a Berlin announcer, speaking English with the clipped precision of a Prussian schoolmaster; a man in Tokio grinds our language between his teeth and spits it out in uncouth, scarcely recognisable lumps; a shrill female from Batavia scolds or cajoles in accents that sicken; and occasionally a dear old gent from Rome bumbles along, making each sentence a perilous voyage through mishaps or eyeglasses mislaid and notes that will get themselves in the wrong order, reaching the end of each sentence on a note of triumph—yet another great Italian victory gained in spite of malignant fate.[48]

Mocking humour typified much of Drake's satire. When Mussolini fell in 1943, Drake's program depicted a Japanese radio voice calling: 'Hullo Lome' again and again. The direction for the actor is: 'Voice grows increasingly distressed, ending almost on a sob.' Then follows the despairing cry: 'We had Lome. And now we have lost Lome!' The 'Japanese' broadcaster goes on to tell a colleague that the last words he heard from Rome were 'Benito *fin*-ito'. The same program went on to depict a radio conversation in which Hitler calls Tojo a monkey.[49] (A carefully cultivated part of allied attempts to split Japan and Germany was the allegation that the Germans referred to the Japanese as monkeys.) On occasion, Drake's own propaganda had a racist tinge. On Christmas Eve, 1943, he recalled Christmas 1941, when the war in the Pacific was little more than a fortnight old, and 'death was being spread over Asia by the little men of Nippon'.[50]

At one stage, Ball asked his deputy, Sawer, for a more consistent approach and emotional tone in broadcasts to the Japanese forces, adding, 'We tend to swing immoderately from threats to cajolery':

In some of these postscripts we take a fierce, minatory tone. We describe the disasters and diseases to which the Japanese forces are subject with a realism and relish that sometimes suggests a little suppressed sadism. And for good measure we may add a few predictions about how we will blast Japanese cities to smithereens. In a postscript the following day we may try to persuade the Japanese soldiers that if they surrender they will find us most kindly and considerate people, with a deep regard for them as fellow-soldiers and a respect for their spirit of bushido. These two lines neither converge nor run parallel. One crosses the other out.[51]

Ball was more specific in a draft memorandum in early 1943 for officers writing news and commentaries for the Japanese transmission (a clear indication that the propaganda lines were to be followed in the news bulletins as well as the commentaries). He said the purpose of the transmission was to weaken and destroy Japanese morale. This morale was built on two things: complete confidence in Japan's final victory; and a deep-rooted sense of duty and honour—a fusion of the strongest religious, patriotic and family sentiments. 'These,' he said, 'are the two beliefs we must try to destroy', and he proceeded to detail the way to go about it. Among the 'don'ts' he listed in this memorandum was:

Don't report stories of the resolution and bravery of German and Italian troops, but play up any reports of their surrender. For example, Russian reports that German units, when invited to surrender, went on fighting until exterminated, should not be carried, for they would only spur on the Japanese to more intense self-immolation.[52]

The American consul-general in Melbourne, Erle R. Dickover, to whom Ball sent a copy of the draft, approved in general, but suggested that ridicule should be added to the armoury of weapons used against the Japanese, who he said were 'perhaps more sensitive to ridicule than any other people on earth'.[53]

While some critics suggested that the shortwave service needed to strengthen its propaganda against the Japanese, others (journalists in particular) accused it of distorting the news. In early 1943 the shortwave service's correspondent covering (allied) general headquarters in Brisbane had to defend himself against an accusation that he was over-optimistic in his despatches. The accusation came from a journalist who headed the Department of Information's Australian News and Information Bureau, based in New York, David Bailey. The GHQ correspondent, Gordon Williams, retorted that every dispatch he sent was an accurate reflection of the daily communiqué and background statements by official spokesmen. If Bailey considered his despatches optimistic, he said, then he must regard the communiqués on which they were based as optimistic. Here, perhaps, Williams had put his finger on the nub of the problem. He said GHQ communiqués in the past fifteen days had claimed that in seventy-seven missions, many against heavy anti-aircraft fire, the allies had lost only one plane. Damage done by these raids was reported to be 'heavy and wide-spread', while at the same time damage done by Japanese raids on allied territory had been described as 'negligible'. After a major air fight over Lae in New Guinea, it had been officially announced that 133 Japanese aircraft had been either destroyed, probably destroyed, or damaged, while allied losses were 'not heavy'. It seems that MacArthur's publicists were trying to do the propagandists' work for them.[54]

A week later, a commentary by Lieutenant Paul McGuire described the battle of the Bismarck Sea (in which allied planes sank most of a convoy steaming towards New Guinea) as 'perhaps the most one-sided blow in history'. If his version had been accurate, it probably would have been. He said Japan had lost ten warships, twelve transports and supply ships, sixty-three aircraft and at least 15,000 soldiers and 3000 seamen, 'probably many more'. The battle, he said, had cost the allies four aircraft and not more than 20 casualties.[55] McGuire was retailing the official version, exaggerated by MacArthur, who was claiming the destruction of the entire enemy fleet of twenty-two ships. The battle was certainly a decisive victory, but in fact, according to Woodburn-Kirby,[56] the Japanese actually lost four warships (not ten), eight transports (not twelve), between twenty and thirty aircraft (not sixty-three) and just over 3000 men (not more than 18,000). At least McGuire's version of allied losses was fairly accurate. (Woodburn-Kirby says five planes were lost out of an attacking force of 335; Long puts allied aircraft losses at six.)[57]

A controversy about one possible means of propaganda arose in mid-1943 when the Allied Political Warfare Committee suggested the use of Japanese prisoners of war in an intensified campaign to induce Japanese soldiers to surrender. The campaign would have included the broadcasting of interviews with Japanese prisoners. When Curtin wrote personally to MacArthur seeking the approval of his headquarters,[58] the allied commander-in-chief showed uncharacteristic caution. Pointing out that the Geneva Convention provided that prisoners be humanely treated and protected, he said he believed its provisions should be practised both in letter and in spirit:

The use for propaganda purposes of broadcasts or statements made under compulsion by prisoners is clearly a violation of the laws of war. Even though this action be voluntary on the part of the prisoner, few Japanese will believe that it is not the result of intimidation or deception; the conclusion of mistreatment will be drawn and may give rise to reprisal action against our own prisoners in Japanese hands.[59]

MacArthur said he had no objection to the use on leaflets of photographs showing the conditions under which prisoners lived, where such photographs did not disclose the identity of prisoners. If features in such photographs were covered in an obvious manner and care was taken to point out that this was done to conceal identities, the effect might well be to modify reluctance to surrender. No doubt MacArthur had been well advised, but in this matter he must be given credit for the wisdom to accept that advice. No more was heard of the proposal to broadcast interviews with prisoners.

Embarrassing discrepancies

The fact that some overseas listeners could also hear the ABC's domestic shortwave programs caused coordination problems for the propagandists. A few days after Japan entered the war, the Director of Information, Charles Holmes, alerted his minister, Senator William Ashley, to the difficulty:

Although the Commission's programmes are specially prepared for Australian listeners, they are broadcast over exactly the same shortwave transmitters as are used at other times by the Department of Information. Moreover, these transmitters when in use by the ABC are beamed in the direction of Darwin. This means that programmes prepared for Australian listeners are in fact clearly heard by very large numbers of foreign listeners throughout East Asia and the islands to the north of Australia ... It is inevitable that many news bulletins and commentaries which it is perfectly proper and desirable to broadcast to Australians are not at all adapted for the presentation of the Australian scene to oversea listeners.[60]

Realising the danger, the chief publicity censor issued instructions that the shortwave news bulletins broadcast by the ABC should be submitted for censorship, but embarrassing discrepancies between the broadcasts continued, and the Japanese made considerable capital from them. In a commentary about fighting in the Solomons in late 1942, the shortwave service was careful not to report that the main airfield had been badly damaged, Japanese troops had made another landing, the Japanese had superiority in tanks and aircraft, the Americans needed reinforcements and the situation was critical. (Here was a clear example of the failure of the service to give 'factual and objective news—no matter how bad—about the war', as claimed in *The Constant Voice*.) But an ABC news bulletin broadcast on domestic shortwave reported all these details, and Radio Batavia, in enemy-occupied Indonesia, drew attention to the contrast in the tone of the two broadcasts.[61] Drake had his counterparts in the Japanese shortwave service. Such discrepancies continued (as Ball put it) to 'embarrass our shortwave propaganda policy',[62] and were periodically referred to by those who thought the Department of Information should take over the domestic shortwave service from the ABC.

A related problem was the occasional inclusion in news bulletins directed to the AIF overseas of items suitable for Australian ears only. In February 1943, Radio Batavia seized on crime stories in an AIF bulletin and made them the basis of a report entitled 'What sort of country is Australia?' Ball was mortified. With uncharacteristic humility he told Henry Stokes, of the Department of External Affairs, 'To include these items was a very grave error in policy, for which I accept full responsibility.' He went on to say that it had been his policy to exclude all crime stories from overseas broadcasts. But in response to a request from the army directorate of public relations for as comprehensive a cover of Australian news as possible, he had told his staff that the reporting of crime was permissible if the story was of general public interest and its presentation did not 'cast a shadow of crime or disorder over the bulletins themselves'. In true chief executive style, his acceptance of 'full responsibility' was immediately followed by a disclaimer from personal blame, when he added that these instructions had clearly not been followed in the case under review.[63]

A much more serious impediment to the effectiveness of the service as an instrument of propaganda was the different news treatment given in broadcasts to the United States (which could be picked up elsewhere) and those to Asia and the Pacific. Very soon after the outbreak of war in the Pacific, Evatt learned of the danger that propaganda broadcasts to Asia would mislead the Americans into thinking Australia was far stronger militarily than it really was. Evatt asked Richard Casey, Australian Minister to the USA, in early January 1942 to 'make some frank confessions of the true position to President Roosevelt himself'.[64]

In March 1943, Radio Batavia ruthlessly exploited inconsistencies in Australia's shortwave propaganda. Ball told Stokes, 'the Japanese propagandists show themselves fully aware of the dilemma with which our shortwave service is faced. Moreover, this comment shows the Japanese determination to exploit our dilemma for their own purposes.' Ball spelled out the dilemma in these words:

I. We want to tell the Japanese and the peoples of the occupied-territories that Japan will be defeated. In our propaganda to Asia we must do this by the analysis of current military operations … We can emphasise Japanese reverses and losses and our own successes … II. In our broadcasts to the USA we must give full prominence to the grave warnings issued by the Prime Minister, Cabinet Ministers and GHQ about Australia's danger; warnings of very powerful Japanese forces on sea, in the air, and on land which continue to threaten Australia's security; warnings of Australia's great danger, and need for additional help from the USA. If, in describing the situation in the Southwest Pacific, we broadcast only the grave warnings of Japanese strength, and Australia's weakness, we cut at the roots of our political warfare campaign in East Asia; if we broadcast news and comment about increasing success in this area and Japanese increasing difficulties, this policy may run counter to the Government's efforts to gain more aid from USA. It would not be satisfactory for us to attempt to confine the gloomy side of the picture to the US transmissions, and the cheerful side to the Asia transmissions, since the Japanese monitor all transmissions and the Americans could, of course, if they desired, do likewise.[65]

It is perhaps ironic that awareness of this dilemma, and the resultant attempts by the Australian propagandists to be reasonably consistent in the story they told to their audiences in Asia and in the United States, helped to 'keep Radio Australia honest' and, by enhancing its credibility, probably increased its effectiveness among its target audiences.

At least one American journalist did not need to monitor Australia's broadcasts to Asia to become sceptical about continued warnings that without increased help from the USA the country was in serious danger. Today, military historians agree that the danger of a Japanese invasion of Australia ended with the battles of the Coral Sea and Midway in May and June 1942, though of course Radio Australia's broadcasters may not have been aware of this at the time.

In March 1943, after the one-sided battle of the Bismarck Sea, Joseph C. Harsch, in the *Christian Science Monitor*, opposed Australian claims for a greater share of American resources. The shortwave service retaliated by broadcasting to the USA a dispatch from Gordon Williams in Brisbane. The dispatch said, in part:

Destruction of the Bismarck Sea convoy has done little to relieve the threat to Australia offered by the enemy's concentrations in the arc of islands north of this continent. This is the considered opinion of persons to whom I spoke today. The shadow of the huge force the enemy has built up throughout his northern occupancies is still falling across this country. Warnings given by Prime Minister Curtin and General Douglas MacArthur retain all their validity … An officer asked, 'What would Mr Harsch consider a threat to Australia? Does he think it is necessary for the enemy to land a force at Sydney before the security of this country is menaced? … Don't make any mistake—the threat to this country is real.' Mr Harsch's statement that Mr Curtin is pouring out appeals which Washington accepts as part of the calendar of fixed monthly events, has aroused resentment in military circles here … The facts in this area today are that we are in the shadow of great danger ... that we have not yet been given the opportunity to develop the blows which we should be raining upon the Japs from our great South-West Pacific springboard. No academic argument or long-distance review can alter these facts.[66]

Yet, within a few weeks, in its 'propaganda lines' to Asia, the shortwave service was hammering the theme of allied 'command of the seas' and 'crushing aerial superiority'.[67]

The transfer of Radio Australia to the ABC on 1 July 1942 coincided with the loss of the relative autonomy enjoyed by Ball for the first two and a half years. In the previous month, Prime Minister Curtin had directed the Department of External Affairs to control the policy of the political warfare broadcasts.[68] Only two weeks after the transfer, the Australian Political Warfare Committee was established, with representatives of the navy, army, air force, Defence Department, External Affairs Department and shortwave broadcasting division. The committee worked through existing Australian organisations, including the shortwave service. Detailed decisions on political policy were made by the Department of External Affairs through its political warfare division, established to act as a secretariat for the political warfare committee.[69] In August 1942, Hodgson, as secretary of the department, wrote to ABC chairman William Cleary, stating that, although the ABC was 'the administrative authority in control of overseas shortwave broadcasts ... the political policy to be followed shall conform to the directives of the Minister in control of political warfare'.[70] This division, controlled by Evatt as minister (though, as Sawer recalled, largely content to relay instructions from London and Washington) was to dictate the policy of the shortwave service much more than the Department of Information had ever done. Later in 1942, an Allied Political Warfare Committee was set up in Canberra, with representatives of Britain, the United States, the Netherlands government in exile, China, Canada and New Zealand. The allied committee decided to work through existing Australian organisations, including the shortwave service. The fact that the Australian government was keen to work in harmony with its allies, particularly the principal ally, the United States, gave the allied committee a great deal of influence over the service in the broader policy issues. In 1988, Sawer recalled:

Shortwave broadcasting was very largely a matter of following general directives which came to us from two directions, one being London, representing in effect European views—predominantly British views—of what general things to say to enemy countries or to neutral countries. When the Americans came in we got a similar set of directives from Washington. These directives came to us through the Department of External Affairs. The Australian department was perfectly at liberty to add its own comments to this or indeed make its own directives. In practice it was a fairly rare event, even under Evatt, for that to happen. For the most part they pushed the overseas directives to us and left it to us in effect to make our own picture of the extent to which, if any, Australian industry was contributing to things or Australian forces were involved in things.[71]

Ball conceded that the Department of External Affairs was in control, assuring the officer in charge of the political warfare division: 'For my part I have, I think, already made it clear that I recognise that shortwave broadcasting is in wartime part of the Government's foreign policy, and that its policy must therefore conform with the Government's policy.'[72] He was even more explicit in an assurance to Hodgson the following month: 'I fully recognise that on all questions of policy your authority is supreme.'[73]

Ball's final protest

The Curtin government won a landslide election victory in August 1943. A month later, Curtin appointed the talented, ambitious and abrasive Arthur Augustus Calwell as Minister for Information. Garnett Bonney, the chief publicity censor, was appointed director-general of information on 13 October. It was Ball's unlucky day. Not only was Bonney his *bête noire*; on the same day the government announced that as part of a reorganisation of the Department of Information, it was to take direct control of shortwave broadcasts directed to persons in enemy-occupied territory.

Ball gained some insight into Calwell's ambition during a chance meeting in Melbourne. Ball told Calwell that, despite his efforts to avoid being taken over by his department, this did not mean any personal hostility towards him. Calwell replied that he wanted to run shortwave for two reasons, first because he believed he could do a good job for Australia, and secondly 'because his ego naturally desired as much power as possible'.[74] Calwell said he personally believed that all of the ABC, not just shortwave, should come under the control of the Minister for Information rather than the Postmaster-General. When he asked Ball how he would feel about remaining under ABC administration, but being responsible to him for policy, Ball replied that this would be satisfactory to him if he could persuade Evatt to relinquish the authority he held over the policy of the political warfare broadcasts. Calwell said he felt sure he could make arrangements along these lines, and that Curtin would agree to them.

But in Canberra a few days later, Evatt told Ball and Hodgson he could not give up the responsibility for policy he already possessed. Indeed, he said, it was necessary for him to extend this responsibility to all overseas broadcasts. Evatt made it clear that he insisted on controlling policy, and that Calwell might, as a consolation prize, control administration.[75] The blow for Ball fell a fortnight later. Curtin announced that the shortwave division was to be placed under the control of the Minister for Information, except for shortwave broadcasts to audiences inside Australia, which would remain (through the ABC) 'under the control of the post-master-general as heretofore'.[76] Ball threatened to resign rather than work under Bonney. To Calwell, he put his cards on the table. He could not work with Bonney because 'there were certain minimum standards of honesty and decency below which the public service should not be allowed to fall. I believed that Mr Bonney's conduct often fell below these standards.' Ball added that he understood that Bonney had expressed his determination to dismiss him at the first opportunity.[77]

After a lengthy rearguard action by Ball, Curtin announced on 22 March 1944 that overseas shortwave would come under the control of Information, with policy coming from External Affairs. The transfer took place on 1 April 1944.[78] Ball resigned, issuing a statement that 'the circumstances in which the transfer is being made and the conditions under which the Shortwave Service will have to operate in future will make it impossible to conduct it effectively in the public interest.'[79]

Having lost a measure of autonomy in 1942 when the Department of External Affairs was given control of the political warfare broadcasts, Ball apparently feared that he would have even less latitude if he were answerable to Bonney. Sawer, who carried on for the next eighteen months as acting controller (but was never confirmed in the position), remarked more than forty years later that the flaw in Ball's character was that he was 'no good at being a lieutenant'. Sawer thought Ball's resignation was unnecessary. 'Mac was quite wrong,' he said, 'in thinking any of these people, Calwell or Bonney, would have interfered.'[80] Sawer and Robert Horne, his news editor, both remembered working with Bonney quite happily.[81] The transition had been a smooth one. Under Sawer's direction, Radio Australia continued do what it had done under Ball: follow the propaganda lines that the government thought would maximise the contribution of the service to the war effort of Australia and its allies.

When he took over the running of Radio Australia, Geoffrey Sawer was thirty-three. Educated, like Ball, at the University of Melbourne, he had tutored in law from 1934 to 1940, when he was promoted to senior lecturer in law. After the war, he was to become the Foundation Professor of Law in the Research School of Social Sciences at the Australian National

University from 1950 to 1974, Pro-Vice-Chancellor of the university in 1975 and Emeritus Professor of Law after his retirement.

As has been shown, the wartime Australian shortwave service suppressed information or gave it differing degrees of emphasis according to the perceived effects on Australia's war effort, and the possible advantage its accounts would lend Japan's shortwave propagandists. There has apparently been no research into the effectiveness of Australia's wartime radio propaganda. Perhaps in the early months of the Pacific war it was no more effective than Japan's propaganda broadcasts to Australia. For most of the war, however, Radio Australia had the advantage of broadcasting from the winning side. Macmahon Ball wrote in 1968:

The main reason for the seeming ineffectiveness of the Japanese broadcasts is very simple. It is that after their first shattering victories the Japanese were steadily and surely losing the war. They were winning for nearly the first six months, then losing it for a little over three years. The Japanese broadcasts commanded a deeply anxious attention in these early months. But you can hardly win a war by radio if you are losing it on the battlefields.[82]

Ball conceded, however, that Australia's radio propaganda was flawed by failure to understand the target audience. He wrote:

It used often to be said that the Japanese propaganda to Australia showed an ignorance of how Australians felt and thought, of our traditional standards of conduct. There is much truth in this. It is also true that Australians were ignorant of how Japanese, and other Asians, thought and felt, and of their traditional standards ... I have a strong impression that we made some bad blunders in our war-time broadcasts to Asia. I recall, for example, that we tried to create moral indignation against 'quislings', as we called them, following our European model. But to many of our Asian listeners their leaders who collaborated with the Japanese were good patriots doing the best they could under the circumstances. They had not been denounced as 'quislings' when they had collaborated with the British or the Dutch or the French.[83]

The Chifley government did not always give a single, unequivocal signal about what it wanted Radio Australia to broadcast. The story of how Geoffrey Sawer became the unwitting victim of tensions over the Indonesian struggle for independence is told in chapter 8. This episode is perhaps the clearest example of how Radio Australia could be affected by internecine conflict between ministers.

As the war ended, the ABC, deprived of even the nominal control it had held over Radio Australia for the two years until 1 April 1944, was calling for the service to 'revert to its care'.[84] But Calwell was determined that his empire should remain intact, and the government ignored the ABC's pleas.

A postwar role

In November 1945, the Ministers for External Affairs and Information (Evatt and Calwell) exchanged letters providing for consultation on all broadcasts affecting Australian foreign policy and for the appointment of an external liaison officer in Melbourne to check the outgoing broadcasts.[85] The agreement was quite specific:

all material which can in any sense be described as political or which otherwise bears on the conduct of Australian external relations should be referred to the Department of External Affairs before transmission. Policy control in regard to such material is to be in the hands of the Department of External Affairs.[86]

But the liaison officer was not appointed until 1950, and in the meantime the amount of consultation actually decreased, partly because of what the director of Radio Australia, Thomas Hoey, described early in 1947 as 'the more settled state of world affairs, particularly those in which Australia is interested', and partly because of Radio Australia's 'increasing avoidance of "external political" subjects'.[87] The first External Affairs Minister in the Menzies government elected in 1949 was P. C. Spender (later Sir Percy Spender—many prominent figures in this story, in government, the public service and the ABC, received the ultimate imperial reward for their services). He said later that in practice, while there had been consultation and liaison, the Department of External Affairs had taken 'no active part'.[88] He complained, however, that, on occasions during this period, Radio Australia had used items despite advice to the contrary by his department.[89]

In 1948, Department of External Affairs secretary Dr John Burton gave 'careful consideration ... to the role which this Department should play in assisting to determine the character of commentaries and news reports broadcast by Radio Australia'. He told Bonney:

My view is that we stand to gain little by directing propaganda broadcasts overseas at the present time and Australian foreign policy can be adequately explained and publicised through the media of United Nations conferences, parliamentary and other speeches. While other countries appear to be overusing propaganda commentaries in their shortwave broadcasting services, I consider that Radio Australia would be well advised to concentrate on building up a receptive listening audience until such time as we have a greater need and perhaps better opportunity of using commentaries of a political nature ... It is not suggested, of course, that the present function of Radio Australia in broadcasting news of and commentaries on Australia should be altered in any way.[90]

The government did use Radio Australia as an instrument of its immigration policy. The somewhat rose-coloured picture of Australia painted in its English-language broadcasts helped to entice English-speaking people (mainly from Britain) who were the most sought-after immigrants. Broadcasts in German were resumed in October 1948, with the sole purpose of attracting 'displaced persons' and others who understood this language.[91] The continuation of broadcasts in Dutch, even after most of the colonial Dutch had left Indonesia, was motivated by the government's desire to attract immigrants from the Netherlands. Pointing out that Australia's defence and foreign policy developed 'largely as a corollary of the White Australia policy', Camilleri says of early postwar immigration policy:

In a sense, the Labor Party's immigration measures were intended as much for defence as for economic purposes. The plan was to give maximum encouragement to European immigration while maintaining restrictions on Asians.[92]

The threatened expulsion of the Indonesian wartime evacuee Annie Maas O'Keefe and her children in 1949 was one sensitive subject on which Radio Australia sought the guidance of External Affairs.[93] (Mrs O'Keefe, a war widow, had been rescued from an Indonesian jungle with her children and brought to Australia as a wartime refugee. Her acceptance as a temporary entrant was subject to the authority of the Minister for Immigration.)[94] A Radio Australia news item in 1949 quoted a statement in the house by Calwell, as Minister for Immigration. On the advice of External Affairs, though, the report made no reference to the Dutch (who were involved because they had not yet transferred sovereignty to the Indonesian government).[95]

A few weeks later, similar embarrassment was caused by the government's refusal to allow Sergeant Gamboa, a Filipino American soldier, to enter Australia. Australia's ambassador in Tokyo, Patrick Shaw, expressed concern that the number of references by Radio Australia to the Gamboa case could perpetuate 'the ill-will towards our country engendered by enemy propaganda during the war'. In particular, he urged that Radio Australia should avoid the use of the term 'White Australia Policy', and merely refer to Australia's 'Immigration Policy'.[96] External Affairs pointed out to Hoey that the items his service had broadcast had been 'unhelpful', and told him 'no reference should be made to the exclusion of Asians from Australia unless it was expected to gain some positive advantage thereby'.[97] ABC chairman Richard Boyer told Burton of External Affairs he was in complete agreement that the term 'White Australia Policy' should be avoided wherever practicable in all broadcasts.[98]

An admission of the extent of External Affairs power over Radio Australia came in 1949, after the department expressed concern that the

Japanese communists had made propaganda use of an item broadcast by an Australian station. The original draft of a secret memorandum to all posts in Asia and the Pacific asserted: 'While we can control Radio Australia transmissions, the transmissions of the Australian Broadcasting Commission are in a different category even though we know they are audible well beyond our coasts.' This was felt to be too frank an admission, or perhaps overstating the case. Before transmission, it was amended to 'Naturally, we, like all other peoples, have ways of speaking among ourselves which we would not employ if strangers or foreigners are present.'[99]

During the early postwar years, Radio Australia remained to an extent part of the international broadcasting operation of the wider British Commonwealth. Among its programs was a transcription from the BBC.[100] When the British closed down their Far Eastern broadcasting service in Malaya in 1949, Radio Australia, conscious of 'an additional responsibility for maintaining and presenting the British Commonwealth case', introduced into its Asian and Pacific services in English a BBC news bulletin relayed direct from London.[101]

In fact, in these early postwar years, Radio Australia's programs were devoted primarily to publicising Australia. By the time Robert Horne returned to the service (as news director) from an overseas appointment in early 1949, Radio Australia staff were under instructions that commentaries were to 'tell the Australian story'. As there were few commentaries on international issues, the Department of External Affairs had lost much of its power over the service, but the government certainly had not. Through the Department of Information it ensured that Radio Australia projected a favourable view not only of Australia, but of its current rulers. Horne recalled in 1988 that comment on Australian politics had been 'of course not likely to be particularly unfavourable to Labor'. 'After all', he said, 'the government was running the Department of Information, and did not expect its department to be particularly critical of its policy'.[102] In parliament in 1947, Calwell had referred to Radio Australia as 'the voice of Australia, which tells the world of the policies of the Australian Government of the day and of the Australian people'. He also assured the parliament that Radio Australia avoided broadcasting 'negative' news about Australia: 'it is an instrumentality that has never brought Australia into disrepute and never aired any internal grievances for the disedification of the world'.[103]

Boyer's biographer, Geoffrey Bolton, says the ABC chairman made several attempts to have Radio Australia returned to the ABC. But, he says, Calwell 'would never surrender it to an ABC over whose running he had no ministerial authority and whose management he had several times criticised in the House of Representatives'.[104]

After the election of the second Menzies government in 1949, some of his ministers were critical of the kind of programs that had been broadcast by Radio Australia under a Labor minister, a Labor-appointed director-general and a controller (Hoey) known to be a supporter of the Labor government. Spender told the House he believed that during the Chifley government 'a great deal of nonsense was broadcast on short wave to foreign countries'. When Calwell interjected: 'That is very unfair', Spender went on:

I have read some of the scripts. Listeners overseas were told about the love life of the koala bear. That is apparently what the honourable member for Melbourne [Calwell] regards as being up to the standard of dignity required for overseas broadcasts from Australia. It certainly does not correspond to my views of what that standard should be.[105]

The defeat of the Chifley government in December 1949 by the man who had opened the shortwave service ten eventful years earlier was to transform it. Just as the Curtin and Chifley governments had used the service for their purposes, the Menzies government tried to use it for its own, but the transfer of Radio Australia to the ABC made the task considerably more complex.

2   A Cold War weapon, 1950–1953

The Cold War culture

The election of the second Menzies government on 10
December 1949 marked the beginning of Australia's wholehearted participation in the Cold War and of determined attempts to use Radio Australia
as a Cold War weapon. At this stage Radio Australia was broadcasting in
English, French, Dutch, Indonesian, Thai and German. The perception of
it as a Cold War weapon was to bring a transformation in the pattern of its
broadcasts, with some languages being dropped and others added.

The political climate in Australia at the time has to be seen in the context internationally of the descent of the Iron Curtain in Europe, the fall of
China to the communists in October 1949 and the outbreak of the Korean
War in 1950. Domestically, Australia had its counterpart (albeit for the
most part less virulent) of the McCarthyism of the United States, with the
attempts to ban the Communist Party in 1950 and 1951, the paranoia
surrounding the Petrov defection in 1954, and the fanaticism of anti-
communists in the Labor Party who later joined the Democratic Labor
Party.[1]

Many in the Australian government, and in the Department of
External Affairs, saw the principal external threat as coming from China.
There was a widespread belief in Australia that China was seeking, or
would seek in the future, to dominate the whole of Southeast Asia, and a
wider area encompassing Australia itself. The proponents of this view
also feared an expansionist Indonesia (until the coup of October 1965,

increasingly in the context of a Beijing–Jakarta axis) and the establishment of Chinese satellite governments throughout Southeast Asia.

As Camilleri says, the discussion of international affairs in Australia from the early 1950s was increasingly conducted in terms of the Cold War mythology of 'the free world', 'the threat from Asia', 'aggressive communism' and 'loyalty to our ally'.[2] This mythology was common not only to those mentioned above, but also, as will be shown, to executives of the ABC and Radio Australia. In this atmosphere, even historian Manning Clark came under surveillance by the Australian Security and Intelligence Organisation, ASIO.[3] To the domestic security organisation was added an overseas equivalent, the Australian Secret Intelligence Service, founded by Menzies in 1952.

Related to this Cold War culture, and to some extent a part of it, was the essentially conservative Department of External Affairs culture. According to Alan Renouf, secretary of the department from 1974 to 1977, the election of the Menzies government was followed by a purge of anyone in the department whose political views were to the left.[4] Casey said in parliament that there was 'a nest of traitors ... somewhere or other in the Public Service',[5] the implication being that they were in the Department of External Affairs.[6] Renouf says none was ever uncovered, but Harvey Barnett, director-general of ASIO from 1981 to 1985, says British evidence 'pointed the finger of suspicion' at James Hill (whose brother later led one of Australia's three communist parties, and who left External Affairs to become a solicitor in private practice) and Ian Milner (who left the department to live in Czechoslovakia).[7]

The Department of External Affairs culture in the Cold War era was basically conservative and illiberal. Its narrow recruitment base (Anglo-Celtic, male, often private school) and elitist attitudes reinforced collective group behaviour and conservative views. The elitism of its officers was in part an outcome of their tertiary education: virtually all were university trained, and many of them had first-class honours degrees. In this respect they contrasted markedly with the journalists against whom they struggled for some control of Radio Australia's news and current affairs programs. Most of these journalists had no university training at all. Some officers of the department would be rewarded with one of the ultimate imperial accolades—a knighthood. Very few journalists even aspired to such an honour.

In the Cold War era, officers of the Department of External Affairs were subject not only to conservative pressures, but also to pressures which made anathema the very concept of the free flow of information, particularly the free flow of Australian information overseas. This obsession with secrecy was deprecated by Dr Peter Wilenski when he became head of the

Department of Foreign Affairs and Trade in 1992. He called for a 90 per cent cut in the number of documents classified as 'restricted', 'confidential', 'secret' and 'top secret', saying the end of the Cold War, with its attendant cooling of national-security paranoia, should be matched by an end to the malaise known in the diplomatic service as 'classification creep'.[8] But despite the end of the Cold War, officers of the department still need security clearance before being employed; it is given by ASIO after an examination of their background. In their work they habitually dealt with classified documents, and strictly preserved their secrecy, on pain of serious damage to, or even termination of, their careers. One career officer in the department, Ric Throssell, son of the writer Katharine Susannah Prichard—a pioneer Australian communist—was never cleared by ASIO to handle top secrets, which in effect set a limit to his career.[9] Evidence against Throssell was given to the 1954 royal commission on espionage, but he was exonerated.[10] It is no coincidence that some of the Radio Australia stories which caused greatest concern in the department involved the broadcast of information which was, or had been, classified. Even during the period of *détente* between the department and Radio Australia, the broadcasting in 1980 of leaked information about a classified report on East Timor by the Australian Ambassador to Indonesia, and about a classified report critical of Mrs Gandhi by the Australian High Commissioner to India, caused grave concern.

It was inevitable, particularly in the atmosphere of the Cold War, that there would be collisions between those conditioned by the Department of External Affairs culture and journalists for whom the seeking out and public disclosure of information was part of their way of life. Journalists are also members of a strongly bonded, separate social group with a unique culture. The distrust of journalists by one of the exemplars of the Department of External Affairs culture, Arthur Tange, was legendary. He once said: 'The power of journalists to divert the executive from seriously addressing real national problems is great and destructive.'[11] The collisions referred to above were aggravated by the determination of some of those in (or aligned with) the department, to influence or even control Radio Australia, and the determination of some of those in (or aligned with) Radio Australia, to preserve what they saw as its integrity.

The contestants

The previous chapter showed how, during World War II and the years that followed under the Labor government, there was a three-way power struggle for control of the shortwave service, a struggle which resulted in the abject defeat of the Australian Broadcasting Commission, the virtual irrelevance of the Department of External Affairs and the triumph of Calwell and Bonney's Department of Information. Just as, on the global scene, war was succeeded by a new clash of power and ideology in the Cold War, the three-way struggle within Australia for control of the shortwave service was succeeded by a two-way contest between the ABC and the Department of External Affairs. And just as the wartime struggle was personified by two proud and determined men, Macmahon Ball and Garnett Bonney, so the later struggle became at times an almost personal contest between ABC chairman Sir Richard Boyer and External Affairs secretary Arthur (later Sir Arthur) Tange, and later between ABC chairman James (later Sir James) Darling and External Affairs Minister Paul (later Sir Paul) Hasluck. Other protagonists in the struggle at various times included External Affairs minister Richard (later Lord) Casey and External Affairs officer Richard Woolcott, on the side of the department, and ABC editor-in-chief Walter Hamilton and Radio Australia editor John Hall, on the side of the ABC. Charles (later Sir Charles) Moses, the ABC's general manager for most of the period, tended to sway with the breeze. As chief executive, the general manager was responsible for the day-to-day running of the ABC, but the government-appointed Australian Broadcasting Commission, headed by the chairman, was in charge of overall policy. (Today, the managing director, who sits on the board of the Australian Broadcasting Corporation, has a much more active policy-making role, and the chairman is more of a figurehead.) The chief executive of Radio Australia (who over the years has had various titles) worked to the general manager, but, in the early decades after the transfer of Radio Australia to the ABC, sometimes had a direct line to the chairman. The editor-in-chief was in charge of the ABC news service, including that of Radio Australia, and the editor of Radio Australia (who like the chief executive has had various titles) worked directly to him. In the 1960s and 1970s, when Radio Australia established a current affairs section, the editor's responsibility was split: he answered to the editor-in-chief for news and the chief executive of Radio Australia for current affairs.

Richard Casey was in many ways more enlightened than his cabinet colleagues, though he had been brought up as essentially a child of the empire. Raised in an establishment family, he had been educated at Melbourne Grammar and Melbourne and Cambridge Universities. Tall, spare and handsome, he was sociable yet shy and a little unsure of himself. Tange believed he was the only member of cabinet who really understood Asia.[12] He had been Governor of Bengal from 1944 to 1946, but his biographer says he was 'instantly converted to the importance of South-East Asia to Australia' during a visit to East and Southeast Asia in 1951.[13] In 1954, Casey lamented that most of his cabinet colleagues were 'unsympathetic to Asia'.[14] He believed it was axiomatic that Australia must as far as possible have friendly relations with Asian states[15] and that it was 'desirable for us to have a representative in Peking as soon as we can'.[16] Casey was also conscious of the fact that Australia 'must live with Indonesia ... for all time'.[17] In America, he was seriously disturbed by McCarthyism, noting in 1951 that 'people hesitate to express even liberal ideas, for fear of being branded'.[18]

On the other hand, Casey saw Australian communists and their associates as agents of foreign powers who, by advocating revolution against liberal democracy, were disqualified from appealing to liberal democratic rights. Hudson says that, given his head, Casey would have banned the Communist Party, sacked communist public servants and trade union leaders and forbidden communist propaganda. He did not recognise that what he wanted in Australia would have amounted to McCarthyism or would have led to McCarthyism.[19] He deplored talks on the ABC by Macmahon Ball, Julius Stone and Peter Russo, intellectuals whom he saw as soft on Asian communism.[20] He complained to Boyer, the ABC chairman, that the ABC was giving too much time to left-wingers, and suggested as alternatives William Stanner, Zelman Cowen, Marjorie Jacobs, Colin Bingham and, later, Frederic Eggleston, B. A. Santamaria and Denys Jackson. Casey's belief that Radio Australia should be run according to the American model rather than the BBC model will be made clear by previously unpublished material later in this chapter. This material will also show how much Casey was influenced by the United States government in his wish to use Radio Australia as a Cold War weapon.

Casey chose Tange, an economist who impressed him as 'a first class officer ... from all points of view', as secretary of the department in 1953, when he was only thirty-nine.[21] Although unashamedly anti-communist, Tange did not think of Asian communism in monolithic terms. He said in 1988 that, although he had been a cold warrior in the 1950s, his stance had been tempered by an attempt to bring about a better understanding of Asian nationalism, which the Menzies government had had difficulty in recognising. After the French defeat at Dien Bien Phu in 1954, his advice was that Australia should keep out of Vietnam. He said that in 1962–3, he had supported the dispatch of Australian military advisers to Vietnam, but he had not favoured the commitment of Australian fighting forces in 1965.[22] Tange was a major contributor to Australia's Cold War effort, both as secretary of the Department of External Affairs from 1954 to 1965 and as secretary of the Department of Defence from 1970 to 1979. In both these positions, he had a powerful influence on the Australian Secret Intelligence Service, ASIS.[23] On the use of Radio Australia as an instrument of foreign policy, Tange was implacable. He said that in 1951, the External Affairs view, and his own view, was that Radio Australia should be used sensitively in a way that supported Australian foreign policy. In 1959, he referred to Radio Australia as the major element of 'Australia's propaganda approach to Asia'.[24] Asked in 1988 what he had meant by this, he replied that, fundamentally, he was not sure there was any role for Radio Australia other than propaganda.[25] Like Casey, he was essentially an advocate of the American model of international broadcasting. The often irascible Tange's long struggle with Boyer, Hamilton and Hall for control of Radio Australia is detailed in this chapter.

Paul Hasluck grew up in the confined atmosphere of a Salvation Army family, with a narrow perspective on the world. According to his autobiography, his parents knew no life except the life of 'The Army' and had very few friends outside it. Hasluck was moulded in childhood by his consciousness of being different, 'marked in infancy to do the work of God and brought up to the strains of sacrifice and duty'.[26] He wrote later, 'I probably was offensive or at least uncongenial to some of my associates and ... others found me difficult to understand because I had been so strongly conditioned by my upbringing in a very unusual household.'[27] Perhaps the narrowness and absolutism of his early upbringing was not unconnected with the relentlessness with which he pursued the American model of international broadcasting for Radio Australia, seeking to place it under the direct influence, and ultimately the control, of his department.

Hasluck recalled in 1989 that during the war, 'I shared the departmental opinion that the service [Radio Australia] was created and funds provided to serve the ends of national policy. The programmes and especially the news broadcasts to Asia should be devised accordingly.' After the war, as Minister for Territories, he became critical of Radio Australia's news bulletins, on which in some parts of Papua New Guinea the European population relied for their news. He feared that 'as a consequence they were receiving some very odd impressions about Australian policy.'[28]

He said that after he had become Minister for External Affairs in 1963,

I heard in nearly every one of our diplomatic missions in southern Asia unfavourable comments on what Radio Australia was doing. Consequently my view in Cabinet discussion was consistently and persistently that in matters affecting our international relations the compiling of news could not be left solely to the mercy of journalists employed by Radio Australia and should pay more regard to Australia's national interests.

Hasluck's recollection that 'I did not worry so much about the transfer of control out of the hands of the ABC as I did worry about the need to establish more clearly constant consultation with the Department of External Affairs and reasonable deference to the views of that department in compiling the news'[29] is not entirely consistent with his actions in 1965, as is shown by previously unpublished documents quoted in chapter 4.

Richard Woolcott had a very different background from Hasluck, and had a very different image. The son of a naval dentist, he was educated at the exclusive Geelong Grammar School, the University of Melbourne and the London School of Slavonic and East European Studies. Brilliant and personable, he progressed rapidly in the department, and Whitlam gave sworn testimony that he wanted him to be secretary in 1974, but at the age of forty-five he was considered too young[30] (though Tange had been appointed secretary at the age of thirty-nine). Woolcott said later that in fact he had declined because, at forty-six, he considered *himself* too young.[31] After two terms as an ambassador (in Indonesia and the Philippines) and one as a high commissioner (in Ghana),[32] Woolcott finally became secretary in 1988. His urbanity and personal charm are a byword in the media and the department. But the records show that beneath his charm towards executives of Radio Australia he was a determined proponent of departmental influence over the service, which he wanted to move closer to the American model of international broadcasting.

Like Hasluck, Richard Boyer had been brought up in a Christian home, though one not so narrow. His father was a Methodist minister,[33] and Boyer himself originally followed his father's calling.[34] Wounded in World War I, he lost much of his religious faith,[35] but not the liberalism and humanism that had gone with it. His belief in the BBC model of international broadcasting will become manifestly apparent—in fact, his commitment was to an idealised version of the BBC model, without the close relationship with the Foreign Office which was known to the department, but hidden from Boyer himself. Boyer's commitment to the imagined BBC model motivated his pressure on the postwar Labor government for several years for the return of Radio Australia to the ABC,[36] and ensured that after the Menzies government carried this out in 1950, he would be on a collision course with proponents of the American model like Casey and Tange.

The evidence from Australian sources, with some corroboration from London, is that collaboration between the Foreign Office and the BBC World Service in the 1950s was very close—certainly far closer than the relationship has ever been between their Australian counterparts since the ABC took over Radio Australia in 1950. That takeover began a long-running battle between the ABC and the Department of External Affairs over the closeness of the relationship in the mother country, which both professed to acknowledge as the model for Australia to follow.

In the late 1950s, after years of argument with ABC executives determined to preserve Radio Australia's independence, the Department of External Affairs sought clarification from the Foreign Office itself. The Foreign Office said, in part:

There is in fact constant co-operation between them [the Foreign Office and the Overseas Services of the BBC] at all levels and both the shape and the content of the various foreign language broadcasts and the nature of the other activities of the Overseas Services are determined as a result of joint consultation.[37]

At no stage since 1950 has cooperation between Radio Australia and the Department of Foreign Affairs been anything but tenuous and perfunctory by comparison. In 1954, the department's liaison officer, Noel Goss, told his superior that Radio Australia's head, Robin Wood, appeared to have little inkling that collaboration between the Foreign Office and the BBC had gone as far as it was shown to have gone in the Foreign Office's memorandum.[38] But not everyone in the ABC was so innocent. One of the most determined defenders of Radio Australia's independence, the ABC's editor-in-chief, Walter Hamilton, told a meeting of ABC and departmental officers in 1955 that he had heard from several sources that the Foreign Office played a big part in determining the activities of the BBC overseas services.[39]

Boyer and a number of ABC executives continued to insist that the BBC was independent of the Foreign Office and that, following this model, Radio Australia should be independent of the Department of External Affairs. He decided to satisfy himself first hand on the former point during a visit to Britain in 1958. Some officers of the department saw their chance: if Boyer could be steered in the right direction in London, he would learn the truth about the closeness of the relationship there.

One External Affairs officer, Charles Kevin, made preparations to have Boyer intercepted in London and told the truth about the vaunted independence of the BBC External Services. In a letter marked 'Personal and Secret' to Owen Davis, a colleague in Australia House, he wrote:

We think it would be useful if in some discreet way you could arrange for Boyer to meet F. R. H. Murray (Foreign Office). You may be able to speak in confidence to Murray beforehand and give him an outline of Boyer's attitude as well as our own in the hope that he can contribute something to correcting Boyer's somewhat unrealistic approach.[40]

Francis Murray was the assistant secretary whose responsibility included dealings with the BBC External Services.[41]

Kevin's carefully laid plan came to nothing. His colleague asked around Australia House whether anyone from the high commissioner down was likely to be entertaining Boyer so that he could 'bring about an apparently accidental meeting' with Murray.[42] But no-one had plans for entertaining him. In a 'Personal and Secret' reply to Kevin, Davis reported that Murray had outlined some of the many BBC pies in which the Foreign Office had its fingers:

Although the BBC Overseas Services sought to maintain the reputation for objectivity, Murray agreed that this was essentially a means to an end, rather than an end in itself. The end was to serve the national interest. To do this it was essential that the point of view of the government of the day should be conveyed to the listeners and should not be unduly exposed to critical comment from other talks or commentaries broadcast by the BBC.[43]

It was probably one of the frankest disclosures of the closeness of the BBC's relationship with the Foreign Office ever made to an Australian.

The planned meeting between Murray and Boyer never eventuated. In a letter to Tange after his return, Boyer continued to retail the official BBC line, quoting the (1957) white paper as saying, 'the BBC enjoys independence of programme content'.[44]

James Darling, Boyer's successor as ABC chairman, was also firmly committed to the BBC model. A product of the British public school system and Oxford University, he had become accustomed to having his own way during thirty-one years as headmaster of Geelong Grammar (where Woolcott had been one of his pupils). When he became chairman of the ABC in 1961, he was not deterred by the collision of his ideas of international broadcasting with those of Tange or Hasluck. He believed that,

by virtue ... of the great integrity of those who operated the service, Radio Australia managed to achieve a reputation somewhat similar to that of the BBC during the 1939-45 war. This was because they followed the general rules observed by the news service of the ABC and included not only the Government point of view but also criticisms of it by the Opposition.[45]

Darling was a staunch opponent of the American model, believing that the Voice of America lacked acceptability in Asian countries because it was 'known to be government-sponsored propaganda'. After his retirement, he said there had been continuing argument between him and officers of the External Affairs Department, and he had resisted strongly its attempts to bring ABC correspondents in Asia under the control of various embassies. He believed that success in preserving the independence of Radio Australia was 'both right in principle and also for the greater good of Australia in the end'. Nevertheless, Darling did not believe in untrammelled freedom for Radio Australia. He later said there had been sufficient liaison with the department to guard against 'any serious expression of views too controversial, and I accepted that the Department might frequently be in the possession of information which could make the expression of views by Radio Australia inappropriate'.[46]

He described Radio Australia as 'the brightest jewel in the ABC crown', and found its officers 'very greatly to be admired'. Hasluck's attempt to wrest this 'jewel' from the ABC and bring it under the control of his department were to bring him into collision with Darling. Eventually, in 1967, the Holt government decided not to give Darling a third term as chairman.[47]

Walter Hamilton was editor-in-chief of ABC news from 1949 to 1959, controller of news from 1959 to 1964, and assistant general manager, news and current affairs, from 1965 until his retirement at sixty-five in 1971. Having been educated at St Joseph's College, Hunters Hill, and the University of Sydney, and after twenty-five years as chief sub-editor of the Sydney *Sun*, he was forty-three when he became editor-in-chief. Physically small but determined, opinionated and at times irascible, he became a formidable opponent of those who wanted to use Radio Australia as an instrument of propaganda. He had an early flirtation with the idea that Radio Australia 'should do what the Government wants it to do',[48] but later became a strong advocate of the BBC model. He said in 1958, 'We have evidence that news organisations, newsagency representatives, government organisations, and in fact government leaders consistently listen to Radio Australia broadcasts, and they know they can be trusted.'[49] A year after his retirement, Hamilton reaffirmed his commitment. Speaking publicly about the 'fairly continuous' pressure on Radio Australia over the years 'from some ministers and many but not all officers of the Department of Foreign Affairs', he said Radio Australia was widely listened to because it was trusted, particularly throughout Asia, where local news media accepted its authority without question:

Aware of this influence, touchy about Australia's reputation, and anxious to avoid policy embarrassments, the Foreign Affairs Department has always wanted the news handled to its liking, to put it euphemistically … we simply could not agree to Radio Australia becoming a propaganda medium, which is what they really meant. Apart from the rape of truth, they could not understand that once we started to tamper with the news people would stop trusting Radio Australia and it would become utterly useless to them anyhow … We knew what would happen because as professional communicators we know how delicate a thing is credibility, how easily it can be lost forever. If we didn't know we always had the example of the Voice of America to guide us.[50]

Hamilton's resistance to the department's attempts to push Radio Australia towards the American model, and his support for similar resistance by its news editor, John Hall, are another major theme of this chapter.

John Hall, no less determined than Hamilton in his resistance of the department's pressure, had an ABC career spanning twenty-five years. A short, thick-set man, he was thirty-nine when he became editor of Radio Australia in 1961. When the department pressured him over the reporting of Indonesia in the early 1960s, he opened files labelled 'attempts at slanting news' and 'censorship attempts'. He was promoted in 1965 to assistant director, programs, a position in which he was no longer responsible for news content. He continued in that position until his retirement with a heart condition eight years later.

Charles Moses, a formidable figure who dominated the ABC for the thirty years he was general manager, until his retirement at the age of sixty-five in 1965, was not aligned with the proponents of either the BBC model or the American model, although at times he paid lip-service to the former. Australian-born, Moses was educated in England, graduating from Sandhurst. Powerfully built, he was a keen axeman, giving his recreations in *Who's Who in Australia* as 'tree felling, walking, music'.[51] A former deputy general manager, Dr Clement Semmler, claimed in 1989 that Moses had told him on a number of occasions that he would have been pleased to see the ABC rid of the overseas service. Moses certainly did not play a notable part in resisting the department's attempts to push the service in the direction of the American model. His vacillation is clear from the hitherto unpublished details revealed in this and the next chapter.

This book does not try to depict Radio Australia's Cold War critics as the forces of darkness, and its defenders as the forces of light. Most of the protagonists on both sides had sincerely held views, for which a cogent case can be argued.

Drastic reductions planned

The body of the Chifley government was scarcely cold before the first attempt was made to enlist Radio Australia as a weapon in the Cold War. Six days after the 1949 election, the acting high commissioner in London wrote to Menzies proposing that Radio Australia should cooperate with international broadcasters in the United Kingdom and the United States in making daily broadcasts in Russian to the Soviet Union. The object was to help circumvent the Soviet attempts to jam the British and American broadcasts. It was suggested that this would not only improve cooperation between Australia and its British and American allies, but also make 'the maximum use in the political field of Radio Australia's transmitters'.[52] The secretary of the Prime Minister's Department, Allen (later Sir Allen) Brown, told his counterpart in External Affairs, Dr John Burton, that the Information Minister, Howard (later Sir Howard) Beale, had told Menzies Radio Australia would have no difficulty in providing such a service. But the Information Minister had said there were certain disadvantages in that the proposal might lead to a jamming war with the Soviet Union.[53]

The Minister for External Affairs, Percy Spender, also questioned the wisdom of the proposal. He told Menzies it would be relatively easy for Russia, China or an even nearer country to jam Australia's broadcasts, adding, 'It would seem, therefore, that in endeavouring to make a small contribution to broadcast to Russia we are likely to damage our broadcast to the whole of South-East Asia.'[54] The proposal was quietly dropped for the time being, though it was to be raised again when Radio Australia was transferred to the ABC.

Initially, the new cabinet was slow to see Radio Australia's potential as a Cold War weapon. With the abolition of the Department of Information imminent, cabinet decided on 9 March 1950 that Radio Australia should be 'transferred to the Postmaster-General's Department [a phrase which many years later the Department of External Affairs was to try to exploit; see p. 86] to be operated by the Australian Broadcasting Commission on a reduced scale for the purpose of the broadcast of important news and information about Australia'.[55] The cabinet committee dealing with the abolition of the Department of Information decided a few days later that there should be a substantial reduction in broadcasting time and areas to which broadcasts were directed. The listening post (which monitored shortwave broadcasts from many other parts of the world) was to be eliminated, or at least substantially cut, and if it did survive it was to be run by External Affairs. Details were to be examined by the Department of External Affairs, the ABC and the PMG Department. The ABC was only too happy to preside over the drastic reduction of the service. Tentatively, it proposed only one broadcast daily (in English) to the occupation forces in Japan, one in Indonesian, one in Dutch, one in French and, tentatively, one in English to the United States.[56] Later the ABC decided to drop its program in Dutch. French too was in danger until Spender, on a visit to New Caledonia, consulted the French governor and concluded that the broadcast performed a very useful function in the absence of adequate local stations.[57] Radio Australia's oldest Asian-language service, Thai, was also reprieved by the department's intervention.[58]

The conference between the Department of External Affairs, the PMG and the ABC agreed that at least half those working for Radio Australia should be dismissed and that overseas broadcasts should be cut drastically, but shortwave broadcasts within Australia and the territory of Papua New Guinea should increase.[59] Apparently without giving the matter serious thought, Moses planned to halve the cost of the overseas service by making it dependent primarily on relays of programs from the home service, including the domestic news bulletins, with additional material as required. Boyer's biographer says that as the date of the transfer, 1 April 1950, drew nearer, some ABC executives began to wonder whether much of the domestic material to be relayed was really suitable for overseas consumption.[60] But there is little evidence of this in the files. The editor-in-chief, Walter Hamilton, claimed that none of the arguments against using domestic news bulletins was unanswerable. He rejected even the contention that the items were not backgrounded well enough for overseas listeners, replying that some knowledge of and interest in Australia must surely be assumed in anyone who would 'go to the trouble of listening to Australian broadcasts'.[61]

More significantly, some officers of the Department of External Affairs perceived dangers and alerted their minister. They began to realise that a weapon of great potential in the Cold War was about to be badly blunted. In fact, it was the department which (for its own reasons) defended Radio Australia from the depredations of the ABC and preserved it relatively unscathed.

Battle joined

Soon, skirmishing began as a preliminary to the battle to control the policy of the overseas service. But in these early stages, the department's territorial claims were modest and Boyer was careful to occupy the high ground. Three days before the takeover, he told his commissioners that the department had asked the ABC to agree to the appointment of a liaison officer in Melbourne 'to advise us on special overseas broadcasts, particularly in relation to news or special talks designed for some particular area'. Burton, essentially a survivor from the *ancien régime*, who was to be replaced less than three months later, 'specifically endorsed the view that the commission itself retain responsibility for all broadcasts, and that the function of his officer was purely to advise and assist'.[62] Noel Goss, the man who was to be appointed to this position, was noted for his dogmatic, obdurate manner; he tenaciously resisted subsequent attempts to consign him and his department to such a subordinate role. (Goss said in 1988 that he had believed his role was 'to add to the news, to censor the news, and to update the news from External Affairs sources'.)[63]

Boyer foresaw that the department might not remain as obliging as Burton had been. He wrote to the Postmaster-General, H. L. (Larry) Anthony, mentioning a difference of opinion between the ABC and External Affairs over the manner in which the department's influence would be implemented, and said, 'I am most anxious that the *directive under which we shall operate* will leave no room for misunderstandings or difficulties of divided responsibilities in the future.'[64] His suspicions were well founded. He told the commissioners a few days later, 'it seems that External Affairs visualise a degree of authority in the actual operation of the service which is much more than agreed on in conference, and certainly more than is desirable.'[65]

By this time Burton (perhaps with prodding from Spender) was having second thoughts. After visiting Radio Australia and the listening post, he asserted that 'recommendations were made to the Government and decisions taken without sufficient examination of some aspects of the work of both organisations ... I have referred the matter to the joint intelligence committee ...'.[66] He told the secretary of the Defence Department that he understood some of the armed services might have had views to express in relation to Radio Australia from a political warfare point of view. 'In making the decision to hand over Radio Australia to the Australian Broadcasting Commission with an indication that the programmes could be substantially cut,' he said, 'the Government probably did not have advice from the Services of their point of view.'[67]

In the meantime, the energetic Goss was analysing ABC news bulletins broadcast in early April to show how unsuited they were to the overseas service. One story quoted a former British Commissioner for Southeast Asia as saying Britain was losing the war in Malaya. Another said the French forces in Indo-China had been fighting a losing war for seven years. Goss commented, 'ABC seems to be giving South East Asia away ... It is thoroughly partizan.' A reference in an ABC story to McCarthy's 'current Communist witch hunt' was condemned by Goss as 'undiplomatic language'.[68] The ABC's reporting of an investigation into the loyalty of 'the State Department's expert on Far Eastern Affairs', accused by McCarthy of being a communist and the leading Russian agent in the United States, evoked from Goss the comment: 'NO. The washing of dirty linen should be left exclusively to the owners.' Goss gave Burton his own prescription for shortwave news bulletins. They should stress the solidarity of Western nations, the internal strength of the United States, and Australia as a strong and prosperous country and a source of material benefits to Southeast Asia.[69]

Another shot across the bows of the ABC was fired by the Joint Intelligence Committee, consisting of the directors of naval, military and air force intelligence, the assistant secretary of the Defence Department and a representative of the Department of External Affairs. The Joint Intelligence Committee concluded that the activities of Radio Australia and the listening post had considerable value from the defence viewpoint, both directly and indirectly.[70]

By this time, Spender had awakened to the opportunity the government had almost missed. He told Menzies that the cabinet decision had been taken before he had had a chance to investigate fully the work that the shortwave division was doing. He continued:

I have now done so, however, and have come to the conclusion that it could make a very useful contribution to the Government's policy in regard to assistance for the co-operation with the countries of South-East Asia. Moreover, I have since ascertained that the recommendations upon which the Committee took its decisions were made without a full examination of the interests of the service departments ... there now exists in Asia and the Pacific a large and receptive audience for Australian shortwave broadcasts and it would seem to be of great importance that this should be maintained in being. There is no need for me to emphasize that the existence of such an audience could be of great importance in combating the spread of communism in those areas. In the circumstances, therefore, I would recommend that the Cabinet Committee be reconvened to give further consideration to the future of both 'Radio Australia' and the 'Listening Post'.[71]

A few days later, Burton spoke to Boyer, Moses and an ABC assistant general manager, A. N. (Huck) Finlay. Apparently all three of them had seen the light. Burton told Spender:

Since I put my submission to you, they have apparently realised that their original transmissions were inadequate, and they are now planning to keep more or less the same number of transmissions as previously. The only point of difference which emerged was on the content of programmes. We had monitored Radio Australia ... and were able to quote examples of news items which gave a completely wrong impression and might have very misleading widespread political effects not only for ourselves but also for the United Kingdom.

The Australian Broadcasting Commission admitted this difficulty and suggested that those items which should be dropped from the national news transmissions be placed at the end of the bulletin, and that special items for the region be substituted. However, in the course of discussion, 'it became quite clear that to adjust national programmes sufficiently to meet overseas requirements would seriously interfere with national programmes and, in many cases, not, in fact, meet overseas requirements'. Burton went on to suggest that the ABC, in conjunction with the Department of External Affairs and the services, should be given a directive providing for specialised transmissions to Southeast Asia, developing in six to nine months into what could be more actively described as 'peace-time political warfare'.[72]

Spender's submission to the reconvened cabinet committee was almost as apologetic as his letter to Menzies. He said the original cabinet decision to gut Radio Australia had been taken before reports from Australian representatives in Southeast Asia and the western Pacific had indicated that Radio Australia had a large and influential audience. Moreover, there had been no discussion with the armed services, which attached considerable importance to the maintenance of Radio Australia as part of their defence planning. The service would be required for political warfare in an emergency, and if anything were done to restrict its present influence, then its value in such an emergency might disappear. He told the committee that the domestic news bulletins in particular were unsuitable for overseas broadcast because the emphasis on local news was too great, the presentation differèd radically, and items intelligible locally were unintelligible to overseas listeners unfamiliar with Australia.

'An instrument of foreign policy'

Spender concluded that it was desirable to maintain Radio Australia as a special overseas service, with a particular bearing on Southeast Asia, to put the Australian viewpoint, to further Australia's policy of 'stabilising conditions in the area by political and economic means', and to meet the needs of defence planning. He recommended that the ABC should be directed to maintain special news transmissions, commentaries and other programs for Southeast Asia and the western Pacific, and to maintain the principal foreign-language transmissions (while dropping Dutch and German). He also recommended that his department 'should be directed to advise on program content, and, *where necessary, the Minister for External Affairs should originate directives in respect of policy aspects of external shortwave broadcasting*'. [emphasis added][73]

The last sentence was symptomatic of the government's increasing push for a measure of control over Radio Australia's programs, at least those that could be used to strike a blow in the Cold War. A few days earlier, Anthony had proposed to Boyer that a committee comprising the ABC, the PMG department and External Affairs should consider 'day to day matters of external political interest'. He added reassuringly, *'Within the framework I have outlined*, your Commission would be in full control of the programme side of the broadcasts.' [emphasis added][74] Spender followed this up by telling Boyer:

I consider it quite essential that I should obtain a right of programme direction as and when it might be appropriate in respect of overseas transmissions ... I seek the whole-hearted support and co-operation of the Australian Broadcasting Commission, its news staff, its commentators and its administration in assisting me in carrying through the foreign policy, which has many vital aspects from a security point of view for Australia.[75]

Boyer was determined to resist these pressures. He replied tactfully to Spender that the commission, which had discussed the matter very carefully, was 'very sensible of the close interest which your Ministry has in the impact of our Australian shortwave broadcasts overseas, and it is our desire to serve in this matter to the fullest extent and to your complete satisfaction.' But after this abject opening came the punchline:

On the other hand, our experience in the operation of this service under the previous Government, as well as the experience of the Canadian and British Governments in facing the same problem, has led the Commission to set out what it feels to be an approach to this matter which will avoid all those difficulties which are inevitable in divided or undefined responsibility, while at the same time achieving what you have in mind.[76]

Boyer enclosed with this letter a statement he had prepared for Anthony the previous day setting out the position. It said the Department of External Affairs was seeking an alteration in the general directive covering the transfer of the service to enable it to exercise a more specifically directive function, 'in view of the disturbed international position and of Australia's especial interests in South-East Asia'. He went on:

We recognise to the full the special interests of the Department of External Affairs in the effect of overseas broadcasts, and it is the Commission's wish to do all in its power to meet these interests ... [but] It is clear that in day-to-day programme building, any division of authority should be avoided, and that the final responsibility for the matter broadcast should be laid squarely at the feet of one or other Commonwealth authority. The Commission's view is, therefore, that statements by the Minister of Government policy in respect of particular countries abroad, would be necessary from time to time for the guidance of the Commission, particularly in view of the existing delicate international situation, but that within this framework the Commission should assume undivided responsibility for the implementation in broadcasting terms of such policy.

As usual, Boyer cited the BBC as a model. He said the BBC was in a position, while assuming specific responsibility for compiling all overseas shortwave programs, to secure at the operational level all required specialised guidance and assistance. In the margin of Spender's copy of the statement, Spender wrote: 'but the ABC is *not* [underlined twice] in this happy position'.[77]

To Anthony, Boyer said the commission's view was that, if the Department of External Affairs felt it necessary to have day-to-day direction of program content, it would be preferable for the department to assume full responsibility for the service. The ABC was prepared to 'give the fullest regard' to all the assistance and guidance which External Affairs could give. Boyer maintained: 'There is a world of difference, however, between assistance and guidance, and direction.'[78] In his attempt to enlist Anthony's support in his struggle with Spender, Boyer made a political point: 'I may mention that the Commission's views on this matter are reinforced by difficulties which we had when formerly in charge of this service under the previous Government.'[79]

Bolton suggests that Boyer refrained from putting to Spender that there was a choice between guidance and direction because Spender might then have insisted on a right of direction.[80] In any case, the chairman's soft words failed to win the support of the minister, who replied: 'I generally agree ... with the need to avoid divided or undefined responsibility in day-by-day operations. At the same time, I do not feel that the present proposals are entirely satisfactory.' He repeated that he should be in a position to authorise whatever changes might from time to time seem necessary, and ended with the ringing assertion:

In other words, I think it is important that Radio Australia be looked at *as an instrument of foreign policy* and that arrangements be made so that it can continually be *brought into line with the requirements of foreign policy.* [emphasis added] [81]

The chairman was unyielding. He replied that the question boiled down to two essentials:

(1) How best can the Overseas Service serve this country at this time having full regard to all the circumstances? As you know, the Commission's view is that even if thought of as 'an instrument of Government policy' [not in fact Spender's exact words], the indirect factual and balanced presentation of Australian life and views is more effective in the ideological struggle than the direct angled approach which is apt to be self-defeating in the long term.

(2) Whichever attitude your Government finally decides to approve, the problem of minute-to-minute [previous references had been to 'day-to-day'] responsibility for the

actual building of programmes will require to be devolved upon the actual radio personnel engaged, whether under the direct instruction of your own Department or of the ABC.

Boyer added an almost obsequious appeal: 'We find it hard to believe that you feel we are unworthy of such a trust, reinforced as we should be with advice, help and information from yourself and your Department.'[82]

Alan (later Sir Alan) Watt, who was soon to take over from Burton as secretary of the department, lent his support to Boyer's case. He told Spender that Boyer's view that the ABC should not be subject to political 'direction' was sound in principle. If a news service were to impress listeners, it was highly desirable to avoid their feeling that the service was 'in some sense a semi-government agency putting forward certain governmental views, however unexceptional these views may be'. On the other hand, he said, having an each-way bet, 'I would ... agree that mere general background appreciations, prepared by this Department, of the international situation, or of international developments in some special area, are insufficient to enable those who are preparing the news broadcasts from day to day to understand sufficiently *how the news should be slanted* [emphasis added].' But he went on to point out that if the department assumed responsibility for 'directing' overseas news broadcasts, it would have to have 'a first-class and responsible staff', which would not be easy to find. Watt concluded that, in principle, the ABC should have control, but should undertake to keep in the closest possible touch with the department for the necessary guidance. This guidance would include daily communication from the political intelligence division, which would give the department's views on what subjects were 'delicate', what subjects should be played up, what subjects should be played down, and so on.[83]

Throughout the debate, it was clear that the politicians and public servants wanted the benefits to their cause of the appearance of an independent international shortwave service, but only the appearance. They were not prepared to accept the disadvantages of a genuinely independent broadcaster.

Selection of news

When at last, two months after the ABC's takeover, the cabinet committee met to consider the future of Radio Australia, it leant heavily towards its operation by the ABC. Its decision on the function of the department's liaison officer was to be often quoted in subsequent years as the battle for control of the content of the key programs of Radio Australia continued to rage:

That a liaison officer from the Department of External Affairs should work in collaboration with the Editorial Staff and *advise on the selection of news items and news commentaries.*
The Minister for External Affairs should give his liaison officer an indication of policy lines
to be kept in mind and the liaison officer will be responsible to *draw the attention of the
Editorial Staff* to matters which appear to conflict with foreign policy. *The formal decision
and responsibility will rest with the Editor,* who will be expected to work in harmony with the
liaison officer [emphasis added].[84]

Some ABC executives had not shared Boyer's concern for Radio
Australia's integrity. Hamilton told Finlay, as acting general manager, that
Radio Australia

must remain essentially a news service, shaped to the interests of the people in the particular target area of each transmission. But, within that broad objective, there still remain opportunities for selection of news which will meet any propaganda ideas the Government or
its advisers have.[85]

Finlay replied, 'As you know, I agree with what you say and when we get
the "all clear", we will go ahead along the lines you have suggested.'[86]
Fortunately for Radio Australia's independence, though not perhaps for the
blood pressure of some officers of the Department of External Affairs, the
'all clear' never came.

Over lunch in Melbourne six weeks later, Finlay assured Goss that the
ABC would give full facilities for close liaison with External Affairs. But
both Finlay and Hamilton, who was also present, were insistent that the
ABC must control Radio Australia. Goss said Hamilton, speaking at times
'with some asperity' (something not unusual for the editor-in-chief) had
shown more concern than Finlay to justify the commission's attitude. But
when Goss said the department's influence would 'acquire a particular
character' only if it wanted a specific news item included, dropped or modified, Hamilton became more receptive. He said he could not imagine circumstances in which 'his people' would refuse to comply with a request of
the kind Goss had mentioned.[87] The same week, Goss gave Watt an idea of
the kinds of news items which he believed Radio Australia should stress.
They were technical assistance news, 'anti-Communist news', news showing the recovery and consolidation of the power of Western democracies,
and news showing American willingness to underwrite Western security.
He also suggested that Australia's attitude to communism in Asia might be
defined in the following way: 'Communism is a new kind of imperialism:

countries that have been colonies and recently won their freedom and independence, should not let memories of the old imperialism blind them to the threat of the new. They might well find themselves colonies again.' This was a theme, Goss said, that could be 'elaborated and repeated in news bulletins and commentaries'.[88]

Spender's determination that Radio Australia should be used as a weapon in the Cold War had been given impetus by the outbreak of the Korean War on 25 June 1950 and the committal of Australian forces a month later. Commitment to the American alliance was formalised the following year with the signing of the ANZUS Pact. Soon Spender was enthusiastically advocating the expansion of Radio Australia to cover further areas and languages, in general coordination with the Voice of America and the BBC. He suggested to the Defence Minister, Philip (later Sir Philip) McBride, that Radio Australia should provide 'a link in the propaganda chain of the democracies'. He agreed with the defence committee that the greatest possible defence benefits should be derived from both Radio Australia and the listening post (now part of Spender's own department). The liaison with Radio Australia, he said, was under the supervision of the head of the political intelligence section, who also represented the Department of External Affairs on the Joint Intelligence Committee, so there was an avenue for effective liaison with the Defence Department.[89]

The same month, the plan for expansion was under way. 'Following discussions' (presumably with the department), Robin Wood, whom the ABC had appointed supervisor of overseas services, sent Finlay a tentative schedule providing for three daily one-hour transmissions in Russian, and three transmissions, totalling two hours, in Mandarin and Cantonese.[90] Two days later, Boyer, Moses, Finlay and Keith (later Sir Keith) Waller of External Affairs decided to investigate further the possibility of extending Radio Australia's broadcasts to Russian and Chinese, throwing in Japanese for good measure.[91]

The move to broadcast in Russian gathered momentum. Boyer told the October meeting of the commission that a request by the BBC and the American State Department that Australia and Canada should cooperate in a 'combined assault' on the USSR had sufficient urgency to justify serious consideration. The ideological issue was of such fundamental and global importance that if there were reasonable grounds for the belief that Radio Australia's contribution would be of significance, it would be 'a grave responsibility' to reject the suggestion. He recommended that, subject to the concurrence and support of the Department of External Affairs, the ABC should agree to make suitable arrangements, as he expected the Canadian Broadcasting Corporation would agree to do. Someone (presumably a commissioner) wrote in the margin beside Boyer's recommendation, 'Won't the Russians jamb us? Surely it is in our interest to deal directly with the effects of R. propaganda in the countries near us than throw our small resources into a campaign for the Soul of Russia!'

The reasoning of the note in the margin was endorsed by the BBC's non-European services, which Boyer had asked to comment. Their view was that the most valuable broadcasts from Radio Australia in present circumstances would be to the Far East and Southeast Asia in Japanese, Indonesian, Malay and English. The BBC had suggested, perhaps not entirely altruistically, that Radio Australia should broadcast in the mornings to avoid clashing with the BBC's evening broadcasts, thus maximising the dissemination of 'the British Commonwealth point of view'. The American State Department had confined itself to urging Australia's participation in broadcasts direct to the USSR.

The head of the Department of External Affairs took a more far-sighted view. He believed the most potent influence Australia could exert was in China and Japan, in that order. Showing considerable foresight, Watt said that, although China was under a communist regime, there was good reason to believe that Chinese communist development might be of a different pattern from that of Russia. It might become Chinese rather than Russian communism, with all that this signified. Boyer agreed that the argument for beginning a Chinese service appeared very strong. The second priority, Japan, seemed only slightly lower in importance. Although Japan was not at the moment threatened by communist domination, the manner in which the Japan of the future developed was obviously of great moment.

Boyer was also impressed by the Defence Department's request that sufficient shortwave broadcasting contacts should be established in peacetime in the countries to Australia's north to enable quick development of these contacts for military purposes in the event of hostilities. In summary, he told the commission he believed Radio Australia should be committed to broadcasting only in Russian, Chinese, Japanese and Malay, with very minor attention to Thai and French. This, he said, would be very modest by comparison with the Canadian Broadcasting Corporation, which broadcast in French, German, Dutch, Italian, Czech, Danish, Norwegian, Swedish, Portuguese and Spanish, as well as many specially-beamed transmissions in English.[92] The commission resolved that Boyer should submit a recommendation to the Postmaster-General along the lines indicated in his report.[93] Shortly afterwards, Boyer told Anthony that the Department of External Affairs believed Radio Australia should be directed most urgently to China and Japan in that order of priority, and that the ABC should consider as a matter of principle the invitation of the BBC and the Voice of America to join with them, and shortly with Canada, in simultaneous broadcasts to Russia 'to pierce the radio curtain of jamming stations erected by that country'.[94]

Goss was more specific than Boyer in his reference to the Defence Department's support. He said the department's plans for psychological war in the event of a third world war assumed Radio Australia's existence and its contact with a wide audience. 'Although independent of Britain and the US,' he said, 'Radio Australia's transmitters are basically part of the Anglo-American apparatus for counter-propaganda.' He claimed that the 'physical [and] mental propinquity' of Broadcast House in London to the Foreign Office served the same purpose as the American system of placing the whole external publicity program of the government under the State Department.[95]

Publicly, Moses claimed that Radio Australia was independent. In the program schedule for late 1951, he wrote:

The Australian Broadcasting Commission, of which Radio Australia is an integral part, is, like the British Broadcasting Corporation, free of government control. Thus, when you are listening to Radio Australia you are listening to the voice of Australia, not of any one political party or other section in Australia.[96]

Calwell, so recently deprived of control of Radio Australia, was no help to those fighting for its independence. He opposed the ABC's control, and even suggested that the service could be run by External Affairs. An alternative, he said, was the Department of the Interior, but the ideal would be control by the old Department of Information resurrected. Calwell's comments, reported in the *Argus*, were made in response to an earlier story in which Casey, as External Affairs Minister, had praised the goodwill Radio Australia was building up in Asian countries. Calwell said: 'A valuable propaganda medium like Radio Australia should not be under the control of such an entertainment medium as the ABC. It is absurd for programmes intended for Australian audiences to be broadcast to people overseas.'[97]

Casey was brimming over with ideas for enlisting Radio Australia in the Cold War. Proprietorially referring to 'our programmes', he told the acting secretary of the department, 'Jim' (later Sir Laurence) McIntyre:

It occurred to me that an innovation that we might well adopt would be to ask each of our relevant posts in the East to send us a daily or periodical telegram recommending any particular lines they think our programmes might take, in connection with political and national matters.[98]

He went on to suggest: 'We might also consider a programme in French directed at Indo-China. I think that there is already a programme in French, but not with Indo-China in mind.'

Casey and his department began to encourage Radio Australia to increase its broadcasts to Asia as part of Australia's contribution to the Cold War. After touring Asia in 1951, he asked the new head of the organisation, Robin Wood, when he contemplated beginning broadcasts in Chinese and Japanese. Wood's reply was that Moses was 'hopeful of having this matter discussed as soon as possible'.[99] But, in reality, Moses was preoccupied with broadcasting within Australia. Wood recalled in 1988 that Radio Australia had been 'rather an unwanted child in a way', and Moses had given it little thought.[100]

In June 1952, Casey decided to seek a cabinet ruling to give his department control of the political content of Radio Australia's broadcasts. The department prepared a draft submission for cabinet that said, in part, 'whatever means be adopted for allocating the responsibility for controlling shortwave transmissions, the division of power should be one that leaves largely in the hands of this Department decisions as to policy and approach'.[101] But for some reason, perhaps because of the fear that such a ruling would confirm listeners' suspicions that Radio Australia was the mouthpiece of the Australian government, the submission never went to cabinet.

Despite Boyer's scruples, Radio Australia, coaxed by Goss, was already doing a good deal to provide the kind of Cold War propaganda the department wanted. Goss reported that in August and September 1952, perhaps twenty-one spoken-word features could be said to have been of political significance. Most had demonstrated the positive approach of the democracies to Asian problems through the United Nations, the Colombo Plan etc., and the remainder had borne directly on current communist propaganda. Two in the latter category had been prepared by Goss himself.[102] Later in 1952 Radio Australia began broadcasting a weekly talk by Spender, then ambassador to the United Nations.[103] On occasions, it broadcast talks by Casey himself.[104] One example is a fulsome talk he gave on the centenary of French settlement in New Caledonia, obviously aimed at the French administrators and settlers rather than the indigenous people. He said, *inter alia*, 'We are gratefully aware that our near neighbour brings to this far region something of the culture and civilising influence of France.'[105]

Liaison with Voice of America

Casey had expanded on his perception of Radio Australia as a quid pro quo in a personal letter to Boyer in July 1952: 'when one gets down to tin-tacks as to what Australia can *do*, as compared with what we can ask the Americans to *do*—there is so little of the former and so much of the latter, that I tend to become a little ashamed.'[106] He made a similar remark in his diary a fortnight later, when he referred to 'development of RA in liaison with the VoA' as one of the 'few things' Australia could offer the Americans in exchange for the 'great many things we could ask the Americans for'.[107] Significantly, the letter to Boyer was written shortly before Casey's departure for Honolulu for the initial meeting of the Pacific Council, which was to implement a tripartite Pacific security treaty. Casey proposed to Boyer much closer collaboration between Radio Australia and the Voice of America in the propaganda war. He began by saying he and Boyer had 'agreed to endeavour to improve the effectiveness of the Radio Australia broadcasts by increasing their political content and otherwise'. He continued:

However, if we are going to make the Radio Australia broadcasts to the East into a real factor in the political situation, I would believe that we have to go on further than we have yet
contemplated. We would need to be closely and continuously informed as to what the
Americans were putting over the Voice of America, so far as the East is concerned—and
our programmes would need to have their content integrated with that of the Voice of
America (although, I would hope, without our material being as blunt and hard-hitting as
the American material) ... This subject of broadcast propaganda (little as I like this word)
seems to be one of the few positive directions in which we could help (particularly in this
Cold War period) without substantial cost to ourselves.[108]

In Honolulu, Casey spoke briefly to his American counterpart, Dean Acheson, about the expansion in Radio Australia's activities. On the voyage home, he wrote to Acheson, with some hyperbole, that the service provided 'a considerable radio bombardment of a number of countries on the Asian mainland, particularly to South-East Asia'. He continued:

I would believe that, in order to make the most of Radio Australia from the political point
of view, we should have some positive link with the Voice of America, so that we are made
aware of the political directives on which the Voice of America operates. I believe that it
would also be possible for us to inaugurate new programmes in local languages if it is

thought that these would be good value. If your people believe that there is merit in what I have said, we would be very glad to discuss with your people how we can best implement it in the general interest.[109]

In a note to an officer of his department to which he attached a copy of his letter to Acheson, he reported his impression that Radio Australia's programs to Southeast Asian countries would need 'an appreciable amount of modification in order to convert them to what we want'.[110]

The possibility of a link between Radio Australia and the Voice of America was followed up by the embassy in Washington. But the aversion of Boyer and some of the ABC's senior executives to the American model was an obstacle. In a secret memorandum, entitled 'Collaboration between Radio Australia and the Voice of America', the secretary of the department told the embassy:

There are several limiting factors which have to be taken into account, since the Department's relation to Radio Australia is quite different from that of the State Department to VOA. While the ABC, which is responsible for Radio Australia, recognises the propriety of presenting the Government's view point on international affairs in its *overseas* service, it is an independent agency. The Department cannot direct: it can only advise—and that from a distance of four hundred miles.[111]

Watt said the department's receipt of the more important VOA directives was the first step towards the desired cooperation, because they enabled it 'to check that our own angle on various international events is generally not inconsistent with that of the State Department'. and because they indicated what subjects were considered important for propaganda purposes and when. But he added:

Needless to say VOA directives as such are never passed to Radio Australia. In fact we do not know whether Radio Australia is aware that we receive them. They have only a limited distribution even inside the Department and when used are incorporated in our regular or ad hoc directives to the Liaison Officer.

Some of the VOA directives, in this filtered fashion, must have found their way into Radio Australia's programs, particularly through the news commentaries.[112] Some VOA propaganda (as well as material supplied directly by the department) may well have been attributed to 'the ABC correspondent in Canberra'. At a meeting of officers of the department and the ABC (including Radio Australia) in 1954, Hamilton said Radio Australia was receiving from time to time 'explanatory material' from the department, but found it difficult to use without 'hanging it on some individual'. He suggested that in such cases the 'explanatory material' might be put into the mouth of an ABC journalist, with the phrase, 'The ABC Correspondent in Canberra states …' The meeting agreed with Hamilton's suggestion.[113] In 1965, the VOA offered to provide 'background material' directly to Radio Australia, as detailed below. By May 1953, a senior officer of the department was able to report to Casey that, during the previous nine months, steps had been taken to increase the political content of Radio Australia's broadcasts. He told the minister that a weekly news commentary was to be introduced on 3 June.[114]

In a confidential note prepared for the Australian planning team discussing psychological warfare at the five-power planning conference at Pearl Harbor in June 1953, the department said Australia was in a position to contribute to propaganda only to a limited degree, *except in the case of radio broadcasting*. The note said that although the final say rested with the editors, Goss was able to 'ensure that the line taken by Radio Australia is in accordance with Government policy'.[115]

3   Moses: 'a gutless wonder', 1953—1964

In the second half of 1953, the Department of External Affairs tightened the screws on Charles Moses. In October F. J. (Blake) Blakeney told him:

Our interpretation of the [1950] directive has been that, while Radio Australia has the formal decision and responsibility, Radio Australia would not, unless in exceptional circumstances, reject External Affairs advice on either the choice of foreign affairs material to be broadcast or the manner of its presentation.[1]

At a meeting between Blakeney and ABC executives ten days after this was written, Moses apparently surrendered without firing a shot. He is reported to have said that, while the ABC would not want to see itself become a 'rubber stamp' of External Affairs so far as its overseas services were concerned,

the ABC would be acting 'irresponsibly' if it acted in defiance of strong External Affairs advice ... Radio Australia should never broadcast anything which is opposed to the interests of Australian foreign policy or which would embarrass that policy. 'Australian foreign policy', in this context, cannot normally be distinguished from 'Australian Government foreign policy'.[2]

But Richard Boyer, as chairman, continued to seek a written directive confirming the ABC's final responsibility for content. In a personal letter to Casey he wrote:

As I think we both agree, it is necessary that either your Department or the ABC should accept the final responsibility for what goes on the air. The present legal position, whereby the final responsibility rests with us, is, I believe, in our best interests mutually, and I feel it should remain so.[3]

The minister responded with a personal and confidential message to Boyer which said, in part, 'There is no doubt, of course, that the Commission has the final responsibility for what goes on the air'.[4] No more formal acknowledgment of this was ever received.[5]

In the meantime, Goss as the department's liaison officer was whittling away Radio Australia's resistance at his level of operations. Reporting on a conversation with Radio Australia head Robin Wood, he told his department: 'I said I thought he had frequently gone further in collaborating with me than his superiors would have approved and would probably have gone further if their attitude had not been so restrictive. He confirmed this.'

In their discussions with more senior ABC executives, officers of the department were using their experience in diplomacy. After the first of a regular series of meetings between ABC executives and External Affairs officers in Canberra in March 1954, the editor-in-chief, Walter Hamilton reported:

The atmosphere was most friendly, informative and co-operative, with not the slightest hint that the department was concerned about anything except to help us. There was no suggestion of interference or direction ... Our approach to the news over Radio Australia— objective without propaganda—was fully endorsed by Mr Plimsoll [an assistant secretary] ... he conceded that Radio Australia could not be *merely* a mouthpiece of Government policy.

The ABC was responsive to this approach:

We emphasised, of course, that the interests of Australia were always an important consideration with us and that we were careful in our handling of racial matters ... We pointed out that we were already doing a great deal to publicise ... the activities of Colombo Plan students.[6]

James (later Sir James) Plimsoll's report to Boyer on the meeting said, in part:

I understand that it went extremely well and that both parties will be able to get some of the things done that they wanted. I understand, for example, that Radio Australia is going to put over more talks of a nature likely to help our foreign policy ... [7]

Behind the scenes, the department was working out the lines Radio Australia should follow to maximise its contribution as an instrument of Australian foreign policy. A document prepared in mid-1954 recommended, *inter alia*, the following approaches to broadcasts about particular issues:

India   With India, more than with any other country of the area, we are confronted with the convolutions of Asian thinking, and criticism based on logical thinking as we know it may not be realistic in India, where it may well be strongly resented and lead to a misunderstanding of our policies.

Pakistan   Pakistan is going through a period of political strain which will probably test to the utmost the Ali Government's ability to hold the two parts together. It is desirable, however, that the recent developments in East Bengal should not be cited as the beginning of the end for Pakistan, but rather as a part of the new nation's evolution. Our sympathy for Pakistan's difficulties should be emphasised …

Arab-Israel relations   Our over-riding objective should be a reduction in tension so that an outbreak of hostilities can be avoided. We should, therefore, strongly condemn all those incidents (usually originated by Israel) involving military or paramilitary forces …

Middle East Defence   Any broadcasts on this subject should … stress that defence is being arranged by the countries concerned themselves—that the impetus comes not from the Western Powers but because the Middle Eastern nations are aware that the real menace to their independence comes from the Soviet Union.[8]

At the third of the regular meetings between External Affairs and the ABC, Casey made it clear that his perception of Radio Australia was dominated by its potential as a weapon in the Cold War. He stressed that Americans in the State Department had mentioned to him from time to time that Radio Australia might well include more political material in its programs than it now did. This was something which 'might be considered'. On the possible expansion of foreign-language broadcasts, he said he thought Radio Australia should begin a service in Mandarin as soon as it could possibly be arranged. This was important because of the large number of Chinese outside China who spoke Mandarin. Casey also stressed the importance of Thailand, which he described as 'one of the important buffers between Communism and our near North'. He thought the weekly Thai service might well become a daily one.[9] On broadcasts about Australia's immigration policy, the ABC executives emphasised that Asian students sent home press cuttings and comments to relatives and friends in Asia. They felt that the bulk of this was adverse comment such as appeared in *Truth*, and there was a need for Radio Australia to counter such reports.[10]

Boyer welcomed Casey's expression of support for a Mandarin service, and followed it up with a recommendation to the Postmaster-General. Casey supported the recommendation in a letter in which he stressed the potential value of the service in terms of the Cold War. Referring to the

Chinese of Southeast Asia, seen as the main target audience, he told the acting Postmaster-General, Sir Philip McBride:

Their international importance stems from their relation with the Chinese homeland. Their financial contributions were a source of support for the Nationalist regime before 1949. They could give equally powerful support to the present Communist Chinese regime and might be brought to do so by Communist propaganda and intimidation ... They constitute a potential fifth column much more numerous and influential than the Japanese fifth column in South-East Asia before the Pacific War.[11]

Casey also referred to the potential audience in China itself, saying it was 'a matter of the greatest importance' that evidence of non-communist viewpoints be available in Beijing. He then gave what was a testimony to the value of the overseas service:

The opportunities that I have had for observation in my trips abroad and the reports that I receive from an increasing number of my Departmental officers have convinced me of the value of Radio Australia as a relatively inexpensive and effective means of making non-Communist views known and of building goodwill for Australia in Asian countries.

Boyer and his commission continued to resist attempts by Casey and his department to use Radio Australia as an instrument of more overt propaganda. Casey suggested that when he made important statements on government policy, brief extracts in his own voice might be interpolated in the news bulletin.[12] After discussing the idea with Hamilton, Goss sent him a draft example in which the insert was clumsily introduced with the words, 'We interrupt this bulletin to give you an extract from the Minister's statement, recorded in Canberra.'[13] The commission declined the suggestion, feeling that 'it might tend to suggest to overseas listeners that the news bulletins are an expression of Government policy rather than an impartial and objective presentation of the news of the day'. Moses said later, though, that it should be made clear to the Department of External Affairs that there would be no difficulty about including occasional short statements by Casey in programs of the newsreel type.[14]

Casey did not acknowledge it in his letter to McBride, but it was not only the State Department that mentioned Radio Australia during his visits to the United States. His diary records that in Washington in 1954 the director of the CIA, Alan Dulles, said his organisation wanted to contribute 'some ideas/material' to Radio Australia.[15] Dulles had proposed that the CIA's station officer in Canberra pass the material to External Affairs through his immediate contacts in Australia, or that the United States embassy in Canberra give it direct to External Affairs.[16] Two years later, Casey recorded in his diary a meeting at his home in Berwick, Victoria, with Dulles, Colonel Harris (a CIA representative) and Alfred Brookes (head of the Australian Secret Intelligence Service). Dulles had expressed interest in the proposed booster station for Radio Australia, a project in which he said the CIA 'might co-operate'.[17]

The piper paid

The year 1955 was an eventful one for Radio Australia, in a number of ways. The government became increasingly concerned about the Cold War, and increasingly determined to use the shortwave service to counter-act communist subversion in Asia. The year was less than a week old when the cabinet considered a top-secret submission from Casey entitled 'Australian Activities in the Cold War'. The submission said a forthcoming meeting of ministers from Manila treaty (SEATO) countries would con-sider not only military planning, but also non-military activities, 'which may well be more important and more fruitful'. The submission was cru-cial to decisions on Radio Australia's future.

Propaganda and information   Here Australia can make a significant contribution through Radio Australia. Radio Australia has built up a valuable reputation for the objectivity of its news sessions and has a wide audience, particularly in Indonesia. Programmes consist mainly of entertainment in order to attract and hold an audience, but a significant amount of political matter (on which the advice of the Department of External Affairs is sought) appears in regular commentaries, etc. ... From a political warfare point of view, it is desir-able to increase the number and length of Radio Australia broadcasts, and to increase the transmitting equipment ... any additional cost of proposals suggested here for winning the 'Cold War'—and attracting American interest in particular into the area—would be small in relation to the military expenditure that we must in any case contemplate.[18]

Casey's submission failed to acknowledge the possibility that Radio Australia's 'valuable reputation for objectivity' would be endangered by its increased use as a propaganda weapon in the Cold War, although later he was to show he was not unaware of this danger. Cabinet accepted the sub-mission's recommendation that the Postmaster-General and Minister for External Affairs prepare proposals for expanding the activities and techni-cal facilities of Radio Australia.[19]

In February 1955, Wood submitted to a secret session of the parlia-mentary Joint Committee on Foreign Affairs a summary of talks programs, indicating how Radio Australia was shaping them to serve the govern-ment's ends. He said the service collaborated closely with External Affairs in the two international talks programs, 'Behind the News' and 'International Report'. The latter, he said, emphasised 'positive measures taken by nations of the free world, working together, to solve social and economic problems'. The program had included a series of talks on Australia and the United Nations, particularly Australia's attitude to issues debated in the General Assembly (using material provided by External Affairs). For 'Australian Editorial Opinion', he said, the service selected 'nothing that would be offensive or likely to be misconstrued, nor do we deal with delicate issues between friendly countries'. Documentaries, he said, had included a new year message to Asia from Casey.[20]

Wood later reported to Moses that, early in the meeting, Senator John Gorton had told him of a decision to spend £90,000 on additional transmitters to step up Australia's shortwave contribution to any future Cold War activities. But he said it was evident that some members of the committee were unhappy about the 1950 cabinet directive which vested the final editorial responsibility for Radio Australia with the ABC: 'Opinions were divergent as to the extent such powers should be exercised by the ABC, more especially in relation to any "cold-war" activities. There was also unanimity in the view that Radio Australia should be taking a more active part in direct propaganda.' Wood summed up his impressions by saying the joint committee saw in the service 'a very great future potential in assisting External Affairs and Defence Departments in the political field'.[21]

Officers of the Department of External Affairs told Hamilton and B. H. (Moley) Molesworth, head of talks, about cabinet's new emphasis on Australia's part in the Cold War, in which Radio Australia must play a big part. In a joint report to Moses, the two ABC executives said one possible development was the posting of an ABC news and talks man in Southeast Asia, for which funds would be provided. One other matter worth mentioning was the possibility of a long-range plan for the removal of Radio Australia staff and studios to Canberra or Sydney 'to gain smoother running and co-operation with the department'.[22]

These were not the department's only plans for Radio Australia. Casey discussed with Boyer a proposal for big increases in foreign-language broadcasts. He envisaged the introduction of a daily program of forty-five minutes in Mandarin to Southeast Asia, the increase of the weekly Thai program to one hour daily and the doubling of the daily one-hour program in Indonesian. Boyer, who had long been seeking such an expansion, welcomed the move.[23]

Most of the staff of Radio Australia, too, welcomed these indications that their value was recognised, and that more resources were to follow this recognition. Many saw External Affairs as an ally against a parsimonious ABC management in Sydney which had done so little for them since the takeover five years earlier. After visiting Radio Australia in March, an officer of the department said his main impression had been of the 'enthusiasm and missionary zeal' of the entire staff, from Robin Wood down. It was entirely due to this zeal, he said, that, despite a critical staff shortage, Radio Australia had been able to build up its overseas audience and maintain such a high standard of program. He reported:

I was very well received everywhere, and convinced that Radio Australia is anxious to cooperate with us in every way—as long as we do not try to have obvious propaganda put over the air. They appreciate our assistance, and accept almost without question our views on the theme and content of talks. Their ready acceptance of our assistance is no doubt due partly to their own staff shortage; but it is also due to their realization that our views and information are authoritative. It is further due, I think, to their feeling of isolation and their desire for a strong ally against both the ABC and Treasury.[24]

The department was not slow to try to capitalise on these feelings. When Wood told Goss he was curtailing the spoken-word content of Radio Australia's programs to permit better presentation and supervision of what was broadcast, Goss replied that he thought the department had more to offer on matters of program content and presentation than it had so far been possible to give. He added that the department was showing an increased interest in the content and presentation of programs, referring rather pointedly to its support for the planned transmission in Mandarin. He suggested that each day's news bulletins should be teleprinted to the department so that the officer most directly concerned with the area would know what was being said and could make suggestions as to what should be said. Goss continued:

I then asked Mr Wood directly if he could let me have a greater share in general programme development. He said: 'No, I can't. It's all too domestic at present.' Mr Wood instanced Sydney's purely negative interpretation of my functions—'to be consulted if and when'. He said we had gone beyond this in Melbourne but he felt this would still be Sydney's attitude.[25]

Two days later, Moses was more malleable when a senior officer of the department, John Hood, proposed increased supervision by the department of Radio Australia's news bulletins. According to Hood's account, Moses accepted the need for this in principle, and undertook to review the staffing position in order to give effect to it. Hood quoted Moses as saying he appreciated that in the Cold War program 'the most effective use should be made of Radio Australia as a special instrument and that this could only be done in the closest co-operation with the Department of External Affairs'.[26]

A submission by Casey to cabinet on 10 May 1955 stated:

In view of its present high standing it is considered that increased use could be made of Radio Australia as a vehicle for promoting the policies of the Australian government and for countering communism in South and South-East Asia, provided that care is taken to maintain its existing reputation for impartiality and accuracy.

Whether or not Casey had previously been aware of the vulnerability of that reputation, apparently he was now.

The submission proposed the foreshadowed extensions to Radio Australia's foreign-language programs (but recommended that the Mandarin service should be not forty-five minutes, but one hour, daily, 'to be increased as soon as possible to two hours daily'). In support of the proposed sevenfold increase in the Thai program, Casey observed that the Geneva settlement in Indo-China had 'brought Thailand into the front line of the Communist advance'. It was considered most important that Radio Australia's audience there should be built up so that 'the Thais might be given unbiassed news and information, and as far as possible encouraged through appropriate propaganda to maintain their resistance to Communism'.[27]

Cabinet endorsed the extensions and approved the appointment (with the concurrence of the ABC) of an ABC representative in Southeast Asia. Cabinet also endorsed daily news commentaries, a program of English lessons for Indonesian listeners, and the technical rehabilitation of Radio Australia at an estimated cost of £110,000.[28] The cost of the ABC's representative in Southeast Asia was to be included in External Affairs estimates and disbursed to the ABC as required.[29] The payments were to be disguised in the ABC's budget under 'sums recoverable from other agencies'.[30] Arthur Tange, the department's secretary, subsequently claimed the cabinet decision had specified that the ABC representative in Southeast Asia (who would also be the Radio Australia representative) was to work 'under the general direction of the Australian commissioner in Southeast Asia (a senior diplomat).[31] No such condition is mentioned in the cabinet minute. Casey's submission to cabinet said it was *proposed* that he should work under the general direction of the commissioner, but noted that this matter was under discussion with the ABC.[32] Moses's successor as general manager of the ABC, Talbot (later Sir Talbot) Duckmanton, drew the commission's attention to Tange's letter in 1965, when the ABC was being confronted by a Minister for External Affairs who was far more predatory towards Radio Australia than Casey had ever been.[33]

A few days after the cabinet's decision, the department took what could have been a decisive step towards control of Radio Australia. According to a handwritten note by Tange in the margin of a secret memorandum to him on the subject of Radio Australia, Casey had told him by phone that Menzies had agreed that 'E.A. must run anything with *"political content".'* Tange's marginal note went on:

Stick firm on this with Boyer.
    I spoke to Minister about need to observe EA connections, particularly provision of funds, lest (a) other govts. identify service & commentaries as directed by Dept (b) MP's give free rein to their own ideas on propaganda in debates on estimates—and do harm (particularly in view of (a)) by raising controversy—from which ABC is virtually immune at present.
    Minister agreed: also agreed that some cover such as 'cultural' aid might prove efficacious. AHT 19/5/55.[34]

Surprisingly, the department seems never to have tried to exploit this agreement between Casey and Menzies. Apart from a passing reference in an inter-departmental memorandum three years later,[35] it appears to have vanished without trace.

Moses concedes

The personal surrender of Moses to Casey in the struggle for control of Radio Australia happened during a chance meeting at Canberra airport. The following day, Casey sent Hood a teleprinter message from Melbourne which said:

I OPENED UP SUBJECT OF RADIO AUSTRALIA WITH HIM AND SAID THAT MY ATTITUDE WAS QUITE SIMPLY THAT EXTERNAL AFFAIRS SHOULD HAVE FULL AUTHORITY IN RESPECT OF THE POLITICAL CONTENT OF RADIO AUSTRALIA BROADCASTS, INCLUDING THE LAST WORD IN SELECTION OF NEWS ITEMS. MOSES SAID THAT HIS PERSONAL ATTITUDE WAS DIFFERENT FROM THAT OF BOYER ON THIS, AND THAT HE QUITE AGREED WITH ME. HE (MOSES) SAID HE REGARDED RADIO AUSTRALIA MERELY AS AN INSTRUMENT OF GOVERNMENT POLICY AND THAT, AS SUCH, THEY SHOULD ACCEPT WHAT WE HAD TO SAY.[36]

Whether Moses was telling Casey the truth, no-one will ever know. Certainly his attitude to the independence of the ABC had varied, depending on whom he was talking to, and under what circumstances. If in reality he was on the side of those who believed the overseas service should be free from political control, he was certainly not prepared to stand up and be counted like Boyer, Hamilton, (Dr Keith) Barry (federal controller of programs) and Molesworth. Dr Clement Semmler, later deputy general manager to Moses, said Casey had told him in later years, when they were reminiscing about Radio Australia, that if he and his department had had only Moses to deal with and not Boyer, the service would inevitably have become an arm of the department. Semmler told the author in 1989, 'I can tell you for certain that Moses never had any interest in RA—he would have been pleased to see the ABC rid of it and he said this to me on a number of occasions.'[37] Semmler described his former boss as 'a gutless wonder when it came to dealing with anyone in authority in the Public Service or Government'.[38]

In July 1955, Casey had little difficulty persuading cabinet that Radio Australia's transmitters broadcasting to Asia should be doubled from three to six over the next two and a half years. No doubt he stressed the potential value of these broadcasts to the anti-communist side in the Cold War. He recorded in his diary: 'Got it through without much argument.'[39]

At a meeting with officials of the United States Information Agency and the Voice of America in Washington in September 1955, Casey reported on Australia's initiatives in the Cold War. He said that, under the Colombo Plan, Australia was distributing radios (both shortwave and medium-wave) to selected individuals, for example headmen, teachers and village leaders. The meeting foreshadowed closer cooperation between Radio Australia and the Voice of America. The director of the USIA suggested better coordination between the two broadcasters 'on the broad lines of approach to certain matters of common interest'. Casey's predecessor, Spender, who was present in his capacity as Australia's ambassador to the United Nations, suggested that too much uniformity could destroy the effectiveness of the programs. But it was agreed that 'in any case the basic policies of Radio Australia and VOA were the same'.[40]

Robin Wood's obligation to the Department of External Affairs was increased early in 1956, when he toured Southeast Asia at the department's suggestion and expense.[41] Barrie Dexter, who proposed the trip, told Tange that Wood had never been to Asia, and was working under a disadvantage because of his lack of first-hand knowledge of the area.[42] The department had another motive: during his visit, Wood was to attend a meeting of the SEATO information committee.[43] Attendance at the meeting would no doubt reinforce Wood's perception of Radio Australia as part of Australia's effort in the Cold War.

The department's assiduous cultivation of Robin Wood was of limited benefit. Shortly after his tour of Southeast Asia at the department's expense, he successfully sought promotion to a position in the ABC's head office in Sydney.[44]

Wood's successor as director was Peter Homfray, an unsuccessful Liberal candidate in the 1953 Tasmanian state election. He arrived full of enthusiasm to expand Radio Australia's services. He suggested that all the languages on Boyer's 'shopping list' of eighteen months earlier should be introduced, in the following order: Japanese, Hindi (which was to be a recurring theme from Homfray), Cantonese, Tamil, Burmese, Urdu and Malay.[45] In his first meeting with Homfray since their days in South Asia, Casey told him he did not see much point in the extension of broadcasts in these seven languages. He did not believe they would have much of a listening audience. Radio Australia's signal would be 'pretty weak' by the time it got to Japan, and 'the number of radio-set owners who could speak only Hindi, Cantonese, Tamil, etc. would be pretty limited'. But an unsigned note in the margin of Casey's memorandum remarks that, in subsequent notes, the minister had expressed the opposite view.[46]

The minister was apparently determined that Homfray, like his predecessor, would be aware of Radio Australia's obligation to the department. According to an account of their meeting, he gave Homfray 'a fair indication of the extent to which the Department is responsible for Radio Australia's development in recent years'.[47]

Boyer versus Tange

The scene was set for a trial of strength between Boyer and the department's formidable secretary, Arthur Tange. The points at issue are clear from a draft statement by Boyer to his minister, Charles (later Sir Charles) Davidson, of 'the relationship between Radio Australia as conducted by the ABC and the Department of External Affairs' and the reactions of Tange, who had been given a copy for comment. Boyer conceded at the outset that 'an external overseas radio service cannot be thought of in the precise terms of an extension of a country's home service'. Tange's comment in the margin beside this admission was: 'Also Govt does not furnish entertainment of foreigners as an end in itself.' On the other hand, Boyer said optimistically:

I believe the Department of External Affairs and its Minister, your colleague Mr Casey, are equally convinced, with ourselves, that Radio Australia should not be the voice of the Government of the day, but should represent the informed opinion of this country as a whole. Further, it is clear from the discussions which we have had extending over a long period with External Affairs that they share our views that our overseas news service should be entirely objective, balanced and factual.

Here, Tange remarked: 'Much depends on definition.' Quoting his favourite example, the BBC in wartime, Boyer went on: 'It was precisely this objectivity which made the BBC news so influential throughout the whole of the belligerent area during the years of the war. Radio Australia has consistently maintained this policy and has been supported by the Department of External Affairs.' Tange's marginal comment here was, 'Broadcasts to Asia in 1958 are not same as broadcasts to European listeners in 1943.' Boyer proceeded to assert that, first, the views of news commentators were not under censorship, and, second, there was a distinct understanding between Casey and himself that the final decision as to the content lay with the commentator, whose responsibility was to the ABC, and not to the department. This was unacceptable to Tange, who asked rhetorically, 'Do these together mean that commentators can employ time provided to attack or undermine objectives of foreign policy of *Govt* and Australia?'[48]

In a letter to Boyer, Tange tried to sugar the pill:

My own personal opinion is that your formulation does not entirely convey the Government's understanding of the objects of Radio Australia news broadcasts and commentaries ...

I confess that I believe that there is a difference of principle which is difficult to bridge with words. I can perhaps illustrate what I have in mind by choosing an extreme example.

Then followed a sentence which, though opaque, is clear enough in import:

I am quite sure that the Government would regard it as an insupportable state of affairs if the objective of the chosen instrument supported and developing its technical capacity to reach Asian audiences with Government finance were to provide entertainment and factual information to non-Australian [*sic*], combined with unregulated commentaries in which there were continued and sustained attacks on Australian foreign policy or representation of views and objectives which were in conflict with the views and objectives inherent in Australian foreign policy.

I believe the basic problem lies in this and also in the Government's belief (endorsed in several decisions of the Government) that *the final objective of Radio Australia is something considerably more* than retaining a reputation for objective news and the conveyance of informed opinions from all quarters of the community on foreign policy questions.[49]

To Davidson, Boyer commented,

I regret to say that the understanding of the Department as expressed in Mr Tange's comments and the understanding of the Commission differ in what we would consider certain essentials ... As I think I mentioned to you, the whole relationship between us, which has at times been difficult while always on a friendly basis, has been rather in the manner of a gentlemen's agreement hitherto, and neither side has attempted to define the relationship and operation.'[50]

A draft letter from Casey to Davidson, obviously prepared under Tange's instructions, said:

Whether we like it or not, all opinions broadcast by Radio Australia will be regarded by overseas listeners, particularly in Asia, as those of the Australian Government … considerations of national interest must, in the ultimate analysis, determine what can and cannot be broadcast by Radio Australia.

Radio Australia has been built up, at official expense, as an instrument of our foreign policy, with the particular task of projecting Australia to the peoples of Asia.[51]

It seems that the letter was never sent.

Boyer later wrote to Tange:

As I see it, the core of this problem is one of very fundamental moment. If, as suggested by you, it were insupportable that Radio Australia should carry views which do not coincide with the foreign policy of the Government of the day, particularly vis-a-vis South East Asia, then clearly we should have to depart altogether from the principle of objectivity. As you know, this question has already arisen in respect of the function of Radio Australia as to whether it should or should not mention in its broadcasts views on foreign policy of the Opposition which conflict with the views of the Government of the day. Quite frankly, we of the Commission feel that if we are to depart from presenting a true view of major responsible Australian opinion in foreign affairs, the usefulness of Radio Australia in the foreign field would rapidly disappear.[52]

Tange replied that he was sceptical of whether principles pronounced as the rule for a global broadcasting system like the BBC were applicable to Asia, 'where there is an ideological and political struggle going on'.[53] (His implication appears to have been that there was *not* such a struggle in Europe.) Speaking of the respect in Europe for freedom of political opinion, he said:

My point of view is that these things have few roots in Asia at present because Asian tradition and educational background are entirely different. Their thinking on political principle is largely shapeless below the level of the literate few. The Communists have the advantage that they recognize this. Their broadcasting follows simplified themes seeking to persuade Asian people to reject the Western democracies, and their foreign policies, and to accept Communism. I do not think it is enough for us to respond to this by demonstrating our liberality of opinion and our freedom to disagree among ourselves. Do Asian listeners regard these things as admirable in the way that you and I do?[54]

It came as a shock to the department when, in November 1958, Moses, the man who had told Casey he thought External Affairs should have full authority in respect of the political content of Radio Australia broadcasts, appeared to bite the hand that fed him. Referring to a letter to

him which had been copied to Homfray, he wrote to Tange curtly pointing out that all mail from the department to the ABC should be addressed
to him. He would pass on copies, 'if it is considered desirable', to the
appropriate ABC program officers.[55]

In 1959 Casey again pressed for his department to have more say in
the content of the broadcasts. He told Davidson:

I think that the goodwill which Radio Australia earns us is a great political advantage and I
think that we must direct our minds to the most useful employment of Radio Australia to
further our political objectives, which can only have a beneficial effect in our part of the
world ... In short, it is my belief that Radio Australia is a weapon of substantial importance
in the ideological war being waged against us.[56]

The previous June, Casey said, the American, British, New Zealand
and Australian governments had agreed at a conference in Canberra that
they all should do everything possible to project their points of view and
augment their counter-propaganda efforts. To do this effectively, they must
continue to build up their broadcasts in the local languages. He had in
mind three additional foreign-language broadcasts to Asia, Japanese,
Hindi[57] and Cantonese.[58] Radio Australia was clearly of high entertainment quality, but he regarded the entertainment content as the 'carrier' for
its political content. He thought the political content could be appreciably
increased, while still stopping far short of what he called 'the too-hard-
hitting type of Voice of America broadcasting'.[59]

Boyer welcomed Casey's interest in expanding the Asian-language
broadcasts. Three weeks later, in a somewhat chummy letter ('My dear
Dick ... Sincerely yours, Dick'), Boyer wrote:

Apropos our recent discussion on Radio Australia programmes, we are going closely into
the balance of their content and will be making changes to ensure more purposeful use of
the medium. I have to admit that your suggestion that such a review seemed indicated, had
real substance. In particular, we are moving toward giving more programme time to our
language broadcasts to Asia and less to the items designed to serve our troops abroad.[60]

The Japanese service was duly introduced in mid-1960; Cantonese was not
to come until several years later.

After this initial acceptance of his ministerial suitor's advances, Boyer
drew back a little. He reiterated his insistence on a policy of objectivity for
Radio Australia. The head of the department's information branch, John
McMillan, told Tange that by this Boyer meant that Radio Australia should
give a substantial degree of coverage to views other than those of the
government.

Following the repeated failure of attempts to persuade the ABC to give Goss some control over Radio Australia's news and current affairs broadcasts (with the exception of the news commentaries, dealt with in chapter 5), the department abandoned this tack. It decided in 1959 to abolish his position. Tange told Moses that liaison work could be carried on from Canberra, with regular visits between departmental officers going to Melbourne and Radio Australia officers visiting Canberra.[61] The failure of the department to control the news broadcasts was attributed by at least one of its senior officers to the determination of the ABC to run Radio Australia according to the BBC model. In a post mortem on Goss's effectiveness, McMillan of the information branch reported to Tange that liaison had not been operative for news items, 'for reasons deriving from professional concepts of objectivity based on analogy with BBC practice'.[62]

Discussing the new arrangements with Moses, Tange said he thought liaison with the Radio Australia newsroom was the weakest point. The secretary later reported :

Mr. Moses said at once that he would like to see more liaison. He said that, after studying a recent account of BBC practice, he understood that it was normal for the Foreign Office to prepare texts for the BBC to use, or not use, as it thought fit. Mr Moses said he saw no reason why Radio Australia should not use such material, attributing it to its 'diplomatic correspondent'.[63]

Tange had replied that there would be difficulties arising from geography which did not exist in London. It was rather more difficult to prepare material when the user was several hundred miles away than when he sat down at a table and had the opportunity of discussing what he was being given. Moses, who appeared to take a different line with different people, told the commission two days later that Tange 'appeared to be agreeable to arrangements which would not prejudice the Commission's responsibilities regarding the content of the Radio Australia programmes'.

Another shot in Tange's battle for greater control was a reminder to Moses that cabinet's decision to approve an ABC (and Radio Australia) representative in Southeast Asia in 1955 provided that he was to work under the general direction of the Australian commissioner in Southeast Asia.

In the meantime, the expansion in Asian-language broadcasts resulting from the department's Cold War offensive was gaining momentum. The duration of the Indonesian service, broadcasting for two hours daily since 1956, doubled between April 1959 and April 1960.[64]

The department now launched a campaign to eliminate from Radio Australia's news bulletins stories unhelpful to the Cold War offensive.

During a visit to Melbourne, the head of the information branch drew the attention of the news editor, E. A. (Ted) Shaw, to news stories which he said 'required comment or correction'.[65] One quoted the president of United Press International as saying that during a visit to Russia he had found no indication of war preparations.[66] A second story quoted six Australian church leaders who had visited communist countries as saying they had found religious services well patronised, especially in the Soviet Union, where there were no signs of restraint on congregations.[67] Another story reported that a pro-communist newspaper in Indonesia had described Australian and American support of the Dutch case for continued control of West New Guinea as 'foreign intervention in Indonesia's affairs'. John McMillan reported to Laurence McIntyre, by this time Australia's ambassador to Indonesia, that for many years Radio Australia's news editor had gone along in his own way without any feeling that liaison with the department was of any use to him. 'I am therefore prepared for a long and slow campaign of infiltration in this field,' he said. 'As a result, it is not very easy for us to tell the news people how they should phrase their news items.'[68] McMillan later told Tange that in his talks with Shaw, the news editor had 'made considerable play of the professional standards of journalism, such as objectivity, impartiality and freedom from Government interference and has conveyed the impression that he can in no way be responsive to direction on lines of policy'.[69]

Darwin booster

By the end of 1959, the department had realised that only a booster station at Darwin would provide the signal strength it wanted in its chief Cold War weapon. Its support for the Darwin station was also to give it another lever to bring pressure to bear on the overseas service.[70] But the commission tried to resist moves to link the Darwin booster and the Cold War. Told by Moses that the booster station would be discussed by the parliamentary overseas planning committee, the commission stated that it was:

> most important that Radio Australia should not come to be regarded as a Cold War weapon. It is the Commission's policy that Radio Australia should present an objective coverage of current events and the Commission believes it is essential that this policy be maintained, both as a matter of principle and because it is necessary as a means of retaining the confidence of listeners overseas.[71]

Boyer, who wanted to have the cake of Radio Australia's independence and eat that of the Darwin station, expressed his concern about the wording of the draft cabinet submission on its construction. He told an officer of the department that the draft submission emphasised too much the role of Radio Australia in the Cold War.[72] But the submission accepted by cabinet the following year stated unequivocally that 'the dangers to Australia of Communist propaganda are a primary reason for proposing the establishment of a booster station in Darwin'.[73]

Cabinet also reaffirmed that the Minister for External Affairs and his department were responsible for 'providing effective guidance' on Radio Australia broadcasts on 'all matters of concern to the Australian government's foreign policy and, in particular, with regard to the objective of the Communist powers'.[74] Davidson quoted these words to the ABC's new chairman, Dr James Darling,[75] and asked him 'to ensure that the Commission maintains as close a liaison as practicable with the Department of External Affairs on all major policy matters [thus, perhaps inadvertently, slightly watering down the cabinet's words] which could affect Australia's foreign policy and our international relations generally.'[76]

Although the department was pressing for Radio Australia to be a weapon in the Cold War, it was wary of proposals for the American message itself to be transmitted from Australia. In 1959, the Voice of America made an informal approach to the Australian embassy in Washington about the possibility of a relay station. Passing on to Canberra what he described as probably 'a trial balloon', the counsellor suggested that if the idea were to be discouraged, it be done fairly promptly.[77] An unenthusiastic Tange replied confidentially that the suggestion was likely to present considerable difficulty. As soon as any such transmission began from Australia, he said, its geographical location would at once be apparent to listeners.

Tange asked the Australian ambassador to try to ensure that the suggestion did not become a concrete proposition.[78] The ambassador failed. Two years later the Voice of America formally asked the government for permission to establish a relay station in Australia. Cabinet discussed the proposal at length, but was obviously swayed by Tange's view. The request was rejected not because of reservations about the anti-communist message of the Voice of America, but on the ground that it would 'cut across' Radio Australia's impact on Asia if two different national voices were broadcasting from Australian territory.[79]

Perhaps Casey's attitude was crucial in the cabinet decision. When Homfray had told him in 1959 of the possibility of a joint American, British and Australian relay station in Thailand, he reacted coolly. He told a senior officer of his department, 'If our Australian signals come out from the same station as a station broadcasting Voice of America material, we are likely to be "branded" with the much too flamboyant American material.'[80]

In mid-1962, someone inspired Labor Senator Patrick Kennelly to question Senator John Gorton (representing the Minister for External Affairs) about the department's influence over Radio Australia's programs. Kennelly asked whether the department had any say in the kind of programs to be broadcast and, if so, on what statutory authority such control was based. After asking that the question be placed on notice, Gorton went on to say he understood that for a long time the programs had been the subject of consultation and agreement, but the department did not have any right of veto.[81] An attempt by one officer of the department to have Gorton state publicly that programs should be in line with foreign policy was unsuccessful. The following words were deleted from the draft reply:

I might add that whilst Radio Australia seeks to maintain a high degree of objectivity and to reflect in its programmes the points of view of all sections of the Australian community, few overseas governments recognise Radio Australia as being other than the official mouthpiece of the Australian Government. It would seem desirable, therefore, that the tone of Radio Australia's broadcasts should not be noticeably at variance with the broad objectives of Australian foreign policy.[82]

Radio Australia's Cold War role was frankly acknowledged in a draft which the department prepared for a cabinet submission on Radio Australia late in 1962. The draft, prepared by Ralph Harry, a first assistant secretary who had been head of the Australian Secret Intelligence Service from 1957 to 1960,[83] stated:

In the general context of the Cold War, and particularly the growth of the Communist threat in the South East Asia area in recent years, it is of the first importance that Australia employ every means at its disposal both to counter Communist influence and propaganda and also to project the Western viewpoint in general and the Australian image in particular, especially in the areas of Australia's 'near north'.[84]

Tange was sympathetic to a proposal to increase Radio Australia's broadcasts in Indonesian. He told Moses: 'It seems quite clear from all the evidence available that Radio Australia's services in Indonesian are widely listened to and very popular. They can and are doing a great deal to project to Indonesia a favourable and sympathetic picture of Australia as a friendly neighbour.'

On the other hand, Tange was infuriated when news of a secret visit he made to the United States in February 1963 was broadcast by Radio Australia. The story said neither the Australian embassy in Washington nor the department in Canberra would discuss the reason for the visit. But it quoted Radio Australia's diplomatic correspondent as saying the main reason was the tension between Indonesia and Malaya over the forthcoming formation of Malaysia. Tange scrawled on a copy of the item: 'This is a "news" item which the Dept of EA should have had the right to say "don't publish". It is the most embarrassing of *all* the speculations that I read.'[85]

Spurred by his embarrassment over this item, Tange made another attempt to bring the operation of Radio Australia more into line with the American model of international broadcasting. He ordered an official of the department to look at his past correspondence and discussions with the chairman of the ABC and 'see whether anything more could be done to achieve some more effective control by the Department of External Affairs over Radio Australia news broadcasting'. The official, Patrick (later Sir Patrick) Shaw (a former ambassador to Indonesia), replied that the department could give 'specific directions on how to handle some particular item of news or how to interpret some current development'.[86] Shaw went on to summarise neatly the attitude of the more hard-line officers of the department to Radio Australia:

The existence of Radio Australia as a Government paid agency must be justified in terms of the extent to which it serves the national purpose. This purpose is the projection of an image of Australia overseas which we consider favourable and which furthers the foreign policy objectives of the Australian Government.

Shaw then referred to the payment of the piper which was to become an increasingly common theme in the department's dealing with the overseas service: 'This is recognised by the extent to which Radio Australia depends upon the judgment and support of External Affairs in obtaining Government money to maintain and expand its services.' He suggested that proposed news items which looked important or controversial be sent to the department by teleprinter before use. Communication problems, he said, might be solved if Radio Australia moved itself to Canberra, which the department should aim for although it would take some time.[87]

Predatory moves

A fortnight later, Patrick Shaw made the first predatory move towards Radio Australia. He told Homfray and Radio Australia's news editor, John Hall, a strong defender of Radio Australia's editorial integrity, that he wanted firmer liaison than could be achieved under the current arrangements. He would like the department to be able to telephone Hall at any time with 'requests' that this or that story should not be used, and to be sure he would comply. Hall enlisted the support of his superior in Sydney, the acting controller of news in Sydney, Gilbert Oakley. 'Obviously,' Hall told Oakley, 'he wants the External Affairs Department to have the right to kill stories on RA news before they are used … The explanations, he said, could be given later.' Shaw also told Hall and Homfray that, for perfect liaison, Radio Australia should be based in Canberra near the department. This, he said, should be the long-term objective.[88] To Semmler, then assistant general manager, programmes, Homfray conceded that listeners as a whole tended to identify Radio Australia as a government-operated organisation reflecting the views and policy of the government of the day:

At all times, [he said,] we show the keenest sense of responsibility and, naturally, refrain from broadcasting anything which is likely to embarrass the government or endanger or jeopardise our national security. [But] if by increasing the frequency of liaison visits it is intended to bring some kind of pressure to bear in the preparation or presentation of our programmes then we would have to resist this form of direct interference.

'Frankly,' he added hopefully, 'I don't think that this was ever intended.'[89]

When Shaw reported on his visit to Melbourne, and said he had asked Homfray and Hall why Radio Australia should not be in Canberra, Tange took off the gloves. In the margin beside the reference to the proposed move, he scrawled: 'Move to bring this about by referring in the next submission to cabinet to the unsatisfactory liaison in present circs.—the liaison which is the *only basis* for the 1955 connection of Radio Aust. with Govt. policy *and* the provision of larger funds.'[90] Ominously, he added: 'The pretence has to stop.' When, three weeks later, the head of the department's information branch, Neil Truscott, suggested, 'It is up to us to ginger up the liaison', Tange retorted:

It seems that you do not grasp my point that if this Dept. finds it inconvenient—as it is— to be running to Melbourne to educate Radio Australia, they are expected—by me—to come here. They are *not* to neglect liaison after enjoying the benefits of the Govt. money and patronage which this Dept. has gained for them on misleading representations to cabinet as to the degree of guidance sought or accepted.[91]

At a meeting with Moses in Canberra a few days later, Tange used the department's support for the Darwin station as a carrot. He told the ABC's general manager that the station was in a way linked with liaison between Radio Australia and the department, especially in the field of news presentation. He would feel more able to recommend to his minister that he should press for this project, involving the expenditure of a large sum of public money, if he could feel sure that Radio Australia was maintaining close liaison with External Affairs and actively seeking guidance. Moses was learning, if he had not learned already, that there is no such thing as a free booster station. He assured Tange of 'his personal wish to do everything possible to ensure that liaison was close so that the risk of embarrassment to the government in its international relationships as a result of anything carried by Radio Australia might be eliminated'.[92]

But when Tange raised the problem of geography, Moses said he was not seriously considering the possibility of moving Radio Australia to Canberra. Apart from the practical problems, he felt Radio Australia would tend to be looked on as just a part of government. The physical separation, he said, helped preserve its independence in the eyes of the outside world.[93]

Now that he had his knighthood (conferred in 1961), Moses was increasingly resistant to the department's pressure. The next time he went to Canberra to see Tange, he brought Hamilton for reinforcement. Hamilton—who, despite his hostility to interference by the department, was apparently not unmindful of the national interest—told Tange that news items were quite often suppressed on his (Hamilton's) initiative, or that of Hall, because it was felt that they were not in the national interest or because some doubt was felt about their accuracy.[94]

Ralph Harry sent Sir Garfield Barwick (who had succeeded Menzies as Minister for External Affairs) a draft submission to cabinet proposing an increase in the amount needed for the Darwin station. In a secret memorandum, he told the minister that, 'in view of this very great increase' (the amount was more than doubled), he felt 'bound to insert in the draft more specific clauses than in past submissions concerning provision of guidance by the Department of External Affairs to Radio Australia'. He felt it essential to establish precisely and to state frankly the extent of consultation, and the extent to which guidance was provided or accepted. 'Guidance and consultation,' he said, 'have not been as continuous nor as detailed as cabinet was entitled to expect following its decision to establish Radio Australia within the ABC in 1950 and subsequently in 1955 to extend its activities.'[95]

Barwick later reached an understanding with Darling on the relationship between his department and the overseas service. In a confidential letter to the ABC chairman, he said meaningfully that he had told his cabinet colleagues of the understanding, 'and news of it was both well received and of critical importance to the ultimate decision'. Apparently overlooking the fact that in 1955 Radio Australia had already been broadcasting in Indonesian, Thai and French, Barwick said: 'The decision in 1955 to endorse the extension of Radio Australia's activities into languages other than English was based on the consideration that increased use could be made of Radio Australia in promoting Australian Government Policies.'

Darling replied that he would refer Barwick's letter to the commission. He could see no possible trouble in the suggestions which he made, nor could the vice-chairman or the general manager.[96] But the department heard nothing more from Darling on the matter. There is nothing on file to indicate that he ever did refer the letter to the commission. Two key executives, Hamilton and Hall, certainly never accepted that the department had the right to 'provide positive guidance on the selection of news items and on the emphasis to be given to particular types of items'.[97]

The department, understandably, felt frustrated and cheated. The stage was set for a confrontation which was to explode two years later in a clash between Darling and a new, more determined, minister, Paul Hasluck.

4   Hasluck's push for power, 1965—1972

Paul Hasluck, appointed Minister for External Affairs in April 1964, became increasingly frustrated over his department's inability to control the content of Radio Australia's programs. Speaking in 1992 as secretary of the department, Dick Woolcott recalled that Hasluck had monitored Radio Australia regularly, particularly on his overseas trips, and about once a fortnight or even once a week would send a note to the department saying that something he had heard on the overseas service was either wrong or damaging to Australia's national interest.[1] This had led him to the course of action to be revealed here publicly for the first time.

Early in 1965, in a draft memorandum for the minister, Ralph Harry, as first assistant secretary, suggested that the department formally advocate the moving of Radio Australia to Canberra, a proposal which had been raised from time to time, but never pursued. He said this would greatly facilitate daily contacts.[2] Some officers of the department already saw such a move as the first step towards the desirable end of separating Radio Australia from the ABC and making it into 'a separate institution'. Others were to oppose it determinedly.

Two months later, Hasluck issued a direction that the department prepare a cabinet submission aimed at ensuring its 'effective control of Radio Australia's activities'.[3] He explained that one of his senior officers said past agreements and understandings had not worked out to the department's full satisfaction. Radio Australia itself was willing enough, he said, but the ABC, and in particular Walter Hamilton, took the line that the department could advise Radio Australia's staff but not tell them what to say.[4] The department's legal adviser reported that Radio Australia had been placed under ABC control in 1950 by a cabinet decision, and although the relevant papers could not be traced, there seemed no reason in law why Radio Australia could not by government decision (without special legislation) be removed from ABC control. If necessary, the Postmaster-General could enforce such a decision by refusing to make shortwave transmitting stations at Shepparton and elsewhere available to the ABC.[5] At the end of March, cabinet brought forward the date for the completion of the Darwin station. The submission from the Postmaster-General said, in part:

The Department of External Affairs considers that the increased gravity of the situation in Vietnam, the greater links between Indonesia and Communist China, the scale of [Indonesian] military operations against Malaysia [two of these problems were to end with dramatic suddenness before the end of the year] ... and the wider commitments undertaken by Australia to Vietnam and Malaysia are sufficient to warrant Cabinet consideration of the timing of the project ...

The political situation in the areas north of Australia have [*sic*] changed considerably since the budgetary considerations which deleted this item from the current financial year.[6]

Hasluck told cabinet that he intended bringing forward a submission on measures which would ensure the effective control by his department of Radio Australia's news and commentaries. Shortly afterwards, he told the Postmaster-General, Alan (later Sir Alan) Hulme, that he had authorised his department to investigate the implications of transferring Radio Australia to Canberra, separating it from the ABC and placing it under cabinet control. He said the shortwave service should be regarded as an important instrument of national policy rather than an independent broadcasting service.[7] Patrick Shaw, who must have found the planning congenial, judging by his previously expressed views on the subject, proposed that the PMG Department be responsible for administration and the Minister for External Affairs for policy direction. He went on:

we would hope that this could be done without legislative action in order to reduce publicity which would make it internationally apparent that it was being taken over as an overseas radio service of the Government. We consider that there would be disadvantages in Radio Australia's becoming obviously a government instrument.

Hasluck wrote at the bottom of Shaw's submission: 'Approved. Do not allow undue delay.'[8]

In the meantime, Woolcott was tightening the screws on John Hall. He told the news editor that for several weeks the department had been following Radio Australia's news bulletins closely, and he felt it might be helpful to pass on some observations made about them. Then came four foolscap pages of closely typed criticism of a number of stories, followed by the thinly veiled threat:

I think you should also know that we shall in the next few weeks be keeping a close watch on Radio Australia bulletins, assessing the accuracy, objectivity and the degree to which Asian audiences are receiving a balanced picture of Australian national policies. This is a subject in which our Minister is at present taking a keen interest.

After all this came the pious statement: 'I hope you do not find these comments unduly critical.'[9] Hall retorted that he was well aware that the bulletins were being examined closely, adding: 'There are, of course, other listeners who watch them very closely, and we strive at all times to discharge the important responsibilities involved.'[10] He said he was quite clear on his role, and what was expected of him under directions from his controller (Hamilton) in accordance with the policy of the commission itself. Hamilton sprang to his news editor's defence. He was surprised that Woolcott should have found it necessary to write to Hall in this manner. 'Broadcasting is our business,' he said dismissively, 'and we take our professional responsibilities most seriously, knowing full well how completely useless to us and to Australia would be an overseas service which was not trusted.'[11] Beside Hamilton's words, 'Broadcasting is our business', Woolcott wrote: 'and external affairs is ours!'[12] Woolcott expanded on this in his lengthy reply to Hamilton: 'As you rightly say, broadcasting is your business and you take your professional responsibility very seriously. Australia's foreign policy and its projection is ours and the same applies.' He went on to say:

While we do not wish to see Radio Australia turned into an *obvious* instrument of government propaganda [emphasis added] ... we are concerned to see that due account is taken of our views and that Radio Australia does not broadcast material which is harmful to our interests or runs counter to government foreign policy.

At the end of his reply, Woolcott, whose personal charm was well known, said he would contact Hamilton when next in Sydney so they could discuss the department's liaison with Radio Australia 'rather than involve ourselves in a lengthy exchange of letters'.[13] Not a hint was given, of course, of the king-hit being prepared by Hasluck. (Woolcott's charm was apparently effective: at a meeting in August—which Woolcott said was intended largely to re-establish personal contact and mend fences— Hamilton said he had no objection to direct correspondence between

Woolcott and Hall, and he had told Hall he could take the initiative in contacting the department.)

'Our own propaganda station'

Some ABC journalists were beginning to suspect that there was something in the wind. In March the ABC's diplomatic correspondent approached Hasluck at a meeting of the Economic Commission for Asia and the Far East and asked him for a taped interview for possible use on Radio Australia. The implacable minister replied, 'I have no wish to be broadcasting on the Government's line of policy over our own propaganda station.'[14] When the journalist expressed disappointment, Hasluck said he had been having consultations about the question of Radio Australia, which he found unsatisfactory for the government's purpose. He added: 'This radio service is the propaganda arm of the Government and I consider it quite untenable that it should be directed from Sydney.' Reporting this exchange to Talbot Duckmanton, who had succeeded Moses as general manager, the acting controller of news, Gilbert Oakley, described Hasluck's reference to 'our own propaganda station' as a further shot in the campaign by External Affairs for the right to decide what should be reported in Radio Australia's bulletins. Perceptively, Oakley mused: 'And when he repeats that the position is "unsatisfactory and quite untenable", and says "Radio Australia must be used for the Government's purpose", I wonder if a really serious move by External Affairs is being planned.'[15]

Duckmanton, a quiet, pipe-smoking, essentially rather shy man, had risen through the ranks by not rocking the boat. He succeeded the more flamboyant Moses at the age of forty-four partly through an unblemished record as a loyal lieutenant. He was happy to leave the running to his chairman, Darling and his assistant general manager, Hamilton, when it came to defending Radio Australia's editorial integrity from Hasluck and his department.

Darling was by now well aware of the threat from Hasluck. At the April meeting of the commission, he drafted a counter-threat to resign as chairman of the ABC. In a draft letter to the Postmaster-General, he wrote:

While I do not consider that the continuation of my services as Chairman of the ABC is a matter of very great importance to anyone I should I think make it clear that it would be impossible to continue in these circumstances. I do not of course speak for the rest of the Commission.[16]

The last paragraph, with its threat of resignation, had been crossed out when he handed the draft to Duckmanton. By 1988, Darling had forgotten that he had ever contemplated such a drastic step.[17] In the letter that he did send to Hulme, Darling wrote:

> There can, of course, be no question of the right of the Federal Government to place Radio Australia under the control of the Department of External Affairs and to use it as an instrument of propaganda in the furtherance of Australian interests among its neighbours. If the Government wishes to do this, it is presumed that it would remove Radio Australia entirely from the control of the Australian Broadcasting Commission and would establish it as a separate organization. I do not know whether such action would need Parliamentary approval. I would, however, urge strongly that such action would be unwise and should not be taken ... I feel fairly certain that the Commission would not accept a half-way position in which, as far as Radio Australia was concerned, it was under the control of a Government department, while supposed to be an independent corporation in its other capacity.[18]

The resignation threat in his original draft was replaced with the milder words, 'For all these reasons I would recommend that the Government should consider very deeply before it decides to alter the existing situation.'[19]

There were officers of the department who were aware of some of the problems in Hasluck's grand scheme. The minister had signed (but not sent) letters to Darling and Hulme discussing the practical questions that would be involved in the separation of Radio Australia from the ABC, its control by the government, and its relocation in Canberra. Against the background of these letters, the department's secretary, Sir James Plimsoll, and some of his most senior officers met to discuss the issue. Patrick Shaw stressed the practical problems that would be involved in taking over *all* of Radio Australia, including its entertainment services. Could the department simply extract the news and commentary sections? Richard Woolcott said the department was at the time not equipped to assume full control, or even to give full guidance, particularly on a 24-hour-a-day basis, to Radio Australia's news services. Meanwhile, he said, the views of Hamilton were a factor working against adequate liaison. It was Hamilton who had instructed John Hall to tell first assistant secretary Ralph Harry, 'I cannot accept as a general policy any obligation to consult the Department before using any story.'

The consensus of the meeting was that the department should try to avoid all the problems associated with a complete takeover. In the short term, it should try to get from the ABC an undertaking that Radio Australia would be obliged to consult the department before using news items on a range of sensitive External Affairs issues and that Radio Australia would be obliged to accept departmental guidance on these subjects. It was also generally agreed that the objective of moving at least the news and commentary sections to Canberra should be kept in view. In fact, the department was back where it had been two years earlier.[20]

Neil Truscott (head of the department's information branch), who was not at the meeting, told David (later Sir David) Hay, who had prepared the draft summary, that the emphasis seemed to have been on not taking over Radio Australia. Hasluck, he said, had also now accepted that the department should not aim physically to take the service over. But the minister apparently had an alternative plan to ensure that Radio Australia was run virtually according to the American model. He now believed it should be taken away from the ABC and in effect left independent in its day-to-day operations, but with the department controlling its policy. Truscott did not think it would be possible to move just news and commentaries. As translators and readers in different languages were involved, they would have to come too. And so would Peter Homfray.[21]

Although Hasluck was in London, he was still on the warpath. He cabled Plimsoll to complain that Radio Australia was broadcasting false statements about a heads of mission conference ascribed to 'journalistic sources' *in spite of the fact that a ministerial statement had been issued*. 'What I object to', he wrote, 'is that government sponsored news service developed solely for presenting Australian point of view overseas should deal in rumours and speculation about such matters.'[22] The minister's cables prompted a further note from David Hay to Plimsoll, reaffirming that Radio Australia's purpose was to reflect the Australian viewpoint, which must inevitably be the viewpoint of the government of the day. Hay continued: 'The Minister for External Affairs and the government must be the one to determine what is or is not the Australian viewpoint and what is helpful or harmful to its presentation.'[23]

With the threat of the separation of Radio Australia from the ABC hanging over their heads, Darling and Duckmanton talked with Plimsoll. They agreed that speculation about Australian government policy or action should be avoided unless Radio Australia had been given a clear lead. (In any case such speculation had almost always been avoided in Radio Australia programs.)[24]

They also agreed (in Darling's case, for the second time) to the stationing of a full-time Radio Australia correspondent in Canberra (though shown as part of the general ABC news service), as well as to the installation of a special direct telephone line between Radio Australia and the department. Copies of news bulletins would be supplied to the department each day after broadcast. Duckmanton told Plimsoll that this was as far as he was prepared to go. Anything beyond these steps would make it preferable to hand over control formally and officially to the department. Plimsoll replied that there was considerable merit in retaining the service independent of government control. But he felt it was now necessary to implement fully the terms of the cabinet decision of 1950 to place Radio Australia under the control of the Postmaster-General, with the ABC simply providing the programs. Duckmanton subsequently drew the commission's attention to the cabinet direction of 1955 that the ABC representative in Southeast Asia was to work under the general direction of the Australian commissioner there. He said that, although the department had never tried to enforce this, he was mentioning it now in view of the attitude of the present minister towards Radio Australia.[25]

Soon there was bad news for the department. Duckmanton's deputy, Clement Semmler, told one of its officers that Hamilton, previously responsible for only the news operation of Radio Australia, was to assume all supervisory responsibility for it. Although Semmler was receptive to the proposal for a direct telephone line to Radio Australia, he thought that if it were used to pipe programs to Canberra, this might savour of 'Big Brother' listening in, and he suggested that this problem be referred to Hamilton when he returned from overseas.[26] Hamilton's reaction was predictable. Plimsoll later told Duckmanton that the department would not now 'insist on' the appointment of a Radio Australia correspondent in Canberra or the direct line. A scrambled telephone link was subsequently installed between the offices of the news editor and the department's Radio Australia liaison officer, a position reactivated (in Canberra) in 1966.[27] Plimsoll suggested that Hay regularly consult a senior executive of the ABC, and Duckmanton replied that Hay could confer with Hamilton.[28]

The Americans, whose diplomats had been expelled from Indonesia, hoped to make use of Radio Australia to get their message through to its Indonesian audience. In mid-1965, Hasluck approved an exchange of Indonesian-language programs between Radio Australia and the United States Information Agency, the parent body of the Voice of America. A senior officer of his department drafted a letter to Duckmanton 'in cautious terms in order to avoid frightening the ABC off the whole thing at the start'.[29] The ABC apparently *was* frightened off, though: the program exchange never eventuated. A different kind of approach followed. In August 1965, the department invited the ABC to meet representatives of the VOA, who said they were concerned that they had no effective impact on opinion in Indonesia because the VOA signal was weak and its program not popular. They felt that Radio Australia offered the only practicable alternative for Indonesians seeking the truth of events inside and outside their country. The VOA officers, unlike some of the hard-line Australians such as Hasluck, did not try to press the American model on Radio Australia. They said they were not seeking to offer their methods or ideas as an objective for Radio Australia. They felt that the Australian service, for which they expressed admiration, should properly appear to be a different voice from the VOA. They did, however, offer to supply Radio Australia with 'background material'. Hamilton said the Americans had admitted that in recent years they had made 'an agonising reappraisal' of their techniques and program content, which 'had not been uniformly successful in the past'.[30] There is no evidence that Radio Australia ever made use of the American 'background material'. Homfray recalled in 1989: 'We probably accepted it politely but didn't use it.'[31]

Shortly afterwards, Hamilton gave Woolcott some good news. He said it was likely that Lachlan Shaw would shortly be appointed news editor of Radio Australia in place of Hall, who had been promoted to assistant director.[32] Woolcott knew Shaw well, and no doubt looked forward to a smoother relationship with him than he had had with Hall. Other officers of the department also hoped for an improvement. The following month, when Woolcott recommended that the ABC be asked to agree to a list of topics on which it would accept an obligation to accept departmental guidance, Truscott of the information branch commented:

Although I feel strongly that without this we shall not have a completely satisfactory control over R/A I continue to be doubtful whether we are likely to get this kind of acceptance. However perhaps we should again hold off until Lachlan Shaw takes over as Editor. John Hall, although pretty cooperative still belongs essentially to the ancien regime.[33]

Hasluck, though, was not prepared to wait. He wrote to Menzies:

I am becoming increasingly concerned at the risks to which we are exposed in the presentation of important foreign policy issues overseas by reason of my department's lack of authority to direct the Australian Broadcasting Commission on the contents of its news broadcasts ... On one recent occasion ... an item was included in a bulletin against the specific advice of an officer in my department whose responsibility it is to conduct the day-to-day liaison with Radio Australia.

At this point in his letter, Hasluck made his push for power:

What is required is that the Government should have the authority, through the Secretary of my Department, to direct the Australian Broadcasting Commission as to the contents of its news services, to the end that Radio Australia would not have the right to broadcast, unless in an approved form, any item which bears directly on the conduct of Australian foreign relations in Asia ... An alternative course of action would be for Radio Australia to be removed from the administration of the Australian Broadcasting Commission and come under direct government control.[34]

Meanwhile, attempts to interfere with the content of Radio Australia's news were being made by Patrick Shaw, by then ambassador in Jakarta. A series of requests from Shaw followed the abortive coup in Indonesia early on the morning of 1 October 1965. In November, Hay asked Hamilton that the ABC check in advance the accuracy of Radio Australia's reports 'about Indonesian matters'.[35] Hamilton rejected the request. He said this would mean that the department was assuming responsibility for the content of news bulletins. This, in his opinion, would be improper.

Attempts were also made to slant news about other parts of the world. The following month, the department told Hall that Radio Australia should not inadvertently give help to the communists in their program of discrediting the Thai government. In its African coverage, Radio Australia was asked to continue to use reports which showed British policies were genuine in their intent to bring down the Smith regime in Rhodesia, and that they were adversely affecting the regime. The department also asked Radio Australia to impress on its African audiences the desirability of refraining from violence.[36]

Hasluck versus Darling

Hasluck, having launched his push for power, was continuing his campaign to erode Radio Australia's image. He asked his ambassadors in Asia about its reception, its audience and the quality of its news and commentaries. At the end of 1965, he sent Postmaster-General Hulme a summary of the responses. They included:

Bangkok: Few listen ... Sometimes news has the wrong slant.

Delhi: Not known who listens but probably few ... The commentaries seem superficial.

Djakarta: ... More people listen to it than to Radio Republic Indonesia and it reaches millions ... opinion was favourable on the whole.

Kuala Lumpur: Not a big audience.

Seoul: Not listened to apart from Australians and a few Americans and Koreans.

Hong Kong: Very small audience.

Singapore: Never heard anyone say he listened to it.

Phom Penh [sic]: Some Cambodians and the whole of the foreign community listen to it.

Colombo: No substantial audience.

Manila: Very few listen.

Rangoon: Some listen, I suspect, but they would do so surreptitiously.

Vientiane: Large audience.

Hasluck added: 'You will appreciate, of course, that these opinions were the result of a quick on-the-spot check from each of the ambassadors, none of whom had previously been warned that the questions would be asked.'[37]

Hulme forwarded the summary to Darling. The ABC chairman was not impressed. He told Hulme that the ambassadors had revealed what they did not know rather than what they knew. In more than five closely typed foolscap pages, Darling quoted mail figures and other evidence that many of their comments were absurd. Of course, he endorsed the positive comments by the ambassador to Indonesia. It was well known, he said, that Radio Australia had an audience of some millions in Indonesia with very great influence. He said a further indication of the prestige of Radio Australia was the recent instruction from the commander-in-chief of the Indonesian army, Major-General Soeharto, that senior officers must listen at least daily to its news broadcasts, reinforcing a similar instruction given in earlier years by his predecessor, General Nasution. Darling noted that the ambassadors had made no reference to China. He said experts on China believed a trickle of letters over several years indicated 'very important, secret listening in China'. Darling ended curtly: 'I am returning Mr Hasluck's letter to you.'[38]

When Hulme sent a copy of Darling's letter to Hasluck, the Minister for External Affairs replied:

I feel it was a pity that the Chairman of the ABC thought there was some need for self-justification. I am sure that our Ambassadors, all of whom are men of considerable experience and trained to report exactly on matters which they observe, offered their opinions in good faith and all honesty.

As for Radio Australia's impressive mail figures, Hasluck pointed out that of the 1965 total of just over 224,000 cards and letters, more than 210,000 came from Indonesia. Excluding China, this left a total of 13,000 items from a population of close on 800,000,000 in the rest of Asia—roughly the same response as if 200 cards and letters had been received in a full year from the population of Australia. He concluded: 'I think the clear fact is that there is a very large audience in Indonesia and a rather small audience in most other Asian countries.'[39]

Darling had the last word. Following a visit to Vietnam and other Asian countries in April by the new Prime Minister, Harold Holt, his press secretary, Tony Eggleton, wrote to the ABC saying, 'The Prime Minister was very impressed with Radio Australia's standing in the Asian countries we visited and we were regular listeners to the RA news bulletins.'[40] On his copy of a resulting memorandum from Duckmanton to the commissioners, the former headmaster wrote the schoolboy retort: 'Ha Ha! So Sucks to Mr Hasluck!'[41]

Inertia policy

Hasluck's attempt to separate Radio Australia from the ABC, bring it to Canberra and put it under External Affairs control, disappeared into limbo. Hasluck said in 1989 that he could not remember what had happened to his initiative.[42] Its fate remained a mystery to the author until a remarkable disclosure by Richard Woolcott, about to retire as secretary of the Department of Foreign Affairs and Trade, in January 1992. Asked whether he had any idea why Hasluck's initiative had failed, Woolcott laughed and replied, 'Oh, absolutely!' After ascertaining that his disclosure would not appear in print before his sixty-fifth birthday the following June, Woolcott said, 'I'll have to phrase this very carefully.' Then he told a story worthy of the television series, 'Yes Minister'. He said Hasluck had directed Plimsoll to prepare a submission for External Affairs to take over Radio Australia and incorporate it as part of his portfolio. Plimsoll had called Woolcott to discuss the direction, and Woolcott had said he thought this would be 'highly dangerous'. Radio Australia was in the public eye, he said, and if run by the department would be seen as resembling Tass or Radio Moscow and its credibility would suffer. Woolcott continued, 'I think what happened then was that he said, "OK, leave it with me," and he put it in the bottom drawer of his filing cabinet and never answered.' Woolcott said he had raised it with Plimsoll a few weeks later. He remembered saying, 'Hasluck will ask about this. Are you ready to prepare some submission on why we shouldn't do this?' Plimsoll had said 'No'—he had been very determined about the course he was taking. Woolcott laughed again as he related how Plimsoll had put his hand on his shoulder and said, 'My boy— inertia policy.'[43]

The inertia policy worked. Presumably preoccupied with other concerns, Hasluck must have lost sight of his grand plan for Radio Australia. He apparently never raised it with Plimsoll again, although he continued as Minister for External Affairs for more than two more years, until early 1969. Woolcott believed Plimsoll's action may have saved Radio Australia from a takeover by the department. He said that if the secretary had made a negative response to Hasluck's direction, the minister would probably have gone to cabinet giving all his reasons for wanting a takeover—and cabinet might have endorsed it.

In January 1968, after the death the previous month of Harold Holt, Hasluck failed in an attempt to succeed him as Prime Minister.[44] A year later, he left the ministry to become Governor-General.

Although the former secretary, Tange, was now high commissioner to India, he was still not slow to criticise when he thought criticism was warranted. In late 1967 he drew Plimsoll's attention to a report in a news bulletin of a 'lecture to Australia by a Chicago parson about our supposed attitude of white supremacy'. He said he did not know whether it was included 'for its value as paradox or irony', but in either case he suggested that the refinement would be lost on 'audiences all too ready to condemn us for racialism'.[45] (Australia was still vulnerable to criticism of its immigration policy. Although this had been liberalised by Holt in early 1966, there was a continuing disparity between the numbers of European and Asian immigrants.)

As Australia's participation in the Vietnam War increased in the late 1960s, so did pressure from the department to influence Radio Australia's coverage. Hasluck's successor as minister, Gordon Freeth, was disinclined to seek radical changes in its relationship with the department. Although 'guidance' continued to be given on the coverage of Vietnam and some other sensitive issues, one officer of the department remarked that, throughout the ABC, extending to the very top of management and to the commission itself, there was 'an inherent resistance to any formal suggestions coming from this department as to how the ABC should do its job'.[46]

One of the 'sensitive issues' that concerned the department was continuing communal violence in Malaysia. The department told the high commissioner in Kuala Lumpur that it would seek in particular to have 'excluded or toned down' stories emphasising the aspects of racial conflict, or lack of impartiality by the authorities.[47] The department was alarmed two months later when the ABC's correspondent in Kuala Lumpur telexed a report to Radio Australia quoting radical Malay student leaders as saying they were about to launch a campaign—violent if necessary—to bring about the resignation of the Prime Minister, Tunku Abdul Rahman, and the establishment of a completely Malay government. The students had said the campaign was necessary and urgent because of the failure of extremist politicians led by Dr Mahathir bin Mohamad (later Prime Minister) to bring about the Tunku's resignation.[48]

Another sensitive issue was Radio Australia's continued use of the word 'native' in its news bulletins, despite the department's attempts over many years to eliminate it because of its racist overtones. After a protest by

Australia's deputy high commissioner in New Delhi,[49] a senior officer of the department at last persuaded the acting news editor that, although the ABC's controller of news had directed that the word could be used as an adjective, though not as a noun, Radio Australia 'should have stricter standards than ABC domestic news'.[50]

But despite continuing concern about Radio Australia's coverage of some issues, Plimsoll, in a draft briefing to the minister, counselled against any fundamental change in the relationship with Radio Australia. Such a change, he said, could raise serious administrative and personnel problems for the department. In the absence of direct departmental control, which he said cabinet had decided against, mistakes would occur. But their frequency could be, and he believed had been, kept down by close liaison.[51]

In a letter to Hulme on the subject, Freeth picked up Plimsoll's point that 'exaggerated or provocative reporting or interpretation of news can do harm to our relations and make more difficult the work of our diplomatic missions.' It was not always easy, he said, to balance the desire of Radio Australia to maintain the '*appearance* [emphasis added]' of an objective, up-to-the-minute and comprehensive news service and on the other hand the government's wish to avoid difficulties that could arise in relations with Asian and other countries because of 'an unguarded use of news items and commentary'. Freeth said that perhaps such problems might be avoided altogether by a further improvement in liaison arrangements. The previous December, he said, Duckmanton and Plimsoll had discussed the possibility of a review of the relations between Radio Australia and the department. It was agreed that this might take place after Peter Barnett (later director of Radio Australia) took over as news editor from Lachlan Shaw.[52]

With Barnett as news editor, the department continued its pressure to slant the news. When President Marcos announced a cabinet reshuffle following student pressure, an officer wrote on the cable from the Australian embassy in Manila: 'Discussed with Barnett. 1. Stress positive. 2. M's sensitivity to change—avoid suggestion that changes grudging.'[53] A few weeks later, the same officer wrote 'Spoke to Barnett' on a departmental release about a treaty of friendship between Malaysia and Indonesia. Underneath, another officer wrote: 'Very important that RA plays this up to Djakarta, KL and Singapore.'[54] There is no indication of whether the pressure succeeded.

While the department continued to try to use Radio Australia as an instrument of foreign policy, the government persisted in its Cold War attitudes to communist regimes in Asia, particularly those of China and North Vietnam. Freeth wrote in September 1969, 'There are unfortunately no signs of any willingness on the part of Chinese communists to abandon their attitude of hostility towards their neighbours.'[55] His successor as Minister for External Affairs, William (later Sir William) McMahon, wrote the following March, 'we still regard Communist China ... as a central obstacle to peace, stability and ordered progress throughout Asia'.[56] But a change was on the way: in May 1971, McMahon announced that his government had decided to explore the possibilities of establishing a dialogue with the People's Republic.[57]

When in 1971 Radio Australia began to seek a fourth transmitter in Darwin, it once again sought the department's help. Perhaps there was an element of hypocrisy in Radio Australia's perception of the department as a friend in times of need but an enemy—or at least a friend to be kept at arm's length—when it felt its integrity to be threatened. Or, on the other hand, perhaps the Radio Australia executives whose attitude to the department fluctuated in this way were simply giving first priority to what they saw as the interests of their organisation. A perceptive paper for Sir Keith Waller, who had replaced Plimsoll as secretary, made the following points:

Radio Australia's statutory position and relationship with the Department:

This is a difficult and sensitive area, and one in which Radio Australia's (and the ABC's) position has historically shifted depending on what it has sought to achieve. When it has needed support to obtain more funds, Radio Australia has been 'a positive vehicle for promoting policies of the Australian Government in the Asian area'. At other times, the right of Radio Australia to take final decision on the content of its programmes has been emphasised, sometimes [to] an annoying degree ... aspects of the relationship between the Department and Radio Australia remain inevitably elusive. Likely future consideration of long term plans and funds requirements—and I would not really put the fourth transmitter for Darwin in this category—could provide a suitable opportunity to restate the role of Radio Australia—and our role in relation to it—in terms which we regard as realistic and appropriate to the needs and conditions of the present.[58]

A series of meetings followed at which the ABC/Radio Australia and the PMG Department tried to win the support of the Department of External Affairs for the proposed fourth transmitter at Darwin. The department's acting assistant secretary, information and cultural relations, reported:

We have repeated almost to the point of exhaustion that, if the need for a fourth transmitter can be demonstrated as essential for bringing existing Radio Australia transmissions up to acceptable standards, we would support it. We would not support it, however, if the object were programme expansion ... Radio Australia made substantial changes in the first part of the Working Committee paper to try to avoid any reference to the role which Radio Australia plays as part of Australia's information activities in Asia and the Pacific and in promoting Australian foreign policy objectives. We pointed out ... that cabinet would need to be convinced it was getting value for its money and that pious declarations about the ABC's independence etc. could be counter-productive. Whether they liked it or not they were considered by their audience as representing the Australian Government.[59]

'Mick' (later Sir Keith) Shann, a deputy secretary of the department, echoed these views. In the margin he wrote: 'The ABC will kill itself if it goes on with the "independence" line. RA is an instrument of foreign policy. If they refuse to accept that, and what goes with it, then we might as well not have it.'[60]

But a fresh wind of liberalism was blowing through the department. With the added impetus of the election of the Whitlam government, it was to bring an era of *détente* in relations between the department and the overseas broadcasting service.

5 News commentaries: a Cold War battleground, 1950–1972

The most open attempt by the Department of External Affairs to use Radio Australia directly to promote foreign policy was through its news commentaries, which were the issue of greatest contention between the department on one hand and the ABC and Radio Australia on the other in the 1950s and 1960s. The news commentaries led to sometimes heated clashes with two commentators who eventually became university chancellors, culminating in the virtual sacking of one of them and the resignation of the other.

The basic problem was that some External Affairs officers tried to use men (there were no women news commentators at that period) such as H. D. (later Sir Hermann) Black, chancellor of the University of Sydney for twenty years until his death in 1990, Creighton Burns, who became foundation chancellor of the Victoria University of Technology in 1990, and Professor (later Sir) Zelman Cowen, Governor-General of Australia from 1977 to 1982, simply to parrot the department's policies. The future governor-general presented few problems, but the other two proved to be the most difficult for the department to handle.

The news commentaries had their genesis in the propaganda talks and commentaries which reflected official policy during World War II. In the postwar years of the Chifley Labor government, under the direction of Arthur Calwell as Minister for Information, they continued to promote government policies, including the drive to attract European (preferably British) immigrants to the antipodean land of opportunity.

After the ABC took over Radio Australia in April 1950, cabinet decided (on 31 May) that one of the duties of the External Affairs liaison officer should be to advise editorial staff on the selection of news items and commentaries. By October, the head of Radio Australia, Robin Wood, had submitted as suggested commentators the names of Professor Geoffrey Sawer (during the war talks editor and then acting controller of the short-wave division), Professor William Macmahon Ball (the first controller of the service, from 1940 to 1944), Eric Ward (a political science lecturer in Ball's department at the University of Melbourne) and Douglas Wilkie (foreign affairs writer for the Melbourne *Sun News-Pictorial*) as the original panel to present a weekly commentary called 'Behind the News'.[1] In a handwritten minute, an officer of the department, Keith Waller, said Ward would be unacceptable. 'Our sponsorship, actual or apparent,' he wrote, 'would be awkward.'[2] No reason was given. In 1989, Waller could not remember why he had considered him unacceptable.[3] Ward was replaced by an apparently more congenial commentator, Zelman Cowen, Professor of Public Law at the University of Melbourne.

Some of the weekly talks were given by External Affairs officers. When the department's first liaison officer with Radio Australia, Noel Goss, wrote one on the Colombo Plan, he asked the department whether it should be introduced as 'by Noel Goss of the Department of External Affairs', simply 'by Noel Goss', or under a pseudonym. He was told that 'by Noel Goss' was sufficient—the department should *not* be mentioned.[4] A talk by Goss a week later on a trip to Southeast Asia and Japan by his minister, Richard Casey, gives an idea of the kind of hyperbole to which the listeners were sometimes subjected. It said, in part:

Perhaps no person in public life in this country knows more about Asia than he does; it's true he hasn't been in South East and Eastern Asia before but he knows the Middle East and Southern Asia. For two years during the war Mr Casey was resident minister in the Middle East for the United Kingdom government. And for two years he was Governor of Bengal. So you see, he has an exceptionally broad experience on which to draw in assessing what he sees and hears in the next four weeks.[5]

Goss castigated both Geoffrey Sawer, one of the most experienced of the news commentators, and Robin Wood, when Sawer made a minor error of fact in a commentary. The talk was corrected and read by an announcer. Referring to Wood's faith in the news commentators, Goss said:

He does not appear to realise that their knowledge may—for his purposes—not exceed that of any intelligent layman ... I think it would help to let Professor Sawer know in a friendly way that he has been caught out in a silly mistake: it might bring him to lean a little more on the Department in writing for Radio Australia in future—even to the extent of sending us copies of his texts.[6]

The last suggestion was a portent of what was to come.

In a later reference to the incident, Goss referred to Sawer disparagingly as 'one of Radio Australia's self-selected experts'.[7] In a private note to his superior, Goss lamented that it was difficult to present his ideas in sufficient detail to make them fairly understood by the talks writers without appearing to determine their talks policy.[8] A few months later, F. J. (Blake) Blakeney, head of the information branch of the department, suggested that Goss should ensure if possible that talks on subjects containing 'possible mischief' were given to 'the least erratic commentators'.[9]

In mid-1952, an officer of the department, Laurence McIntyre, asked the ABC's controller of programs, Dr Keith Barry, whether Radio Australia would be willing to program daily news talks from scripts provided by the department. Barry replied that it would be difficult if only because scripts had to be written especially for broadcasting, and 'those who were not in the broadcasting game mightn't quite appreciate some of the techniques'. He also said Radio Australia had to beware of regular broadcasts of material which might be *detected* as purely official statements. Wood agreed with Casey's view that the department should have first call on the weekly 'Behind the News' session if 'certain administrative difficulties' could be overcome. In a confidential file note, Goss identified one of these difficulties as 'the absence of an agreed list of tame commentators who could be trusted to take basic material and hammer it into shape and produce a talk acceptable to us'. Goss recorded in this file note that he had proposed a new style of news commentary. Wood had seemed receptive, and had listed a few names, including Ball, Sawer, Cowen, Wilkie, Paul Freadman (who had been senior researcher with the Australian Broadcasting Control Board since 1949 and was a news commentator on ABC radio) and Professor (later Sir) Samuel Wadham (then professor of agriculture at the University of Melbourne).[10]

The ABC subsequently submitted a proposed panel of speakers,[11] but the department found it 'too large and unwieldy', and some of the suggested speakers unacceptable. Certain of the speakers proposed, said Blakeney, 'would almost certainly be unwilling to accept departmental suggestions on policy'. After pruning it down to about a dozen, he suggested that the ABC's proposed panel could be retained 'for appearance sake' as long as the ABC accepted the department's restricted list. The most notable of the names deleted by the department was that of Macmahon Ball. Geoffrey Bolton, the biographer of Sir Richard Boyer, attributes the exclusion of the former controller of the shortwave division to ABC officials, who he said 'thought Ball's material too "dangerous" for overseas broadcasting'.[12] But the records show that on this occasion it was the department that was responsible. Another of the names deleted by the department was that of Melbourne *Argus* journalist Dr Peter Russo, an expert on Japan who had broadcast regular propaganda talks for Radio Australia early in the war. In fact, Menzies had once tried to get Russo dropped as a commentator on the ABC home service but Boyer had successfully resisted this move.[13] Obviously his views were too left-wing for the department in 1953. He had come under unfavourable notice two years earlier when he was one of three panellists in an ABC program about Communist China which Goss said smacked of special pleading and which led to a Dorothy Dix question to Menzies in the House. Another 'leftist' panellist, the authority on China Professor C. P. (Pat) Fitzgerald, was also proposed by Wood as a news commentator, and was also weighed in the balance by the department and found wanting.[14]

Blakeney proposed that the department should decide each week on three or four topics, to be passed on to Goss with the 'line' to be taken and perhaps in some cases a suggestion as to the speaker.[15] The news commentaries, he said, were the exception to the rule that Radio Australia retained responsibility for the final decision on the content of its programs. It 'was instituted as a programme designed specifically to reflect Government policy and which has to be approved by the Department before broadcast'.[16] In an extreme case, a commentary could be 'suppressed by the Department and not broadcast'.[17] On 8 June 1953, only five days after the first of the new-style 'Behind the News' commentaries began, a departmental note asserted that Goss was able to ensure that the line taken by Radio Australia in talks and commentaries was in accordance with government policy.[18]

Black versus Goss

A collision between the ABC and the department was inevitable, especially as at least one of the news commentators was not prepared to be 'a passive puppet mouthing Australian foreign policy'. Hermann Black, the skilled broadcaster whose warm, kindly voice with its greeting, 'Hullo girls and boys', became familiar to a generation of postwar schoolchildren as he told them about 'the world we live in', had an implacable hatred of censorship. In fact, the maternal ancestor from whom he had inherited his first name was an editor who had fled Germany after incurring Bismarck's displeasure by publishing Heine's poems when Jewish writers were in disfavour. On a prewar visit to Germany, Black had seen how the propaganda of Goebbels had made convinced Nazis of two of his young cousins, both of whom were later killed fighting for Hitler. His personal experience of censorship had begun during World War II when he was a commentator on the ABC's home service. In 1988 he recalled a wartime experience which had 'stirred me up emotionally about the stupidity with which the censorship was being applied'. He was two-thirds through reading a script when an army officer entered the studio, stood behind him, reached over his shoulder and, with a thick pencil, crossed out two words he was about to read. He finished the broadcast, but recalled that this experience, and others, had left him with a feeling that censorship tended to get 'arrogant, self-centred and out of hand'.[19]

Black, who believed that victory in Europe should be the first priority, remembered in 1986 how he used to sidestep sharp directives to emphasise the war in the Pacific:

> It is possible to do it by writing your script in such a way that, though you might give the Pacific great emphasis naturally enough, nevertheless, you could convey the significance of the European theatre by the use of your voice and by the pauses that you made or the extra emphasis that you put. In this way, no attempt to conscribe free thinking can ever succeed. The listener would hear behind the lines the real thoughts of the news commentator.[20]

Black, then a lecturer in economics at the University of Sydney, believed that he and the other postwar news commentators should collectively give the impression of speaking 'from a country where diversity of opinion was in fact an element of our culture'.[21] This belief, and his determination to remain his own man, led to a concerted move by the department and Moses to drop him from the panel of regular commentators. On 2 September 1953, an ABC officer in Sydney told Black that his original script for that day was not acceptable, and heavy amendments to it by Goss could be accepted or not at his discretion. Goss arrived a few minutes before air time with the substantially modified script. One paragraph, which said, in part, that Australians had 'read with pleasure the encouraging reports emanating from Indo-China relating to the progress being made in France's relations with the Associated States of Vietnam, Laos and Cambodia', had been deleted altogether. In the margin, Goss had scribbled, 'This carries the implication that we are urging the French on, and we don't consider that utterances of this kind help at the present juncture.' To replace the offending section, Goss had written his own commentary on the first policy statement by Indonesia's new Prime Minister, Ali Sastroamidjojo.[22]

In a long report the following day to Molesworth, the head of talks, Black reported that 'this prickly man' had 'rather glowered in putting the script before me'. When he had refused to accept some of the changes, Goss had 'ventured the suggestion that *he* might read *his* script!!' In a 'rapid fire of argument', Black told him no commentator would take direction as to what he was to say, and went on to broadcast his original script. (So upset was he by the confrontation, though, that his customary aplomb was noticeably absent, and he made several 'fluffs'.) 'In the last analysis,' Black told Molesworth, 'I am not a "voice" broadcasting what Mr Goss thinks I should.' Did Goss, he asked, have the right to order the *withdrawal* of part of a script, or to insist on a *modification* of it? Was Radio Australia confined to the explanation of official Australian foreign policy? If so, what role was envisaged for the commentator? Goss himself scribbled the answer on a copy of the report: 'He is primarily an explainer of important issues and of the Australian point of view thereon. If this does not commend itself to him, he should not be employed.' Black's report went on to state his belief that Radio Australia should present a variety of viewpoints: 'The fact of the possibility of a variety of viewpoints and their expression is an important fact about a democracy like Australia and needs to be (and could always be) "got over" to listeners.' Black went on to say he could not accept any future invitations to broadcast over Radio Australia until he was quite clear where he stood.[23] The department was only too ready to take advantage of this ultimatum. Already Goss had telexed Blakeney saying this episode was the climax of a series which had marked each of his visits to Sydney and which indicated that 'Sydney is psychologically unprepared for periodic participation in the panel.'[24]

Some of the department's answers to the questions Black had asked Molesworth were a classic example of Orwellian doubletalk. The response to the question whether Goss had the right to order the withdrawal or modification of any part of a script was 'No. But the ABC has and in such matters, it should follow External Affairs advice.'[25] In other words, the ABC had the freedom to choose, so long as it chose what the department told it to choose! Blakeney subsequently wrote to Moses spelling out the department's interpretation of the rather vaguely-worded decision of the cabinet committee on 31 May 1950, which ended with the words, 'The formal decision and responsibility will rest with the Editor who will be expected to work in harmony with the liaison officer.' Blakeney told Moses, in part:

Our interpretation of this has been that, while Radio Australia has the formal decision and responsibility, Radio Australia would not, unless in exceptional circumstances, reject External Affairs advice on either the choice of foreign affairs material to be broadcast or the manner of its presentation.[26]

At a meeting with Blakeney a few days later, the response of Moses was at first evasive. He thought it undesirable to commit to writing the

Richard Boyer

Richard Casey

Paul Hasluck

James Darling

Arthur Tange

Richard
Woolcott

Charles Moses

Wally Hamilton

John Hall
(© ABC)

Warwick Beutler
(© ABC)

Creighton Burns

Arthur Calwell

David Hill
(© ABC)

Philip Koch

Richard
Broinowski

Derek White

Prime Minister Robert
Menzies: 'The time has come
to speak for ourselves.'
(National Library of Australia)

The ramshackle building at Lyndhust, Victoria, housing the transmitter from which Radio Australia began broadcasting in 1939.
(© Radio Australia)

Director Peter Homfray, one of the few chief executives with a regular program, with Radio Australia journalist Hock Khoo.
(© Department of Foreign Affairs and Trade)

The author interviews President
Soeharto in Jakarta in 1971—a
'soft' interview (see page 225).

Pius Bonjui,
broadcaster with the
Papua New Guinea
service, with students
of Tintern Church of
England Girls'
Grammar, Ringwood,
Victoria, who had
penfriends in PNG.
(Courtesy Post
Newspapers)

Foreign correspondent
Don Hook interviews
Buddhist monks in Laos.
(© Radio Australia)

Foreign correspondent
Andrew Swanton talks
to slum-dwellers in
Thailand who face
eviction to make way
for development.
(© Radio Australia)

Foreign correspondent
Peter Couchman
interviews a Khmer
Rouge commander in
Phnom Penh.
(© Radio Australia)

ABC's understanding of its function and the department's in the matter. He had in mind, *inter alia*, the probability that members of the commission could not accept a written formula such as that contained in Blakeney's letter which 'might appear to give the ABC no more than a "rubber stamp" function'. No doubt the likely reaction of Boyer to such a formula was very much in his mind. The oral response of Moses at this meeting, though, amounted to a complete surrender. He accepted the department's answers to the questions asked by Black of Molesworth, including the doubletalk about the ABC's 'right' to follow External Affairs advice (but not to reject that advice) on the withdrawal or modification of any part of a script. It was a slap in the face for Barry and Molesworth, who were present at the meeting, and who had previously taken a much stronger line in resisting the department's depredations.[27]

A few days later, Moses (perhaps prompted by Blakeney) suggested that, after the next commentary by Black, the department write to Moses himself,

> pointing out the inconvenience and expense of continuing the Sydney commentaries and suggesting that henceforth they be confined to Canberra and Melbourne. Mr Moses would then be in a position to explain to Black that it was purely the difficulty of making the necessary administrative arrangements that was causing the ending of the Sydney commentaries.[28]

Molesworth, regarded by many in the ABC as something of a radical (he had once given a lecture on Marxism in Broken Hill), mounted a rearguard action a month later, after Blakeney was posted to the Australian embassy in Washington. The ABC talks director wrote to Wood:

> I don't think we should agree to dropping a Sydney speaker from the panel of commentators. Up to the present, the commentaries from Sydney have been given by H. D. Black, who is a particularly good commentator, and especially so for overseas broadcasts. The Department of External Affairs hitherto has not raised any question of difficulty and expense in sending a man to Sydney. I would think that the matter is now being raised because of the recent friction with Mr Goss.[29]

Belatedly, Moses came to Black's defence. To a letter from an officer of the department, Owen Davis, suggesting that the commentaries be confined to Melbourne and Canberra, he replied:

> Such an arrangement would prevent us from using H. D. Black, who is recognised generally as a particularly good commentator. We think he is so good that he should not be left out of any roster of commentators on our overseas service ... We have full confidence in Mr Black as a commentator who would do nothing to embarrass the Government of his country.[30]

But Black *was* dropped from regular use (although he did continue to record occasional programs). It is clear in retrospect that the reason was not the clash between the 'prickly' Goss and the independent-minded Black, but Black's refusal to accept the department's 'guidance' on every point, together with the genuine liaison difficulties in Sydney, which, unlike Melbourne and Canberra, did not have an External Affairs officer within easy reach to look over the commentator's shoulder.

The minister, Richard Casey, was not yet satisfied about the extent of his department's control. He wrote to one of its officers the following April that he would feel much happier if the whole of the 'political content' of the commentaries—as well as the selection of news items—was 'completely in our hands'.[31] After the elimination of Black as a regular news commentator, most of the other speakers were comparatively compliant (though an even more troublesome commentator was just over the horizon).

In May 1955, on the initiative of the government's Cold War planning committee, cabinet decided that, as part of 'the Australian programme to help counter communist subversion in the South and South-East Asia area,' news commentaries of three to four minutes should be broadcast five days a week in addition to the weekly 'Behind the News' commentary. A secret cabinet submission said: 'It is envisaged that this commentary would reflect Australian policy and attitudes, and that it would be prepared in close consultation with the Department of External Affairs.'[32]

The daily programs began on 1 August 1955. Wood (with the approval of the ABC in Sydney) had proposed six rostered commentators for the daily program, Frederick Howard, Douglas Wilkie, Zelman Cowen, Norman Harper (associate professor of history at the University of Melbourne), Ian Shannon (research fellow in economics at the University of Melbourne) and J. A. C. (Jamie) Mackie (lecturer in history at the University of Melbourne).[33] Originally, Peter Russo had been invited to take part, but he declined, because, according to the Radio Australia talks assistant who initially produced the daily program, 'he knew External Affairs'.[34] The department accepted Wilkie, Cowen and Harper, but not the other three. In place of Howard, Wood proposed, and the department approved, Creighton Burns, a reader in political science at the University of Melbourne.[35] It was a decision they were to regret. Burns, aged thirty, was a man with strong opinions who insisted on his right to express them. A former Rhodes Scholar, he had been educated at Scotch College and Melbourne and Oxford Universities. He was later to become Southeast Asian correspondent of the *Age* (1964-7), Washington correspondent (1975-81) and finally editor of the paper from 1981 to 1989.

Three months later a confidential report to the secretary, Arthur Tange, from Malcolm Booker, by then head of the information branch, listed Cowen, Harper and Burns as 'permanent commentators' and Wilkie and Reginald Neal, Radio Australia talks assistant, as 'ad hoc commentators'. Booker reported that, generally speaking, the commentators had accepted the department's guidance and used much of the material it provided, though they had usually added material of their own which had 'sometimes blurred the impact of what we were trying to say'. Only very rarely, though, had there been any direct conflict of views between the department and a commentator as to content. He gave Tange the following pen-pictures:

Professor Cowen: Co-operates fully and has sufficient background knowledge to grasp particular points made by department.

Mr D. Wilkie: Co-operates fully and is happy to accept fairly full departmental guidance.

Mr Harper: Co-operative, but with some fixed ideas of his own. Not always sufficiently well informed to understand some of the pitfalls involved in particular subjects.

Mr Burns: Recently co-operative, but with strong ideas of his own. Owing to his lack of knowledge of some aspects of international affairs, he tends to oversimplify some of the subjects dealt with (e.g. he could not see why [Malayan Prime Minister] Abdul Rahman should not negotiate with [Malayan Communist Party leader] Chin Peng). His insistence on putting 'both points of view' sometimes blurs the intention of the commentary.

Booker went on to remark that Burns, while best kept off Malaya, was good for commentaries on the Colombo Plan. Finally, however, Booker recommended that the entire panel be dropped, and replaced with 'a professional commentator, employed by Radio Australia but working either in this Department, or in Melbourne in close liaison with us'. He recommended that the department seek the ABC's concurrence.[36] Tange espoused the idea with enthusiasm.

A request to posts in Asia for their reactions to the daily commentaries had brought a mixed response. The head of public relations in the Australian commissioner's office in Singapore, Ian Hamilton (later to head the Australian News and Information Bureau), reported that 'the number of Europeans and English-speaking Asians who have gone out of their way to tell me how much they appreciate "these short, interesting talks after the news", indicate that the sessions have a fairly wide—and selective—audience.'[37] The Australian legation in Bangkok, on the other hand, reported that listeners in Thailand had plenty of choice from both local and international stations, and the average listener 'tends to turn up Dinah Shore and Bing Crosby rather than Creighton Burns, Douglas Wilkie, Norman Harper or Zelman Cowen'.[38]

After a trial period of five months, Tange told Moses that the commentaries were placing a heavy burden on his staff, and he was not satisfied that they were achieving the purposes for which they had been conceived. These purposes, he said, were 'to combat Communist falsification of events ... to rebut specific Communist propaganda lines ... to persuade Asians not only of the need but of the practicability of effective resistance to Communism ... to encourage the free Asian countries to believe that their own national traditions and institutions should be preserved against Communism ... to expound Australian attitudes and policy in a consistent way', and 'to build up a regular listening audience for the commentaries'. Tange, with the concern about secrecy typical of those steeped in the Department of External Affairs culture, was also concerned that the commentators would 'gain an insight into confidential policy without being under any official obligation of secrecy'. Tange said he and Boyer had agreed that, where it seemed desirable that there should be a fairly 'straight' commentary on government policy, this should be delivered by someone described as a 'government spokesman'. Conceding that this would emphasise the official nature of the contents, whereas the purpose was to avoid the labelling of views with a government tag, Tange put forward Booker's suggestion that the solution lay in the appointment of a single professional commentator to replace the panel. This commentator could work either in Melbourne in close liaison with the department, or in the department itself. But 'he would not of course be publicly linked with this Department in any way'.[39] The reaction of some senior ABC executives was, predictably, hostile. The director of talks, Alan Carmichael, and controller of programs, Keith Barry, questioned his assertion that the briefing of the commentators placed 'a heavy burden' on External Affairs staff. Carmichael pointed out to Moses:

SEATO has charged Australia with a major role in the campaign against false Communist propaganda; 'Radio Australia' is a key organ in this struggle; therefore the Department should regard as thoroughly justified the few hours spent each week in furthering this cause.

In response to a claim by Tange that the commentators tended to be 'too long and discursive' and that the 'presentation is not good,' Carmichael said, 'I regard these men not merely as good, but as extremely good broadcasters.'[40] Robert Horne, who was acting director of Radio Australia while Wood was touring Southeast Asia, saw overriding disadvantages in Tange's proposal:

(a) It would make all our commentaries single person affairs and from this it would be a very short step to the identification by listeners of this person as a spokesman for the government. (b) The broadcaster, though a member of the Commission's staff, would be directly responsible to another department. (c) The broadcaster, having publicly identified himself with the views of an existing government, would have to be replaced if the government changed, or proceed to express opposite views on certain issues. We feel that no commentator would accept a position on such terms.[41]

Beside these points, Moses scrawled three words: 'I agree entirely.'[42] The commission, led by Boyer, decided that as a matter of principle it must adhere to the policy whereby controversial issues were normally dealt with by a panel of speakers rather than by any one commentator.[43] In his reply to Tange, Moses voiced a philosophy for the news commentaries very different from that which he had accepted from Blakeney only a few months earlier. It was, in fact, an overstatement:

I am sure that the short-wave listener—the person we are striving to win—derives most of his confidence in 'Radio Australia' from his belief that it comes from a country that is so free and straightforward that it is willing to put on all sorts of people and give them full rein to say what they think about Australia and all the countries in the world.[44]

Predictably, Tange was not prepared to take this lying down. In a reply to Moses stamped 'Secret', he observed:

while the principle of impartiality must be the overriding one as far as the Home Service is concerned, I am not sure that we can be quite so detached in matters involving our international relations and ultimately our security. As far as the overseas audience is concerned it consists largely of Asians, and is quite unlike the average Australian audience. Its standard of education is much lower, it is lacking in political discernment, and it is exposed continuously to Soviet and Chinese Communist propagandist themes.

Apparently accepting as inevitable the continuation of the panel of commentators, Tange suggested that it should be announced at regular intervals over Radio Australia that the commentator was expressing only his own views.[45]

After his return from Southeast Asia, Wood reportedly agreed privately with the department that none of the commentators was good, although, wrote Booker, 'we cannot of course quote him to the ABC'. Booker went on to say that the audience could be held only by brief, simple and direct comment, and by the personal style of the commentator. 'Neither of these requirements are being met by the present arrangement,' he wrote, 'and consequently a very valuable opportunity for influencing Asian opinion is being missed.'[46] After Wood made his criticism of the commentators at an ABC meeting, Carmichael told Moses he regarded Cowen, Burns and Harper as 'very adequate commentators'. He proceeded to suggest that, because of their broadcasting ability, Geoffrey Sawer and H. D. Black 'might well be included occasionally in the panel'.[47] Wood, to whom this memo was copied, replied that the four commentators (Wilkie was the fourth) had been given coaching, and were lifting their standards. 'Harper,' he said, 'is speaking slower and getting more light and shade ... Cowen has improved considerably.' He said he was in favour of the occasional use of Sawer and Black, but for the time being he thought it best to concentrate on the Victorian panel.[48] A few days later the 'considerably improved' Cowen wrote to Tange suggesting that the commentators should aim to reach the more educated (English-speaking) Asians, rather than aiming for the masses. Tange retorted, 'I think you will agree with me that when we are addressing ourselves in English to other groups ... we must speak in simple and straight forward terms if we are to be understood.'[49]

The stormy career of Creighton Burns

The first skirmish in the brief, stormy career of Creighton Burns as a news commentator took place on 4 August 1955, only three days after the daily commentary began. Discussing a crisis in Indonesia, Burns said, 'Of course, Indonesia isn't the only nation which has had unsettled relations between the Army and the Government in recent years.' He then proceeded to quote the sacking of General MacArthur by President Truman five years earlier. Booker asked that this be deleted, as it might give offence to America. Burns described this as 'rather a silly reason', but agreed to drop the offending reference when two Radio Australia officers said they felt the disputes in the US and Indonesia were not similar, and for that reason there was no point in quoting the American incident.

Then, on 1 September 1955, Booker asked that the news commentary deal with Casey's guarded statement in the House the previous day about an apparent thaw in the Cold War. He commented to Reginald Neal (the Radio Australia talks officer dealing with the broadcasts), 'I don't know how Creighton Burns will feel about this,' referring, Neal said, to the department's line.[50] Burns readily agreed with the *subject*, but wanted to balance Casey's statement with a few lines on the less cautious view of the Opposition leader, Dr H. V. (Bert) Evatt.[51] Evatt had maintained that a real chance of international peace and cooperation had opened up. Burns's script concluded:

Some Australian commentators believe that there is no necessary conflict between Mr Casey's counsel of caution and Dr Evatt's optimism. They feel that while we must still

look for positive proof of the Communists' peaceful intentions, we should also seek immediately to widen further the existing area of economic and social co-operation.[52]

External Affairs was scandalised. The reference to Evatt's view was
expunged from the script, whereupon Burns retorted, 'If these two paragraphs are deleted, I cannot allow my name to be used.' After seeking
approval from Wood, who checked with Moses, Neal himself read the
commentary, without the offending words. In his report to Moses on the
incident, Wood remarked, 'It is clear that if the External Affairs
Department is disposed to follow the rigid line it took in demanding the
deletion of Burns' last paragraphs—which we considered fair comment—
we will have considerable difficulty in finding suitable people willing to
undertake this assignment.' He said Burns was not the only commentator
who was unhappy. At a briefing meeting in Canberra on 1 June, Cowen
and Harper had emphasised that their commentaries could not be merely
a reflection of government policy, and that they would insist on being able
to express their own views. Cowen felt there was a tendency on the part of
External Affairs to 'tell the commentators what to say'. Although Harper
would 'readily amend his script if a reason is given', he had told Wood in
strict confidence of his concern over a conversation he had had with Casey
in August. He had cited to Casey a couple of verbal brushes with Booker
and said that the commentators must preserve their individuality. Casey
had contested this vehemently. As Harper had described it, Casey had had
'the bit between his teeth'.[53]

Keith Barry entered the fight wearing Burns's colours, and those of
the ABC's independence. The reference to Evatt's statement, he said, was
not only reasonable, but would do something to counteract any thought
that Radio Australia was merely giving official handouts in its commentaries. In a memo to Moses, he said,

We all agree, I think, that if Radio Australia is to have its continued influence in the target
areas, it is essential that it not be thought merely a medium of propaganda. If, and when, it
is thought to be that, so will its influence correspondingly decrease. It seems clear that
External Affairs is taking the view that they, and not the ABC, have the final authority to
say what is to go in the special News Commentary.

Secondly, he said, he felt it was extremely embarrassing when 'outside'
speakers received what were tantamount to instructions from External
Affairs when they were engaged and paid for by the ABC:

Men of the calibre of a Dean of a Faculty of Law, Senior Lecturers at a University, an
expert foreign affairs writer in a responsible newspaper, may well reach the point where they

feel they cannot continue working under the present arrangement, and it could be that they would feel it sufficiently important to issue a statement on the matter. If we—and External Affairs—want the audience value of the names and positions of such people we will, I think, have to face the fact that they are not the sort of people to be content with a position in which their names are used but their overall opinions are silenced.

Thirdly, he said,

we are now faced with a situation where, in a News Commentary, our commentator was instructed not to give the view of the Leader of the Opposition. This, of course, in a democratic country, is a very serious matter, and one frankly doubts whether such a policy is known to, or would be endorsed by, Parliament.[54]

Barry's signature at the foot of this memo had more than its customary flourish. It was he who now had 'the bit between his teeth'!

The commission meeting to which his declaration of independence was submitted resolved:

That the Chairman should see the acting Minister for External Affairs to explain the Commission's point of view about this matter, particularly the fact that the Commission believes it is essential that the news commentaries given in the overseas service should be objective and should not give the impression that they are designed as propaganda or are expressing only the official view of the Government.[55]

Boyer subsequently reaffirmed that it had been agreed with the secretary of the department that the ABC would have the final responsibility for the content of the news commentaries.[56]

But this was by no means the end of the struggle between the department and Creighton Burns. After briefing the three 'permanent commentators' in Canberra a few weeks later, Casey told Tange that he had found Burns (who was thirty) 'rather juvenile'.[57] Burns, for his part, was growing increasingly irritated at what seemed to him the intrusiveness of External Affairs into what he had seen originally as a Radio Australia venture.[58]

The next exchange of shots came the following May (1956), when Burns was asked to broadcast a news commentary on the breakdown of talks on self-government for Singapore. Concerned about the strength of communism in Singapore, Britain was insisting on retaining some control of internal security. Senior officer Owen Davis objected to Burns's penultimate sentence, which read:

I, for one, believe that the people of Singapore should *have* the right to decide *when* they want the help of Britain and the rest of the Commonwealth, and just what sort of help they want.[59]

Davis said it was undesirable for the commentator to express this point of view, as it was diametrically opposed to the point of view of the British and Australian governments, and in effect said Britain was wrong and David Marshall (the Chief Minister of Singapore) was right. He discussed the serious risk of communist subversion in Singapore. Burns, though, had insisted that the sentence was an expression of his opinion, and said he would not be prepared to give the commentary without it. Davis later reported to Tange that Wood, in an attempt to reach a compromise, had 'referred to the fact that the Chairman of the ABC, Sir Charles Boyer [sic] had in a circular which had been sent to commentators stated that they were entitled to express their own views and not necessarily the view of the government of the day'. Radio Australia had suggested as a compromise the insertion of a reference to the fact that Evatt had disagreed with Casey's statement on the matter, that 'most of the press had supported Mr Casey but that there was a minority opinion in favour of Mr Marshall's point of view'.[60] Burns had then proposed that in place of the offending paragraph he substitute:

This is clearly a difficult problem. We need to balance the legitimate claims of the people of Singapore for independence against the security needs of the area as a whole.

More fine tuning followed. Davis objected to the use of the word 'legitimate'. Burns agreed to change his final sentence to:

We need to balance the demands of the people of Singapore for independence against the security demands of the area as a whole.

So, after prolonged casuistry worthy of mediaeval theologians, the compromise commentary went to air. Tange scrawled in the margin of Davis's report: 'Why was this Singapore question allowed to drift into the hands of Burns of all people?' It is perhaps ironical that the government that emerged in an independent Singapore could give lessons to Britain in the handling of internal security!

At a meeting between officers of the department and the ABC three weeks later, both parties agreed 'that the panel of commentators would be reviewed with a view to increasing its efficiency and that over a period of time the number of talks given by Mr Crighton-Burns [sic] would be reduced and in due course he might be dropped from the panel'. [61] Barry asked the External Affairs representatives if they would like to indicate any order of preference for speakers, adding that 'we ourselves felt that Zelman Cowan [sic] was the least effective broadcaster'. There was an immediate reaction to this aspersion on the commentator whose views the department apparently found most compatible with its own. Barry reported:

The Departmental officers expressed some alarm at the thought of Cowan's name being removed from the list, saying they felt his material was the best of all. Although it was indicated that they would not be prepared at that point to give any official list of preference, it seemed clear that they thought that Wilkie and Cowan were the best of the speakers and that perhaps Howard and Harper followed. There was uneasiness about Burns, and it was felt that his subjects should be very carefully chosen.[62]

Soon, though, the source of the uneasiness was removed. Burns wrote to Wood asking that he be dropped from the panel. 'I am now convinced,' he said, 'after a year's experience, that my independence as a commentator is largely nominal. The policy requirements of the Department of External Affairs have become increasingly restrictive and coercive. And I find myself less and less in sympathy with the emphasis of official departmental policy.'[63] A postscript to the affair was that, nearly two years later, Wood reported to the commission that in his opinion, Burns's decision to leave the panel had not arisen 'directly from criticisms of certain of Mr Burns' commentaries made by the Department of External Affairs but had been due primarily to other reasons'.[64] Asked in 1989 what these 'other reasons' were, Wood replied, 'He wouldn't conform, and he had problems with that.' Burns, he said, was 'too left—too radical' for the particular role.[65]

Burns recalled in 1988 that he had been very proud of an angry letter he had written to James Plimsoll as acting secretary of the department saying he was not prepared to be called an independent commentator when it was quite clear that he was no longer independent, and saying this was damaging to his integrity as an academic. Plimsoll had sent a one-paragraph reply simply thanking him for his 'great contribution to the independent news commentaries of Radio Australia' and expressing regret that he was 'unable to continue'.[66] Boyer flew to Canberra to see Casey about Burns's resignation and reportedly 'thumped the table' and told the External Affairs Minister the ABC would not have its commentators dictated to.[67] There was, however, no attempt to persuade Burns to return. Boyer's biographer, without the benefit of the confidential files now released, says that through Radio Australia's experience with the news commentaries, the ABC chairman 'established his point that the ABC could be entrusted with overseas broadcasting without any direct censorship by External Affairs'.[68] Burns's experience shows that this assessment is well wide of the mark.

After the removal of this thorn in its side, the department had little further trouble with the commentaries. Wood's successor as director of

Radio Australia, Peter Homfray, recalled that at one stage a commentary by Zelman Cowen on Israel had been rejected because his personal beliefs had been too intrusive. Radio Australia had played five minutes of music instead.[69] In 1988, Cowen himself had no recollection of this, though he conceded that it might well have happened. There appears to be no record of the incident in the files. Cowen was usually very cooperative with the department. He said in 1988 that, though he had never had the disposition to be used as the voice of the government, he had conceded that the voice of Radio Australia could not be significantly different from Australian foreign policy.[70]

'The party line'

The other surviving commentators, too, were fairly accommodating, and the message got through clearly. In a personal letter to Davis, David Hay, then ambassador to Thailand, reported that the standard of commentaries had been 'very satisfactory'. 'The boys are right on the ball,' he wrote, 'and the party line has been coming over well.'[71] At least one respected outsider, though, was far less enthusiastic. Macmahon Ball wrote:

In these last weeks I have been stunned by the news commentaries I have heard. They follow a fixed official pattern. They seem designed to persuade Indians, Indonesians and others that Britain and France know what is best for East Asia, and that Australia knows they know what is best. The commentaries seem also designed to foster Asian resentment against Egypt and other Arab countries ... I cannot imagine that the voice of Australia can get any response but amusement, derision or fury from Asian listeners.[72]

Some commentators were willing accomplices in putting over what Hay referred to as 'the party line'. Some merely converted the department's notes into a script, though others were becoming restive about a tendency for the department to provide 'notes' which were virtually complete scripts. Not infrequently, quotes from Casey turned up in them. Betty Cook, the personal secretary to whom Moses was increasingly delegating, told him: 'What is happening seems to me to be fairly remote from the panel of independent commentators the Commission envisaged. Except for the look of the thing, we might just as well be using a speaker from External Affairs.'[73]

Douglas Wilkie said laughingly in 1988, 'By that time I had become a cypher.' He described himself as 'an amenable Pom in my politeness and general cooperation with them'. His rounded English accent and clear articulation (his father Allan Wilkie had been a celebrated Shakespearian actor) no doubt helped commend him to the ABC in an era when its leading broadcasters had to *be* English or to *sound* English (though Wilkie said, 'I suppressed the worst artificialities that I might have inherited from an English public school education'). In any case, he said, his personal viewpoint had been very close to that of the Menzies government. When the department had taken issue with something he had written, it had 'always ended in a compromise in their favour or in my surrender, because it never seemed to matter that much'. Increasing 'compromise in their favour' or surrender had been needed, he said, because External Affairs had wanted the propaganda to be more and more overt.[74]

In a letter to Postmaster-General Charles Davidson in mid-1958, Boyer reaffirmed that the final decision as to content lay with the commentator, whose responsibility, he said, was to the ABC, and not to the Department of External Affairs.[75] Tange, who was given a copy of the letter, was quick to counter-attack. It would be 'an insupportable state of affairs,' he said, if 'the chosen instrument supported ... with Government finance' were to provide

unregulated commentaries in which there were continued and sustained attacks on Australian foreign policy or representation of views and objectives which were in conflict with the views and objectives inherent in Australian foreign policy. Foreign policy is the policy of the government of the day, there being no unity on many fundamental issues ... It is pretty difficult to interpret what the informed opinion of the country as a whole is except as the expression of all shades of opinion held by reputable people ... the Government view would be that this is not enough.[76]

The man who took perhaps the hardest line in the battle with the ABC over Radio Australia, Malcolm Booker, launched a full frontal attack three years later, when he was ambassador to Thailand. It was another foray in the long campaign by Tange and others for control of the commentaries. As reported by a colleague, Booker attacked on several fronts:

(a) the present news commentaries are useless; no one listens to them; (b) the voices of the commentators were, on the whole poor, and their material not well-prepared; (c) what was required was one or two highly qualified broadcasters—specialists in presentation, with excellent voices ... who would give a lively and convincing presentation of the Australian viewpoint; (d) there was no point in being 'objective'; Asians would prefer to get the 'Australians Government' line [*sic*] ... (f) the commentaries should be unashamedly by official Government spokesmen, so that listeners would know what our policies were ...

It sounded like a formula for the Voice of America. But Booker added another sour note:

(g) it would, of course, be almost impossible to secure such a change in arrangements, because of ABC opposition ... [77]

This initiative came to nothing.

The following year, another commentator was dropped. Guy Harriott, then associate editor of the *Sydney Morning Herald*, was leaving for three to four months overseas. Noting that he had 'shown some reluctance to accept amendments suggested by the Department', Ralph Harry, a first assistant secretary, remarked, 'It is possible Radio Australia will take no initiative to contact him on his return.'[78] These words proved prophetic.

A new commentator who joined the panel at this time, Stuart Sayers, assistant leader writer of the *Age*, was less difficult. Although he did not always conform exactly with what External Affairs asked, he said many years later, 'You recognised that you were speaking to an audience outside Australia who would tend to think you were speaking officially ... In a way you were giving a government view.'[79]

A later recruit to the panel, Monash University politics lecturer Max Teichmann, had 'a few rows' with External Affairs over the content of his commentaries, but was always able to reach a compromise. He later said he believed he had been dropped not because of anything he had said, but because he had become very active in the anti-war movement as Australia sent first military 'advisers', then regular army troops, then conscripts, to Vietnam. Teichmann said he had become 'something of a guru' to the Save Our Sons movement.[80] Finally, External Affairs apparently could no longer suffer the embarrassment of a news commentator who publicly opposed a major aspect of Australia's foreign policy. Teichmann was dropped from the regular panel in the mid-1960s.[81]

By 1965, the department's control over the content of the commentaries had become tighter than ever. The head of the information and cultural relations branch, Neil Truscott, was able to report that Sayers, Wilkie and Harper had recently accepted material prepared almost wholly within the department on issues where its officers had aimed at a particular point. If a commentator was unwilling to accept a complete briefing or extensive changes, he reported, the department had on occasion had the commentary read by an officer of Radio Australia.[82] William Pinwill, the Radio Australia journalist who in the 1960s became producer of the news commentaries, recalled in 1989 that 'some commentators—more often academics—would be quite happy to read what was put in front of them'.[83] In 1966, the public information officer, Richard Woolcott (who in 1989 became secretary of the department) asserted, 'Commentaries are, as you know, virtually under our control.'[84]

Long after Plimsoll had replaced Tange as secretary, the department was still insisting that the news commentary 'was instituted as a programme designed specifically to reflect Government policy and which has to be approved by the Department before broadcast'. But there was a note of greater realism:

> Radio Australia will not be able to keep good commentators if they are too circumscribed and the point of having a commentary by an apparently independent commentator is defeated if the commentaries are too stilted. It is a fairly delicate process to find the best way of serving the Government's purpose with news commentaries.[85]

The paper containing these words was drafted by C. R. (Kim) Jones, the former Radio Australia liaison officer who brought a new liberalism to relations between Radio Australia and the department.

In any case, by this time the very idea of a news commentary, in which a 'high credibility' figure gave a more or less authoritative interpretation of issues and events, had become an anachronism. In the ABC's domestic broadcasts, such commentaries had already been replaced by current affairs interviews in which a range of interpretations was presented.

This trend, with the increasing liberalism in the department, eventually spelled the end for the news commentaries that had been such a point of contention between the ABC and the department for almost two decades. After his appointment as editor of Radio Australia in 1972, Philip Koch joined Homfray in an approach to Sir Keith Waller, then secretary of Foreign Affairs (renamed in 1970). The commentaries were no longer of value, they argued; international issues could be better treated within Radio Australia's expanding current affairs programs. Waller agreed. Shortly afterwards, ABC general manager Talbot Duckmanton told Waller that he had decided to discontinue the commentaries from 30 June 1972.[86] Relief must have been felt not only in Broadcast House, Sydney, and 529 Lonsdale Street, Melbourne (the Radio Australia building), but also in not a few offices in the Administrative Building, Parkes, ACT, the headquarters of the Department of Foreign Affairs.

6 Vietnam: 'one of the chief agencies for radio propaganda', 1956—1973

It is only to be expected that the Department of External Affairs tried to influence Radio Australia's coverage of the Vietnam War. It is true that such attempts were not nearly as numerous as attempts to influence its reporting of Indonesia. Nevertheless, the department did try to intervene throughout the period of Australia's military involvement in Vietnam (1962 to 1972).

The scene was set when the director of the service, Robin Wood, visited South Vietnam in 1956 during his trip to Southeast Asia at the expense of the Department of External Affairs. In Saigon, where he described the work of the United States Information Service as 'impressive and worthy of special comment',[1] he had a long talk with the deputy chief of the Voice of America, Robert E. Button. Button told him he regarded Radio Australia as 'one of the chief agencies for radio propaganda in S. and S.E. Asia because it was probably "less suspect than the Voice of America" '. Button's advice was that Radio Australia should transmit to South Vietnam in Vietnamese, rather than French, advice which the Australian government was to follow a few years later.

On one occasion, early in the second (post-Dien Bien Phu) stage of the war in Indo-China, the department became concerned that Radio Australia had inadvertently weakened the Australian position in a disagreement with the United States. Australia had advocated support for the moderate Prince Souvanna Phouma in Laos rather than for the American-backed General Phoumi Nosovan. When Souvanna decided to recognise the Beijing government, and Beijing (not surprisingly) welcomed this step,

Radio Australia gave extensive cover to the Chinese statement, as broadcast by Radio Beijing. The report quoted the statement verbatim:

The Chinese Government considers that the present unstable situation in Laos is a result of United States imperialist support of the Phoumi Nosovan rebel group.

The Chinese Government sternly condemns the crude intervention by the United States imperialists in the internal affairs of Laos and supports the lawful Souvanna Phouma Government.[2]

The department was embarrassed by this publicity for Beijing's unwelcome support for the Australian policy. One of its officers commented:

At a time when we are having serious policy difficulties with the US the latter could be seriously misled, as could the communist bloc, and the cause of the latter is in any case gratuitously advanced by the dissemination of the attached news report over Radio Australia.[3]

A senior officer of the department, F. J. (Blake) Blakeney, added: 'This is completely bad in my view. Surely RA can draw a distinction between "news" and propagating Chinese anti-American propaganda.'

The secretary of the Department of External Affairs, Sir Arthur Tange, sent a confidential letter to ABC general manager Charles Moses, which said, in part: 'It would be a major misfortune if Radio Australia through inadvertence were to be used as a vehicle for Communist propaganda.'[4] The ABC's acting controller of news, Gilbert Oakley, told Moses that almost anything from Radio Beijing had a propaganda angle, and Radio Australia watched this as closely as possible, but there were times when official statements must be given in the interests of impartiality and balance. He conceded, though, that the direct quotations should not have been used.[5] Moses replied to Tange that Oakley had discussed the matter with those responsible, reiterating 'the need for vigilance in matters of this kind,' adding, 'I hope that you will not have further cause for concern.'[6]

The department again took issue with Radio Australia over its reporting of the fighting in Laos in early 1961. The Laos government had shown correspondents arms, ammunition and equipment bearing Soviet and Chinese markings which it claimed had been captured from the Pathet Lao forces, and had also produced two prisoners. Noting that the prisoners had both been born in Laos, a Radio Australia correspondent said the display 'did not prove outside intervention, but did illustrate that the communist bloc was supplying the Pathet Lao forces'.[7] An External Affairs officer noted on the script: 'This is *shocking editing*. NO "intervention" proved but Communist bloc "supplying" is "illustrated".' Another officer of the department who raised the issue with the Radio Australia editor, John Hall, reported that Hall had 'accepted (vaguely) the criticism about "intervention"'.[8]

Radio Australia's introduction of broadcasts in Vietnamese was a direct result of the Vietnam War, and the Australian government's willingness to enlist the shortwave service as part of the West's psychological warfare. Although the possibility of broadcasting in Vietnamese had been discussed within the Department of External Affairs, the first formal suggestion to Radio Australia was that made to Robin Wood in Saigon by the deputy chief of the Voice of America.[9]

The first proposal from the department came in January 1962, when Tange told Moses that the department favoured the introduction of broadcasts in Vietnamese as soon as possible. In a follow-up letter, Tange told Moses:

There are 30 million people in the whole of Viet Nam who are exposed to strong propaganda pressure from Communist radio stations. In both North and South Vietnam the official news services are heavily censored and slanted. Vietnamese programmes from Radio Australia, by providing reliable news, would help to raise morale in the south, and provide an alternative to Communist programmes received in both halves of the country. The survival of a non-Communist Government in South Vietnam is of much political importance to Australia.[10]

Significantly, these words were later incorporated into a cabinet submission by the ABC on Radio Australia.

The ABC responded with unusual speed. Little more than two months later, Moses told Tange that the commission had agreed to include funds for the Vietnamese broadcasts in its 1962-63 budget, provided the government gave its financial approval.[11] When a new language was required for political reasons, the government, as well as the ABC, could act with alacrity. As outlined in chapter 2, the treasurer, Harold Holt, notified the Postmaster-General within a few weeks that, because both the ABC and the department considered that a program in Vietnamese should begin as soon as possible, approval had been given for the necessary expenditure.[12]

At the suggestion of Radio Australia's director, Peter Homfray, South Vietnam's national day (26 October 1962, the seventh anniversary of the founding of the Republic of Vietnam) was chosen for the opening broadcast. Homfray said that on a visit to Saigon he had found the choice of this date was 'more than appreciated by all the members of the Vietnamese government to whom I spoke'. The Australian embassy in Saigon offered to arrange for President Diem to record a message for inclusion in the opening broadcast.[13]

Two years after the service opened, the Australian ambassador in Saigon wrote approvingly of its impact as an unbiased source of news to South Vietnam:

Radio Australia news broadcasts are frequently quoted as sources by Vietnamese-language newspapers which are unable to afford access to wire services ... Radio Australia, together with the BBC, seems to be regarded as the most unbiased source of news and comment (rather than the Voice of America which is considered to broadcast somewhat 'slanted' news).[14]

'Generally,' he wrote, 'I consider that Radio Australia's impact in Viet Nam is substantial and that it is one of the most effective means of keeping Australia's name and interests before the public in Viet Nam.'

Woolcott versus Hall

But the department's public information officer in Canberra, Richard Woolcott, was less satisfied with Radio Australia's coverage of the war. A long letter to John Hall, editor of Radio Australia, in March 1965 listed several stories which the department had found wanting. Generally, Woolcott criticised Radio Australia news bulletins for making 'rather too much' of the pressure for a conference.[15] He continued:

For listeners used to the techniques of Communist propaganda the impression could well have been gained that the Australian Government, through Radio Australia, was covertly pushing the case for a conference on Indo-China. You will appreciate that this is not the case, and in our guide-lines we specifically caution on the use of items suggesting that South Vietnam may be ready to negotiate a settlement or the dissemination of pro-neutralist statements.

One of the stories the department thought should not have been used reported a suggestion by Arthur Calwell that Australia should seek to promote a Geneva-type conference to find a peaceful solution in Indo-China. Woolcott criticised another story because it said American air strikes on the North had hit 'what were described as military targets', showing Radio Australia as 'doubting or even discrediting the official US version of events'. Another criticism was that a report of protests by North Vietnam to the international control commission for Vietnam over the provision of more Australian military advisers was 'a clear case' where it was suggested that official Australian comment should have been sought and used to balance the report.

Woolcott also took issue with the use of a report that a South Vietnamese company had fled in the face of a Viet Cong propaganda offensive which asserted that the Viet Cong only wanted to kill the Americans:

It is unfortunate that isolated reports of poor morale in the Vietnamese Army should be disseminated over Radio Australia. On the whole the Vietnamese Army has done well as a fighting force and such incidents are quite rare. This sort of report can only contribute to the lowering of morale in an already difficult situation and *we feel that consideration should be given to excluding them from at least the Vietnamese language service* [emphasis added].

Another item deplored in Woolcott's letter was a report of a joint American–South Vietnamese operation in Phuoc Tuy province. The second sentence had said baldly, 'The operation was apparently a complete failure.' Woolcott did not think the insertion of this judgment so near the beginning of the story was 'necessary or desirable'. He also thought a reminder, on the same day, that the Viet Cong had inflicted the biggest defeat of the war on government forces in this area last December was unnecessary.

Woolcott was concerned that another story made it appear that the American Defense Secretary was deciding and announcing the policy of the South Vietnamese Army. He added:

We feel that *we* should try to avoid as far as possible the impression that the Vietnamese have no say in running their own affairs [emphasis added]. I suggest that in general a good deal of discretion might be used in quoting American military spokesmen as sources.

Woolcott wrote on his copy of the letter: 'Radio Australia's record has been far from good recently and this may serve to remind them of our interest in their bulletins and underline the need for consultation.' The note said the ABC's editor-in-chief, Walter Hamilton, had recently told Hall not to take the initiative in consulting the department.

Hall's reply was unequivocal:

For my part, I am quite clear on my role and what is expected of me under directions from my Controller in accordance with the Commission itself. In providing overseas listeners with a news service directed to many target areas, we are conscious of our national responsibilities and, in the interests of factual and objective reporting do, I suggest, take a close expert interest in what we broadcast, closer than perhaps anyone else.[16]

He referred the letter to Hamilton, who told Woolcott that, although 'in one or two marginal cases a phrase might be in doubt', overall he rejected the criticisms.[17]

Hamilton's rejection of his earlier criticisms did not deter Woolcott from further attempts to influence Radio Australia's coverage of the war. When, in a comment on talks between Air Vice-Marshal Nguyen Cao Ky, of Vietnam, and the American Secretary of Defense, Robert McNamara, Radio Australia said, 'America appears to have no choice … but to pour money, weapons and men into the country', Woolcott told Hall this 'could be damaging'.[18] It would be preferable, he said, to 'take the opportunity to emphasise the increasing pressure from the Viet Cong made possible by increasing assistance from Hanoi as a reason for United States build up'. He also told Hall that speculation in the same bulletin about possible argument between the Americans and the South Vietnamese on the command of troops was 'undesirable and at this stage not justified by the facts'. Woolcott commented to a first assistant secretary of the department, David Hay: 'This seems to me to be the type of report which, in the process of news gathering, Radio Australia should check with us in advance.' In mid-1965, the Minister for External Affairs, Paul Hasluck, went so far as to question Radio Australia's right to report the Opposition's criticism of the government's Vietnam policies: 'While this would be proper for an Australian audience,' he wrote, 'do we have to publicise it externally?'[19]

It was the Vietnam War which was the immediate stimulus for Hasluck's attempt to take control of Radio Australia, discussed in chapter 4. He directed that a letter be prepared for Menzies asking him to consider giving the secretary of the department power 'to direct Radio Australia not to broadcast, or to broadcast only in an approved form, any item which bears directly on the conduct of Australian foreign relations in Asia'.[20] In response to this direction, Hay told Hasluck one of the courses open to him was:

to seek, on the basis of the special circumstances which now exist with Australian forces engaged in warlike operations in Viet Nam, a special arrangement with the Australian Broadcasting Commission whereby government control is accepted freely by the Commission, for the purposes envisaged by you.

Fortunately for Radio Australia's editorial integrity, the proposal never came to fruition.

A document sent to Hall in December 1965 criticised the extent of the recent coverage of anti-war demonstrations in the West. The document said it was 'desirable not to contribute to the belief that these demonstrations in Western countries—particularly the United States—against

American policy in Vietnam, are a sign of significant opposition to policy.'21 The document also said it was 'Desirable to look for and make use of items which show that Laos is the victim of North Vietnamese attacks ... The statements by the Laotian Minister for Information when out here about North Vietnamese interference in Laos might have been used more extensively with good effect ...'. Hall's handwritten comment in the margin said: 'Story was used extensively in foreign language and English bulletins. There may have been cause for complaint if we had ignored this story.'

Tim Bowden, then an ABC talks officer, reported after a brief tour of central South Vietnam that both the anti-government, Buddhist-inspired 'Struggle Movement' and representatives of the South Vietnam government had told him they had found Radio Australia's reporting to be 'fair and impartial', particularly when compared to the BBC and the Voice of America.22 Bowden said that, as the South Vietnam government had virtually no political control of the region, this could be counted as something of an achievement. (Presumably Viet Cong representatives were not asked *their* views of Radio Australia's impartiality.)

Greater exposure for South Vietnamese government figures was an inevitable result of the Australian government's support for the Saigon regime. When Ky visited Australia in early 1967, Radio Australia broadcast extracts from his two news conferences and his address to the national press club, and two Vietnamese broadcasters accompanied the official party and reported daily for the Vietnamese service. Their programs included interviews with Ky, his wife, Foreign Minister Tran Van Do, and two members of the constituent assembly of South Vietnam. Radio Australia's French service also broadcast an exclusive interview with Ky.23

Radio Australia's message was getting through to listeners in North Vietnam as well as the South, according to an assistant director of the United States Information Agency, who visited Melbourne in mid-1968 after a tour of South Vietnam. He said it was apparent from the interrogation of North Vietnamese prisoners that Radio Australia's Vietnamese program was widely listened to in the North, despite the fact that such listening carried heavy penalties.24 He said that, of all Vietnamese-language services, Radio Australia probably had the biggest audience.25

Concerned about the sensitivity of the Paris peace talks on Indo-China in 1968, the secretary of the department, Sir James Plimsoll, asked the ABC chairman, Sir Robert Madgwick, to agree to a step which had been resisted by Walter Hamilton for years. He wanted reports on the peace talks for Radio Australia's news bulletins to be submitted to the department in advance. Despite Hamilton's opposition, Madgwick agreed, 'with the idea that External Affairs may be able to supply additional information or warn about any pitfalls they may see'.[26] No right of censorship was conceded: Madgwick said the ABC would retain the right to use material at its discretion. But it would have been a courageous editor who had rejected any departmental advice about 'pitfalls'. Madgwick told Clement Semmler:

> I know that we can trust our officers to interpret the arrangements in the spirit as well as in the letter, because I have come to the arrangements in what I regard to be the best interests of the nation and of the ABC.
> I would hope that the whole matter might be kept strictly confidential.

The arrangement, which applied to news bulletins in all languages, had originally been intended to cover only those in Vietnamese. In the original draft of the agreement between Madgwick and Plimsoll, the words 'in Vietnamese' had been crossed out.[27] Hamilton, by then assistant general manager of the ABC, wrote to Semmler 'to place on record my very strong disagreement with the proposal, and advice against it, as given verbally to you and the Chairman'.[28] Hamilton cautioned Lachlan Shaw, who had replaced Hall as news editor of Radio Australia:

> I can only advise you to take the closest heed of any advice given you by the department— for addition, deletion or amendment. You should always seek the reason for the advice given you and then make up your own mind, but on no account must you feel any obligation to alter a news story against your better judgement. I would be disappointed if you yielded in this way, although please do not think I fail to appreciate the problem.[29]

At a meeting of the commission two days after his agreement with Plimsoll, Madgwick tried to justify the decision. He said Plimsoll had emphasised 'the extremely delicate nature of the issues involved in the Paris peace talks and explained that the department, from its own sources, might be able to supply additional information and advice'.[30] Madgwick said that, in the discussions which had followed, he had reached 'a compromise arrangement which he felt would be in the best interests of the nation and the ABC while still preserving the integrity of Radio Australia'. He was now submitting his report to the commission for confirmation or otherwise of the action he had taken.

At Madgwick's invitation, the commissioners heard statements from Duckmanton and Hamilton. After lengthy discussion, they agreed 'that nothing should be done which would prejudice in any way the integrity and credibility not only of Radio Australia news broadcasts but of the whole ABC news service. However commissioners thought that in the present international situation the proposed arrangement was acceptable.' The commission resolved

that it has agreed to this action only because of the singular situation which now exists in relation to the Peace Talks being held in Paris, and that this agreement must not be interpreted as any weakening of its determination to maintain the independence, integrity and credibility of the ABC News Service in general and the Radio Australia News Bulletins in particular.

A year later, the department complained about a Radio Australia story on Indo-China which 'even if true' could damage Australian interests. The embassy in Phnom Penh took issue with the linking of two facts which officially were supposed to be unrelated. The lengthy summary at the beginning of a news bulletin read:

At the same time as United States Secretary of State William Rogers announces in Washington the resumption of diplomatic relations between United States and Cambodia, United States and South Vietnamese military commanders in Saigon announce that allied artillery and bombing attacks will be carried out against North Vietnamese army positions within Cambodia.[31]

The embassy said that Radio Australia was 'considered the official mouthpiece of the Australian Government here whether we like it or not' and the deliberate 'linking of' the two stories would scarcely escape attention in Phnom Penh. Its telex to the department continued: 'You will appreciate the mischievous effects of Radio Australia carrying this report, even if it's true the Vietnamese Communists themselves could scarcely have done better.' The department agreed that the linking of the items was 'inappropriate and potentially damaging'. It replied that Radio Australia's acting news editor (John Nelson), who had been absent on sick leave when the bulletin was broadcast, had been told in detail of the embassy's objections and acknowledged their validity.[32]

A mole in Radio Australia

Soon afterwards, the department had something more serious to complain about. Radio Australia broadcast in a bulletin targeted to North America a story beginning: 'The National Union of Australian University Students is going to raise funds at universities throughout Australia to rebuild schools bombed by the United States in North Vietnam.'[33]

Radio Australia apparently had a 'mole' in its ranks: an External Affairs officer, Pierre Hutton, said he had heard about the use of the item from a 'private' source.[34] The Radio Australia Liaison officer, Richard Broinowski said that Alan Tye, who was in charge of Radio Australia news during Nelson's absence, agreed that the department should have been given 'a courtesy call to seek our opinion'.[35] But he thought he had been justified in using the item, pointing out that the national union was the official organisation of the Australian student body, and its discussions and activities were news. Sir Laurence McIntyre, deputy secretary of the department, exercising some journalistic judgment, underlined these last six words and wrote in the margin: 'But are they *really*? Isn't it the case that it is the newspapers that think they should be news and make them into news?' Tye went on to say that a report that an Australian student organisation disapproved of the Vietnam War 'would hardly be treated as serious or unique by a sophisticated audience in the United States, where student reaction to the American commitment was much stronger than here'. Reporting on the incident, Broinowski said that the department had 'at least indicated to the News Section quite usefully that we have a means (unspecified) of knowing what appears in their Bulletins other than those we monitor or get the texts for'.[36] Asked in 1990, by which time he had become general manager of the service, if he could remember whether the department's 'private source' in Radio Australia was a journalist, a translator or perhaps Homfray (who, as he no doubt knew, had a background in intelligence), Broinowski said he could offer no clarification 'without seeing the letter I allegedly wrote to Pierre Hutton'.[37] A photocopy of his memo to Hutton was sent to him with an accompanying letter, but neither this nor a follow-up letter was ever answered. Homfray denied that *he* had been the source of the leak, saying that, as he had not been editorially responsible for news, he had had nothing to do with its content.[38]

The Australian embassy in Phnom Penh suggested in September 1969 that Radio Australia should be 'steered away' from comments on border incidents which could exacerbate relations between Cambodia and its neighbours.[39] One example was a remark by the Thai ambassador in Australia that those killed in the Phnom Melai incident near the Thai border had been 'only innocent woodcutters'. A first secretary in the Phnom Penh embassy, Mack Williams, said Radio Australia's reporting of the remark was 'not helpful to the interests of an improvement in relations' between Cambodia and Thailand. He also instanced a report of a border incident between American–South Vietnamese forces and Cambodians on the border with South Vietnam.

A few weeks later, the Phnom Penh embassy was complaining about two reports damaging to the fiction that North Vietnamese forces were not using Cambodian territory. The first said a document captured by the South Vietnamese detailed an agreement by Cambodia giving North Vietnamese forces freedom of action in a Cambodian province. The other item complained of was a report (which led a news bulletin) that American aircraft had attacked North Vietnamese positions inside Cambodia for the second day in succession. A handwritten note on the Phnom Penh complaint said Peter Barnett, then news editor of Radio Australia, had agreed that 'such items should *not* be given prominence but rather tacked on to other VN stories'.[40]

The following year, the embassy in Phnom Penh was complaining again. It said Radio Australia had consistently headlined reports of alleged massacres of Vietnamese civilians by Cambodian armed forces. The complaint was not that the reports were wrong. 'As you will know from our reports,' the embassy said, 'these allegations appear unfortunately in most cases to be well founded.'[41] The telex continued:

WHILE NOT CONDONING WHAT HAS HAPPENED, RADIO AUSTRALIA, WE SUGGEST, MIGHT PLACE THESE REPORTS IN THE CONTEXT OF THE TRADITIONAL CAMBODIAN HATRED FOR VIETNAMESE (CAUSED IN GOOD MEASURE BY VIETNAMESE HARSHNESS IN PAST), OF THE FACT THAT IT IS VIETNAMESE WHO ARE INVADING CAMBODIA AND OF THE WELL-KNOWN 5TH COLUMN ACTIVITIES BY VIETNAMESE IN CAMBODIA ...

WHILE WE EXPECT THAT INTERNATIONAL PRESS AGENCIES AND FOREIGN CORRESPONDENTS WILL CONCENTRATE ON THESE STORIES WE HOPE THAT RADIO AUSTRALIA CAN MAKE SOME ATTEMPT TO MODERATE THEIR REPORTING ON THIS PARTICULARLY DELICATE TOPIC. THE VIETNAMESE COMMUNIST MILITARY OPERATIONS HERE (RATHER THAN THIS CAMBODIAN REACTION) SEEMS TO US THE MAIN NEWS STORY HERE.

The department replied that Radio Australia had accepted that the main news story was as the embassy described, but was hampered by the paucity of reliable information on Vietnamese communist military operations.[42]

Radio Australia's contribution to the anti-communist information offensive in Vietnam was not unappreciated by the Americans. In 1971, in a paper for a meeting between Radio Australia and the department, one of its senior officers, John McCredie, said the Americans had shown some gratitude for 'the independent commentaries of Radio Australia, beamed globally, on Indo-China'.[43] Pointing to the problem of assessing the impact of international broadcasting, the paper continued: 'Their content is unexceptionable but, regrettably, we have no evidence of how many conversions they have effected.'

Next, the department turned its attack on the ABC's correspondent in Vietnam. Keith Shann told an assistant general manager, Charles Buttrose, that the department, and particularly its secretary, Sir Keith Waller, regarded Andrew Swanton's reporting as 'inaccurate, callow and damaging'.[44] Shann said Swanton 'caused a great deal of trouble by his tendency to report as fact the first thing that seemed to come into his head'. Buttrose had made 'an interesting comment' that in the old days news media allowed people to become war correspondents only when they had had a great deal of journalistic experience, but this was no longer the case. Buttrose said he would be glad to get from the department instances of its dissatisfaction and would do something about it if the commission were convinced that what it was saying was soundly based. The department's resultant search, if any, for instances of 'inaccurate, callow and damaging' reporting by Swanton was apparently unsuccessful: the files contain nothing further on the matter.

The Australian embassy in Saigon noted in November 1972 that a speech by South Vietnam's Foreign Minister foreshadowing the end of the war had been 'picked up accurately by Radio Australia and will no doubt elicit unfavourable attention elsewhere'.[45] But this time there was no complaint: at least some of the department's officers were recognising the inevitable. The fact that within a month Australia seemed likely to have a new government opposed to its participation in the war might have had something to do with the deathbed conversion.

The broadcast of allegedly inaccurate information remained a matter of concern. Three months later, Waller told Duckmanton that the ambassador in Saigon was concerned about 'certain aspects' of Radio Australia's news broadcasts about developments following the ceasefire agreement in Vietnam. One recent instance, he said, was that Radio Australia had reported that all main roads out of Saigon had been cut, whereas three highways were in fact open. Waller said that, for many people, including those in South Vietnam who relied on Radio Australia for their basic news, such errors could create a wrong impression of what was actually occurring. He was sure Duckmanton would appreciate that it was important that Radio Australia's news broadcasts should be as accurate and up-to-date as possible.[46] But this was the department's last hurrah over coverage of the Vietnam War. The era when it tried to tailor the news to make Radio Australia in some measure part of the government's war effort was finished.

Even after Australia's military involvement in the Vietnam War began in 1965, the department made more frequent attempts to influence Radio

Australia's reporting of Indonesia than to influence its reporting of Vietnam. This raises the question of why this should be so. In Vietnam, Australian forces were fighting in a war. In Indonesia, after the end of the border skirmishes in Borneo following the downfall of Soekarno in 1965, Australian forces were not directly involved.

One reason for the department's preoccupation with Radio Australia's coverage of Indonesia was undoubtedly its perception of the relative importance of the two countries to Australia's national interest. The department had long maintained that Indonesia should have first priority among Radio Australia's primary target areas.

A second reason may have been that Radio Australia's coverage of the Vietnam War was comparatively circumspect because of the heavy dependence of its correspondents on Australian military public relations. The correspondents in Indonesia made far wider use of independent sources.

A third reason for the department's greater concern with coverage of Indonesia is that, largely because of Radio Australia's huge audience in Indonesia, the Indonesian government was increasingly sensitive to its reporting of Indonesian affairs, especially issues which, through self-censorship or outright suppression, were not covered in the domestic media. In later years, Radio Australia's coverage of such issues, including the invasion of East Timor and subsequent events there, and allegations of corruption involving some of the country's leading figures, led to the expulsion of the ABC's correspondent in 1980, described in chapter 9. One suspects that, even if the department had not perceived relations with Indonesia to be of crucial importance to Australia's long-term interests, the frequent, niggling attacks on Radio Australia's broadcasts by an influential neighbour would have preoccupied its senior officers considerably more than the reporting of a war in a country which, officially at least, ignored those broadcasts. The files contain not one mention of any official complaint from South Vietnamese leaders. Not only was Radio Australia's audience in Vietnam too small for its impact there to have been of any real significance; those leaders, of course, had far more pressing concerns.

7 | The coming of *détente*, 1970–1991

In 1970, after twenty years of attempts to use Radio
Australia as a Cold War weapon, the service was broadcasting in eight
languages, English, Indonesian, Standard Chinese (Mandarin), Cantonese,
Vietnamese, Thai, Japanese and French. The changes in this pattern over
the next two decades resulted from various factors: a growing realisation
that the people of Papua New Guinea were an important target audience;
the transformation of Australia's relationship with the countries of Indo-
China; a change in the perception of the audience in Japan; and shrinking
budgets. For Radio Australia, Cold War themes and tensions never re-
emerged, although some regional tensions did emerge, in particular with
Indonesia.

Not only were the two decades an era of progressive *détente* on the international scene, culminating in the collapse of European communism in
the early 1990s; they were also an era when, apart from the odd skirmish,
Radio Australia had won its war of independence from the Department of
Foreign Affairs (renamed on 5 November 1970). This resulted partly from
a generational change to more liberal, or less combative, officers in the
department. At the same time, though, the war intensified between the
ABC and Radio Australia officers who felt the parent organisation was
starving it of the resources it needed to do its job adequately.

It is no accident that periods of *détente* in Australia's relations with the
communist powers have tended to be accompanied by a slackening in the
struggle for control of Radio Australia. With the easing of the Cold War, or
at least Australia's participation in it, there was less incentive, and less

political pressure, for the Department of Foreign Affairs to use Radio Australia as a Cold War weapon. But the slackening in the Cold War saw not so much an acceleration in the disengagement of the Department of Foreign Affairs and Trade from Radio Australia as a continuation of a progressive process of divergence.

Regardless of the state of the Cold War on the global scene, though not unrelated to it, the most notable period of *détente* for Australia began with the election of the Whitlam Labor government on 2 December 1972. It was not accidental that the election of a government which in its first few days announced Australia's pending withdrawal from the Vietnam War and recognition of the government of the People's Republic of China coincided with the ascendancy of a more liberal spirit among officers of the Department of Foreign Affairs.

But the accession of the Whitlam government did not bring as radical a change of direction as is sometimes believed. The American alliance remained central to Australia's foreign policy. Opposition to the renewed American bombing of North Vietnam in December 1972 was confined to a confidential letter of protest from Whitlam to Nixon.

Furthermore, the new wind of liberalism in the department's attitude to Radio Australia did not begin overnight on 3 December 1972: it had already begun to blow. This was apparent in a draft paper prepared for a departmental discussion of the overseas service in 1970. The paper, setting out 'the conclusion which might be reached by the proposed meeting',[1] said Radio Australia should provide a 'balanced, attractive picture, taking care to avoid cutting across, or speculating on, government policies in foreign affairs, trade investment and other areas'. But it then went on to say:

The use of Radio Australia for pointed advocacy should be kept strictly in reserve for emergency situations: broadcast of direct propaganda could only impair Radio Australia's reputation and thus its current and potential usefulness.

Other indications of a growing acceptance by the department of the appropriateness for Radio Australia of the BBC model of international broadcasting came in the closing section of the paper, headed 'Relationship with the Department of External Affairs'. The section stated:

Radio Australia operates somewhat uneasily within the Australian Broadcasting Commission, and senior Radio Australia officers feel that it would benefit from greater autonomy, either within that organisation or as a separate entity ... Whatever the administrative context, however, Radio Australia's independence should be carefully safeguarded both for substantive reasons—as the basis of its reputation—and for reasons of international presentation.[2]

The draft conclusions prepared on the basis of the paper included: 'No attempt should be made to alter Radio Australia's status, and its reputation for objectivity and accuracy should be scrupulously safeguarded.'[3] The last of a series of meetings which substantially adopted the draft paper accepted the need for more transmitting facilities, including a fourth transmitter in Darwin. (It was to be a long time coming.)

Another evidence of a new, more liberal attitude to Radio Australia was the reaction to criticism of a news item in mid-1972 by the high commissioner in London, Sir Alexander Downer. The item reported that, on the eve of a meeting of the council of SEATO in Canberra, a 'distinguished Australian academic' had urged that Australia scrap SEATO and reconsider the value of the ANZUS Pact and the Malaysia–Singapore defence arrangement. The academic, Professor Hedley Bull, said the only thing that kept SEATO alive was that it operated as a continuing justification for the American, Australian and New Zealand presence in Vietnam.[4] As for the five-power arrangement, this should be seen not as a new relationship with Malaysia and Singapore, but as 'the last dying gasp of the British Empire in South-East Asia'. Downer was outraged. He described the statement as inflammatory and damaging and hostile to Australia's interests.[5]

Commenting on Downer's criticism, Richard Woolcott wrote to the new news editor of Radio Australia: 'If one is trying to run an objective news service one needs to broadcast from time to time criticism of the Government by authoritative persons. As you know, I would not contest this.'[6] The secretary, Sir Keith Waller, commented to Woolcott: 'The short answer is that the commentaries [the news item had been written from a news commentary by Bull] are about to cease—But even so, can we stop RA broadcasting news that conflicts with Govt policy? I should have thought not.'[7] Woolcott replied:

We cannot 'stop' RA broadcasting news which conflicts with Government policy as we have no editorial control over RA. But we do have *influence* and I hope this will grow … While I do not entirely share Sir Alex's attitude to this particular case I see no reason why we should not send a copy … to Hamilton and Koch [the Radio Australia news editor], simply so that they will be alerted to the reaction to including this type of item in R/A news.[8]

Woolcott's hope that the department's influence over Radio Australia would grow, in other words that the service would move closer to the American model, was of course a familiar theme, expressed at frequent intervals down the years. But his acceptance of the need for Radio Australia to broadcast criticism of the government, and of the department's powerlessness to stop this, was comparatively new (for Woolcott as well as for the department in general).

Within three weeks of becoming Prime Minister (and Foreign Minister), Gough Whitlam roundly endorsed Radio Australia's independence of government (although, as previously mentioned, he was badly astray when he attributed the same policy to all of his government's predecessors):

The Australian Government—the Government which has just been defeated in the election as much as my own Government—has never used and shall never use Radio Australia as a propaganda machine. There has never been any difference between our Australian political parties about this. Radio Australia will continue to be completely independent, completely free to report the news as it truly is. Radio Australia is not the voice of the Australian Government.[9]

The Minister for the Media, Senator Douglas McClelland, took a similar line in his Arthur Norman Smith memorial lecture at the University of Melbourne the following year:

The policy is quite clear: Radio Australia is the voice of Australia, not the voice of the Australian Government. We will not interfere by any form of pressure on the station's staff to enforce conformity with Government thinking or policy. We are adamantly opposed to any measures which would militate in any way against RA's reputation for impartiality, objectivity and reliability.[10]

Homfray versus the ABC

The accession of the new government appeared to offer hope for a new deal in the allocation of resources. In April 1973, Whitlam directed McClelland to make a 'critical analysis' of the overseas service.[11] McClelland concluded that Radio Australia had become a 'lost division' of the ABC. Peter Homfray had told him that Radio Australia 'gets what's left of the cake' after the domestic service had had its meal. The Department of Foreign Affairs reported that personal relations between Homfray and Charles Buttrose, the assistant general manager to whom he was responsible, simply could not be worse. Homfray had reported that they had not spoken to each other for months. The department said lack of liaison and contact would not necessarily be of concern had it not reached a point where some important policy matters were being affected. The fact that personal animosities had developed and produced such bad overall relations suggested that there was a real need to change the administrative arrangements under which Radio Australia operated. It was Australia's shortwave service with special responsibilities, yet it was 'buried in an organisation whose primary concern is a domestic media service'.[12] Against this background, McClelland suggested to Whitlam that Radio Australia be put directly within his ministerial responsibility and attached to the Department of the Media.[13] This, of course, would not only have removed the service's funding from the parsimonious ABC; it would have constituted a return to the American model of international broadcasting, placing it under the direct control of a government department. Even if McClelland himself (or the government in which he was a minister) did not try to exercise this control, the way would have been open for future ministers, and future governments, to do so.

Whitlam, who at this stage was also Foreign Minister, consulted the Department of Foreign Affairs. On its advice, he replied to McClelland that Radio Australia must be able to demonstrate its comparative freedom from direct government control.[14] This could be jeopardised by the incorporation of Radio Australia into the Department of the Media. Despite the reservations indicated by his use of the word 'comparative', Whitlam was opposed to the direct control of the shortwave service by a government department, as in the days of Calwell's Department of Information.

In July 1973 Homfray burned his bridges. Without telling Buttrose, his immediate superior in the ABC hierarchy, he wrote directly to McClelland, proposing that Radio Australia be made a separate statutory authority. He suggested that the authority be controlled by a commission of seven, three of whom would be nominated by the Minister for the Media, the Minister for Foreign Affairs and the Treasurer.[15] McClelland replied to him in 'friendly but non-committal terms'.

A crucial meeting was held in McClelland's office in North Sydney on 13 August 1973 to consider the proposal. It was chaired by McClelland, and attended by representatives of the Department of Foreign Affairs, the Public Service Board and the Postmaster-General's Department as well as the chief executives of the ABC and Radio Australia. When Duckmanton met Homfray beforehand, he asked for an indication of the agenda. Homfray stalled, and the ABC general manager did not realise the real purpose until the meeting began, and Homfray handed out to each participant an outline of his proposal for an independent statutory authority. In the event, Homfray's bold move failed: after an exhaustive inquiry, Radio Australia remained a part of the ABC.

A position paper by the Department of Foreign Affairs commented that Radio Australia was an important instrument for helping to achieve

Australia's overseas information objectives, and played 'a valuable role in presenting an objective and credible Australian voice and view in the regions of immediate concern to us.'[16] The paper stated: 'It is of continuing interest and concern to the Department that Radio Australia should at all times be able to present itself as a credible, independent short-wave broadcaster, and not an instrument of Australian Government propaganda.' The department concluded that, although it could not take a firm stand on the suggestion of a separate authority until it had a better idea of what was envisaged, the idea did have some appeal. When compared with the proposal that Radio Australia become part of the Media Department, a separate authority had the obvious advantage that the service would clearly be seen to be independent of direct government control. The recommended position was that, bearing in mind the apparent unwillingness of the ABC to give Radio Australia a 'fair go', the department saw some merit in the idea of a separate statutory authority. It was concerned at the state of relations between the ABC and Radio Australia, not, it claimed, through any wish to interfere in the internal affairs of the ABC, but because the situation was reducing, or could reduce, Radio Australia's effectiveness as a shortwave broadcaster. But the Department of Foreign Affairs was told later that Whitlam did not favour the idea of a separate statutory authority for Radio Australia, and concluded that therefore this possibility was out.[17]

Later in 1973, the department prepared a report on Radio Australia which said, 'It would not be appropriate for Foreign Affairs to circulate at a future meeting any paper containing our views on the administrative arrangements between the ABC and Radio Australia.'[18] The report added that it was 'clearly in the department's interests that Radio Australia not be hindered by an administrative structure which might in any way limit its effectiveness as a short-wave broadcaster'.[19] On liaison arrangements with Radio Australia, the report said it was of continuing interest to the department that Radio Australia

should be able to present itself as a credible, independent shortwave broadcaster, and not as an instrument of Australian Government propaganda. At the same time it is in our interests that Radio Australia should not carry commentary which is openly critical of Australian Government policy or other material which could embarrass us in other countries.

Unfortunately, the report said, it had never been made clear exactly how far the department could go in providing 'effective guidance'. In correspondence with the department, Duckmanton had stressed that the final responsibility for deciding the content of programs rested with Radio Australia. But historically, the report said, the ABC's position had shifted depending on what it had sought to achieve. When it had needed more funds, Radio Australia had been 'a positive vehicle for promoting policies of the Australian Government in the Asian region'. At other times, the right of Radio Australia to take a final decision on the content of its programs had been emphasised.

On the subject of news items critical of government policy, the report made a proposal which represented a significant retreat from its former position that such news items should not be used—yet another indication of the more liberal spirit prevailing in the department after the election of the Whitlam government: 'Where a news item is by itself critical of Australian Government policy or where it could give a wrong impression of policy, Radio Australia should, as far as possible, balance the report with a brief factual re-statement of the policy in question.'

The department then proceeded to take a considerably more cautious line than it had often taken in the past:

We would need to put these suggestions in delicate terms for while Radio Australia remains an integral part of the ABC it is within its rights to operate under the terms of the Australian Broadcasting Act which, of course, gives the ABC independence of Government control of its programs. It would probably be best to present the suggestions in terms of improving existing arrangements rather than give the impression of breaking new ground or wanting to exert some control over Radio Australia's programs, something to which we are not in any case legally entitled.

Under the microscope

In the three years from 1974 to 1976, Radio Australia was subjected to no fewer than three inquiries, the Public Service Board–ABC review and the Waller inquiry into Radio Australia, and the Green Committee's examination of Australian broadcasting. In April 1974, McClelland initiated a review by a joint team from the Public Service Board and the ABC. The team looked at three possibilities—complete independence, placement as a largely autonomous unit within the Department of the Media, and reorganisation as a more distinct management identity within the ABC. Showing a clear preference for the BBC model of international broadcasting, the team favoured the third approach, partly because it would maintain the existing management structure, 'which is recognised as assuring freedom from political direction'.[20] But it also favoured the establishment of a standing Radio Australia review committee of five, three of them representatives of government departments. The three outsiders would be from Foreign Affairs, the Department of the Media and the Australian Post Office.

Such a committee would have given governments more power over Radio Australia policy than they had had at any time since the transfer of the service to the ABC. The proposed functions of the standing committee were to 'review programme policies in the light of Radio Australia objectives', to consider reports by Radio Australia's board of advice or individual standing committee members, and to consider plans and policies for the continuing overall development of the service. The proposals of the Public Service Board–ABC report were approved by the commission without any qualifications.

The union covering most ABC employees, the ABC Staff Association, made a strong protest to Duckmanton. The association described as 'both reprehensible and amazing' the fact that it (the association) had not been consulted by the review team.[21] In a badly spelled submission, it objected strongly to the proposed inclusion of senior officers from the Departments of Foreign Affairs and the Media on the standing review committee. This objection was based 'on the policy that Radio Australia should be independant of any "Department of State" in terms of programme policy and it's objectives'. The inclusion of these officers on a committee that reviewed program policies would 'seriously weaken the integrity of Radio Australia and could ultimately be used to discredit it as a mere propaganda tool of the Government'.

Before the Minister for the Media had approved the report, Whitlam announced that he had appointed the former secretary of the Foreign Affairs Department, Sir Keith Waller, to inquire into Radio Australia. The Waller committee, whose deliberations and conclusions were to develop further the *détente* between the department and Radio Australia, met for the first time on 4 June 1975. By this time the problems of Radio Australia had been exacerbated by the total loss of its Darwin station in Cyclone Tracy on Christmas Day 1974. The Waller committee considered three options:

(a) That Radio Australia should be under the control of a government department.
(b) That Radio Australia should be a separate agency, removed from the ABC, with its own board of directors or commissioners.
(c) That a reorganised Radio Australia remain within the ABC.[22]

Homfray made a submission of twenty pages in which he urged the committee to consider his proposal for a separate statutory authority. He forthrightly blamed the ABC's senior management in Sydney for the fact that Radio Australia had failed to keep abreast of its main competitors.

Homfray also criticised the ABC news service for failing to consider Radio Australia's requirements. He pointed out that news had been placed outside his area of responsibility (the news editor being responsible to the controller of news in Sydney). He proceeded to list major news events in Asia which had not been covered by ABC foreign correspondents.[23]

It was Homfray's last thrust against Duckmanton and the Sydney ABC establishment, in which he saw Foreign Affairs principally as an ally. On 11 July 1975, he was transferred to a nominal position created for him in the Victorian branch of the ABC, and Philip Koch, Radio Australia's news editor, was made acting director of the service. Koch was an experienced foreign correspondent (Indonesia, Vietnam, Japan), whose career had been in the ABC news service The department had a high regard for the quality of his reporting from Indonesia, especially in the aftermath of the attempted coup of 1 October 1965. In some ways he was the model for Guy Hamilton, the hero of the novel *The Year of Living Dangerously* by his brother Chris (although Phil Koch was short, dark and handsome, whereas Hamilton had been portrayed as tall, fair and handsome).

Koch prepared for the inquiry a thoughtful draft statement of Radio Australia's basic objectives which was endorsed by the ABC's Sydney management without significant amendment. No less aware than Homfray of the importance of Foreign Affairs support, he said that Radio Australia recognised the department's 'special responsibility ... for policy proposals about the role of Radio Australia within the total canvas of Australia's external relations'.[24] Expressing the view that it was perhaps more important in 1975 than in the previous thirty years that Australia should have a quality radio presence in its major target areas, Koch continued:

It is not simply that British influence has decreased and that the United States is re-examining its Asian policies, but that the views expressed in BBC and VOA programmes to Asia concerning events *in Asia* may not necessarily be shared by Australians. In the 1950's and 60's, there tended to be a common view. Today, there are differences and tomorrow there may be deep divergences ...

Analysing reasons for Radio Australia's popularity in Asia, particularly in Indonesia, the statement said:

Listeners refer to the impartial, accurate news and enjoyable music programmes to account for their preference.

We believe there is more than this. We believe Australia is acceptable to Asian listeners for wider reasons. We are not seen as a colonial power. Our record is good in supporting independence movements ... In broadcast terms, Australians don't talk down to listeners or speak from outside the region ... Our programme policy, with the liaison assistance of Foreign Affairs, is to represent clearly the Australian viewpoint in foreign policy and explain events in terms that are readily understood by our listeners.

Koch blamed the previous government for the recent stagnation in the development of Radio Australia. He said that, in 1970, the government had instructed the ABC that no further development in Radio Australia was to take place. The allocation of resources, he said, had been within that framework. His draft paper said the preferred alternative, proposed by the report of the joint inquiry by the Public Service Board and the ABC, and approved by McClelland and the commission, was for a reorganised Radio Australia within the ABC. The most important advantage of this option was that it would maintain the position of the service as conforming to the British model, free from immediate political direction.

Waller endorsed Radio Australia's conformity to the BBC model by approving a slightly amended version of Koch's draft paper, thus endorsing the ABC's preference for the overseas service to remain part of the ABC, rather than become a separate statutory authority, as proposed by Homfray.

In concluding that Radio Australia was effective, the Waller inquiry drew on four sources. One was a summary of responses from overseas posts, which strongly endorsed Radio Australia's contribution as an instrument of foreign policy. Asked by the Waller committee whether it would matter if Radio Australia were closed down, all posts with the exception of Tanzania considered that, on balance, the service should be maintained. Nearly all posts believed that the news service was probably its most valuable contribution, and some made pleas for an increase in 'more serious' programs to try to reach more influential circles in Asian countries.[25]

A second source of information on Radio Australia's effectiveness was a report of the results of surveys by the BBC and the Voice of America, which indicated that the Australian service was doing well in ratings in India, Indonesia, Thailand and Malaysia in comparison with other external broadcasters.[26] A third source was information about Radio Australia's mail, which totalled 315,000 letters in the twelve months to June 1975. The fourth was 'the steady demand by stations in the region for relays and transcriptions of Radio Australia's programs'.

The civil war in East Timor and its subsequent invasion by Indonesia heightened the appreciation of at least some Foreign Affairs officers of the value of a clear signal for Radio Australia, something which Cyclone Tracy had made increasingly rare in Asia. Richard Woolcott, by then Australian ambassador in Jakarta, asked the department to bring one of his cables to Canberra to the attention of Waller and those ministers who were involved in the consideration of Radio Australia's future:

THE NEED FOR AN AUDIBLE AUSTRALIAN EXTERNAL BROADCASTING SERVICE WITH A GOOD SIGNAL HAS RARELY BEEN MORE CLEAR TO BOTH SENIOR

AUSTRALIAN AND INDONESIAN OFFICIALS HERE AS IT HAS BEEN DURING THE
LAST FORTNIGHT WHEN WE HAVE BATTLED WITH STATIC, INDIFFERENT
RECEPTION, FADING, AND SHADING BY THE MORE POWERFUL TRANSMISSIONS
OF OTHER COUNTRIES TO HEAR RADIO AUSTRALIA REPORTS ON THE
SITUATION IN TIMOR. THE PRIME MINISTER'S CALL TO THE PARTIES IN TIMOR
FOR A CEASE-FIRE AND THE ENDING OF THE BLOODSHED IN THE HOUSE ON
26 AUGUST WOULD NOT HAVE REACHED MANY EARS IN THIS PART OF THE
WORLD ON RADIO AUSTRALIA WHICH I WOULD HAVE THOUGHT TO BE THE
PRINCIPAL INSTRUMENT BY WHICH HIS MESSAGE MIGHT HAVE GOT ACROSS.[27]

The ABC's submission of basic objectives to the Waller inquiry acknowledged the consultative role of the department in the operation of the
shortwave service. The submission gave the following definition of these
basic objectives:

Radio Australia should be required to provide, in consultation with the Department of
Foreign Affairs, (N.B. not under its direction) a short-wave service designed to attract an
international audience.
    Its purpose should be the development of international awareness of Australia and the
Australian identity through programmes of entertainment and enrichment, which reflect
the realities and quality of Australian life and culture, Australia's national interests and policies and the full spectrum of Australian viewpoints on domestic and international affairs.[28]

The Waller committee endorsed this paragraph of the submission with
minor amendments, and it became a definitive statement of Radio
Australia's *raison d'être*. The amendments slightly strengthened the statement in Radio Australia's favour: the words 'entertainment and enrichment' were replaced by the words 'high quality news, current affairs,
entertainment and cultural enrichment'.[29] The words 'Australia's national
interests and policies', which could have given the Department of Foreign
Affairs a pretext for pressing the broadcasters into placing emphasis on
government policies, were deleted.

The ABC listed seven guidelines for program policy.[30] The committee accepted four of these, including one stating that Radio Australia
should aim at 'accuracy and balance in presenting foreign and Australian
affairs'[31] (avoiding any suggestion that only the policies of the government
of the day should be presented).[32] Another guideline said the service should
have 'an overall objective of providing an accurate, coherent and appealing
reflection of Australian life, viewpoints and cultural values', and a third said
the aim should be to 'achieve balance between conflicting views in a single
transmission or programme'.[33] The references to 'Australian viewpoints'
and 'conflicting views' made it apparent that the Waller committee believed
that Opposition as well as government policies should be reported.

Koch foresaw the danger that the officers of the Department of Foreign Affairs who wanted Radio Australia to move closer to the American model would try to use the Waller inquiry to increase their influence over Radio Australia's news and current affairs content. He suggested to Duckmanton in June 1975 that perhaps the new Minister for the Media, Dr Moss Cass, should be aware that the inquiry intended to examine the liaison relationship between the department and Radio Australia. He reminded Duckmanton that the department had claimed that 'shortcomings' in the selection of news items on Radio Australia could in part be attributed to 'deficiencies in the existing liaison arrangements'.[34] The 'critical study' by Foreign Affairs which had followed the meeting at North Sydney on 13 August 1973 had reported that 'the Department is working towards defining a more useful liaison relationship and will be making suggestions as to how this might be achieved'. Koch prepared a draft on the 'Role of Radio Australia' which said the ABC welcomed the department's liaison role to provide background briefing:

> But should there be any development towards 'selection' rather than 'briefing', then it is felt listeners would quickly notice important shifts in Radio Australia's coverage, particularly interpretation of news events concerning Australia's interrelationship with other countries.[35]

An exchange of correspondence followed between Koch and the acting assistant secretary of the department, Charles Mott, about proposed new guidelines for the liaison. The initial draft by Mott, approved by the secretary, Alan Renouf, was symptomatic of the new spirit of *détente* between the department and Radio Australia, and the department's acceptance of the desirability of the BBC model. The power it sought for the department was much more modest than would have been acceptable to Tange, let alone Hasluck. It began by stating that Radio Australia was 'an important instrument for helping to achieve Australia's overseas information objectives and can play a valuable role in presenting an *objective* Australian voice in the regions of immediate concern to us [emphasis added].'[36] The draft went on to concede that Radio Australia should be able to present itself as 'a believable, independent broadcaster and not an instrument of Australian Government policy', and spoke of the value of a 'close, flexible and equal relationship'. The draft guidelines also conceded that the final editorial decision would be for Radio Australia to take. But Koch took exception to a guideline which gave the department 'a right and a duty' to provide factual information and background to Radio Australia on matters of foreign affairs, and to bring to its notice 'cases where we believed their reporting might damage Australia's foreign policy interests'.[37] He feared that this might be interpreted to mean that Radio Australia would be obliged to amend the news on the basis of such advice. He persuaded Mott to weaken the phrasing to give the department merely 'a liaison responsibility to keep Radio Australia briefed' about such matters. Koch also persuaded the department to delete the guideline:

We should encourage Radio Australia not to carry reports about the Department without first checking with us and, where a news item is critical of Government policy or where it could give a wrong impression of policy, to balance the report with a brief factual statement of the policy in question.

Koch argued that guidelines should not assume that Radio Australia would not provide a balanced coverage of any broadcast criticism of government policy. In the spirit of *détente*, Renouf accepted Koch's amendments, and Duckmanton accepted the new guidelines. It was agreed that both the department and the ABC should keep the details completely confidential.[38] The guidelines were endorsed by cabinet when it considered the Waller report in 1977.[39]

Of more pressing concern to Radio Australia than liaison with the department was the rehabilitation of its transmitters. In a private and confidential letter to the ambassador to Japan, Koch described the Waller inquiry as 'the last shot in the locker'.[40] If Waller could not persuade the government to rehabilitate the service, he said, 'then RA dies a miserable slow death':

And as you are aware, previous submissions to Cabinets on RA have failed; the reason I believe has been that there was never a vote in them. This remains the case, so in the corridors of Canberra, Sir Keith will need to be at his persuasive best. If it were for a 'rock' station in Sydney, he'd breeze it in!

In fact, the inquiry agreed that the service was declining because of deteriorating technical capacity, and reported that if obsolete equipment were not rapidly replaced, Radio Australia would 'no longer be viable as an effective external broadcasting service'.[41] Waller recommended a major, six-year program of rehabilitation estimated at 1975 values to cost $69 million.[42] Unfortunately for Radio Australia, the recommendation was made in December 1975 not to the big-spending Whitlam government (which in any case had become much more circumspect about its expenditure by late 1975), but to the new Fraser government, determined to wield the financial razor with vigour. The report was not released until early 1977, when Post and Telecommunications Minister Eric Robinson, noting that the price had by then grown to $80 million, announced that the government 'felt unable to make a commitment of this order of funds at the moment given the present difficult economic situation'.[43] (The Whitlam government had turned down a proposal by the BBC to build transmitters on Christmas Island in the Indian Ocean, to be shared with Radio Australia. The proposal could have given Radio Australia a strong signal into Asia without costing the government a cent in construction costs.)

A new threat to the independence of Radio Australia emerged with a recommendation of the Green committee, appointed by the Fraser government in April 1976 to examine Australian broadcasting. This recommendation was:

Because of the necessity to co-relate Radio Australia program content and target areas with other components of Australia's overseas influence and cultural activity, it is considered essential that guidelines concerning strategy and target audience and coverage of target areas of Radio Australia be set by Foreign Affairs in conjunction with Overseas Trade;

Programs for Radio Australia should be presented by the ABC in conformity with these guidelines.[44]

Koch suggested to Clement Semmler that these points were unacceptable to the ABC. 'We have for years resisted department interference and have successfully avoided the propaganda tag,' he said; '... these guidelines could turn Radio Australia into just that—a propaganda service.'[45] Semmler agreed, and this time, Foreign Affairs was an ally. Together with the Prime Minister's Department, it opposed the recommendations, believing they would harm the independence of the service. Ultimately, the opposition of the two departments, the ABC and others prevented the adoption of Green's recommendations.

The Green report's recommendations were hardly surprising, in view of the personal opinions of the committee's chairman, Frederick Green (secretary of the Postal and Telecommunications Department), expressed later to a meeting of an inter-departmental committee to consider proposals for rehabilitating Radio Australia's transmitters. At that meeting, he showed himself to be firmly on the side of the American model of international broadcasting. He said his personal opinion was that the government, particularly through the Department of Foreign Affairs, should have the right to lay down general guidelines 'for the information of Radio Australia broadcasters' in regard to certain target areas and to the content of programs 'where political embarrassment could be caused between the Australian Government and another country by the broadcasting of certain controversial broadcasting matter'.[46] On this occasion though, Green was in a minority of one. After his departure from the meeting, the committee unanimously decided to reject the Green inquiry recommendation on guidelines, and to convey this view to Green. The meeting recommended that the only guidance given to the ABC should be 'that presently available'. It endorsed the ABC view that Radio Australia's programs should be 'independent of direct control by any outside group'. The government later endorsed this stand, saying it did not accept the recommendations of the Green report as they related to the control over broadcasting by Radio Australia.[47]

Despite its reluctance to spend enough money to keep Radio Australia competitive with other international broadcasters, the Fraser government pledged to maintain the service, and to maintain its independence. In December 1976, the Minister for Foreign Affairs, Andrew Peacock, said:

I simply say with the support of the Prime Minister ... that if any officials want to put a recommendation to us that Radio Australia be abolished, then that recommendation will fall on deaf ears ... It will remain independent and will not come under the control of the Department of Foreign Affairs.[48]

Cabinet endorsed the continuing need for an independent Australian external service, committed funds for the limited rehabilitation of the Shepparton station and the complete restoration of a station in northern Australia (Darwin), and agreed that 'the present liaison and co-ordination arrangements between Radio Australia and the Department of Foreign Affairs continue'.[49]

Despite the spirit of *détente* in relations with the broadcasters, there were still a few desultory attempts by the department to influence Radio Australia's news and current affairs coverage. In May 1977, the department's liaison officer, Peter McCready, asked Koch to have Radio Australia play down the story of the arrival of twenty-five Vietnamese boat people in Western Australia. McCready said the department did not want to encourage Vietnamese to think that they might gain easy entry into Australia, thereby encouraging them to flee Vietnam. But Radio Australia continued to cover the arrival of the boat people in its news programs,[50] and the department became increasingly concerned about the effect of its reports. In mid-1978, the department's assistant secretary, information branch, David Evans, remarked:

It seems pretty clear that the Vietnamese refugee problem is going to get a lot worse before it gets better. It seems to me that the handling of reporting on the issue internationally by Radio Australia is probably one area where we ought to guide Radio Australia in the right directions.[51]

McCready's reply was cautious.[52] He said Radio Australia's reports on Indo-Chinese refugees were confined to information on their arrival, and statements by various people on the problem. Official statements by ministers and government officials far outweighed the statements of others, for example heads of refugee organisations or members of the Opposition. On balance, McCready said, he thought the reporting was largely unbiased, unless, he added with a touch of irony, the greater attention given to official statements could be construed as bias.

In early 1978, Radio Australia prepared to resist any attempt to make it an instrument of anti-apartheid propaganda in response to a resolution by the United Nations General Assembly. Australia's delegation had voted for the resolution, which asked member states whose broadcasts could be heard in South Africa to cooperate in a regular program based on the United Nations campaign against apartheid and in support of the right of self-determination. Increasingly confident of the independence of the service, Radio Australia's board of management decided that any suggestion that the ABC should undertake such broadcasts would not be agreed to.[53] But no such suggestion had come from Foreign Affairs. David Evans said the department would not try to encourage Radio Australia to carry out the resolution.[54] A less permissive department could have made this an issue, but in the prevailing atmosphere of detente with Radio Australia, the proposal was quietly buried.

Alliance with Foreign Affairs

In fact the department, now one of Radio Australia's strongest allies, again gave practical support to the service when its minister expressed concern at the lack of any announcement that the station at Cox Peninsula, west of Darwin, was to be restored. Describing Radio Australia as 'an important part of the accurate and timely projection of Australia overseas', Peacock told the new Minister for Post and Telecommunications, Anthony Staley, 'Numerous foreign broadcasting organisations, some with interests inimical to ours, direct services into the Asian and Pacific area and I think we may be losing audiences through poor reception and that it could take us some time to re-establish and hold sizeable audiences in important countries.'[55] Peacock's fears were justified: Cox Peninsula had some powerful opponents, and the location of the Darwin station had to be considered by a joint parliamentary committee before its restoration was certain. Peacock wrote in almost identical terms to John Howard as acting Minister for Finance, affirming his 'substantial interest in an effective external broadcasting service and in the restoration of such a service to full strength as soon as possible.'[56] Affirming the importance of the service as an instrument of foreign policy, he told Howard:

Radio Australia is an important means of disseminating accurate and prompt information about Australian policies and Australian interests to overseas audiences and attitudes towards international issues. It is, accordingly, an important instrument in the furtherance of Australia's foreign policy.

The committee on Australia's relations with the Third World, chaired by Professor Owen Harries, which reported to the government in April 1979, expressed support for Radio Australia's independence. The report concluded: 'It is particularly important that Radio Australia's services should be as free as possible of all political bias and should be seen to reflect neither official Australian Government policies nor the view of atypical minority groups.'[57]

Strong support for Radio Australia's role also came from Allan Griffith, a special adviser to the Prime Minister. After conferring with the author, as acting director of the service, in April 1979, Griffith dictated a note to Fraser putting a strong case for the inclusion of an amount in the next federal budget to enable work to begin on the reconstruction of the Cox Peninsula station. He linked the reconstruction with the growing demand for Radio Australia's service in China, pointing out that a signal from Darwin to China, particularly the politically significant northern part of the country, would be less subject than the Carnarvon signals to interference from Radio Moscow, Radio Pyongyang, NHK (Japan) and the Voice of America.[58]

The remarkable mail response from listeners in China in 1979 was one of the causes of new respect for Radio Australia in government circles, including the Department of Foreign Affairs. For many years the Chinese programs were known to have a large audience among the 'overseas Chinese', as shown, for example, by the total of nearly 43,000 Chinese-language letters in 1972–73, almost all of them from Southeast Asia. At the time, the audience in China itself was hard to estimate. A confidential paper by the Department of Foreign Affairs in 1974 had guessed that 'Although it is doubtful if the audience is very large it would certainly be greater than that indicated by the five letters received last year from China.'[59] Subsequent events made it obvious that this was a gross understatement. In 1978, Radio Australia received twenty-five letters from the People's Republic (twenty-two in Chinese, two in English and one in Japanese). The following year, the total was well over 100,000.

Because of the overwhelming response, it was decided to pulp tens of thousands of unopened letters from China in early 1980, and to discourage mail. The federal Labor spokesman on post and telecommunications, Senator Susan Ryan, described the decision to halt the mail service as 'disgraceful'.[60] She said it seemed that ABC management had shown 'a dreadful failure of imagination' in allowing the service just to die out. ABC sources told the *Age* that the ABC radio management in Sydney had agreed orally to cover the costs of maintaining the service but had later refused to provide funds. One ABC source described the pulping of thousands of letters established on goodwill as 'a bloody disgrace'.

Some of the most liberal statements ever made by the department were included in its submission to the Committee of Review of the Australian Broadcasting Commission (the Dix committee) in April 1980. The submission came down firmly on the side of the BBC model of international broadcasting, though making it clear that this did not give Radio Australia complete independence, or freedom from the department's guidance or liaison.

The submission stated the two extreme positions in the organisation of external broadcasting institutions as:

(i)   Handling external broadcasting through a fully Government-controlled instrumentality, such as the Australian Information Service. The Voice of America is such a body. The advantages of this approach are that it ensures that the Government's purposes in its international relations are directly served and that embarrassing material or material which could damage the broadcasting country's relations with other countries is not disseminated. The principal disadvantage is that the material broadcast under such arrangements inevitably sounds like Government propaganda, to use a strong term, and it is taken by most listeners to be such, with the risk of an adverse effect on the credibility of the broadcasts.

(ii) Allowing the external broadcasting organ to operate completely independently of the Government without providing any guidance or liaison arrangements ... This approach avoids the credibility problems suffered by completely Government-controlled external broadcasting bodies but its disadvantage is that the national interest may not be served in any way by the activities of such a station.[61]

The department believed that the appropriate arrangements for Radio Australia lay somewhere between the two extremes of 'complete control or complete licence'. After arguing that, because of its monopoly position, Radio Australia had a special responsibility to provide internal balance in its programming and not to follow its own unfettered editorial policy, the submission added a sentence which would have been anathema to some of the department's cold warriors of an earlier era: 'Nor, we believe, is it acceptable in a democracy such as ours that the only viewpoint broadcast by Radio Australia be that of the federal government of the day.' The submission suggested the adoption of guidelines, including:

Radio Australia should respect the target priorities decided on by the Government; In its news and commentary programs Radio Australia should aim to achieve accuracy and balance ... it is desirable that Radio Australia should not adopt persistent attitudes damaging to Australia's foreign policy interests ...

Then followed a paragraph, drafted by the department's assistant secretary, public affairs, C. R. (Kim) Jones, which has since been quoted by some Radio Australia journalists as a virtual charter of independence for the organisation, but which was actually a recognition of reality:

The Department recognises that, despite the existence of such guidelines, there will be, as long as Radio Australia broadcasts are not directly controlled by the Government, occasions where items broadcast will irritate governments with which Australia had good relations or in other ways will inconvenience the conduct of Australian foreign policy. These occasions should be minimised by the requirements for balance and by the maintenance of effective liaison between Radio Australia and this Department. However, such occasions will occur and we believe that this possibility has to be accepted as part of the price paid for the greater credibility and influence achieved through operation outside the direct control of the Government.

The department's tolerance of 'such occasions' was to be tested in the ensuing months.

The Dix report, *The ABC in Review*, supported Radio Australia's independence. The report came down firmly in favour of continuing to operate the service on the BBC model:

Radio Australia, like most broadcasting organisations directing their output at audiences the greater part of which have no relationship with the broadcasters' funding, serves purposes of policy. In many cases of overseas broadcasting such purposes of policy mean government or party propaganda. Australia's overseas radio service, like that of the BBC on which it has been modelled, is built on a much wider concept of policy. This concept assumes that the broadcaster which is seen to be independent of the particular views and concerns of sectional groups or the government itself will be the most credible and effective.[62]

But the report proceeded to qualify what could have appeared to be a prescription for complete freedom:

this independence cannot mean, however, that the overseas broadcasting body can operate with indifference to Australian objectives and purposes in the international environment.

Its accountability is to the Australian public which funds it, not to a diffuse international one. These characteristics and the nature of its audience set Radio Australia apart from the domestic services of the national broadcasting organisation.

The Dix committee concluded 'that Radio Australia's editorial policy should not be "fettered" but that Radio Australia should take into account the purposes it is being financed to undertake in the development of its editorial policy on all matters.' But this apparent hint that its editorial policy should favour the government line was qualified by the statement that government policies should be 'among a wide range of factors influencing Radio Australia's editorial policies.'[63]

The Dix committee agreed with a long-standing proposal by the Department of Foreign Affairs which, while ostensibly motivated by the desire for administrative efficiency, was in fact to increase the department's influence over Radio Australia and to some extent lay the ghost of Walter Hamilton.[64] This proposal was that the editor of Radio Australia should be responsible for news content to the controller of Radio Australia rather than the ABC's controller of news.

The Dix committee's recommendations led to the Australian Broadcasting Corporation Act of 1983, which, according to the 1989 *Radio Australia Review*, 'clearly established' the editorial independence of Radio Australia and of its operation.[65] Noting that the formal relationship between Radio Australia and the Department of Foreign Affairs and Trade now involved two meetings per year, the review said such consultation could only be based on 'an absolute recognition of Radio Australia's editorial and operational independence'. The department stressed the need for Radio Australia's independence in its submission to the review, which endorsed the operation of the service according to the BBC model.

Although embarrassed by the Indonesian government's constant criticism of Radio Australia, and its expulsion in 1980 of the ABC's correspondent in Jakarta (chapter 9), the department defended the coverage by the service of events in New Caledonia, even though this drew periodic criticisms from the French authorities. Praising the accuracy of Radio Australia's Pacific news stories in early 1981, the deputy head of the South Pacific section, William Fisher, remarked that Foreign Affairs had seen nothing to justify any of this criticism.[66] The French, he said, were concerned about such items simply because they were accurate, and hence embarrassing to the colonial authorities.

But Indonesia was another matter. Allegations by the Indonesian government that Radio Australia was engaged in a campaign against Indonesia led to renewed political pressure for the department to have the right to censor sensitive news stories. The issue was raised by the Minister for Communications, Ian Sinclair, in January 1981 in a letter to the ABC about procedures for assessing news and current affairs stories about foreign countries intended for broadcast by Radio Australia.[67] The commission replied that any requirement that Radio Australia refer news copy to the Department of Foreign Affairs for clearance before broadcast would destroy the programming independence of the overseas service, and of the ABC.

Two months later (on 24 March 1981), Sinclair made a similar approach to the Minister for Foreign Affairs, Tony Street, in a letter which was leaked to the *Age*. The paper reported that Indonesian officials were particularly concerned that Radio Australia's Indonesian-language service carried reports about political events in Indonesia which the country's own news media were banned from reporting.[68] The same day, the Melbourne *Herald* quoted the former ambassador to Indonesia, Thomas Critchley, as saying Radio Australia reports were sometimes incorrect, and that Indonesians believed there was a deliberate campaign against their country in the Australian media.[69] The Opposition spokesman on communications, Senator John Button, responded to the leaked letter by telling Parliament that the Labor Party would oppose control of Radio Australia's broadcasts by the Department of Foreign Affairs, adding that Radio Australia would 'lose all credibility' if this happened.[70] Street replied that there was no question of Radio Australia's being censored by government officials.[71] Referring to the *Age* report, Street told the parliament there was liaison between his department and Radio Australia, but this was only to keep the service 'informed of developments'.

Foreign Affairs was not the only government department concerned during this period with Radio Australia's news coverage. The head of the Department of Immigration and Ethnic Affairs, John Menadue, telephoned the author, as editor of Radio Australia, late in 1981 to discuss fears that some foreign broadcasters were giving information about the shipping lanes in which boat people from Vietnam had been picked up. He said such information would help future boat people to set their courses, and perhaps encourage them to leave Vietnam.[72] The author replied that Radio Australia did not go into this sort of detail in stories about the boat people. But he told Menadue that the service had covered his department's announcement that Australia expected to accept 36,000 Indo-Chinese refugees over the next three years, and suggested that, if the department did not want announcements of this kind broadcast, they should not be made. Menadue said that in future his department would be careful about what was said publicly about plans for the acceptance of refugees. When Menadue asked whether Radio Australia broadcast anything which would be likely to encourage Vietnamese to come to Australia, the author said the very fact that Australia was accurately projected as an increasingly multi-racial society with a general attitude of goodwill towards its Asian neighbours, and with a high level of economic prosperity and social harmony, would inevitably make the thought of flight to Australia attractive to Vietnamese who would contrast this picture with the poverty, factional hostility and political repression of their own country. He stressed, however, that the picture of Australia was presented 'warts and all', and that a recent program about resentment towards Vietnamese settlers in the Sydney municipality of Fairfield might have given some potential immigrants pause for thought.

One Radio Australia initiative that had the strong support of the department was launched by the author in 1983. The proposal was to introduce a current affairs program about Pacific events and issues which would use voice reports from Pacific Island journalists. Radio Australia news bulletins had for years been the major source of international news, including news about the Pacific, in Pacific Island countries. By early 1983, the broadcasting organisations of ten of these countries were relaying one or more Radio Australia news bulletins, recording them for later rebroadcast, or transcribing them for partial incorporation into their own bulletins. An eleventh country, American Samoa, was added to the list later in the year, when it began relaying Radio Australia news bulletins in place of news from the Voice of America.[73]

Plans for the proposed current affairs program were developed in consultation with the first secretary, information, in the Australian high commission to Fiji, Warwick Cooper, who was enthusiastic about its potential. Cooper consulted his immediate superior, the Australian high commissioner to Fiji, Colin McDonald, and high commissioners and consuls-general in other parts of the South Pacific. Their reaction was unanimously positive. Cooper later quoted them as saying the proposal would be 'one of the most significant aspects of Australia's current thrust into the region'.[74] They believed that the broadcasting of a program tailored specifically for the Pacific audiences would bring a dramatic rise in the number of Pacific Islanders tuning directly to Radio Australia. Furthermore, they said they would expect many broadcasting organisations in the region to 'pirate' the best items from the program and rebroadcast them on medium wave. This would do Radio Australia no harm, as listeners to the local stations would soon find that they could hear the items before their friends and neighbours by listening to Radio Australia on shortwave. Cooper summarised the reaction of Australian diplomats throughout the South Pacific as 'Everyone will benefit, but Australia most of all.' For some reason, however, Radio Australia's director, Peter Barnett, vetoed the proposal and it came to nothing.

The Hawke Labor government which came to power on 5 March 1983 legislated the following June to transform the Australian Broadcasting Commission into the Australian Broadcasting Corporation.[75] This began the process by which most of the recommendations of the Dix committee for the ABC were implemented, including most of those on Radio Australia. It was the end of an era for Australia's international shortwave broadcasting service.

Independence affirmed

The latest in a long series of reviews of Radio Australia, the Revill review in 1989, went farther than any of its predecessors in asserting Radio Australia's independence from Foreign Affairs. There was no Foreign Affairs representative on the committee, which consisted of three ABC executives, assistant managing director Stuart Revill (convenor), managing director David Hill and director of radio Malcolm Long, with Dr Rodney Tiffen, senior lecturer (now associate professor) in the University of Sydney's Department of Government, as consultant. The review's report, *Radio Australia Review*, stated that, 'Certainly since the ABC Act of 1983 the editorial independence of Radio Australia and of its operations have been clearly established.'[76] The report went on to say that the formal relationship between Radio Australia and the department now involved two meetings a year, at which both parties freely exchanged views. It noted that 'such consultation, and the regular use by Radio Australia staff of the department as a source of information, could only be based on an absolute recognition of Radio Australia's editorial and operational independence'. In fact, by 1992, even these meetings had been abandoned, at least temporarily. The acting first assistant secretary of the department's public affairs division, John Campbell, said in mid-1993 that liaison with Radio Australia had 'fallen into a hole in the past 18 months'.[77] But when it was pointed out in July 1993 to the general manager of Radio Australia, Derek White, that no liaison meetings had been held since his appointment in 1992, he replied that there would be such a meeting in Melbourne later that month, at which the department would brief Radio Australia on Indo-China, and Radio Australia would brief the department on its service to Indo-China.

White said in mid-1993 that Foreign Affairs did not make suggestions about programming, merely getting Radio Australia's copy after broadcast. Another senior executive said that the department's input was down to occasional questions about the content of programs.

Nor was the editorial independence asserted by the Revill review in 1989 opposed by the department. Its submission to the review stated fairly unequivocally (though with an apparent reservation in the second sentence of the passage quoted below):

We believe that Australia's national interest is served most effectively by Radio Australia's status as an independent broadcaster, which delivers a product with balance and objectivity. In this context, we see it as essential that Radio Australia not be seen *merely* as a Government mouthpiece [emphasis added]. To be perceived as a propaganda organ for the Australian Government would very quickly devalue its impact among Radio Australia's considerable audience.

That is not to say that the Department believes that Radio Australia need engage in tendentious coverage of regional countries' internal affairs in order to demonstrate its independence, nor to suggest that they have done so.

However, on occasions, items which have been broadcast on Radio Australia dealing with volatile political issues have caused difficulties with neighbouring countries. In these circumstances, Radio Australia's independence needs to be accompanied by the highest standards of editorial control and professionalism to reduce the risk of misunderstanding.[78]

But the submission went on:

On the other hand, we see it as fundamental to Radio Australia's reputation that the Government be able to assert to the governments of neighbouring countries that Radio Australia is beyond the editorial or programming control of the Australian Government. In the end Radio Australia's independence, along with a record for accuracy, has been the source of its authority and, we judge, a major reason for its large audience. National interest, apart from liberal principles, suggest that we should not interfere with that.[79]

The department's submission stated that 'no other instrument of Australian society' reached more people in Australia's neighbouring region than Radio Australia, adding, 'The Department of Foreign Affairs and Trade sees Radio Australia as an important continuing asset for Australia, and one which needs continuing encouragement and support.'[80]

Radio Australia's independence from government control was endorsed by Foreign Minister Gareth Evans in a book he co-authored in 1991. He wrote:

Radio Australia plays a particularly important role in informing the region about Australia. For many it is probably their only link with Australia. Here, as elsewhere in public diplomacy, credibility is crucial to success, and Radio Australia's independence from government control is the touchstone of its credibility. Were Radio Australia to be seen as a tool of the Australian government, its credibility in Asia and beyond would be diminished. Even though its broadcasts sometimes create difficulties for official bilateral relations,

Australia's overall and long-term interests are better served by a Radio Australia which is valued for its independence, and for the window which it opens on to Australian society, than by a broadcaster of government propaganda.[81]

Richard Broinowski said in late 1991 that he talked with his Indonesian staff quite frequently about the stories they covered and did not cover, and 'I am satisfied that they do give a fair run to stories antipathetic or antagonistic—or perceivably so—to the regime ...'.[82] Asked what sort of stories he thought Radio Australia's news and current affairs programs should conceal, he replied, 'I can't think of any. If we are talking about foreign policy stories or international stories, RA has a duty to report stories that are accurate and newsworthy. There are only two criteria as far as I am concerned.' Asked about stories that could prejudice relations with other countries, he replied:

As far as I am concerned, if it's news, if it's accurate, we don't conceal it, we broadcast it ... even though it might prejudice our relations with another country. Look, we have got a foreign service that I know quite well and regard as being very professional. It's their job to maintain diplomatic relations with other countries—it's our job to provide the news.

When it was suggested to him that on occasions Foreign Affairs had been very embarrassed by Radio Australia's reporting, he replied, 'Sure—No, no—certain diplomats have been embarrassed, certain ministers have been embarrassed, certain ambassadors have been embarrassed.'

During the past decade, Radio Australia has probably been closer to the idealised BBC model of international broadcasting than the BBC external services themselves. Even in the first three decades after its takeover by the ABC in 1950, it was able to retain its relative independence and operate according to that model. Many factors played a part in bringing this about. Without the dogged resistance of Boyer, Hamilton and Darling, the Department of External Affairs would probably have gained control of the service during the Cold War, so that it would have reverted to the American model. If the takeover move by Paul Hasluck in the mid-1960s had succeeded it would certainly have had that result.

Having survived the Cold War with its independence relatively intact, Radio Australia was able to continue to operate according to the BBC model, in its idealised form, partly because of the increasing liberalism of the department. As this chapter has shown, periodic attempts to increase the department's influence over its news and current affairs programs during this period of *détente* were resisted with considerable success by journalists who, like Hamilton before them, believed that Radio Australia's usefulness to the national interest depended on its credibility, and that this, in turn, depended on its perceived independence from government control. More often than not, those journalists had the support of an increasingly liberal department.

Although Radio Australia has won the long struggle for freedom from attempts by Foreign Affairs officers to distort its editorial processes (with the help, it must be said, of the more liberal-minded of those officers), it will maintain that freedom only if it keeps up its guard. The danger of interference by the politicians who hold the power of the purse is perhaps a greater potential future threat than the danger of interference by officers of their departments.

Gulf threat

An astonishing example of the danger of interference by a politician was the thinly veiled threat in 1991 by Defence Minister Robert Ray that the ABC's budget could be cut if Radio Australia did not broadcast personal messages to Australian servicemen and women serving in the Gulf War. Ray was not alone in attacking Radio Australia. Opposition and government senators joined in the criticism, and the Senate passed a motion condemning the ABC.

When Iraq invaded Kuwait in August 1990, a number of Western civilians, including some Australians, were taken hostage. Little more than a week after their capture, word reached Australia that morale among the hostages was poor. Radio Australia decided to send to the Middle East a two-hour program of messages and entertainment specifically for them. Australian naval personnel serving in Middle Eastern waters also heard the program, and a few messages were sent to them as well. The program was additional to Radio Australia's regular 24-hour English-language program. The Department of Transport and Communications provided additional money to pay the overtime needed to keep the transmissions going.

As well as sending personal messages, Radio Australia drew on entertainers and public figures to do guest spots. Some of them sent camouflaged messages: for example Victorian football legend Ron Barassi reminisced about coaching teams out of tough spots.

After about six weeks, the pressure on the hostages was lessening, and the women and children were released. The Australian consul in Kuwait said transistor batteries were in short supply, and the Department of Foreign Affairs and Trade was becoming concerned about the cost of the service. After the male hostages were released about 14 December, there were only a few messages from the families of naval personnel, and the service was cut to an hour and a half a day. Then, on 21 December, it was dropped altogether. Special transmissions to the Middle East continued, but these carried the regular English-language programs.

At this stage, Ray intervened. He had heard the message service while visiting the naval personnel on one of the vessels, and expressed interest. His office approached the ABC in Sydney about the decision to drop the service. Meanwhile, the political temperature was rising. David Hill, saying Canberra was putting pressure on him, asked the acting general manager of Radio Australia, Geoff Heriot, for briefing notes giving the strongest possible arguments against running a message service. The briefing notes also pointed out that there were reasons why such a service could be justified. The overall judgment was that the message service was not justified at the time, but program options needed to be kept open if war broke out. The notes were leaked to a reporter for the *Age*, whose story fuelled press speculation about hidden reasons for dropping the service.

Hill told the ABC current affairs program 'AM' that 'the view that RA took was, a message service for Australian military personnel serving overseas had never been a function of RA. It had fought hard for its credibility internationally by being independent of the military and independent of the government. It did not want to see itself as an American services radio or a Radio Moscow.'[83] He said later that 'the risk of upsetting Middle Eastern listeners' had also been a consideration.[84]

A member of Ray's staff attacked Radio Australia, saying the overseas service could be in breach of its charter if it failed to provide a special service for Australian service personnel in the region. Hill responded with a letter to Ray in which he said,

We do not believe it is appropriate to establish such a service solely for Australian naval personnel ... To do so would involve a significant change in current Radio Australia practice ... The recognition of Radio Australia's editorial and operational independence has characterised the relationship between governments and Radio Australia for many years.[85]

The *Age* said it was believed that senior ABC staff were concerned that any move to provide a special service to members of the Australian navy could undermine the broadcaster's independence from the government's foreign policy decisions.[86]

Heriot, who had been acting head of Radio Australia at the time of the announcement that the message service was being dropped, said later that there were concerns about the overall tone and balance.

If you had a special two-hour service hinged on news and current affairs purporting to be dispassionate and impartial and uncommitted, and after close to an hour of this you then had half an hour of messages to our boys in the field, there's a real tonal issue there ... Once Robert Ray came out heavying us, there was a principle there too.[87]

Heriot said that because of the conviction that it was not Ray's role to tell Radio Australia what to do, whatever ground there may have been for movement became less once he started going public. Heriot had said in the briefing notes, sent to Hill on 23 December:

Editorial independence—real and perceived—is a delicate matter. It is one thing to identify with civilians caught suddenly in crisis. It may be another to respond to pressure seeking Radio Australia's overt support for a government political/military endeavour.[88]

General manager Broinowski agreed. He said later that the message service 'could be seen to be uncomfortably close to being a kind of government propaganda service. We could be seen to be propagandising Australia's political commitment to the Gulf war.'[89]

Ray's veiled threat followed in the Senate on 9 January 1991. He said one of the reasons advanced for the cessation of the message service was that ABC management and the Australian Journalists' Association were concerned that Radio Australia would become a propaganda arm of the government. He continued, 'It is not true to say that families sending messages to their loved ones in the Gulf can in any way be construed as militaristic or propagandising.' He warned that, although he did not often make threats, he could not see why, 'if Radio Australia cannot serve its country in this way, it should continue to deserve its current level of funding'.[90]

The ABC's intransigence ended with the Senate resolution condemning its stance. Hill and Ray worked out a compromise. From 28 January, an hour of music and messages packaged by the navy was transmitted each night outside the normal Radio Australia schedule. The navy sent the messages to Radio Australia, which, in the words of Broinowski, 'simply became a production house for the navy'.[91] Heriot said later, 'It was broadcast by RA but was not RA, which was a fiction of course.'[92] There was a brief pause between the regular program and the special program for the naval personnel, which Heriot said later would not have fooled anyone.

The ABC was also attacked by Prime Minister Bob Hawke over its coverage of the Gulf War. He accused it of using 'so-called experts' who were 'loaded, biased and disgraceful',[93] largely because of the use of an opponent of Australian participation, Dr Robert Springborg, as an analyst. But Broinowski said later that this criticism had not been directed at the overseas service. Radio Australia, he said, had not used Springborg to the extent that the ABC home service had done, particularly on television. In fact, Radio Australia bowed to an extent to the prime ministerial criticism, and used Springborg even more sparingly after it.

Although Radio Australia had won its war of independence from Foreign Affairs by the early 1970s, its experience during the Gulf War showed that there remained the potential for political pressure on the overseas service.

8   Uneasy Indonesian honeymoon, 1945–1974

Of the critics of Radio Australia who believe it has done more harm than good, many refer to the occasions when its broadcasts to Indonesia about Indonesian issues and events have aroused the hostility of the authorities, and even strained relations between the two governments. Radio Australia has broadcast to Indonesia at various times in five languages: English, Dutch, Indonesian, Standard Chinese (Mandarin) and Cantonese. The language with by far the largest audience, hence the language in which the broadcasts have been most sensitive politically, has been *bahasa Indonesia*,[1] the lingua franca from 1928 of the diverse ethnic and cultural groups which made up Indonesia's independence movement, and, from the declaration of independence on 17 August 1945, the national language of Indonesia.

The Indonesian-language programs have had huge audiences, numbered in the millions. There have been several reasons for this. Because of the distances to be covered in a country stretching over a huge archipelago, a great deal of domestic broadcasting by *Radio Republik Indonesia* has been in shortwave. Most of the radios owned by Indonesians have shortwave bands, so that turning to Radio Australia is just a matter of twiddling a dial. Radio Australia has been popular because of the quality of its programs, including lively music, and the popularity of its presenters, some of them nationally known personalities who have been mobbed at the airport when they have visited their home country. And an important factor in the popularity of Radio Australia's programs has been its news and current affairs coverage, through which its listeners have been able to hear about events and issues that are censored or glossed over in the local media.

Recent audience surveys show that Radio Australia's English-language program also has a substantial audience in Indonesia, many of whom have learned some English from the popular English-teaching programs on the Indonesian transmission.

The attitudes of the Indonesian authorities to Radio Australia have differed at different times, and have not always been hostile. As mentioned in chapter 4 (page 89), at different stages two commanders-in-chief of the Indonesian armed forces, General Nasution and General (later President) Soeharto, instructed their senior officers to listen to Radio Australia's news broadcasts.

The next three chapters show how Indonesian official attitudes to Radio Australia have varied at different times. They also show how, for most of the half-century that Radio Australia has been broadcasting in Indonesian, the Indonesian programs have been the greatest source of contention between Foreign Affairs and Radio Australia.

Radio Australia's wartime broadcasts in Dutch, which began in 1940, and in 'Malay' (Indonesian), which began in 1942, presented a colonialist point of view. These broadcasts were not even controlled directly by the Department of Information or (from July 1942 to March 1944) by the ABC or the Department of External Affairs. The direct control of the programs was largely, by default, in the hands of the officers of the Netherlands Indies Government Information Service (NIGIS) who staffed it—by default because neither Macmahon Ball nor any of his staff understood Dutch or Indonesian. Translations into English were provided to Ball, so that he did have *post facto* control, although even this was contested by the head of the NIGIS, Lieutenant Commander Huibert Quispel. Nevertheless, the NIGIS operated under Australian censorship and, from mid-1942, under basic directives approved by the Allied Political Warfare Committee.[2] So trusted were Australia's colonial Dutch allies that late in 1944 the shortwave division requested, and was given, security clearance for live broadcasts in Dutch.[3] Clearance for live broadcasts in Indonesian followed six months later.[4]

Not all the programs broadcast in Dutch and Indonesian originated with NIGIS. Many were prepared in English, and merely translated and broadcast by the NIGIS officers. But broadly the message was the same, reflecting the basic agreement between the governments of Australia and the Netherlands East Indies: the Dutch were the rightful rulers of the East Indies, and would resume control of their colony when the Japanese usurpers were defeated.

This common policy can be seen clearly in a script written in English, translated into Dutch, and broadcast in both languages on 7 March 1942,

the day after the invading Japanese forced the closure of the official shortwave station in the Netherlands Indies. It said, in part:

We have long regarded the Netherlands Indies as a great bastion defending the North of
Australia. The Dutch are our close neighbours, and already the Japanese are using Dutch
territory for air attacks upon North Australia ... Nothing in the British tradition and nothing in the exploits of our own Anzacs is more glorious than the way the Dutch of the Indies
have met their enemies in these last days. Everyone in Australia feels the deepest reverence
for the example which the Dutch have set all free peoples ... During these last weeks we in
Australia have come to identify ourselves very closely with the Dutch, and now we feel that
the restoration of the Indies is as much a part of our national task as the protection of
Australia. The freedom of the Indies [sic] and the freedom of Australia are inseparable ...
For to the Dutch of the Indies these islands were not colonial territories to be developed—
they were their homes, part of the very fabric of their lives ... We in Australia feel proud to
have such a people for our neighbours.[5]

A script prepared and broadcast in Dutch a few days later for the Dutch of
the occupied Indies, though somewhat more effusive, expresses the same
message:

Have courage and do not despair! The forces now being concentrated in Australia, and the
war material being assembled here, are increasing day by day before our eyes ... When all
is ready, in a few weeks, days perhaps, the great blow will be struck, which is to assure for
you and for us an existence worthy of civilised nations in the future ... All Netherlanders
in Australia, as well as in the old Motherland, are thinking of you day and night ... The
Netherlands and the Netherlands Indies will rise again![6]

A senior NIGIS official pronounced: 'These examples of propaganda are
excellent indeed. They have just the right tone of grave sympathy. The
promise to contribute to the restoration of the NEI [Netherlands East
Indies] is given in the right tone: quiet determination.' He suggested, however, that the forecast that 'the great blow' would be struck 'in a few weeks,
days perhaps', was 'too optimistic and therefore creating disappointment'.[7]

The transfer of control to the ABC on 1 July 1942, had no practical
effect on the government's use of the shortwave service as an instrument of
propaganda, according to the American model. On the contrary, with the
Japanese threat at its peak, the formation of the Australian Political Warfare
Committee in Canberra gave the Department of External Affairs ultimate
control of the service (although Ball continued to press, with some success,
for moderation, accuracy and credibility). The committee issued weekly
'propaganda lines' to Ball telling him what to stress, what to play down and
what to avoid in his broadcasts.

Prompted by a report from Quispel stressing the simplicity of the indigenous people, Ball also became concerned that the Indonesian-language

broadcasts should be easily understood by them and 'directly tie up with their hopes and fears'.[8] He told Quispel:

I feel that the news bulletins we have been handing on for translation presuppose a much wider knowledge of world geography and the existence of sophisticated mental processes which do not, in fact, exist among these people. ... should we not plan, in a deliberate long-term way, a greatly increasing emphasis on all the discomforts Japanese rule brings to the Indonesians?

The Dutch broadcasters overestimated not only the simplicity of the Indonesians, but also their loyalty to their former colonial masters. (Robert Horne remembered that in January 1943, the Indonesian news often began with the progress of Princess Juliana's confinement. Horne said the Australian broadcasters would ask the Dutch if this news was really so important, in the middle of a war. The reply was that the Indonesians would be very interested: they were 'terribly loyal to the Dutch'.)[9]

In late 1942, the Netherlands East Indies authorities in Australia prepared a set of directives for broadcasting to the territory for the guidance of American broadcasters. Needless to say, these guidelines reflected the same policies which had been apparent in the Australian broadcasts. Among the stated aims of such broadcasts were:

To convince the inhabitants of the Netherlands Indies that the United Nations will inevitably win the war.

To convince them and especially the Indonesians, that they would have nothing to hope from a Japanese victory except slavery; to stimulate discontent and hatred of the Japanese.

To convince them that the Netherlands Indies as the natural mediators between the Orient and the Western world will have an important place in the new world order, and that their future will be the brighter the more they contribute to their deliverance from the Japanese.

To prepare them, in the first stage of the war for passive resistance, and in its last stage for popular revolt [only against the Japanese, of course!], promising them the necessary assistance and support.[10]

Among the propaganda themes listed in the directive were:

Stress that the GEA [Greater East Asia] sphere of co-prosperity means ruthless squeezing of all the countries concerned for the benefit of Japan. Bring out facts proving that 'Asia for the Asiatics' means 'Asia for the Japanese', but *do not mention the slogan* 'Asia for the Asiatics'. Always speak of 'Asia for the Japanese' ...

Express complete confidence in the special ability of all parts of the population—the Dutch, born as a nation from a struggle for tolerance; the wise and tolerant Chinese; the Indonesians with their gift for creating harmony and their understanding and respect for others, and their mode of life and thought—to establish a model Commonwealth, invaluable to the new world.

In 1943, the Netherlands Indies government began using the Dutch transmissions to send code messages to its agents (with Indonesian code-names). These messages were included as items in the news bulletins on the 5th, 10th, 15th, 20th, 25th and 30th of each month.[11]

In a policy speech in August 1943, the Minister for External Affairs, Dr Evatt, showed no evidence of an awareness of the nationalist movements in the colonies to Australia's north in his references to post-war security arrangements. (Two years later, he was to become a supporter— albeit an equivocal one—of the Indonesian struggle for independence.) He said, in part:

The arc of islands north of us from which Japan has launched so many attacks must be secured against further aggression. Arrangements will be made with such Powers as Holland, Portugal and France, as well as with Britain and the United States, in order to establish a great South-west Pacific zone of security against aggression … Once relieved of Japanese domination, the many millions of people in these areas will look to Australia just as we shall look to those areas for new markets for our own Australian products.[12]

The secretary of the political warfare division of the Department of External Affairs, Henry Stokes, suggested to Ball that these references, in conjunction with previous statements by Evatt, might well be used in political warfare to the area, the speech itself as a news item and its policy background in the composition of news commentaries. He added that, in references to Australia's interest in the political and economic welfare of the area, and of responsibility towards it, great care should be taken to avoid giving any colour to charges of economic imperialism.

Ball, apparently far more aware of Asian nationalism than Evatt, was cautious. He prepared for the North American transmissions a draft script based on Evatt's remarks, but submitted it for approval to John Hood, a senior officer of the Department of External Affairs.[13] Hood did not veto the script, but, perhaps mindful of American opposition to colonialism, said it was not in itself a particularly suitable subject for a North American transmission. On the other hand, he said it would be 'eminently suitable' for transmission to the enemy-occupied territories.[14] Ball replied that he would have no regret at all in not using the item. He had suggested it for the North American transmission because he felt it was not suitable for the enemy-occupied territories. Demonstrating the extent of External Affairs control over the shortwave service, even during this period when it was nominally run by the ABC, Ball said: 'If you really want us to use it for the EOT we shall of course cheerfully do so …' But he went on to spell out his reasons for considering it unsuitable for these listeners:

1. Japan has made explicit and comprensive [*sic*] promises of 'independence' to Thailand, Burma, the Philippines, with various degrees of independence to other occupied territories. If we are to compete with them in this kind of promise, then these statements fall very far short of what they have said. They are very milk-and-waterish. 2. It struck me that the specific reference to Holland, Portugal and France, 'as well as with Britain and the United States', expressed very clearly that European angle on Asiatic affairs which we particularly want to avoid. If Portugal is to share these heavy responsibilities why not Thailand, and above all, why not China? The scheme as expressed ... in the letter of August 6 looks very much like a return to the status quo. 3. I feel that the last sentence in the statement by Dr. Evatt ... rather suggests too nationalistic an Australian attitude. Will the many millions of people in East Asia really look so eagerly towards Australia?[15]

Ball's perceptive insight prevailed. The shortwave service never told the outside world of Evatt's rather limited vision of post-war Asia.

The return of the shortwave service to the Department of Information on 1 April 1944, and the associated resignation of Macmahon Ball, made little difference to its operations. It continued to be a direct instrument of government policy, along the lines of the American model of international broadcasting. Hardly surprisingly in a country fighting total war, the ultimate authority in matters of programming remained the Political Warfare Committee of the Department of External Affairs. There was a gradual shift, however, in the message to Indonesia, as some Australians, including the acting controller, Geoffrey Sawer, became more aware of the strength of the independence movement and the need to counter Japan's desperate promises of independence.

The Department of Information's control over the shortwave service was certainly less than absolute. On 11 May 1945, the department suggested, as guidance, that the word 'Indonesian' should not be used. But, a few days later, Sawer told the political warfare committee that he was not at present observing this. He said both the Dutch and Indonesian advisers in the shortwave division considered that 'a sudden dropping of the expression would be unfortunate'.[16] A week later, he reported that, on further advice from the Department of External Affairs, and pending further consideration, the service was continuing to use the expression 'Indonesian' as previously.[17]

War of independence

The delicate issue of Australia's policy in Indonesia's war of independence was to lead to the sudden sacking of Sawer by the Prime Minister, J. B. (Ben) Chifley—an action which left no doubt that the shortwave service was operating under direct (though not tight) government control. The government itself was divided on the issue of Indonesian independence: on the one hand, it was anti-colonialist but, on the other, it espoused the white Australia policy, and some ministers saw continued Dutch rule in the Indies as conducive to the preservation of a white Australia. Evatt, who, according to Edwards, 'aspired to mediate between the two sides and simultaneously to woo Dutch support in his campaigns for the presidency of the General Assembly',[18] was at loggerheads with Calwell, Minister for Information, who wanted the reinstatement of some form of Dutch colonial rule. Although Edwards says Chifley was 'fairly consistently anti-Dutch', it seems from Sawer's account that the Prime Minister was trying to keep the peace between the different factions in his cabinet. External Affairs had given Sawer some guidance about the problems, but none at all on what to say.[19]

Sawer said that, late in 1945, Evatt had telephoned him to say that the shortwave service ought to be criticising the Americans. He had said the government knew that the Americans were supplying the Dutch with weapons after having the American markings removed from them. The minister had said the government did not want to offend MacArthur, but Australia should be saying that it was up to the great powers to come to an agreement over Indonesia, and obviously the agreement should provide for the rapid development of Indonesian self-government. Sawer and another writer, Michael Keon, prepared five programs, which Sawer said had been 'particularly cautious'. None mentioned the covert supply of American arms to the Dutch, although they did suggest that the Americans should reconsider the extent to which they were helping the Dutch forces. The first three had already been broadcast when two Melbourne newspapers found out about them, and reacted with outrage.

The three scripts had apparently fallen into the hands of the colonial Dutch, who shared the same building as the Australian broadcasters. Alarmed by their tone, they 'leaked' them to the Melbourne *Argus* and *Sun*. On 16 November, the *Argus* led its front page with a story under the two-decker banner headline:

**PM REPUDIATES
BROADCASTS
ON INDONESIA**

**D of I Scripts Made Offensive
References to Great Powers**

The story read, in part:

MR CHIFLEY LAST NIGHT REPUDIATED THREE BROADCASTS ON THE INDONE-SIAN CRISIS MADE BY THE DEPARTMENT OF INFORMATION SHORTWAVE BROAD-CASTING DIVISION IN MELBOURNE BETWEEN NOVEMBER 5 AND NOVEMBER 8 ...

Their gravity lies in the fact that, emanating from a government station, and therefore, purporting to give the Government's view on incidents of the utmost international delicacy, these scripts accused 'all the great powers' of hypocrisy, and specially named Britain and USA ...

Nominally the policy of the Department of Information short-wave broadcasting station is supervised by the Department of External Affairs, though the Department of Information conducts the station.[20]

The partial text of the offending broadcasts on page 3 of the *Argus* quoted Sawer as saying:

Australia cannot be blind to the fact that 40 million Indonesians in our near north may well, in the long run, be more important to our security, not to mention our trade and commerce, than a few thousand Dutch who have hitherto controlled that area, and whose control is now being disputed. Moreover, a Labour Government in Australia is necessarily influenced by the conception of emancipation and advance to self-government of subject peoples.

The *Sun* ran a long story on page 6 under the headings:

Not Government Policy, Says Mr Chifley

**STIR OVER BROADCASTS
ON INDONESIA**

The story said that, although the government had refrained from defining publicly its policy towards the 'Indonesian disturbance', the broadcasts implied that the government view was pro-Indonesian. It said that, because the shortwave talks had been under the sponsorship of the Department of External Affairs and the Department of Information, many people overseas had assumed that they reflected official government policy. The *Sun* quoted Sawer as saying that the United States had tried, like Pontius Pilate, to wash its hands of the matter, but was in practice underwriting the policy being pursued by Lord Louis Mountbatten.[21]

The *Sun* also devoted its main editorial to the subject, under the heading 'Insulting Our Friends'. More vehemently pro-Dutch than the *Argus*, it said:

Mr Chifley's statement that the views expressed do not represent the Government's policy renders the situation even more fantastic. The service which sent these views overseas is conducted by the Department of Information in collaboration with the Department of External Affairs and so is accepted as expressing the Government's considered opinions. A Mr Keon and a Mr Sawer are designated as having prepared the commentaries. Who these gentlemen are we have not the remotest idea. But even in the absence of the globe-trotting

Dr Evatt, pronouncements on foreign policy presumably are not made by minor officials without ministerial approval. Who, then, was the Minister who sanctioned this latest contribution to the Government's policy of 'neutrality' toward the Indonesian affair?[22]

Chifley summoned Sawer to Canberra. On his arrival, the broadcaster found himself facing not only the Prime Minister, but also Evatt and Calwell. Sawer told Chifley that he had understood from Evatt that there was an Australian view about Indonesia, and that the shortwave service should convey it. As Sawer recollected the meeting, the Prime Minister, characteristically sucking at his pipe, replied that he could see Sawer was trying to construct policy where in fact policy did not exist. He said he understood Sawer was on leave of absence from the University of Melbourne, and asked him when he would like to go back there. When Sawer suggested 31 December, Chifley, who Sawer said was 'quite charming' throughout the interview, replied that this would suit him.[23] He told Sawer to carry on in the meantime, but not to say anything more about Indonesia or the Dutch. Throughout the brief interview, Evatt, who publicly was straddling the fence, remained silent: Sawer said Evatt had made no attempt to speak in his defence, and had certainly given no indication that it was he who had originally proposed the offending broadcasts. Six weeks later, Sawer went back to full-time teaching at the Melbourne University law school. There is no question where Calwell stood. His wholehearted commitment to the white Australia policy was well known, and he undoubtedly saw the Dutch East Indies as a bastion of European power between Australia and the Asian hordes. In his autobiography, Calwell was quite frank about his racial attitudes:

All nations—black, brown, yellow and white—are racist, simply because the world consists of different races and nations. All races suffer from a deep feeling of xenophobia and all are determined to preserve the homogeneity of their own people. They all reject the brotherhood of man concept. Some people call me a racist because I am proud of the blood that flows through my veins. I am proud of my white skin, just as a Chinese is proud of his yellow skin, a Japanese his brown skin [sic], and the Indians of their various hues from black to coffee-coloured. Anybody who is not proud of his race is not a man at all.[24]

A few months later, the NIGIS was disbanded, and direct control of broadcasts to Indonesia in Indonesian and Dutch passed to the shortwave division of the Department of Information. The Australian government's support for Indonesian independence (albeit lukewarm), together with the more militant attitude of some shipping and transport unions (including the communist-led waterside workers, who refused to load arms for the Dutch forces), left a legacy of goodwill towards Australia which, according to a later director of Radio Australia, still remained in 1975.[25] Evidence of the reality of this goodwill was the Indonesian republic's choice of Australia as its representative on the good offices committee of the United Nations, and later the United Nations commission for Indonesia.[26] Australian support of Indonesia continued (initially) under the Menzies government, when Indonesia was admitted to the United Nations as a result of sponsorship by India and Australia.[27] Radio Australia itself played a role in peace negotiations between the Dutch and the Indonesians. The Dutch embassy in Canberra gave Radio Australia the wording of the Dutch peace proposal, which it broadcast to Indonesia. The Indonesian response was conveyed through the Australian embassy in Jakarta. (When Indonesia became independent in 1949, an overenthusiastic Indonesian announcer on Radio Australia shouted into the microphone '*Merdeka*! [Freedom!]'. He was sacked.)[28]

The Department of External Affairs was slow to realise that the transfer of Radio Australia to the ABC in 1950 had brought a significant change in the control of the overseas shortwave broadcasts, with a diminution in its own power. Broadcasts to Indonesia became a source of continuing concern to a department determined to maintain tight control of such programs. An early and continuing problem was coverage of the dispute over West New Guinea, which the Dutch refused to relinquish to the new nation despite the fact that it had undeniably been part of the Netherlands East Indies.[29]

By 1957, the department's concern about Radio Australia's coverage of the continuing dispute over West New Guinea (which one of its officers was still suggesting at the end of 1958 should be referred to in broadcasts as 'Netherlands New Guinea')[30] led to an official complaint by Casey to the Postmaster-General, Charles Davidson. He told Davidson that a Radio Australia report of a statement by the Indonesian delegate to the United Nations, Ali Sastroamidjojo, had been 'unnecessarily loaded in favour of the Indonesian case'.[31] The Indonesian delegate had made a statement expressing 'deep regret' over the announcement by Australia and the Netherlands of a joint policy on developing the peoples of New Guinea towards self-government. He accused Australia of trying to undermine the forthcoming United Nations debate on West New Guinea and of supporting a colonial policy there. Showing little understanding of the difference between news and propaganda, Casey said: 'A positive Australian lead at least rather than an Indonesian lead might have been expected.' In a long letter of explanation to Davidson during the absence of Boyer on a sea trip, the ABC's vice-chairman, Edgar Dawes, said Sastroamidjojo's statement represented a responsible Indonesian reaction, which the ABC felt should have been used. He pointed out that the item was part of continuing references to the subject, and that the announcement of the joint Australia–Netherlands policy had been fully covered two days earlier. Dawes was apparently determined to hold the line established by his absent chairman.[32]

In January 1958, Casey fired another shot in his department's campaign to prevent Radio Australia from maintaining an independent stance in its reporting of Indonesia. In a secret telex to the secretary of his department, Arthur Tange, he said the subject of the rebellion (by separatists based in Padang, in West Sumatra) in Indonesia was:

ONE ON WHICH THE POLITICAL INTERESTS OF THE AUSTRALIAN GOVERNMENT ARE SO STRONG THAT WE CANNOT ACCEPT THE RISK THAT AN AUSTRALIAN INFORMATION SERVICE WHOLLY SUPPORTED BY THE GOVERNMENT SHOULD SET UP ANY INFLUENCES CONTRARY TO THE ACHIEVEMENT OF GOVERNMENT POLICY.

INSIDE OUR OWN DEPARTMENT WE SHOULD ENSURE THAT GUIDANCE AND, IF NECESSARY, SUPERVISION COMES FROM A SENIOR LEVEL. I STRESS THAT WE ARE NOT REQUIRED TO MEET THE INDONESIAN VIEWS OF WHAT IS DESIRABLE BUT WE ARE REQUIRED TO ENSURE THAT AUSTRALIAN FOREIGN POLICY INTEREST PREVAILS IN THIS DELICATE SITUATION.[33]

A fortnight later, as acting general manager of the ABC, 'Huck' Finlay struck a blow for Radio Australia's policy of accuracy and impartiality. He wrote to Tange: 'I have no doubt you will be interested to hear something of the reaction to Radio Australia's reporting of recent events in Indonesia.'[34] He went on to state that the ABC's (stringer) correspondent in Jakarta, Mrs Christine Cole, together with its Singapore office, under the direction of Colin Mason, had 'combined to give us factual and balanced reports of the Indonesian crisis'. He said the Jakarta area commander had given Cole a 'laissez passer', permitting her to report and take film anywhere in the capital and its neighbourhood, in direct consequence of the ABC's reputation for impartiality in its reporting. One tangible result was that Cole had had 'a remarkable number' of letters asking for the Radio Australia program guide. Finlay's obsequious expressions of gratitude to Tange and his department were a sugar coating on his assertion that Radio Australia's policy of independence had proved successful:

We cannot help but regard this as a most gratifying reward for the work and thought put into our Radio Australia broadcasts, in which of course we have been fortunate to have the support of you and your officers, which we have valued greatly. There could hardly be a better token of appreciation of our policy, and I rather feel too that despite the turmoil and confusion of recent events in Indonesia, Australia's standing may be even higher than ever.

If we have helped your department's efforts in any way in achieving this gratifying result, you may be sure the opportunity to be associated in such a worthwhile work is highly rewarding to us.

A few weeks later, Mason reported to Moses on a visit to Indonesia. He said Laurence McIntyre, the Australian ambassador, had told him it was the Australian government's view that all possible measures should be taken to keep the Padang rebel movement alive, and the government felt that Radio Australia was an important instrument in achieving this, because of its very large audience throughout Indonesia.[35] Mason had replied to McIntyre that it was his function, until he received instructions otherwise from Moses, to present the facts from both sides as accurately as his sources of information permitted. He added that when he had first arrived in Jakarta he had faced a wall of official obstruction. Mason (who was later to become an Australian Democrat senator for New South Wales) went on to say he had no doubt whatsoever that communism was very bitterly hated and opposed by the majority of influential Indonesians, especially the army officers, who had very wide powers under the current state of war. Proposing that Radio Australia take a deliberately anti-communist stance in its reporting of Indonesia, Mason said:

The truth, *and the angle which it would serve us best to follow* [emphasis added], is that Communism is a foreign ideology attempting to make capital by creating disturbed conditions in Indonesia. That while most Indonesians are not Communists, there is a strong and growing Communist influence, which has been directly responsible for the anti-Dutch, anti-Seato and anti-Australian demonstrations recently. The Communist influence is an alien one, is financed by direct contribution from the Bank of China, and has everything to lose and nothing to gain by the success of Padang. It is, in fact, direct foreign intervention in Indonesia's internal affairs.[36]

He recommended to Moses that the ABC should try to maintain a reasonable balance of material coming from the central government and from Padang radio, and that it should continue to point out the degree to which China was intervening through its control over the Indonesian Communist Party.

The ABC's editor-in-chief, Walter Hamilton, told Moses that, although Radio Australia had taken no 'line' in dealing with the Indonesian revolt, but had pursued its policy of objectivity and balance, it was impossible to ignore the extent of the communist influence in the affairs of the central government.[37] But he said that, although the intervention of China was doubtless a most important factor, it was not the proper function of news bulletins to 'point this out', as Mason had suggested. 'Inference and commentary of our own,' he said, 'does not belong in the news.'

McIntyre's assessment of Australia's interest in the rebellion in Indonesia was confirmed by Charles Kevin in the department's Canberra headquarters. The ABC's controller of programs quoted Kevin as saying that

the Padang attempt—presuming it was successful—would be of most benefit to our way of thinking, it was highly unlikely that the central government would not come out on top; and seeing that we have to live with the Indonesians, it was only tactful to keep a balanced view and at least be fair to both sides ... which, as I understand it, is precisely what the News Department has been endeavouring to do.[38]

Moses reported to the commission a few weeks later that both news bulletins and commentaries in foreign languages were to be checked periodically on the point of accuracy of translation. These checks (by Australian security officers) were to be made at irregular intervals, care being taken that the dates were not known to the members of staff concerned.[39]

The ABC's annual report of 1957–58 appeared to turn back the clock in the patronising remark it made about Radio Australia's broadcasts to Indonesia (with an oblique reference to the rebellion). It said:

The Commission believes that in the long term, our neighbourly relations with the Indonesian people will be greatly strengthened by the degree to which the historic riches of British political and cultural life can become available to this large new Republic, for whose problems and difficulties we in Australia should have special interest and sympathy.[40]

Radio Australia again incurred the wrath of Indonesian government officials in early 1962, over its reports of an attempt to assassinate President Soekarno during a visit to Macassar. Some officials alleged that Radio Australia had got the news from a secret Dutch radio transmitter, and complained that it had speculated that the Darul Islam movement was involved, instead of accepting the Indonesian government's statement that 'Dutch henchmen' were to blame. The acting spokesman for the Foreign Office was Ali Alatas (a future foreign minister—who Tange said a few months later had struck him in some ways as 'rather a silly chap')[41]; he told ABC correspondent Colin Hann that he considered Australia to be pro-Dutch, and Indonesia was concerned that Radio Australia would carry 'the wrong type of propaganda'.[42] Hann was the first of many ABC correspondents to be threatened (though obliquely) with expulsion. He reported that officials at the army information centre, 'in their usual happy, joking way', had said: 'You won't disregard our request, will you? We wouldn't like to expel our dear old friend from Australia.'[43] Relations between Indonesia and Radio Australia were exacerbated a few months later when an attempt was made to assassinate Soekarno in Jakarta, and a Radio Australia news bulletin carried a report by United Press International that the president had been killed. Repeated retractions were subsequently broadcast, together with an apology, and on this occasion there were no reprisals against Radio Australia, though the correspondent for United Press International was expelled.[44]

West Irian

It was understandable that Australia, whose government tended to side with the Dutch in the dispute over West Irian, would be widely regarded in Indonesia as 'pro-Dutch'. It was perhaps understandable that some of this bias would creep into Radio Australia's programs. In 1962 its Indonesian staff wrote to the ABC's acting director of programs, Arthur Wyndham, asking that Dutch reports be balanced by Indonesian reports. When Tange asked Moses about the claim of the Indonesian staff that there was a pro-Dutch bias in Radio Australia's news about West New Guinea, 'Sir Charles did not appear to know about this development, and offered no substantial comment.'[45] Tange said that it sounded like political blackmail, and expressed the hope that the ABC would take a firm line with its Indonesian staff. In the margin of the department's report of their meeting, Tange scribbled: 'Employ Malayans ... '.

At least one member of Radio Australia's Indonesian staff took unilateral steps to try to redress the balance. Complaints began flowing in from Dutch sources. One allegation was that, after playing the song 'Stranger on the Shore', an announcer (one of Radio Australia's most popular, Ebet Kadarusman)[46] had said, 'They must mean by that the Dutch in West Irian, because they have no business there.'[47] Another was that Kadarusman had wished 'Good fighting!' to Indonesian volunteers in West Irian. He was also accused of referring to 'all listeners in Indonesia from Sabang [Sumatra] to Merauke [the southeasternmost township in West New Guinea]'. Yet another allegation was that an announcer had referred to the Indonesian volunteers as 'freedom fighters'. One of these criticisms appears to have been an inference drawn from the phrase 'selamat berjuang! [good fighting!]', which Kadarusman did not deny using. A Dutch newspaper translated his closing announcement on 4 July 1962 as 'This is Evereth [sic] Kadarusman of the Melbourne studio wishing you a good morning and a good fight until the next time from Radio Australia.'

There is little doubt that the phrase was a reference to Indonesia's struggle in West Irian. A somewhat naive report by the ABC's assistant general manager, administration, Talbot Duckmanton, on the allegations against Ebet Kadarusman concluded that *selamat berjuang* was a greeting widely used in Indonesia, which could be translated not only as 'good fighting', but also as 'good hunting', 'good endeavour', 'good wishes for a successful end to the struggle' or 'keep up a good effort'. Presumably he had been told this by the staff of the Indonesian section, and had believed it: the greeting had been common during the struggle for independence, but the most widely used Indonesian–English dictionary of the period records 'fight' and 'struggle' as the only meanings of the root word, *juang*.[48] Kadarusman also did not deny that he might have referred to listeners in Indonesia from Sabang to Merauke, but he claimed, not very convincingly, that he meant listeners to the Indonesian *program* from Sabang to Merauke. (The phrase, 'Sabang to Merauke' had been widely used by Indonesian nationalists from colonial times to refer to the territory they regarded as theirs.) As for the song 'Stranger on the Shore', it had been broadcast on 27 June in a program of listener requests. Kadarusman denied that he had used the words complained of, and the officer monitoring the program had not heard them. In the absence of a tape recording, the allegation could not be proved true or false.

Moses sent Duckmanton's report (without criticism) to the Postmaster-General, Davidson, saying it showed there was no justification for the sweeping criticisms which had been made. The general manager pointed out that it was the first complaint received from Dutch authorities in more than twelve years, whereas, on the other hand, there had been a number of complaints ('equally unjustified') from Indonesian sources claiming that Radio Australia had been broadcasting anti-Indonesian propaganda.[49] Davidson later put an added gloss on the dismissal of the Dutch complaints when he said 'top level investigations which he had instituted had satisfied him that there was no substance in the charges'. Going a step farther than Duckmanton, who had simply found the 'Stranger on the Shore' charge 'not proven', Davidson said he was satisfied that the announcer had not used the words complained of. The minister said all translations of scripts, commentaries and news bulletins were pre-recorded before transmission (omitting to mention that this precaution had been taken *after* the Dutch complaints).[50]

Other government instrumentalities were increasingly involved in the monitoring of Radio Australia's Indonesian broadcasts. For many years, officers of the Joint Intelligence Bureau[51] had been 'spot' monitoring the foreign-language broadcasts, including the Indonesian ones, but Moses later concluded that these checks had been made 'at no better than six monthly intervals'.[52] When the issue of West New Guinea had come prominently into the news, the ABC had asked the bureau to increase the frequency of its monitoring. In June 1962, the bureau's regional director in Melbourne had been told that the ABC wanted Radio Australia's Indonesian broadcasts monitored continually. But the Joint Intelligence Bureau was dilatory, and the increasingly impatient ABC had finally turned to the Department of External Affairs, which had arranged for the regular monitoring of the Indonesian transmission by intelligence officers at the RAAF's language training school at Point Cook, Victoria.[53]

A few days later, the ABC decided to pre-record programs in Indonesian, Thai and Chinese, and check the recorded programs against original scripts. The ABC's acting chairman, Edgar Dawes, told Davidson that the Thai and Chinese programs were being pre-recorded as well because the introduction of direct monitoring of the Indonesian program was 'a delicate operation'.[54] Another reason for monitoring the Chinese program was that it appeared from some on-air monitoring that the nationalist Chinese employed as broadcasters were using 'abusive phrases' which it was thought were 'inappropriate for Radio Australia broadcasts'.[55]

In mid-1962, Tange compiled a secret report entitled 'Indonesian Attitude to Radio Australia'. He said there was not much doubt that for many years Indonesian officials had been less than happy with Radio Australia's influence in their country, and probably also with Australian efforts to increase it. They had shown unmistakable signs of sensitivity to the news services and commentaries during the Permesta rebellion (in Sumatra) and since the dispute over West New Guinea this sensitivity had become acute. The most recent official complaint had been directed at a broadcast referring to an 'alleged' attempt to assassinate Soekarno in Jakarta. Tange pointed out that by the time of the broadcast—ten days after the attempt—the ABC news service should have been fully conversant with the fact that the attempt had been genuine.[56] Tange's conclusions about Indonesian concern over Radio Australia's influence were borne out in a report by its editor, John Hall, on a visit to Indonesia with its director, Peter Homfray, and the ABC's Southeast Asian representative, Lachlan Shaw, in mid-1962. Hall said two leading Indonesian officials had told him privately that they and others agreed that Radio Australia probably had more impact on public opinion than all the other communication media in the country.[57] Hall said the main criticism of the news at that stage was, in essence, 'that we give the Dutch as well as the Indonesian side of the West New Guinea dispute'.

During this period, Indonesia's Foreign Minister, Dr Subandrio, was keeping a close check on Radio Australia's news bulletins in Indonesian. Peter Barnett, who had replaced Hann as the ABC's correspondent in

Jakarta, reported that Subandrio had a transcript of the morning and evening bulletins on his desk every morning, and that during the Cuban missile crisis Soekarno had taken a bundle of the copies away with him, saying he wanted to study them closely.[58]

In mid-1963, Gordon Jockel (a senior officer of the department, later to become Australian ambassador to Indonesia) tried to persuade Radio Australia to slant its coverage of riots in Indonesia. He had three requests:

(1) Do not give undue importance to the Indonesian riots. Mention them, but not as a major item.
(2) Report any Indonesian Government statements expressing concern at riots.
(3) Do not play up dissatisfaction with Indonesian Government, or any suggestions of political instability.[59]

When Hall asked why Jockel wanted the story handled in this fashion, he was told: 'We do not want to be accused of hindering the Indonesian Government. We do not want to offend them in this way.' Hall explained to Jockel that the story of the riots was in the realm of straight news and as such would have to be reported without suppression. He said Radio Australia would not use the riot stories as a means of campaigning to whip up dissatisfaction against the government. It did not campaign on any issues. It kept to the facts, treating all stories on news value. Jockel stepped back a pace, and told Hall that this approach 'would do'. Hall placed a written report of the approach in a new file which he labelled: 'attempts at slanting news'.

Hall opened another new file, labelled 'censorship attempts', in which he noted a number of occasions over two weeks on which the department tried to have parts of news stories deleted to avoid offending Indonesian sensibilities. When Menzies announced an increase in defence expenditure in May 1963, the head of the department's information branch, Neil Truscott, suggested that Radio Australia delete the Prime Minister's reference to concern about Indonesia as the cause of increased defence expenditure. He also wanted Radio Australia to play up the increased expenditure on the air force and the navy, rather than on the army. The figures for the army, he said, would only serve to emphasise that Australia's army was so much smaller than Indonesia's. Hall replied that he could not and would not censor the Prime Minister, whose statement would be treated strictly on news value.[60] Menzies had in fact mentioned West Irian and made a point of saying Australia would defend its New Guinea territory as it would defend the Australian mainland. Both points were included in Radio Australia's story.[61] A few days later, External Affairs Minister Barwick, speaking in New Zealand, referred to Indonesia in regard to

Australia's defence expenditure. In a story broadcast in Indonesian as well as English, Radio Australia quoted him as saying Australians were becoming more conscious of 'having a land border with Indonesia', which he described as 'a power that had shown a disposition to expand'.[62] An officer of the department's information branch suggested that Radio Australia play down this angle, or drop it from the story. Hall retorted that if the department wanted to take a certain line, surely its minister would be informed about it.[63] The officer told him (somewhat shamefacedly, one would assume) that in fact the department *was* cabling the minister.[64] After several such rebuffs, attempts to censor the news became less frequent.

At this stage External Affairs doubts about the advisability of reporting Indonesian affairs to Indonesia in Indonesian began to surface. Such doubts were to proliferate in the 1980s after the expulsion of the ABC's correspondent from Indonesia. (They were not confined to Foreign Affairs officials: in 1987 the ABC's managing director, David Hill, went to Indonesia apparently prepared to discuss the abolition of such reports as the price of the return of an ABC correspondent to Jakarta.)[65] Jockel asked Hall during a visit to the department whether the aim of Radio Australia's Indonesian-language service included conveying to the Indonesian people a news coverage of Indonesian affairs. When Hall replied that it did, Jockel said he had some personal doubts about the 'proprietary [*sic*]' of a foreign radio station having an objective of conveying to another country its own internal news.[66] Jockel later reported that he had referred to a recent report from Barnett on the riots in Indonesia: 'I repeated that I did not question the facts but the proprietary of Radio Australia disseminating them in such terms and detail. There were elements in this report which could clearly cause offence to the Indonesian Government.' Jockel's views were certainly echoed by some Indonesians. Anthony Cane, who succeeded Barnett as ABC correspondent in Jakarta, reported that the Foreign Office in Jakarta had several times asked him: 'Why does RA broadcast so much Indonesian news back to Indonesia when Indonesian people have their own radio and papers to give it to them?'[67]

Confrontation

The next in the series of crises in relations between Australia and Indonesia was that caused by Britain's plan to consolidate its territories and former territories in Southeast Asia, Malaya, Singapore, Brunei, Sabah and Sarawak, by joining them together as an independent Malaysia. As Indonesia's 'confrontation' of Malaysia intensified, Australia's ambassador

in Jakarta, Keith Shann, became concerned about the effect on his diplomacy of Radio Australia's broadcasts. He told the department that it should
be clearly realised that Radio Australia was 'an instrument that we may
need to use which we should not damage'.[68] Shann, who had sent the wives
and children of diplomats to Singapore, was concerned at a report that, as
a result of a talk he had had with Foreign Minister Subandrio, he had said
he had advised that it was safe for them to return. In a confidential cable
to the department, he said:

THE INDONESIANS ARE ANNOYED THAT WE FELT THAT OUR DEPENDANTS WERE
UNSAFE AND TO SUGGEST THAT SUBANDRIO AND I DECIDED THAT IT WAS NOW
PRUDENT THAT THEY SHOULD RETURN IS NONSENSE, DESTROYS A USEFUL PART
OF THE EFFECT OF THE EXERCISE, AND WILL *NOT* ENHANCE THEIR SECURITY
WHEN THIS INSTRUMENT OF POLICY IS USED AGAIN, AS IT WILL BE ...
    THE INDONESIAN GOVERNMENT IS FAIRLY SENSITIVE TO RADIO AUSTRALIA,
AND IT COULD GET AROUND TO JAMMING IT. IT, AS WELL AS 1947-48, GIVES US A
VERY SPECIAL POSITION HERE, AND IT IS SOMETHING WHICH WE SHOULD
EXERCISE GREAT CARE OVER.

The department replied: 'we have in recent months been in much closer
contact with Radio Australia in an effort to ensure treatment of news
stories which would support Government policy'.[69]

The ABC began to consider what it might do if relations with
Indonesia deteriorated to the point where it was necessary to replace Radio
Australia's Indonesian staff. Truscott reported in mid-1964 that replacement possibilities included: Malaysian students, 'particularly those with
some knowledge of Bahassa [*sic*]', Point Cook graduates '(not very satisfactory because of the high military content of the vocabulary taught
there)'; loan officers from Radio Malaysia; and Dutch-Indonesian immigrants.[70] Homfray later revealed that, through his 'spooky friends' in the
Australian Secret Intelligence Service,[71] he had arranged in 1963 for 'Kuala
Lumpur' to supply Malay broadcasters to carry on Radio Australia's
Indonesian broadcasts if it had been necessary to replace the Indonesian
staff.[72] As it happened, such desperate measures were never necessary.

In the meantime, the conflict in West New Guinea (by now known in
Australia as West Irian) was continuing, despite its eventual transfer to
Indonesian sovereignty through the New York Agreement of 1962. Several
years later, as secretary of the Department of External Affairs, Sir Keith
Waller looked back on the confrontation era as a time when Radio
Australia had been particularly useful. He told Duckmanton:

Radio Australia news broadcasts formed an invaluable service, particularly to the
Indonesians, in providing accurate, impartial news of what was actually occurring. In many

cases Radio Australia enabled the Indonesians themselves to obtain a real picture of what was happening in their own country. This was of great importance to us in our efforts to maintain contact with the then Indonesian regime and more particularly with the Indonesian people.[73]

But at least the crisis over Radio Australia's coverage of confrontation was about to end. The abortive coup of the early morning of 1 October 1965 and its sequel, the downfall of Soekarno, at first transformed official Indonesian attitudes to Australia's international broadcaster. The delicate manoeuvres between Soeharto and Soekarno, however, led to new tensions between Radio Australia and the Department of External Affairs, which for the most part had been allies in adversity at the height of confrontation. Shann was happy about Radio Australia's reporting of the coup and its immediate aftermath. A few days after the murder of six generals, he described the coverage as 'completely admirable'.[74] The ABC was also happy. In a cabled tribute to Radio Australia's staff from Jakarta, ABC correspondent Philip Koch said, 'Radio Australia's coverage has won us enormous prestige. Impact of proven accuracy of our coverage in outer islands is incalculable.'[75] Walter Hamilton remarked that what Koch had not said was that this result was due largely to 'his own magnificent efforts'. His coverage, Hamilton said, had been outstanding for its balance and thoughtfulness.

Although Shann himself was happy with Radio Australia's coverage, the department immediately began trying to slant it. Its public information officer, Richard Woolcott, stressed that the attempted coup, the army counter-coup and the strife between the PKI (Indonesian Communist Party) and the army, were all internal domestic matters. Although they were of concern and interest to Australia, he said, Radio Australia must avoid giving the impression that Australia was in any way involved. He also urged Radio Australia not to jump to any premature conclusions that Soekarno was implicated, that he was finished as a political force, that he had fully restored his authority or that a nationwide civil war was imminent.[76] Woolcott said Radio Australia should, by careful selection of its news items, not do anything which would be helpful to the PKI. It should highlight reports tending to discredit the PKI and show its involvement in the losing cause of the 30th September movement.[77] A week later, Shann (through Woolcott) made six requests. One was that Radio Australia not refer to Soeharto as anti-communist because this could be harmful to his efforts in Jakarta. It was better to call him non-communist. Hall agreed to this. Another request was that Radio Australia use factual stories pointing up the involvement of the PKI in the coup, and the strength of feeling opposed to communist China. Hall told Woolcott there was no need for such advice: all facts of the situation would be broadcast. Shann also asked that Radio Australia avoid implication (at this stage) of Soekarno in the plot, although it was thought he was implicated. Hall replied that the service would not run stories implicating—or absolving—Soekarno unless they were official and properly sourced. Another suggestion was that it would be 'helpful' to run stories that Subandrio's name (implicating him along with the communists in the plot) was appearing on slogans in Jakarta. Hall said one such reference had already been made, run briefly without interpretation.

A few weeks later, a senior officer of the department, David Hay, said that, although the Radio Australia service had been satisfactory, there were still incidents in which greater accuracy would have conveyed the news more effectively to the Indonesian audience. He told Hamilton that,

given the special delicacy of what we say in respect of Indonesia at present, particularly about Indonesian matters, and given the rapidly changing picture, we would hope that the ABC would agree to Radio Australia checking over with us in advance, so that factual accuracy could, as far as possible, be guaranteed, in the items on Indonesia in the Indonesian news service.[78]

After clearing his response with Duckmanton (now general manager), Hamilton rejected this request, saying it was impracticable, and acceptance would be improper both from the ABC's and the department's point of view.

The following month, Hall received a document from the department listing 'points for discussion' with Radio Australia. It stated, *inter alia*:

We consider it is desirable to avoid giving indirect assistance to Subandrio in trying to maintain his influence. Perhaps emphasis in selection of news items could be given to those voicing criticism of Subandrio ...
    Desirable to avoid presenting the Indonesian Army as defying Sukarno. At the same time we do not wish unnecessarily to enhance his position. Sukarno's statements supporting the PKI and China should be played down as far as possible.[79]

Beside this last comment, Hall, asserting the supremacy of news values in positioning stories, wrote: 'Sukarno's statements, particularly of substance, cannot be ignored. Natural to lead an Indonesian bulletin.'

More moves to muzzle

The situation in West Irian again led to attempts by the department to muzzle Radio Australia when fighting by rebels intensified as the date for the 'act of free choice' approached in 1969. The full story of the fighting might never have been told had it not been for a news-gathering trip by Hidayat Djajamihardja, the ABC's Indonesian journalist based in Jakarta. His first report, broadcast after his return to Jakarta, said an air strike had been made against rebellious tribesmen in the town of Enarotali. The following day, Radio Australia quoted the Indonesian Information Minister as saying that an aircraft carrying the provincial military commander of West Irian had been fired on as it made a low pass over the Enarotali airstrip.[80] The Australian embassy in Jakarta reported that a good deal of the story was accurate, but not necessarily everything. Jockel, now ambassador to Indonesia, was concerned about Radio Australia's independence of the Department of External Affairs. He said his political officers told him that the Radio Australia office thought of itself very much as a news-gathering body on the same basis as the other external news agencies in Jakarta, and shared the same attitude to stories and scoops as those agencies. The office had had no contact with the embassy before filing these stories and conducting its interviews.[81]

Jockel said there were at least two specific causes for concern in this. One was that the Indonesian authorities would not want it widely known in the territory that various outbreaks were occurring, as this would encourage further outbreaks. The other was that the publicity would encourage the armed forces and local authorities to take more suppressive measures. The minister, Gordon Freeth, was told that, without making firm recommendations, Jockel questioned the role of the Radio Australia office in Jakarta as a news-gathering source. But an official of the department, who apparently appreciated the implications of Radio Australia's move away from the American model of international broadcasting, said it would be neither wise nor profitable to ask Radio Australia to discourage its Jakarta correspondent and his staff from carrying out what he considered to be a legitimate news-gathering role. Under the present arrangements, he said, the department guided and advised the news editor, but was not empowered to direct him by vetoing news content.[82]

Freeth agreed with this advice, which was conveyed back to Jockel. The department told him it needed to bear in mind the danger that an approach to Radio Australia or the ABC might leak and give rise to more publicity through allegations that the government was trying to whitewash the Indonesians and to repress unpalatable facts. The department's message continued:

WE HAVE ALREADY OBSERVED TO THE ABC THAT IT IS UNFORTUNATE AND UNHELPFUL THAT SO MUCH PROMINENCE IS BEING GIVEN TO THEIR BEING THE SOURCE OF THE ORIGINAL STORY ...

YOU WILL NO DOUBT CONSIDER WHAT OPPORTUNITY MAY BE OPEN TO YOU IN
JAKARTA TO TALK DISCREETLY AND PRIVATELY TO RADIO AUSTRALIA/ABC
CORRESPONDENT THERE ABOUT THE IMPLICATIONS FOR AUSTRALIAN/
INDONESIAN RELATIONS OF REPORTS HE SENDS AND OF THEIR HANDLING.[83]

Freeth agreed that the ABC should not be reproached for having discov-
ered unpalatable facts, but the department mentioned to the ABC that it
was unfortunate that such prominence was being given to the attribution
of the story to its correspondent.

Freeth complained to Hulme, the minister responsible for the ABC,
that 'highly coloured and inaccurate' reports such as one that 30,000
tribesmen were in revolt 'could have a bad influence in West Irian'.[84]
Earlier, the department had told Radio Australia that if the reports were
broadcast they could do a good deal of damage even if they proved
substantially accurate.[85] Advising on a further letter from Freeth to Hulme,
McIntyre said the ABC could not argue against the department's 'very
substantial say' in what Radio Australia reported.[86]

Jockel was now proposing that the department suggest to
Duckmanton that 'a mature and experienced person' was needed in Jakarta
to replace the current ABC correspondent, Michael Carlton,[87] who continued to be a thorn in Jockel's side until he was replaced in early 1970.[88]
Shortly before he returned to Australia, Carlton filed a story that led to an
official complaint to the Australian embassy by Brigadier-General Ali
Moertopo, special assistant to the president and head of operations of the
national intelligence agency. A member of Moertopo's staff visited the embassy to complain that his superior had been mentioned in a report by
Carlton on allegations of corruption made by the editor of the newspaper
Indonesia Raya, Mochtar Lubis, against prominent officials in the government. In reporting this to the department, the embassy said Moertopo was
one of the more influential men in Indonesia, and actually was not widely
accused of corruption. In fact, although Carlton's story had mentioned
Moertopo, it had not said he was an object of Lubis's allegations. The
department sent the full text of the report to Jakarta to enable the embassy
to convince Moertopo he had not been libelled. The department also told
Homfray that it regarded the report as sensational, speculative and
potentially damaging to relations with Indonesia, and the department
should have been consulted before the report was broadcast.[89]

Late in 1974 came the first rumblings of the crisis that was to bring
relations between Radio Australia and Indonesia to an all-time low, and
cause the exclusion from Indonesia of a Radio Australia officer and the
expulsion of the ABC correspondent. Several Chinese in East Timor wrote
to Radio Australia saying they feared trouble following the referendum on

independence the following April and inquiring about the possibility of emigrating to Australia. The (renamed) Department of Foreign Affairs suggested that Radio Australia tell them briefly on air that priority was given to the immigration of sponsored family members and people with special skills. Those who felt they might meet these conditions were directed to write to the Department of Labour and Immigration.[90]

9   Collision with Indonesia, 1975–1988

In 1975 Bruce Beresford's bedroom farce *Alvin Purple* on ABC television was creating a major stir. Mrs Grundy and her cohorts were outraged by, *inter alia*, the sight of Alvin's bare backside on the screen.

At the same time, an Australian planter from East Timor went to the United Nations to make a direct attack on Radio Australia, and, as a result, the UN scheduled a debate on Radio Australia's coverage of the war. The director of Radio Australia, Philip Koch, phoned from Melbourne to tell the ABC's assistant general manager, Dr Clement Semmler. Koch suggested that the commission, meeting that day in the ABC's Sydney headquarters, should be told. But the commission was discussing the controversy over Alvin. Semmler's reply was: 'Philip, they've got their heads up Alvin Purple's bum, and they don't want to know!'[1]

Koch told the author about this exchange as an illustration of how little the ABC cared about Radio Australia's coverage of the East Timor war, and, indeed, about Radio Australia. The commission was to care far more four years later when Radio Australia's reporting of Timor and other news about Indonesia led to the expulsion of the ABC's correspondent in Jakarta, Warwick Beutler. That was in 1980, and apart from the occasional brief visit, the ABC was to be frozen out of Indonesia for eleven years.

The Department of Foreign Affairs was certainly far more aware of Radio Australia's coverage of East Timor, and its possible consequences for relations between Australia and Indonesia, than the myopic commissioners, for whom Alvin's bum loomed so large. The department, which at the height of the Cold War had been determined to use the external broadcasting service as an instrument of foreign policy, had adopted a more liberal stance in the early 1970s. But Timor caused mounting tension between officers whose prime concern was the damage Radio Australia's Timor coverage was doing to relations between the two countries and those who affirmed the value of the credibility of the service. As the damage done by that coverage increased, so did doubts about whether it was wise for Radio Australia to report Indonesian affairs to Indonesia in the Indonesian language. Such doubts were to proliferate in the 1980s after the expulsion of the ABC's correspondent.

East Timor was not the only issue that raised the anger of the Indonesian authorities. This chapter examines the ways in which the reporting of events in Indonesia to Radio Australia's millions of listeners in that country created a serious rift between Jakarta and Canberra. In retrospect, it seems remarkable that Jakarta tolerated for so long an intrusion that many of its leaders regarded, not without cause, as cultural imperialism.

The outbreak of civil war in East Timor in 1975 created enormous problems for all Australian news-gathering organisations, particularly for Radio Australia. Initially, no journalists were allowed into the territory, and all communications were cut until the Fretilin (Revolutionary Front for Independent Timor) party began sending lengthy messages by radio to its supporters in Darwin, who sent them on by telex to the Radio Australia newsroom in Melbourne. The cables set out the party's position on negotiations with the Portuguese authorities and sought Australia's support. Radio Australia began using the messages as a news source, though being careful to attribute them to Fretilin. As a result, the official government spokesman in Jakarta alleged that the broadcasts were pro-Fretilin. The situation was finally alleviated when the ABC's correspondent in Jakarta was able to cover the Indonesian and UDT (Timor Democratic Union) side of the struggle from the border between East and West Timor.

The Australian government took the attitude that some form of incorporation into Indonesia would be in the best interests of Australia. Journalists obtained a number of documents, some through Freedom of Information legislation, including the department's briefing for the Minister for Foreign Affairs before an ANZUS Pact ministerial meeting in April 1975, which said, in part: 'The best result from our point of view, would still be some form of association with Indonesia, but this is still unlikely to command popular support in Timor or to be easy for the Indonesians to contrive.'[2]

The Timor Gap, with a seabed potentially rich in oil, was a factor in Australia's policy. Richard Woolcott, Australia's ambassador in Jakarta during the period immediately before and after Indonesia's invasion of the territory, was notable for his emphasis on appeasing Indonesia. In August 1975, he wrote:

IT WOULD SEEM TO ME THAT THIS DEPARTMENT MIGHT WELL HAVE AN INTEREST IN CLOSING THE PRESENT GAP IN THE AGREED SEA BORDER AND THIS COULD BE MUCH MORE READILY NEGOTIATED WITH INDONESIA BY CLOSING THE PRESENT GAP THAN WITH PORTUGAL OR INDEPENDENT PORTUGUESE TIMOR. I KNOW I AM RECOMMENDING A PRAGMATIC RATHER THAN A PRINCIPLED STAND BUT THAT IS WHAT NATIONAL INTEREST AND FOREIGN POL- ICY IS ALL ABOUT ... [3]

(The Australian and Indonesian Foreign Affairs Ministers signed the Timor Gap Zone of Cooperation Treaty in an aircraft above the Timor Sea in December 1989, and it came into force in February 1991.)[4]

A week later, Woolcott was advising the department:

WE SHOULD KEEP IN MIND THAT THERE IS NO INHERENT REASON WHY INTEGRATION WITH INDONESIA WOULD IN THE LONG RUN BE ANY LESS IN THE INTERESTS OF THE TIMORESE INHABITANTS THAN A HIGHLY UNSTABLE INDEPENDENCE OR CONTINUING FACTIONAL FIGHTING.[5]

Although pressure by the Department of Foreign Affairs on Radio Australia increased as the crisis deepened, it never reached the intensity of the middle and late 1960s, when Australia's involvement in the Vietnam War had been at its height and Paul Hasluck had been Minister for External Affairs. The moderation of the Whitlam years was apparent in the response to a letter from the department's assistant secretary, information, Charles Mott, to Woolcott, as civil war raged in East Timor in September 1975.[6] Mott's call on Radio Australia to take account of reports from Jakarta about East Timor was queried by Whitlam, as acting Minister for Foreign Affairs. Whitlam's private secretary, Alan Oxley, said it would be 'at least fair to describe it as an intervention about Radio Australia's reporting'.

Oxley said one of the more common criticisms of the government's policy towards East Timor was that it had paid too much heed to Indonesian interests. The risk in intervening in Radio Australia as a result of Indonesian complaints was that, were the intervention to become public, this line of criticism of the government's policies would be given more credibility. He went on to say:

Of course, at any time, intervention with either the ABC or Radio Australia about their re- porting, carries a substantial political risk for any Australian Government, but more so in the case of the current Government since one of its major policy aims has been to promote the independence of the ABC.[7]

Those in Radio Australia, he said, had been rather put out at the suggestion that their coverage of events in East Timor was not balanced. He understood that a review by the department of Radio Australia's recent reporting demonstrated that it had, in fact, been balanced.

In a secret message to the minister in reply, the secretary of the department, Alan Renouf, spoke of his department's 'close working relationship with Radio Australia' and its frequent, almost daily, contact with the overseas service. 'In the case of Timor', he wrote, 'we exercise especial care in our dealings with all members of the press—so much so that a fairly common criticism is that we are withholding information that we should be releasing.'[8] In this case, he said, the department's contact in Radio Australia had commented that it would not be surprising if the Indonesian sources of Woolcott's report were trying to bring pressure to bear on Radio Australia, through the embassy and the department, for their own policy purposes.

Philip Koch said that, during his term as director of Radio Australia from 1975 to 1979, there was no direct attempt by Foreign Affairs to interfere editorially. But there was an extraordinary attempt at interference from within the government. Dr Moss Cass, as Minister for the Media, had asked ABC general manager Talbot Duckmanton to explain why Radio Australia appeared to be pro-Indonesian in its Timor broadcasts. This was in 1975, when most critics were accusing Radio Australia of being pro-Fretilin, because, Koch says, it was being 'showered with cables by Fretilin' and because its reporters could not get into East Timor from the Indonesian side. Koch says that at this stage, Radio Australia was simply trying to prevent the lack of information from the Indonesian side from causing a pro-Fretilin bias in its coverage. He had what he later described as 'a quite amazing meeting' with Cass in Melbourne at which he was 'more or less asked to explain'. He told the minister he could hardly believe his questions: the greatest difficulty for Radio Australia, he said, was to appear not to be biased *against* Indonesia.[9]

Perhaps surprisingly, the files seem to indicate that the Indonesian authorities made no complaint to the Australian embassy about Radio Australia's coverage of the killing of five television newsmen at Balibo on the border of East and West Timor in October, 1975. If they did, that complaint was apparently not conveyed to Radio Australia. The newsmen, on assignment for Australian networks, were killed by Indonesian soldiers taking part in the invasion of the territory.[10] Journalists working for Radio Australia shared with other Australian journalists a feeling of anger and outrage at the killings. The fact that the Indonesian authorities apparently did not complain about Radio Australia's reporting of the incident may be an indication that its reports were measured and factual. Or they may be an indication that those authorities, conscious of the guilt of the troops responsible, thought the less said the better.

Secret message

In late 1975, Woolcott, as ambassador to Indonesia, pressed to have Radio Australia moderate its coverage of the fighting in East Timor in a way that would minimise offence to the Indonesian government. Later attempts by the author to have a secret message from Woolcott to his department, and associated documents, declassified under Freedom of Information legislation, were rejected on the grounds that the documents were 'of a particularly sensitive nature'.[11] In January 1991, Woolcott, then in his last few months as secretary of the department, told the author there was probably no longer any reason to prevent their disclosure. He said he had not been involved in the original decision not to release the documents, which had been taken by a political officer at a lower level. The author's subsequent persistent attempts to have the documents released dragged on for more than a year. In November 1992, by which time he had retired, Woolcott had told the author that there should no longer be any difficulty about the release of the documents, as many more sensitive documents about Timor had been made public. A further approach to the department did result in the release of five associated documents. But Woolcott's secret message pressing for the moderation of Radio Australia's coverage to minimise offence to the Indonesian government had all but one of its five paragraphs deleted. A second secret message from Woolcott to the department also had all but one paragraph deleted, and a third was not released at all. The department apparently felt that the release of these documents would have an extraordinarily damaging effect on relations with Indonesia.

The one paragraph of a secret cable from Woolcott that was released said Radio Australia was coming in for some criticism for its reporting of Fretilin activities. He said Radio Australia had been referred to by one of the embassy's main media contacts as 'the voice of Fretilin'. The department conveyed this to Radio Australia, but made no complaint and did not suggest any particular action.[12]

In 1977, Woolcott, an old friend of Philip Koch, supported his proposal to visit Indonesia to explain Radio Australia's Timor coverage to Indonesian officials.[13] Koch wanted to say that Radio Australia was trying desperately to be very fair and impartial, but could give a much improved coverage if the Indonesians would let the ABC's Jakarta correspondent into East Timor, and would respond to Fretilin statements. In Jakarta later the Foreign Minister, Adam Malik, told Koch he accepted that the ABC had not taken an editorial viewpoint on Timor, but said Indonesia was concerned that the Australian media's 'concentration' on the East Timor issue (which he called 'a small issue') could damage relations with Australia. Koch replied that one of Radio Australia's greatest problems in providing a balanced coverage of East Timor had been the difficulty of getting a fast and authoritative response in Jakarta to Fretilin claims and other allegations against Indonesia. Malik conceded that Indonesia could have handled its information dissemination better, and gave Koch 'a firm assurance' that in future he would ensure that an Indonesian comment or reply would be readily available to Radio Australia in Jakarta.[14] This assurance, which seemed to have little practical effect, was similar to one made in 1978 by Malik's successor as Foreign Minister, Dr Mochtar Kusumaatmadja.[15]

Dr Edward Sinaga, the personal assistant to the Minister for Defence and Security, General Panggabean, was less conciliatory. When he met Koch in Jakarta in June 1977, he accused Radio Australia of being subversive by broadcasting an interview with the former Australian consul in Dili, James Dunn, in which he said internal support in Indonesia for an independent East Timor was possible, and by reporting an attempt by left-wing unionists in Australia to send a shipload of arms to the Fretilin resistance. Sinaga also referred to the fact that, after the Australian government had closed the Fretilin radio link in Darwin and declared its operation illegal, seven members of the federal Opposition, including three former senior cabinet ministers, had broadcast messages to Fretilin to which the ABC had given considerable prominence.[16] (Indonesia's sense of grievance at the lack of Australian support for the annexation of Timor perhaps partly resulted from false expectations. Whitlam is reported to have told Soeharto at Jogjakarta in September 1974 that an independent East Timor would be 'an unviable state and a potential threat to the area'.)[17] The director of Indonesia's Centre for Strategic and International Studies (a government 'think-tank'), Harry Tjan, later accepted Koch's assertion that, had Radio Australia not reported the Opposition members' messages to Fretilin, it would have clearly been censoring news of Opposition activities. He also appreciated that Radio Australia could not have avoided reporting fully Dunn's allegations of Indonesian atrocities in East Timor which finally were made in evidence before the international relations sub-committee of the United States House of Representatives. Koch later reported that he felt he was able to give Tjan a clearer picture of some of the material that had annoyed or confused officials in Jakarta.[18]

Koch reported that it was the Australian embassy's view that, if a special relationship between Australia and Indonesia had ever existed, it certainly did not now, because of Australia's stand on Timor, and its refusal to accept Indonesia's annexation of the former Portuguese colony.[19] Koch told Woolcott that he thought his visit to Indonesia had been successful in re-establishing goodwill towards Radio Australia, and that he believed a better understanding among ABC executives of Indonesia's situation would result.[20] Woolcott replied that this was helpful, as the close and substantial relationship with Indonesia which successive governments had built up over three decades, notwithstanding several setbacks, had been adversely affected by the Timor situation and, inadvertently or otherwise, Radio Australia had played a part in this. The integration of East Timor was now an established fact and, while continuing opposition from certain groups in Australia would not change this reality, it could continue to undermine Australia's long-term interests in maintaining its relations with Indonesia and with the ASEAN region.

The ambassador agreed with Koch that all Radio Australia could do was ensure that its coverage was carefully balanced. He added: 'Perhaps you might also bear in mind that it is the policy of the left-wing professional anti-Indonesian lobby to keep the Timor issue alive so that they can continue to exploit it in their anti-Indonesian campaign.' Presciently, Woolcott doubted whether Malik's promise of quick Jakarta responses to Radio Australia questions would hold good, but said the embassy would do its best to help. He commented that the new ABC correspondent, Warwick Beutler, seemed to be settling in well and some Indonesians had commented to him that recent Radio Australia news had been more balanced and more positive in its approach to Indonesia.[21] Koch's belief that his visit would bring a better understanding of Indonesia's situation among ABC executives proved illusory. He sent a report to Duckmanton for presentation to the commission, but there was no response.

Warwick Beutler's honeymoon with the Indonesians was a brief one. Radio Australia continued to report Indonesian events regardless of official displeasure. On 23 January 1978, the *Indonesian Observer* said several of the elite had learned from Radio Australia that six Jakarta newspapers had been banned.[22] Two days later, the ABC's manager, Asia, J. A. (Peter) Hollinshead, reported that Beutler had been warned through the Australian embassy that the generals were displeased with Radio Australia's reports of the arrest of students and the sacking of generals in the wake of the 1977 national elections.[23] At this stage, in reaction to student demonstrations and a wave of criticism by others, including the Jakarta press, the Indonesian authorities were becoming increasingly intolerant of the media, both domestic and foreign.

The year 1978, however, saw the removal of one source of friction between the Indonesian government and Australia, with the Fraser government's *de facto* recognition of Indonesia's annexation of East Timor. Australia changed its vote at the United Nations to oppose the regular resolution criticising Indonesia on the issue.[24] But a continuing problem was the slowness of the Indonesian authorities to respond to claims by rebels both in East Timor and Irian Jaya.[25]

In September 1978, Radio Australia broadcast a report by Beutler which appears to have been an attempt at appeasement. The report was about Indonesian claims that Radio Australia was carrying stories about Irian Jaya based on unsubstantiated allegations by the Free Papua Organisation (OPM). He stressed that this concern was also expressed by Australian diplomats and intelligence sources who discounted many of the OPM's claims as ridiculous. Beutler said the Indonesian government admitted that, by saying nothing about the Irian Jaya issue, it had probably contributed to the problem.[26]

In November 1978, Beutler and the Radio Australia officer based in Jakarta, Alan Morris, had a two-hour session with Sukarno (no relative of the late president), the official directly responsible for the foreign media, who suggested that foreign correspondents in Jakarta, particularly Australians, were in collusion with groups wanting to overthrow the Indonesian government. Beutler felt the suggestion was being made that action might be taken against them, but Sukarno refused to admit that there were any such plans. Beutler described his approach as 'paranoid'.[27]

Australian government pressure on Radio Australia intensified. The Joint Parliamentary Committee on Foreign Affairs and Defence decided that the Minister for Foreign Affairs should seek a meeting with the chairman of the ABC 'to emphasise the extreme sensitivity not only of Radio Australia programs but also of ABC domestic programs, particularly from Darwin'.[28]

The pressure continued in Jakarta as well. Beutler told the author (as acting controller of Radio Australia) in early 1979 that the Australian ambassador, Thomas Critchley, had 'complained most bitterly' to him about a Radio Australia story which had referred to Indonesia's 'invasion' of East Timor. Beutler said that, personally, he did not quarrel with the use of the word: Indonesia *had* invaded East Timor. But he tended to agree with Critchley that it was 'an unnecessary word at a time when Australia was doing everything it could to smooth out relations'. Beutler suggested that Radio Australia could have said 'since East Timor became part of Indonesia' or 'since East Timor was incorporated into Indonesia'. He thought that 'sometimes a little more care in the choice of words would help us a little'. He added, 'Frankly, we don't seem to be winning our case here, and I don't put all the blame on Javanese stubbornness.'[29]

Beutler's fears about 'not winning his case' were justified. In April 1979 Sukarno asked for a statistical breakdown of the Indonesian transmission showing what proportion of news and information programs dealt with Indonesian domestic subjects. The implication was clear: it was the increasingly familiar theme that Radio Australia's coverage of domestic subjects, in the Indonesian language, constituted Australian interference in Indonesia's domestic affairs.[30]

The next day, without waiting for the statistical breakdown, an Indonesian intelligence officer told the embassy that a survey of Radio Australia's Indonesian service had shown that much of what was broadcast was either propaganda or took an anti-government line. In some cases, he said, the broadcasts were similar to those between two hostile nations. The authorities had almost decided to ask that all Radio Australia staff in Indonesia be withdrawn. Apparently offering the Australians one last chance, the officer said that no action had yet been taken, but the question was still under review.[31]

The Department of Foreign Affairs and Radio Australia were surprised at the strength of the Indonesian moves, particularly in view of the steadily improving relationship as the Timor issue had abated. The assistant secretary, information branch, David Evans, said there had always been an element of bluff in Indonesian criticism of Radio Australia, but recent approaches were being examined seriously.[32]

Radio Australia's Indonesian-language supervisor, Peter Moore, had his own theory about the cause of the Indonesian dissatisfaction, which the author passed on to the department. On a visit to Indonesia, Moore had been told by the Information Minister, General Ali Moertopo, that the government was very concerned at the groundswell revival of Islam in Indonesia. At the end of their meeting, the minister had thrown up his hands and said that eventually 'we [presumably the generals] may all drown under the wave of Islam'. Moore believed Radio Australia's reporting of recent developments in the Islamic world might be at least part of the reason for Indonesia's current concern. He said no Indonesian papers, radio or television had reported developments in Iran, particularly the execution of former generals. No prominence had been given, either, to the execution of the former Prime Minister of Pakistan, Zulfikar Ali Bhutto. (Another possible motive for the curtain drawn over the Iran story on the national broadcasting stations, however, is that, if it had been reported, 'ordinary listeners could have understood this to be giving official imprimatur to the revolution.')[33]

It soon became clear that, in the absence of major concessions by Radio Australia, Beutler's fate was sealed. Probably only an about-face by the ABC and an agreement to broadcast only 'good news' on Radio Australia could have saved him. Joe Coman (as supervisor of Radio Australia's Indonesian broadcasts) said some years later that it still amazed him that action had not been taken sooner to remove ABC representatives from Indonesia, given the criticism of the service and the depth of feeling against Radio Australia in certain military circles in Jakarta.[34]

David Evans told the minister that the department believed the ABC had a point in being somewhat indignant over claims of imbalance in its Radio Australia coverage. Under a certain amount of probing, Sukarno had been unable to sheet home the precise nature of Indonesian sensitivities, even on the two issues of reporting from Jakarta—the Papua New Guinea border and student agitation—which he claimed were relevant. Evans added that there was probably no answer to the problem 'short of a Government takeover of Radio Australia or alternatively its demise', neither of which, he said, was practicable.[35]

Foreshadowing the most permissive paragraphs of the department's submission to the Dix committee of inquiry into the ABC the following year, another senior officer told Critchley that the department believed it inevitable that the ABC's reporting would cause occasional Indonesian dissatisfaction because of different interpretations of events or because of the choice of issues covered. Indeed, reporting which might cause the Indonesians offence could well be quite accurate and fair.[36] But the ambassador was not so permissive. Referring to a recording of a 'Variations' program on Timor broadcast by the ABC home service (not by Radio Australia), he said:

I appreciate that the media cannot be controlled. But surely an organisation dependent on the Government should be expected to attempt to give a balanced broadcast and not embark on an exercise designed to engender hatred of a country with which we need to have good relations.[37]

Early in 1980, the Indonesian government told Beutler it would not issue a visa to Joe Coman, who was to have replaced Morris as Radio Australia officer in Jakarta. The exclusion of Coman and the prospect of becoming the first ABC reporter to be expelled from Indonesia did not deter Beutler from reporting contentious items. Less than a month after the announcement that Coman's visa would not be issued, Beutler filed a report about a statement by President Soeharto defending attacks on his integrity. Beutler's suggested studio introduction stated unequivocally (if ungrammatically): 'Indonesia's President Soeharto has said that groups seeking to remove him from power are spreading vile rumours about he and his wife.'[38]

The head of military intelligence, General Benny Moerdani, told Beutler Indonesia's complaints and objections lay solely with the Indonesian-language news bulletins: 'You can say any hurtful thing you like about Indonesia in English,' he said, 'but not in Indonesian.'[39] Moerdani said the decision to exclude Coman had been taken at a very high level by a committee. Those on the committee had been very resolute in their opinion that Radio Australia had carried stories about Indonesia that could upset political stability. Moerdani had admitted that Timor had been the beginning of the 'prejudice' (Beutler's word) against Radio Australia, but transcripts he produced covered many other issues. Among the major complaints about Radio Australia, Moerdani said, were that it covered 'sensitive' subjects. Beutler mentioned the possibility that Indonesia would refuse to renew his visa the following month, but Moerdani gave him 'a strong assurance that that would not happen', adding, 'We want you here.'

'On the run'

Assessing the situation after his meeting with Moerdani in early May 1980, Beutler wrote:

He would judge, I believe, that he has us on the run and that maybe RA will think twice before it runs stories about Indonesia. I'm not suggesting we should do this; I'm saying only that he thinks we will ... It's patently obvious that the Indonesian government wants to muzzle RA. Every other form of media in Indonesia is controlled. RA is a big embarrassment to them. They want to stop us reporting sensitive matters. The list of examples shows this: the student troubles leading up to the last Presidential election, Timor starvation, Irian Jaya bombings, the President and Vice-President and relations with China—all the most sensitive issues in Indonesia. Their objections go beyond the question of errors and analysis. They touch on our right to report on these subjects at all. From where I sit, [Beutler added] many of Indonesia's complaints are justified and have my sympathy. There was bad editorial judgement used in a number of the stories listed in the document. They were not checked with me. As the head of RA's news and public affairs department [the author] knows, I have complained loudly and bitterly about this, yet the practice continues.

Apparently taking at face value Moerdani's assurance that he was not in danger of expulsion, Beutler suggested that, if he could go back with some definite assurance that Radio Australia was as concerned about its mistakes as the Indonesians were, and that it had instituted changes, they might be satisfied, and, in a few months possibly, they would let Coman in. The transcripts which Moerdani handed to him covered a wide range of stories but, whether accurate or inaccurate, all had a common thread—political sensitivity. They were from two periods, February to June 1978 and November 1979 to April 1980.

The stories from the first period dealt with student troubles before the 1978 presidential election; people fleeing Indonesian bombing raids in Irian Jaya; the decision of Malik to resign as Vice-President; a famine on the island of Sumba; and a story by Beutler saying Soeharto's visit to the Middle East to secure petro-dollars was a failure ('which it was,' said Beutler in his report, 'but the government doesn't like us to say it was').[40]

Half of the stories in the second period were on the hypersensitive issue of Timor. They included:

- A report that the Australian Government was providing $300,000 in aid to East Timor 'following reports of widespread starvation there'.
- A mistaken news agency report that Mochtar had compared the situation in Timor with that in Biafra or Kampuchea.
- Comments by the secretary-general of the Australian Red Cross after a visit to Timor.
- A report by Beutler on the number of deaths in one division in the East Timor campaign, saying Timor was the biggest of the three major campaigns which Indonesian troops had fought, and it had taken the heaviest toll of life.
- A roundup of editorials calling on the government to explain what was going on in Timor.

The fact that several of the stories complained of were not about Timor strongly suggests that the concern of the authorities was not confined to the one issue. They included:

- A mistaken news agency report that Indonesia was going to repatriate one million Chinese.
- A report by Beutler about Soeharto strongly advocating that the armed forces should retain their political role. The objection was to a comment by Beutler that this was contrary to the views of ministers,

parliamentarians and members of the ruling Golkar party. (Apparently suggesting that comment should be censored from news in Indonesian, Beutler said it was arguable that the Indonesian section should have 'cut it out'.)

- A report by Beutler about Malik resigning as Vice-President. The major complaint here was his comment that Malik was unhappy in the job. (Again, he said this comment was 'perhaps unnecessary for the Indonesian service', claiming that 'everyone' knew it anyway.)
- Beutler's story about Soeharto's denial of the 'vile rumours about his personal life'. The objection, Beutler said, was to his comment that the President's outspokenness had led to speculation that he had decided 'to run again for the presidency'. This, said Beutler, was the most sensitive subject in Indonesia. Again, he questioned whether it should have gone out in the Indonesian transmission.

Glossing over the 'many complaints' which Beutler said were justified and had his support, Peter Barnett was dismissive when he later reported on Moerdani's complaints in a draft answer to a question in parliament. He devoted one sentence to them: 'Independent experts who analysed the comments said they were minor in character.'[41] The Minister for Communications, Ian Sinclair, reproduced this sentence word for word in his reply in February 1982 to the Labor member for Fraser, Ken Fry. Fry had asked three months earlier whether the Indonesian government had protested about the content of any of Radio Australia's broadcasts in the previous five years and, if so, had they been investigated, and what had been the result.[42]

Before Beutler's report on his meeting with Moerdani reached Melbourne, the author told the sub-editors he believed two incorrect agency stories run the previous November were a factor in the decision to refuse a visa to Coman. These stories, both among those in the list Moerdani had handed to Beutler, were the report that Mochtar had compared Timor with Kampuchea, and the report that, according to an Indonesian parliamentarian, the head of the national intelligence agency had said that about a million unnaturalised Chinese were to be housed in specially designated areas pending their deportation. The author said the sub-editors responsible had been negligent, and issued an instruction that, where 'humanly possible', a phone check should be made with the Radio Australia correspondent on the spot.[43]

Alan Morris, as acting supervisor of the Indonesian section, supported Beutler's complaints about the use of agency reports without checking. But he strongly opposed Beutler's suggestion that reports in Indonesian be toned down. If Radio Australia were to have any integrity, he said, it must have it in all languages.

With more experience of Indonesia than any of the ABC's correspondents, Morris expressed the view that, no matter how careful or expert were Radio Australia's sub-editors and translators, the Indonesian government would not be satisfied. Some Indonesian officials were insatiable, he said: nothing short of abject fawning would satisfy them. Morris believed that it was not errors of fact and translation that really irritated the Indonesians: it was the accurate analysis and interpretation of the facts that they did not like, because they saw it as 'negative'. He went on:

Either we leave out analysis and interpretation (and thus render most Indonesian news utterly meaningless) or we cease broadcasting the news entirely.

A complete blackout of Indonesian news in the Indonesian language would probably please the government. Of course, it would not please our listeners, but the government is not concerned about that.[44]

The acting controller of Radio Australia endorsed Morris's opposition to Beutler's suggestion that reports should be sanitised for use in the Indonesian service. He said bilingual Indonesian listeners compared the English and Indonesian broadcasts, and would soon notice discrepancies.[45]

Beutler's days were numbered. In mid-May 1980, a petition was presented to the Indonesian parliament expressing concern at Soeharto's recent speeches. The fifty prominent Indonesians who had signed it included two former prime ministers, the former head of the emergency revolutionary government of 1949 and former armed forces commander Nasution. One of the petitioners, Mohammad Jasin, later produced a document of his own criticising the alleged hypocrisy and corruption of the Soeharto government. There was a domestic news blackout on both documents. Beutler filed the stories, and Radio Australia broadcast them. To make matters worse, Radio Australia broadcast the story of corruption charges made against Soeharto by Kartika Tahir, the widow of a former executive of the state oil company.[46] Rumours began to strengthen that the ABC's Jakarta office would be closed down and Beutler expelled.[47]

Expulsion

In June 1980, just before his visa was due to expire, Beutler was told there would be no extension. The Australian Foreign Minister, Andrew Peacock, protested to the Indonesian government, expressing his 'disappointment and disapproval'.[48] The federal Opposition leader, Bill Hayden, described the decision as 'outrageous', and 'obviously aimed at stifling proper open commentary'.[49] But they were merely going through the motions: they would have been naive to expect their protestations to have any effect. On 28 June, Beutler left for Singapore, where it was proposed that he would continue to cover Indonesia by telephone.[50]

An editorial in *Suara Karya*, the paper of the Indonesian government's political party, Golkar, said Indonesia did not greatly need relations with Australia. Friendly relations had developed primarily because of 'an intimate spiritual tie with the Australian people', but if the Australian government felt that Radio Australia must be allowed to broadcast 'offensive news and commentaries', it must accept the consequences.[51]

Beutler continued to file stories about Indonesia from Singapore, although his output dropped by about half. The Indonesian Information Minister, Moertopo, invited a senior representative of the ABC to visit Indonesia to discuss the commission's representation there, but shortly afterwards was admitted to hospital with heart trouble. (A voice of moderation in Indonesia's dealings with Radio Australia was silenced when Moertopo died on 15 May 1984.)

An intelligence officer in the Department of Foreign Affairs who specialised in Indonesian affairs reported that the decision to expel Beutler had been made at a very high level, a month before it had been implemented. He said the hope had been that Australian reaction would not be too strong. The risk was considered worth taking if it meant minimising the impact of Radio Australia in Indonesia. The intelligence officer said direct discussions in Indonesia could only reinforce what was already known—that 'negative news' in Indonesian was not acceptable, notably criticism of the President.[52]

The Australian government's commitment to the independence of Radio Australia was severely tested by subsequent developments. Senior Indonesian officials were threatening a 'major falling out with Australia' unless Radio Australia stopped broadcasting in Indonesian. There was talk of rejecting all Australian military and civil aid, cutting the size of the Australian embassy staff and even forcing the withdrawal of the ambassador. One official said a generalised feeling of unhappiness with Australia had been latent until Radio Australia had stirred everything up. But David Jenkins wrote in the *Far Eastern Economic Review* that the Australian Prime Minister, Malcolm Fraser, might be inclined to disregard the advice of those in Foreign Affairs who could be expected to argue, at the very least, for a full-scale review of Radio Australia's aims and objectives. Moreover, Jenkins said, Fraser was known to believe that a relationship, if it were to be at all meaningful, must be able to withstand the occasional difference of opinion. According to Jenkins, Indonesian officials admitted that it was the Jasin and Tahir stories that had brought the affair to a head, but said the issue went well beyond this: what they objected to was the whole notion of Radio Australia 'airing Indonesia's dirty linen in public'.[53]

A month after Beutler's expulsion, a former supervisor of Radio Australia's Indonesian section, Burt Millane, raised the dirty linen issue. In a letter to Radio Australia's new controller, Peter Barnett, he asked, 'What gives Radio Australia the right to meddle in the internal affairs of Indonesia? What is the gain or advantage of this unfriendly action to the taxpayer and the Government?'[54] Millane wrote in similar terms to the ABC chairman, John Norgard, and later to Communications Minister Ian Sinclair.[55]

Norgard's reply, drafted by Barnett, was a spirited defence of the independence and integrity of the service. It quoted the Foreign Affairs submission to the Dix committee in 1980, saying that although there would be occasions when items would irritate governments with which Australia had good relations, this was the price to be paid for the greater credibility and influence achieved through operation outside the direct control of the government.[56] The government closed ranks with Radio Australia in its response to Millane. In a clear indication of its commitment to the independence of the service, Sinclair wrote that even though Radio Australia had become an embarrassment in relations between Australia and Indonesia, the government affirmed that, on balance, it was more a help than a hindrance to the national interest. Sinclair added:

On the contrary, it is the Government's opinion, re-enforced by the Department of Foreign Affairs—that Radio Australia's foreign language broadcasts do a great deal to buttress Australia's international position and to encourage foreign listeners to appreciate the Australian way of life. When considered against its overall cost, the number of listeners gained by Radio Australia demonstrates clearly that the Australian taxpayer is gaining an investment return of considerable national and international benefit.[57]

Some officers (and particularly some former officers) of the Department of Foreign Affairs were by no means as supportive of Radio Australia as Sinclair. A former Australian ambassador in Jakarta, Sir Keith Shann, said Australia's relations with Indonesia were worse than they had been at the height of its confrontation with Malaysia in the early 1960s. He said the relationship had soured in part because of the Australian media's presentation of Indonesian affairs and also because a new generation of Indonesians had grown up unaware of Australia's role in what he euphemistically called 'the Dutch departure from the area'. In particular, he was critical of 'Radio Australia's presentation' and with the continuing focus of the Australian media on East Timor and the deaths of the five Australian-based newsmen there. Speaking of Radio Australia's huge audience in Indonesia, he asked: 'If we were in the same position and we heard remarks that were critical of our country and the tone derogatory, can you honestly imagine that we wouldn't react very violently if that were our main source of news?' He said that, 'while he did not for a moment advocate censorship of Radio Australia, the service could be more aware of the positive aspects of the relationship, such as Australia's aid program'. A report in the *Sydney Morning Herald* said Shann's views were 'known to be widely shared by the Department of Foreign Affairs'.[58]

The Indonesian government was not happy to have Beutler reporting on Indonesia from Singapore, and apparently brought pressure to bear on its ASEAN neighbour. Singapore's immigration department told Beutler in September 1980 that his application for an employment pass had been rejected. No reason was given. But Prime Minister Lee Kuan Yew had told Australian journalists on a flight from New Delhi to Singapore the previous day that 'he had an understanding with the Singapore press about coverage of Indonesia'.[59]

The expulsion of Beutler brought an end to the long period of *détente* between the department and Radio Australia which had begun a decade earlier. The trouble began with the leak of classified American documents which mentioned, *inter alia*, the substance of a critical report from the ambassador, Critchley, following a visit to Timor in May 1980. Senior members of Radio Australia's current affairs staff believed it was a story that should be covered (not least because Radio Australia's credibility would suffer a serious blow if others covered it and Radio Australia was seen to have censored it). The current affairs journalists interviewed an official of the organisation Action for World Development, who confirmed some of the ambassador's observations. The journalists also sought to 'balance' the report by interviewing Dr Peter McCawley, of the Australian National University, who could usually be relied on for a comment sympathetic to the Indonesian government. McCawley did not disappoint them: he said it was time Australia stopped emphasising the Timor issue and began to concern itself more with its overall relationship with Indonesia.

The full text of the item was sent to the department, before broadcast, with an invitation to comment. Instead of accepting the invitation, the department telephoned senior executives of the ABC, including Peter Barnett, claiming that the item was 'unbalanced and negative'. Barnett apparently wanted to 'kill' the story, but could not think of a valid journalistic reason to justify such a step. Instead, he and the author (as editor of Radio Australia) changed the studio introduction, to give the item a more 'positive' emphasis, highlighting the fact that the documents showed the ambassador had a generally favourable view of the Indonesian presence in East Timor. Overruling the protests of the author and Radio Australia's executive producer of current affairs, Warren Wilton, Barnett also insisted that McCawley's comment should *precede* the report of what he was commenting on! Whether this astonishing piece of editorial judgment did anything to mollify the Indonesians was not apparent. But the Radio Australia journalists had compounded the offence. A statement critical of the resettlement in East Timor, made in the leaked documents by an American political officer, was wrongly attributed to the Australian ambassador.[60] The secretary of the Department of Foreign Affairs, Peter Henderson, concluded that there were 'clear limits to the capacity of current arrangements to bridge differences of view between the Government and Radio Australia on what should or should not be carried in news or current affairs programs'. He said the broadcast of the item on the leaked documents seemed to him to show a 'disturbing lack of control by the ABC and Radio Australia management'. While discussions with Radio Australia and senior levels of management in the ABC had resulted in a slight restructuring of the story for broadcast to Indonesia in Indonesian, he said, it was the view of the Radio Australia and ABC management that any attempt to alter significantly the content of the report would have invited 'a strong and probably unacceptable reaction' from the journalists concerned and possibly also from the Australian Journalists' Association. In a confidential note, Henderson wrote:

In effect, and even after exerting all the influence it could within the scope offered by the existing guidelines, the Government was unable to achieve a real adjustment of what my Department considered to be a significant imbalance in the news story.[61]

The secretary of the Department of Communications, Bob Lansdown, told Duckmanton that, while his minister, Ian Sinclair, was under no pressure to bring up a cabinet submission, he was clearly intending to do so. He said the incident reflected the particular issue of programming control which was causing unease in a number of quarters.[62] Duckmanton replied that he could not accept Henderson's suggestion that the incident showed a lack of control by the ABC and Radio Australia management. Barnett and the author, he said, had concluded that the report was 'balanced and fair'. As for the factual error in the report,

Duckmanton said the fact that it had gone to air resulted from a break-down in the normally smooth working of the liaison between Radio Australia and the department. If, after the text had been telexed to the department, the story had been checked against the ambassador's report, and the department had pointed out that he had not made the statement attributed to him, this part of the story would not have been broadcast.[63]

After his retirement, Henderson wrote more frankly than at any time during his career about his attitude to Radio Australia and Indonesia. He said:

I believe that on occasion individuals within Radio Australia, whose cast of mind was hardly pro-Indonesia or pro its government, have broadcast to that country over Radio Australia material gratuitously critical of the Indonesian government ... I remember being told by an Indonesian that what he found offensive about Radio Australia was deliberate use in Indonesian language broadcasts of words known to be offensive to Indonesians, words whose connotation and true shades of meaning would be clear only to Australians expert in the Indonesian language.

Henderson revealed here his ignorance of the way in which Radio Australia works. News and current affairs items are translated not by Australians, but by Indonesian members of its staff. Any systematic attempt, by the Australian linguists who sometimes checked the translations, to introduce offensive words—and there is absolutely no evidence of any such attempt—would inevitably come to the attention of senior executives of Radio Australia. He continued:

But choice of unsuitable language apart, should we not ask ourselves if it is the proper role of an officially, publicly-funded Radio Australia to broadcast critical or even hostile material to Indonesia? None is obvious to me ... I would be very surprised if Radio Australia did not still claim the right ... to reject guidance or instructions from outside, including from *the government which foots the bill for Radio Australia's existence* [emphasis added].[64]

Further trouble between Radio Australia and the Indonesian govern-ment in early 1981 brought an attempt by the Australian government to assert control. The trouble concerned Radio Australia's reporting of anti-Chinese riots in Central Java. After Duckmanton had told Sinclair that the reports had not been referred to Foreign Affairs prior to broadcast, Sinclair asked that this be done in future with items the department thought were 'highly controversial'. If the department disputed the right of Radio Australia to broadcast such an item, Sinclair said, the item should be referred to both him and Street. If the ABC had agreed to the proposal, it would have been the first time it had conceded the department's right to see Radio Australia stories prior to broadcast, with a view to their possible censorship. But the commission replied:

Any requirement by the Government that Radio Australia refer news copy to the Department of Foreign Affairs for clearance prior to broadcast would destroy the programming independence of Radio Australia, and of the Australian Broadcasting Commission.[65]

Norgard, staunchly defending the independence of Radio Australia from government interference, subsequently told Sinclair that any reaction to the Indonesian situation restricting Radio Australia's broadcasts would, in the commission's view, be a severe blow to the credibility of the service, and in fact would 'harm Australia's image as a whole in the eyes of our near neighbours'.[66]

The *Age* supported the commission's stand, saying in an editorial that any suggestion that Radio Australia's news be vetted in an effort to please the Indonesians 'represents a complete about-turn on the Government's previous stated policy'. The paper asserted that, as Street had said in parliament on 1 April, this policy was 'that Radio Australia and the Australian Broadcasting Commission retain editorial responsibility for deciding what material is broadcast and how it will be used'. Street had added, 'As far as I am aware, Radio Australia's broadcasts to Indonesia are treated and handled in the same way as those in any foreign language.' The editorial went on to sound a warning:

But he then added that the report of the Dix Committee, which is inquiring into the ABC, might cause the Government to give the matter 'further consideration'. Under certain circumstances, 'the Government would look at what arrangements under which Radio Australia is established and conducts its operations' [*sic*]. This statement is not very reassuring. It sounds as though Mr Street is carefully leaving open the possibility that the Government might step in.[67]

In December 1980, Barnett and the ABC's assistant general manager, radio, Keith Mackriell, had gone to Indonesia to discuss the possible return of an ABC correspondent. They met Sukarno, who was in charge of foreign media, and he indicated at the outset that he was concerned about Radio Australia's coverage of the anti-Chinese riots in central Java, news of which had been blacked out in the domestic media 'in the interests of national stability'. Initially, he asked that Radio Australia stop broadcasting any news at all about Indonesia in Indonesian. But he later modified this to any 'negative' items about the country. His euphemism for what he was asking was 'freedom with responsibility'. Replying that this would amount to a form of censorship, Mackriell countered with a proposal that any correspondent would be well-briefed and 'sensitive to Indonesia's problems', and would send balanced reports. Critchley tended to support Sukarno's views. Mackriell later said Critchley would clearly prefer Radio Australia not to broadcast 'any stories unfriendly to Indonesia'.[68]

The department's heightened sensitivity to Radio Australia's reports in Indonesian was apparent in the concern of the new ambassador, Rawdon Dalrymple, over a report of a statement by the Australian minister, commercial, in Jakarta, John Allgrove, made in Darwin. Allgrove had told Darwin businessmen that bribery was a fact of life when dealing with businessmen and government officials in Indonesia.[69] (The Radio Australia report also included Allgrove's statement, which might well have minimised any Indonesian offence, that such payments were merely regarded as gratuities and it was senseless to pretend that similar circumstances did not exist in Australia.) Dalrymple questioned Radio Australia's motivation in reporting the statement, which he said Allgrove had thought was off the record. He said it was hard to see that the intent could have been other than mischievous. The ambassador added a threatening note: 'In any discussions about Radio Australia's future following the Dix Report departments might wish to consider how pointless and damaging Radio Australia Indonesian language activity of [this] kind can be minimised or prevented.'[70]

The Australian embassy again expressed concern in October 1982 about a Radio Australia program dealing with human rights in East Timor which it said 'could well exacerbate difficulties in the relationship in areas affected by East Timor, particularly perhaps family reunions'. The embassy told the department that, while it was true that the program had included some views favourable to Indonesia's record in East Timor, the balance of the program was heavily on the side of allegations of human rights breaches and criticisms of the Indonesian administration there. It concluded: 'It would be interesting to know whether the Department of Foreign Affairs was consulted in connection with production of the program.'[71]

The author, as editor of Radio Australia, replied that a program about human rights in East Timor *ipso facto* was going to upset some officials in Indonesia, but he did not believe this was a reason that such sensitive topics should be avoided. The author also pointed out that such a program unavoidably devoted more time to detailing the allegations than to denials of these allegations. There was a limit to how many times pro-Indonesian government participants in the debate could reiterate that there had been no breaches of human rights. The author said that, although the subjects of forthcoming programs were normally discussed with an officer of the department during his daily liaison telephone call, the officer had not phoned on the days before the two broadcasts, adding, 'This is not to suggest, of course, that subjects should be "cleared" with Foreign Affairs before broadcast.'[72]

In 1986, a story published in the *Sydney Morning Herald* caused a more serious setback in relations between Australia and Indonesia than anything Radio Australia had broadcast. The article, linking Soeharto and his family to corruption in Indonesia, was written by a former correspondent in Jakarta, David Jenkins. According to some accounts, what caused the greatest offence was the headline (not written by Jenkins) comparing Soeharto with the disgraced President Marcos of the Philippines. Jakarta downgraded its relations with Canberra, a plane-load of tourists arriving in Bali from Australia was refused entry, defence cooperation was curtailed, and official visits were cancelled. Several Australian journalists, including Jenkins of course, were put on a list of those forbidden to receive visas.

Hill's abortive visit

But despite the problems created by Jenkins's article, criticism of Radio Australia by the Indonesian authorities and Australia's Department of Foreign Affairs abated in the mid-1980s. Perhaps the Indonesians were finding that the expulsion of Beutler, together with their pressure on Radio Australia to be circumspect in its coverage of news embarrassing to Jakarta, was having the desired effect. (It is understandable that if journalists perceive that their careers may be damaged by full and frank reporting that antagonises a 'friendly' government, they will tend to exercise a degree of self-censorship.) As for the department, perhaps it found Bill Hayden, who became minister after the election of the Hawke government in March 1983, less sympathetic than his predecessor to attempts to mute the voice of the overseas service. Hayden certainly staunchly defended the independence of the service following a visit to Indonesia by David Hill, the second managing director of the Australian Broadcasting Corporation (which had replaced the Australian Broadcasting Commission on 1 June 1983).

There were some who believed that Hill favoured the cessation of news broadcasts in Indonesian about Indonesian domestic matters. His two-day visit to Jakarta was made in March 1987 to try to persuade the Indonesian authorities to readmit an ABC correspondent. During his visit, he discussed ways in which Radio Australia could, as he put it, work more 'satisfactorily'. He came away 'with some optimism that the ABC may be allowed back into Jakarta next year'.[73]

During Hill's visit to Indonesia, he excluded various people from his discussions with Indonesian officials: the two ABC officers who accompanied him; the ABC's general manager, Asia, Ian Macintosh (eventually—more than four years later—appointed as the ABC's next correspondent in Jakarta); and the assistant head of Radio Australia's Indonesian-language service, Alan Morris. Morris reported that Hill, on his return from his last appointment, with Sukarno, was 'in high spirits and optimistic that the ABC would be back in Jakarta within a matter of months'.[74] Hill told Morris in his hotel room that Radio Australia would continue to broadcast international news in Indonesian, including international news items on Indonesia itself. But as editor-in-chief he insisted on news being handled 'with sensitivity and responsibility'. He said he would be 'putting to the board the fact that Radio Australia had been broadcasting *domestic* news to countries for 30 years, and it was now time for the ABC to make a decision as to whether this should continue. He will insist that the ABC make an assessment of RA's news service.'[75]

On his return, Hill is reported to have taken the view that Radio Australia's charter did not authorise it to broadcast to Indonesia about Indonesian domestic matters. On the other hand, at least one executive of Radio Australia, the controller of news and current affairs, Geoffrey Heriot, with the support of Foreign Affairs, was arguing that, as the charter did not proscribe it from doing so, it could, and should.

Hill told the secretary of the department, Dr Stuart Harris, that he and 'his board' would appreciate a greater input from the department on Radio Australia's role and content. Harris retorted that his department neither wanted nor sought such a role. He said that would be contrary to the best interests of both Radio Australia and the department. He viewed Radio Australia as a 'very important vehicle, not for the promotion of Australian foreign policy or for the views of the government of the day but, in a wider sense, for the promotion in our region of Australia's cultural, political and social values'. He said the department put a very high value on Radio Australia, adding that, for all the problems it sometimes caused, the benefits far outweighed the costs.[76] Harris was supported by his minister; Hayden said his view was, in essence:

Radio Australia should not become a mouthpiece for any government of the day, its independence and ethical standards should be preserved, the latter of a high order, that its responsibility, inter alia, is that its broadcasting must be factually correct, and that in my view it was pointless having a Radio Australia broadcasting to countries in the region but not broadcasting domestic matters of interest arising from within those countries to listeners within those countries … If Radio Australia is to be muzzled or converted into some sort of government propaganda utility I would rather that it be closed down as a waste of taxpayers' funds and apply the funds to something more beneficial.[77]

Several months later, Hill denied that he had sought to restrict Radio Australia's broadcasts to Indonesia as a way of persuading the Indonesian government to allow an ABC correspondent back into Jakarta. Repudiating the views attributed to him by the minister and the department, he told the *Age*, 'My personal view is that you would destroy the credibility of Radio Australia as an independent news broadcaster the minute it came under the control, or even the appearance of control, of the Department of Foreign Affairs.'[78] Whether this had been his view a year earlier, or whether he had travelled on the road to Damascus, is a matter for conjecture.

In retrospect, it is clear that some of the Indonesian complaints about Radio Australia's reporting were justified. Needless offence was caused at times by sub-editors ignorant or uncaring about Indonesian sensitivities. The use of unconfirmed news agency stories was clearly the source of some legitimate complaints. The agency story foreshadowing the deportation of a million Chinese, run before Beutler's expulsion, touched on a particularly sensitive issue, and had the capacity to exacerbate racial tensions and cause alarm and panic among the unnaturalised Chinese. In retrospect, the author wishes he had not waited until after this reprehensible mistake had been made to instruct the sub-editors not to use such agency reports without checking with Beutler.

But such issues were peripheral by comparison with the coverage of Timor. It is clear that after the invasion of East Timor, Radio Australia's reporting of events in Indonesia to Indonesia in the Indonesian language was one of the greatest irritants—perhaps the greatest irritant—in relations between the Soeharto regime and Australia. The Department of Foreign Affairs did little to try to minimise the damage by 'leaning' on the ABC. This was partly because key officers, and at least one minister, believed, in the words of the department's submission to the Dix committee in 1980:

there will be, as long as Radio Australia broadcasts are not directly controlled by the Government, occasions where items broadcast will irritate governments with which Australia had good relations or in other ways will inconvenience the conduct of Australian foreign policy … we believe that this possibility has to be accepted as part of the price paid for the greater credibility and influence achieved through operation outside the direct control of the Government.[79]

Some of the officers of the department who support Radio Australia's independence point out that short-term irritants in relations with a particular regime are not necessarily long-term impediments to friendly relations. Although there are opposition figures in Indonesia who, like those in power, see Radio Australia's reporting of their country's domestic affairs as unwarranted interference, others welcome the reporting of events blacked out in the country's own media. In theory, those favourably disposed to Radio Australia may one day be in power.

Having an independent overseas service trying to report objectively on the affairs of a friendly country clearly has its disadvantages. Whether these disadvantages have to be accepted as part of the price of the 'greater credibility and influence achieved through operation outside the direct control of the Government' will continue to be debated whenever the subject of Radio Australia's relative independence of government is discussed.

10 Indonesian massacre, 1991—1993

In the late 1980s and early 1990s, the signals from the Indonesian authorities to Radio Australia gradually became warmer, and the ABC came to believe that the time was right to make formal approaches to them. In June 1991, Indonesia's Foreign Affairs Department told Australian journalists in Jakarta that approval had been granted for the ABC once again to base a correspondent in Indonesia. The ABC chose for this delicate assignment one of its most experienced foreign correspondents, Ian Macintosh (who, as general manager, Asia, had accompanied Hill on his abortive visit to Jakarta more than four years earlier).

Macintosh, who took up his position on 8 October 1991, had been reporting for barely a month when a storm erupted, in the form of the Dili massacre in East Timor. An analysis of how he, and Radio Australia, covered this explosive story shows that, after a cautious start, both were surprisingly forthright in reporting an issue of extreme sensitivity.

Asked a few days before the Dili massacre if he had any idea why the Indonesians had let an ABC correspondent back, the general manager of Radio Australia, Richard Broinowski, said he guessed the Indonesians probably felt a bit more relaxed about Australia. He said the ambassador in Jakarta, Philip Flood, had said that Radio Australia seemed to be 'in good odour'.[1] This may have been partly a result of self-censorship, or to use another word, sensitivity, by Radio Australia. The Australian embassy commented in May 1989, 'Experienced RA broadcasters, both Indonesian and Australian, appear to have exercised more sensitivity and caution in the Indonesian programming segments in recent years, a fact quietly appreciated by Indonesian decision-makers.'[2] The following April, Flood told Broinowski he had received no complaints from the government or anyone else since taking up his appointment fourteen months before.

Broinowski said in October 1991 that he could not imagine Hill giving the Indonesians any undertaking about what Radio Australia would broadcast and not broadcast. 'If he did it in 88, and I don't think he did, Hill would have probably changed his mind now ... I am not sure that there's any way in which Hill would make such an undertaking today.'[3] He said Macintosh had not been given any 'riding instructions'. He was supposed to be reporting the news as he saw it. Broinowski had no knowledge of any threats the Indonesians may have made. 'Mind you, I think that Macintosh is living in a fairly dangerous or unstable environment to the extent that it would take one story by him they disagreed with to get rid of him again [sic].'

Three days after his arrival in Jakarta, Macintosh recorded for a domestic ABC radio program a piece which was also used by Radio Australia. It was a scene-setter in which he spoke of the changes that had taken place since Beutler had been, as he tactfully put it, 'officially requested to leave the country'.[4] He reported that, during that time, Indonesia had 'steadily developed its economy and made significant progress in improving the lives of the 180 million people who inhabit the vast archipelago'. But it was not just a good-news story. He reported, in Jakarta, 'Chronic traffic jams, persistent air pollution, a seriously depleted and contaminated water table, electricity and telephone systems which regularly fail, and no sign of any letup in new arrivals from around the country, who increasingly burden an infrastructure already close to breaking point.'[5] But, he added, there was a bright side. 'There is little about Jakarta which an outsider would term attractive or comfortable, and yet amid the abuses and wrongs, dust and rubbish, mud and carbon monoxide, one senses an unstoppable energy that could well fuel yet another Asian economic success story.' Drawing attention to a development which was to provide Australia with an alternative means of communicating directly with the Indonesian people, Macintosh reported that the satellite television revolution was rapidly changing the way Indonesians saw the world and their place in it. Previously the playthings of the rich and powerful, satellite dishes could now be seen in ever-increasing numbers atop the houses of Indonesia's rapidly expanding middle class and even in poor areas, 'notwithstanding the efforts of a dire and determined Department of Information, which [as he said euphemistically] still fights the good fight to keep the nation's own media under careful control'. Then, touching gently on a delicate point, Macintosh reported that 'on the more sensitive domestic subjects, such as the big gap between rich and poor, there is still little public debate'.

In Dili early on the morning of Tuesday, 12 November, Indonesian soldiers fired their semi-automatic weapons into a crowd of well over 3000 East Timorese demonstrators, killing dozens and wounding many more. The demonstrators were commemorating the death of one of two youths killed a fortnight earlier in a clash with pro-integrationists, later revealed to have been under-cover security agents. Estimates of the number killed ranged widely, as is usual in such situations—from the original military figure of nineteen to an estimate of 271 by Dr George Aditjondro, of Satya Wacana University, Central Java. Aditjondro, a former journalist, said another 200 people had disappeared.[6] Australian journalist John Pilger, who visited East Timor in secret in 1994, estimated that 'the total number murdered or missing totalled more than 400'.[7] An Australian authority on Indonesia, Professor Herbert Feith, of Monash University, after a careful assessment of the evidence, estimated a few weeks later that 'probably well over 100 people were killed on and immediately after 12 November'.[8] Indonesia's national investigation commission, the Djaelani commission, reported that about fifty were dead, more than ninety-one wounded and about ninety missing. Feith says the group described as missing may well include the sixty or so said to have been secretly buried at Hera, near Dili, three days after the massacre. Macintosh believed several months later that the death toll had probably been more than 100, and possibly even more than 200.[9]

In order to assess Radio Australia's coverage of the massacre, and that of Macintosh, it may be helpful to examine the accounts of eye-witnesses. (It must be appreciated, however, that the journalists who arrived in Dili the day after the massacre had little initial access to eye-witness accounts. The foreigners had left East Timor, and the Timorese witnesses who had not gone to ground were, in Macintosh's words, 'terrified, traumatised or both'.[10])

In December 1991, the month after the massacre, *Inside Indonesia*, the bulletin of the Indonesia Resources and Information Program (comprising academic specialists on Indonesia and members of overseas aid agencies, development action groups and trade unions), also estimated the death toll to be at least 100 civilians. The magazine assembled the testimony of seven witnesses to the killing, including three journalists, a camera operator and a photographer, which directly contradicted official claims that the soldiers had fired in self-defence at a 'brutal mob' attacking them with stones, guns and machetes.

An American journalist, Amy Goodman, said the demonstration march had stopped at the Santa Cruz cemetery, and people were just standing around, when a military truck had come down one road, blocking that way. A long line of soldiers had come from another road. The soldiers had then opened fire on the defenceless people, and had just kept shooting. Her companion, Alan Nairn, also an American journalist, corroborated her version. He said that the soldiers on foot, hundreds of them, had brandished their M16s and walked very deliberately. 'There was a kind of stunned silence, and people started back-pedalling into the cemetery.'[11] Nairn estimated that many dozens had been killed. 'There was no provocation, no stones ... thrown. The soldiers issued no warning. They simply shot several hundred unarmed men, women and children. They chased down young boys and girls and shot them in the back.'[12] Nairn said three army trucks with bodies stacked up on them had then driven away. Both Goodman and Nairn were beaten by the soldiers.

Stephen Cox, a British photographer, reported that the soldiers on the truck had leapt off, formed a line and jogged towards the people (presumably these were not the soldiers Nairn had seen 'walking very deliberately'). Without warning, they had opened fire directly into the crowd, indiscriminately, killing all in their view. Survivors had fled down the surrounding streets, and many had been shot in the back. Cox said the sound of automatic gunfire had continued uninterrupted for between two and three minutes, followed by sporadic bursts of gunfire.

Bob Muntz, a project officer for Community Aid Abroad, an Australian overseas development agency, said intense fire had continued for about two minutes. Thousands of rounds had been fired. Renato Stefani, an Italian missionary visiting Dili, said the soldiers had fired perhaps a thousand rounds. In the cemetery, a soldier had taken out a knife and plunged it into the belly of a young Timorese and ripped it about until he died. 'It was a sea of blood. Hours after the massacre I saw bloodstains on the road—even though the soldiers had tried to scrub them out.'[13]

A quantitative analysis of Radio Australia's Indonesian news and current affairs programs in the seven days after the massacre (conducted by Radio Australia) shows that the story was given extensive coverage. In that week, of the 626 news stories in the (international) news bulletins in Indonesian, forty-five were about the Dili shootings, compared with twenty-three on other Indonesian issues. In terms of time taken up by the stories, 15.8 per cent of the total was about East Timor, and 4.5 per cent about other Indonesian issues. In the current affairs program, 'International Report', of forty-eight new items, eighteen dealt with the Dili killings and one with another Indonesian story. In terms of duration, the East Timor story took up 37.5 per cent, and the other Indonesian story 2 per cent.[14]

The following qualitative analysis of Radio Australia's coverage in the two weeks after the massacre results from a careful examination of transcripts of every one of the thousands of words broadcast, both in English and in Indonesian. An analysis of Macintosh's stories about the massacre shows that, after a cautious start, his reports were progressively more blunt. Like any good journalist, he was careful to source contentious aspects of the story, but as the story developed, he did not shy away from them. Nor did Radio Australia shy away from using his reports, and other reports guaranteed to raise the blood pressure of listening Indonesian officials. In fact, an analysis of both the news and current affairs stories about the Timor massacre on ABC radio and Radio Australia shows that Radio Australia's coverage was just as forthright as that on the home service. There was no attempt to disguise the fact that eye-witnesses and reliable sources generally presented a picture of the events greatly at variance with the version given by the Indonesian military. And the story told by Radio Australia was basically the same in the English-language and Indonesian-language programs. Most, though not all, of the stories broadcast in English were also broadcast in Indonesian. Any serious discrepancies between the versions given in the two languages would have been bad for Radio Australia's credibility, as some Indonesians listen in both languages, and would have noticed the differences.

'Shooting incident'

One minor respect in which the coverage differed in the two languages is that for the most part the Indonesians (all but one of the broadcasters and translators who staffed Radio Australia's Indonesian Section are Indonesian-born) scrupulously avoided literally translating 'massacre'. An authoritative English–Indonesian dictionary gives only one translation of 'massacre', *pembunuhan besar-besaran*, literally 'large-scale killing'.[15] But Radio Australia's Indonesian programs usually translated 'massacre' as *insiden penembakan puluhan orang sipil*, 'shooting of dozens of civilians'; *pertumpahan darah*, 'bloodshed'; *peristiwa berdarah*, 'bloody incident'; *insiden penembakan* or *peristiwa penembakan*, 'shooting incident'; or just as *penembakan*, 'shooting', or *insiden*, 'incident'. On only a few occasions did they use the words *pembunuhan massal*, 'mass killing', which is another way of saying 'massacre'.[16] Asked why the term for 'massacre' had mostly been avoided, an officer of the Indonesian section said it was 'emotive'. Apparently it was thought that its use could upset the Indonesian authorities. Asked whether he regarded the word 'massacre', used in the English-language programs, as emotive, he replied that he did. (To be fair, Radio Australia had told a parliamentary subcommittee in 1992, 'Rigid rules of verbatim translation may result in the use of language considered inappropriate by Indonesians.')[17] In their coverage of the killings in Beijing on 4 June 1989, the Indonesian broadcasters used the word *pembantaian*, literally 'butchery' or 'slaughter'. The executive producer of Indonesian programs explained that this word was not used in reports of the Dili massacre because, with perhaps fifty people killed, it was on a much smaller scale than that in Beijing, where tanks and cannons had been used, and hundreds, perhaps thousands, had been killed.

The use of euphemisms like 'shooting incident' or just 'incident' in translating 'massacre' would once have been detected by the external 'monitors' paid by Radio Australia to detect mistranslations or misreadings of prepared news scripts (deliberate or otherwise). The monitors, given scripts and tapes chosen at random, checked the accuracy of translation and delivery. But they were dispensed with in 1985, ostensibly as a cost-cutting measure.

Macintosh, reporting in English, was initially sparing in his use of the 'emotive' word, 'massacre'. In most of his early reports, he referred to the incident as 'the shooting', although in two voice reports he used the word 'carnage' to describe what had happened, and in a later one he referred to 'the Dili slaughter'. Later, when the facts became clearer, he frequently, though not always, referred to the incident as a massacre.

Macintosh's first report, sent from Jakarta on the afternoon of 12 November, was cautious. ('Cautious' here is not meant to be pejorative, but Macintosh does not consider it an accurate assessment. He made the point that 'It was to be some days before our own probing, the accounts of eye-witnesses and the military's explanations began to give us a handle on what happened and how Jakarta was reacting.')[18] Radio Australia's story quoted unconfirmed reports that there had been many deaths and injuries when Indonesian troops had fired on mourners at a cemetery in Dili. Then followed Macintosh's voice report, which began, 'Although Indonesian officials are yet to give their version of events, reliable sources here say a number of people were seen lying on the ground after the shooting,' and ended, 'Latest reports say the authorities made a number of arrests and the streets of the East Timor capital are now said to be deserted.'[19]

The following day, Radio Australia was running a report from Agence France Presse (AFP) quoting unconfirmed reports from London and Lisbon as putting the death toll at between fifty and sixty. Then it ran a report from London quoting the national campaign director of Amnesty International as saying early reports that dozens of mourners had been killed indicated 'a military out of control',[20] and Australia must immediately send a fact-finding delegation to East Timor. Shortly after this report reached Melbourne came the second account from Macintosh, this time for the current affairs program 'International Report'. Again the report was circumspect, though Macintosh later said it contained what little information was available. It began, 'It's been impossible to obtain official Indonesian comment on the shootings, and details about the incident, the events which preceded it, and the casualties resulting, remain to be confirmed.'[21] The next news agency story run by Radio Australia news quoted the Indonesian military as saying 'several people' had been killed and wounded when security forces in Dili opened fire to defend themselves from rioters. Shortly afterwards, 'International Report' reported that the Portuguese news agency Lusa had quoted an East Timorese church official as saying fifty were dead, while some estimates were even higher. The report, used in both English and Indonesian, went on to say that thousands were reported to have died in East Timor since Indonesia's military intervention in 1976 (*sic*). Meanwhile, an Radio Australia news story was saying the Australian Foreign Affairs Department had asked for urgent information from Indonesia on reports that between twenty and fifty East Timorese had been killed. Radio Australia news reported Prime Minister Bob Hawke as describing the incident as 'an appalling tragedy'.[22]

AFP was now saying some reports were claiming that the death toll could be as high as 115. At this stage, Radio Australia did not refer directly to this estimate, but Indonesia's military chief, General Try Sutrisno, provided an opportunity to make an oblique reference to such reports. Try said in Jakarta that foreign press reports that 100 were dead were far too high. At the most, he said, fifty had been killed and twenty wounded (an uncommonly high ratio of killed to wounded). He also said several people had been arrested and hand grenades, guns and knives seized. He claimed that on their march the demonstrators, shouting hysterically, had pelted shops and a police post along the way. The security forces had tried to impose order through what he called 'sympathetic and persuasive means',[23] but had failed, and the situation had become worse when an army major had been stabbed. (The story of the stabbing of the major was confirmed by an eye-witness, a Timorese student who told the Australian *Catholic Leader* by phone that it had occurred after the major had grabbed one of the flags the demonstrators were carrying.[24] But the incident took place well before the marchers reached the cemetery.) Radio Australia news quoted Nairn and Goodman as saying the shooting had been completely unprovoked, and it was not a situation that had spiralled out of control.

By now, the day after the massacre, Macintosh had arrived in Dili. With few hard facts available, his first report from the East Timor capital began on a low key. He said attempts to piece together the events which had led to the killings and their aftermath had so far provided little new information, but what had been learned appeared consistent with the official account given in Jakarta by General Try (when he had conceded that there could have been fifty deaths). But although the voice report was low-key at the beginning, Macintosh gave a pathetic account of seeing, at the back of the dusty cemetery, piles of clothing, some shoes, schoolbooks and a man's belt, all lying in the dirt. He reported that some of the items were bloodstained, though he had found no bullet holes in the clothing.

Meanwhile, the London-based East Timorese human rights organisation, Tapol, had claimed that the death toll in Dili had risen to sixty with the death of five people from injuries. Tapol also claimed that, after the massacre, several people had been rounded up and taken to the district military command, where they had been knifed to death. These claims, from a source often regarded as less than reliable, were not used by Radio Australia.

In Dili, late on the night of the day after the massacre, Macintosh gave an interview to an ABC journalist which was broadcast on the program, 'International Report'. The item began innocuously (if clumsily) enough with Macintosh's words, 'What we've seen is a town which is a good deal more heading towards normal than I understand from local residents from what it was yesterday when the place was deserted.'[25] But the interview ended with his description of finding, at the back of the cemetery, 'a pile of clothing of all sizes, some shoes, some school ... what appeared to be school exercise books'. A translation of the interview was broadcast in Indonesian.

Two days after the massacre, a report from Jakarta by the Associated Press contrasted Try's statement that no more than fifty people had been killed or hurt (sic) with an estimate by the Indonesian Legal Aid Foundation that the death toll was 115, and a statement by the Indonesian Institute for the Defence of Human Rights that independent sources said more than fifty were dead. Radio Australia did not use this report. A report that a Swiss delegate of the International Committee of the Red Cross had seen the army fire into the crowd without physical provocation of any sort was used in English, but not Indonesian. Also not translated was the word 'murders', used by Professor Herbert Feith in an interview broadcast in English, and in translation.

On the same day as the Feith interview, Radio Australia broadcast an interview which could have enraged the Indonesian authorities. The interviewee was Shirley Shackleton, the widow of Greg Shackleton, one of the five newsmen killed by soldiers at Balibo near the border of West Timor during the Indonesian invasion in 1975. Since then, Shackleton had been an unremitting campaigner against the Indonesian presence in East Timor. In the interview, she said the Australian government should quickly tell the Indonesians that they had to get their military out of East Timor. 'The military is out of control,' she said, 'and that cannot be allowed to go on.'[26] The interview was translated, and broadcast in Indonesian, though her reference to 'when the Indonesians go' in the original English was not used in the Indonesian version. The report in Indonesian which incorporated a translation of the Shackleton interview quoted Macintosh as saying it was still difficult to establish the number of victims, and he had not been able to get clarification from leaders in East Timor. But, he added, details of the shooting and the surrounding events given by local people were usually no different from the reports sent from Jakarta.

An overview of East Timor, broadcast in English and Indonesian, included an interview with Fretilin spokesman José Ramos Horta, in Portugal, in which he said Fretilin was planning a new strategy to oppose what he called Indonesia's takeover of East Timor. Much of the interview was translated into Indonesian, but not his statement that Indonesian military and intelligence officers were 'murdering the women and children in East Timor'.[27] (The journalist in charge of Radio Australia's current affairs programs said in mid-1993 that there was a ban on using Ramos Horta unless in 'a balanced package'. He said current affairs was 'circumspect' in its treatment of East Timor.)

Hawke's ultimatum

Meanwhile, Prime Minister Bob Hawke, announcing that the massacre had thrown into doubt his planned visit to Indonesia the following February, said it was time for Indonesia to sit down and talk with the people of East Timor, including the resistance. He said his visit could go ahead only if Indonesia carried out a genuine inquiry into the killings. (As it happened, Hawke never had to decide whether to make the visit: he was replaced as Prime Minister by Paul Keating the following month.) The

Indonesian-language translation of this story also quoted Bishop Carlos Belo of East Timor as saying that, although the military were saying that nineteen had been killed, the militant separatist group had told him that the death toll was 180. A fuller account of Hawke's remarks was broadcast in an Indonesian current affairs program the next day, but it did not include the damaging assertion by the bishop.

On the evening of Thursday, 14 November, Radio Australia news broadcast Macintosh's account of a news conference in Dili at which the two senior military officers in the area announced that 19 people had been killed and 91 wounded in the shooting two days beforehand. The journalists were told that some of the wounded were in a critical condition. They were shown a display of weapons, knives, guns and hand grenades, together with pro-independence banners. The generals said their troops had first fired into the air after someone in the crowd had fired a pistol into the air. They also claimed that a hand grenade had rolled from the crowd. Macintosh reported that 'The generals' account contradicted the East Timor Roman Catholic Bishop, Carlos Belo's earlier charge that no warning shots had been fired.'[28] After the news conference, he said, reporters had been escorted to a small public cemetery 12 kilometres from Dili, where they had seen 19 fresh graves, grey mounds of earth marked only by small rocks. Their military escorts told them it was not known which victim was buried in which grave.

The following morning, a fuller account from Macintosh was broadcast in 'International Report' in both languages. This time, his account said the military commanders had reported *two* officers had been stabbed, and the hand grenade that had reportedly rolled from the crowd had also become plural. Macintosh reported:

The military's version of events said there were three and a half thousand people on the streets on Tuesday morning, and as they moved through Dili in a noisy demonstration, two Indonesian officers were stabbed. One was said to be in a serious condition.

A short time later, the press conference was told, a pistol was fired into the air from within the crowd, which had reached the cemetery. Crudely modified hand grenades were produced, and we were told these had rolled from the crowd.

The officers claimed that warning shots had been fired in the air before troops and police, said to number 85, opened up on the crowd. It was claimed that a junior officer had advised them not to shoot, but that his order had been misunderstood.[29]

Macintosh was still being careful to source all his reports, but made his doubts about the military account clear by the use of words like 'the military's version', 'the press conference was told' (edited out of the broadcast version) and 'claimed'.

Ramos Horta was quoted again in a news item that Friday morning. This time he was saying that the troops had killed 'at least 100 people', and that 'the death toll could rise to 150 because some of the wounded were in a critical condition'.[30] The item then reminded its listeners that the Indonesian military said nineteen people had been killed and ninety-one injured, 'but witnesses put the number of dead at well over fifty'.

On the same morning, a special current affairs round-up, broadcast in both languages, reported a selection of estimates of the death toll. The roundup began by saying unconfirmed reports had put the death toll as high as sixty, and reports from other sources said between fifty and sixty people had died. It went on to quote the estimates of more than fifty by the Portuguese news agency, sixty by Tapol, and finally more than 100 killed or injured, by Fretilin's chief spokesman in Portugal.

Strong words were quoted in news items later that day. A report by ABC correspondent Matt Peacock in Washington said the chairman of the Congress Foreign Relations Committee had said 'the atrocity casts doubt on Indonesia's ability to be a civilised nation'.[31] A bulletin of Australian news reported angry demonstrations in Darwin and in Melbourne, where the crowd had torn down the flag at the Indonesian consulate and set it alight. The secretary of the Victorian Trades Hall Council, John Halfpenny, after saying the massacre demonstrated that the Indonesian regime was aggressive and inhuman, threatened a union boycott of Indonesian products.

Macintosh's next current affairs report from Dili would not have pleased the authorities, but he was careful to source it. And the source itself was authoritative. He quoted the East Timor governor, Mario Carrascalao, himself Timorese, as blaming the armed forces for the bloodshed, and accusing the military of using right-wing terrorists against those who favoured independence for the province. He said these terrorists often made use of their weapons and training to settle old scores. A news report in Indonesian quoted the governor as saying that, although the official death toll was nineteen, local reports said far more people had been killed. A news bulletin the following day quoted the governor as calling for a neutral investigation. He had told a leading Jakarta newspaper that the root of the problem was that a group of rioters had been able to win the hearts of many East Timorese. Two weeks later, Radio Australia news quoted the governor as again questioning the official death toll, saying he had a feeling he had seen a number of corpses in a truck, although he did not have any experience in counting bodies.

A story in a bulletin of Australian news broadcast by Radio Australia on the night of 15 November quoted the Community Aid Abroad project worker Bob Muntz, who had returned to Melbourne that day, as disputing both the official death toll and claims by the Indonesian authorities that the soldiers had opened fire after being provoked. He said that from what he had seen, there had been no provocation. He said a nurse whom he had visited several times in Dili for treatment for his own wounds had told him military authorities had estimated late on the day of the massacre that eighty-four people had died on the spot, at or inside the cemetery, and that thirteen others had died after being taken to hospital. The following morning, Radio Australia news, once again repeating the military death toll of nineteen, said that according to other sources, at least 100 had been killed.

On the Sunday after the massacre, Radio Australia reported the highest estimate of the death toll it had yet quoted. A news item reported that 'other sources', including a Portuguese priest who had witnessed the incident, had said at least 200 people had been killed. According to a report by Reuter quoted in the same item, government and military officials in East Timor were admitting that the tragedy had seriously set back their sixteen-year campaign to integrate the province into Indonesia.[32]

Some careless journalism followed. A subsequent report by Radio Australia news, apparently telescoping eye-witness accounts and estimates of the death toll by others, said 'Timorese and several Westerners' who had witnessed the shooting were saying that *more than* 100 people had been killed.[33] Later in the morning, another news bulletin reported that a priest who had been in Dili at the time of the incident (presumably not the eye-witness referred to earlier) had quoted the British cameraman who had seen the shooting as saying that *at least* 100 had been killed. Later in the day, RA news was attributing the estimate of 115 dead, originally made by the Indonesian Legal Aid Foundation, to 'eye witnesses and civil rights groups'.[34]

Macintosh, now back in Jakarta, reported on the Sunday night that Indonesia was to conduct a national inquiry into the massacre. Now that the facts were becoming clearer, his reporting was becoming more blunt. He said the decision to hold the inquiry had followed a wave of international protests, editorials in Indonesia calling for a full investigation, and persistent eye-witness reports that the carnage (a word used in the studio introduction but not in his voice report) was far worse than initially admitted by Jakarta. His voice report, after referring again to the official accounts that the troops had opened fire after being provoked by demonstrators, continued, 'But various eye-witness accounts presented a very different picture of events. As protests continued to pour in, Jakarta started a painful re-assessment of its predicament—in the words of one senior official last night, "... some of us didn't quite believe the seriousness of the matter ...".'[35]

In a voice report on the following day, Monday, 18 November, Macintosh said that, as the number of protests had continued to increase, Jakarta had started to reassess its position. 'Clearly,' he added, 'President Soeharto did. Reliable sources say he was embarrassed and upset by what he had learned.'[36] This report was broadcast in both languages.

Second massacre?

At this point, allegations of a second massacre started coming in. Timorese groups in Darwin, Sydney and London said they had received reports that up to eighty East Timorese had been killed in a shooting outside Dili. They claimed that the killings had come after hundreds of people had been picked up by the military after the original massacre. On the ABC's home service radio news, the story began bluntly with the words, 'The East Timorese news agency—based in Sydney—says it's received word of a second massacre near Dili. News agency editor Antonio Sampaio says his sources in Dili report Indonesian troops took about seventy Timorese from a local police station to a rifle range outside the city and shot them.'[37] In a subsequent story, the figure was revised to 'up to eighty'.[38] Radio Australia news was more cautious, beginning with the 'softer' lead, 'Australia's Foreign Affairs Department says that it has no information on reports of a second massacre in East Timor.'[39] The story continued by quoting a Foreign Affairs spokesman in Canberra as saying the Australian embassy in Jakarta would be asked to investigate the reports. In a story later that day, Radio Australia news reported that Australian diplomats in Indonesia had been unable to confirm the allegation. It said an Australian diplomat who was in Dili at the time reported that he had heard nothing of a second massacre. The following day, Radio Australia news quoted the military in Jakarta as strongly denying a charge by Tapol that eighty prisoners had been executed three days after the Dili shootings. Later that day, the Indonesian edition of 'International Report' quoted General Try as denying the charge. He said it was a lie whipped up by those who wanted to besmirch Indonesia. The AFP news agency later quoted witnesses in East Timor as saying the reports might have been based on the secret burial by the military of victims of the massacre the previous Tuesday.[40] A week after the report of a second massacre on 15 November, Radio Australia news reported that Fretilin's representative in Australia was alleging that another ten people had been shot outside Dili on 17 November, and seven more the following day. He alleged that they had witnessed the earlier execution of the eighty. (Macintosh, who was in Dili at the time, later said that neither he nor other reporters and diplomats in the town were able to confirm claims of a second massacre.)[41]

Radio Australia news gave detailed coverage to a picket outside the Indonesian embassy in Canberra organised by the Trades and Labour Council. The report said the picketers had set up placards reading, 'Timor … Indonesia's killing fields', together with 119 wooden crosses. True to Radio Australia's usual practice of broadcasting the same reports in both languages, these details were also reported in Indonesian.

Meanwhile, in Jakarta, Macintosh filed a story that Australia had urged Indonesia to allow the Red Cross access to those wounded in the massacre (a word he again refrained from using). He reported that Australia had also asked Jakarta to furnish the Red Cross with the names of those killed. Macintosh understood that the Red Cross had already obtained lists of people wounded and detained by the military.

Macintosh himself made news when he was one of two Australian journalists detained and questioned by police when they tried to talk to East Timorese activists who staged a peaceful protest march down Jakarta's main street. The journalists were questioned for twenty minutes about how they had learned of the demonstration, and why they were covering it. The marchers had handed a petition to the United Nations representative in Jakarta and to diplomatic missions, including the Australian embassy, calling for Indonesia to withdraw from their province. The protest, and the arrest of Macintosh and the other journalist, were reported in both English and Indonesian. One news agency reported that about fifty of the demonstrators had been arrested, but this was denied by a military spokesman, even though they had been seen being put into vehicles after their protest.[42] An Indonesian legal aid group later said seventy demonstrators were in police custody.[43] Jakarta police subsequently made nonsense of the military denial of the arrests by announcing that forty-nine of the seventy students being held would be released immediately.

The following day, Macintosh reported that the man appointed to chair the national investigative team, Supreme Court Judge Djaelani, had a strong military background. He was a military lawyer who had risen to the rank of major-general before retiring from the armed forces three years earlier. Macintosh reported that several other members of the team had armed forces connections and there were no nominees from non-government organisations or other independent bodies.[44]

Radio Australia news reported that the military commander of East Timor had announced that he would allow independent observers to visit the wounded. But they would not be able to do so until the military had finished interrogating them, because, he said, 'the sight of foreigners could make them start talking about wild rumours'.[45] So far, the report said, even relatives had been banned from visiting the wounded. The following day, another condition was reported. The commander said that, although the observers would be allowed to visit the wounded, they would not be allowed to speak to them. The International Red Cross rejected this condition as unacceptable.

By Thursday, 21 November, nine days after the massacre, Macintosh was retailing a report by the official Indonesian news agency that, according to Home Affairs Minister Rudini, life in East Timor had returned to normal. 'According to the official Antara news agency,' Macintosh continued, 'the minister, who met here yesterday with East Timor's provincial governor … said the Timorese were no longer gripped by fear.'[46] He reported that, according to Antara, Rudini had described the Dili slaughter (Macintosh's word) as 'only a small incident', and urged people not to be influenced by foreign press reports. All this was duly broadcast in Indonesian as well as English, but with the word 'slaughter' translated as *peristiwa penembakan*, 'shooting incident'.

The next day, it was reported in both languages that the chairman of the Australian parliament's new sub-committee on human rights, Senator Chris Schacht, had announced plans to hold public hearings on the massacre. A voice report by a current affairs reporter in Canberra said Schacht had described the massacre as 'this extraordinary abuse of human rights', and said it was clear that after sixteen years the people of East Timor had not accepted incorporation into Indonesia. The report continued:

Senator Schacht said it was quite clear that the excuse that the soldiers suddenly panicked and started shooting did not really stand up—the video coverage gave a fair indication that there was some forethought given to the shooting that took place.
    The Senator also said he was appalled by reports that the Indonesian Armed Forces Commander, General Try Sutrisno, had said East Timorese dissidents should be wiped out. [This statement had been reported in some Australian newspapers, but not by Radio Australia.]
    And he was equally angered by reported comments from the Indonesian commander in Dili that it was all right for his troops to keep firing for 10 minutes.[47]

Even stronger words were used a few days later in a Radio Australia news report of a Labor Party resolution which referred to Try's comments about the massacre as 'nauseating'. This story was translated literally into Indonesian, 'massacre' being translated as *pembunuhan massal*, 'mass killing'.[48]

Nairn and Goodman were back in the United States, telling their story to anyone who was interested. Nairn was reported to have a fractured skull. Goodman said the fact that she was American and not Australian may have saved her life. When she was lying on the ground, the soldiers had pointed M16s to her head:

Ms Goodman says the soldiers repeated 'Australia' several times, while she and Mr Nairn kept on saying that they were from the United States. She says she has little doubt the soldiers would have treated them much worse if they had been Australians.[49]

The report was broadcast in both languages.

Two weeks after the massacre, Amnesty International presented Indonesia with a list of the names of 60 people it said had been killed, repeating the claim that the total death toll was more than 100. Most of the sixty dead named by the organisation were said to be schoolchildren aged between fifteen and twenty. Macintosh's voice report was one of the few at that stage in which he used the word 'massacre'. But the Indonesian translation of his piece referred, as usual, to the 'shooting incident'.

The next day, a BBC report from New York said an Indonesian government report on the massacre suggested that the death toll might be higher than admitted by officials. It had said there were many more soldiers and demonstrators present than previously reported. The BBC's United Nations correspondent, who claimed to have seen the official report, said it appeared the Indonesian government had publicly played down the number of protesters to suggest a lower level of disaffection in East Timor.

As the evidence mounted, Macintosh's reporting was progressively becoming less cautious. Reporting on Try's evidence before a parliamentary committee hearing in Jakarta, he said the commander-in-chief had restated his subordinates' previous claims that troops and police in Dili on 12 November had been provoked, 'a charge which has been consistently contradicted by eye-witnesses to the killings'.[50] He went on to report that, 'illustrating the unchanged state of the military's version of events in Dili, General Try at one stage broke from his presentation in *bahasa Indonesia* to say of the Dili crowd, in English, "Peaceful demonstration? Bullshit!" '

The commission of inquiry handed down its preliminary report late in December, more than six weeks after the massacre. President Soeharto ordered that it be made public. Not surprisingly, it contradicted the official armed forces death toll. The commission found strong grounds for believing that about 50 people had died, more than 91 had been injured and another 90 were still missing. It also criticised the actions of the military in

Dili on 12 November, although it concluded that the killings were not the result of an order or policy of the armed forces. But it supported the claims of the armed forces that the troops had fired in self-defence after being provoked by the demonstrators.

Sentenced to Harvard

The treatment of the preliminary report by Radio Australia news was forthright. The story led with the finding that about fifty people had died, and contrasted that figure with the earlier official death toll of nineteen. It went on to list the figures of more than ninety-one wounded and about ninety missing, quoting the preliminary report as saying the ninety missing could either be dead, wounded or in hiding. Although the story was based on Macintosh's report, his name was not mentioned in the version broadcast except in a 'throw-away line', 'Ian Macintosh says President Soeharto is expected to comment on the report's conclusions within the next few days.'[51]

Radio Australia current affairs treated the story more cautiously. The day after the news reports (which were broadcast on the Boxing Day public holiday in Australia), 'International Report' began:

> More than six weeks after Indonesian troops fired on a crowd in the East Timor provincial capital, Dili, the commission of inquiry established by President Soeharto has handed down its preliminary report. The initial conclusions of the seven-member commission ... contradicted the official armed forces tally of people killed and wounded in the bloodshed and contained other criticisms of the military's actions in Dili on November 12th.[52]

It was not until two minutes into the voice report that Macintosh mentioned the toll of dead, injured and missing. But he said later that this was not a result of self-censorship. He pointed out that, as these details had been run in every news bulletin for twelve hours, 'it was clearly good radio current affairs style to take a different tack'.[53]

The inquiry's final report was said to be six to eight weeks away. But it was never released. Macintosh said in September 1992 that it had been in Soeharto's hands for more than a month, perhaps in his too-hard basket. He said that maybe the authorities were hoping people would forget.[54] Later, it was explained that the interim report was in fact the 'executive report', and that the final decisions rested with the president and the government. In mid-1993, Macintosh reported that the military had revised the number of people still 'missing' down to sixty-four. He pointed out discrepancies in various figures previously cited by the Indonesian authorities, and said the latest statement had been greeted with scepticism by some foreign diplomats.[55]

The treatment meted out to those responsible for the clash was uneven, to say the least. Thirteen demonstrators were charged—eight in East Timor and five who took part in the peaceful demonstration in Jakarta a week later. Four of them, two in Dili and two in Jakarta, faced charges under Indonesia's controversial anti-subversion law, which carries a maximum penalty of death. One of the Dili pair was gaoled for life, and the other was sentenced to fifteen years' gaol. In Jakarta, the two East Timorese charged with subversion were gaoled for ten and nine years respectively. The other nine men were convicted of criminal charges, their prison sentences ranging from ten years to six months.

As for the military, one of the generals responsible and two other senior officers were dismissed. The second general went to study at Harvard, and has since returned to Indonesia. Three other senior officers were removed from active duty, two permanently and one temporarily. According to *Tempo* news magazine in Jakarta, one other senior officer was to be pensioned at the youngest permissible age, three were returned to their units and 'given further guidance', and a fifth was exonerated.[56] In mid-1992, nine soldiers of lower rank and one police corporal were sentenced to gaol terms of between eight and eighteen months.

Despite their caution, Macintosh and Radio Australia were criticised both by some Australians and by Indonesian officials for their reporting of the massacre. According to the *Jakarta Post* newspaper, the speaker of the Indonesian parliament, Kharis Suhud, told visiting Australian Foreign Minister Gareth Evans that Radio Australia's reports on East Timor 'hurt our ears'. He was not convinced by Senator Evans's assurance that Radio Australia was independent. 'It is receiving grants from the government', he retorted, 'so it could still be controlled, though not 100 per cent.'[57] Indonesian officials were even more unhappy with some other accounts. Dozens of foreign journalists, including some Australians, were banned from entering the country in response to international media coverage of the massacre. Jakarta-based foreign correspondents were kept out of East Timor for most of 1992. They were readmitted in numbers only when the trial of captured Fretilin leader Xanana Gusmao began early in 1993.

Officials of Evans's department were reported to be happy with Macintosh's coverage. Asked his opinion in February 1992, the assistant secretary, Southeast Asia, of the Department of Foreign Affairs and Trade, Kevin Boreham, said Macintosh had been 'a model example of how to handle reporting from Indonesia over such a sensitive issue like East Timor'.[58]

Asked in 1993 what his aims had been in covering the story, Macintosh replied, 'Purely to report as comprehensively as I could what was happening there. I took the view that the shots had to be called from the scene.'[59] As soon as word of the massacre had reached Jakarta, he had flown to East Timor, without waiting for permission from the Indonesian authorities. The result was that, for the first time in many years, perhaps for the first time ever, voice reports had been sent direct from East Timor and heard in Australia (and by Radio Australia's millions of listeners) on the same day. Asked if it was possible that the massacre was a military conspiracy, Macintosh replied that this was possible, as the army had known that the demonstration was planned.

Some believed Macintosh's reporting was circumspect as a result of his delicate position. Broinowski said in 1992, 'I know that he has taken a fairly measured approach towards certain stories. He realises I imagine that he could very easily get removed from Jakarta. At the same time, we are satisfied that he is covering the news in an objective and responsible way.'[60]

Tiffen (referring to Indonesian journalists) wrote in 1990:

In Southeast Asian journalism, there seems to be wide acceptance that news reporting should pay attention to its likely consequences, that if a story were likely to cause a race riot or religious violence, it should not be published. There is what we might broadly label a culture of caution, an ethic of restraint, based upon the experience of fear of widespread social conflict and disorder.[61]

Tiffen went on to quote Geertz: 'There can be very few Indonesians now who do not know that, however clouded, the abyss is there, and they are scrambling along the edge of it.'[62] Although both were writing about Indonesian journalists, what they have to say applies, to a lesser degree, to foreign journalists working in Indonesia.

Some self-censorship is inevitable when correspondents are working in an authoritarian country. When David Jenkins (then working for the Melbourne *Herald*) and the author were based in Jakarta in the early 1970s, both were well aware of stories of corruption in high places, and knew that the President's wife, Tien Soeharto, was widely referred to in private as *Ibu Tien Per Sen* (Mother Ten Per Cent), a reference to the percentage she was reputed to demand for her support for commercial ventures.[63] But none of the foreign correspondents, including Jenkins, wrote about either: they were well aware that such an indiscretion would have brought about expulsion from Indonesia, and probably the closure of their offices.

Jenkins said in 1986 that foreign correspondents who wanted to remain in Indonesia were obliged to trim their sails to the Ministry of Information wind, or face the consequences. In particular, they were 'under

Hu Ring, exchange
broadcaster from
Beijing Broadcasting
Institute, 1988–9.
(© Radio Australia)

Indonesian
broadcaster Ebet
Kadarusman—
'Stranger on the
Shore' (see page 170).
(© Radio Australia)

An armchair ride for
Margaret Wood,
compère of the forces
request program which
was broadcast daily to
Australian forces
overseas.
(© Radio Australia)

A student in Beijing
listens to Radio
Australia.

A correspondence
officer with part of the
avalanche of mail from
Chinese listeners in
the 1970s, before
Radio Australia asked
them not to write.
(© Radio Australia)

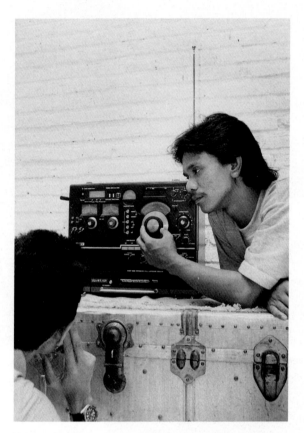

Listeners in Jakarta
tune in to Radio
Australia.

Indonesian
broadcaster Hidayat
Djajamihardja and
Director Peter Barnett
during a prime
ministerial visit to
Radio Australia.
(© Radio Australia)

Keith Glover, compere
of 'Mailbag' for
twenty-five years.
(© Radio Australia)

John Royle (seated), the ABC announcer who put Radio Australia to air in 1939, with George Ivan Smith, who arranged the first broadcasts. Behind them is Rudi Munir, now executive producer of the Indonesian service. (© Radio Australia)

Top: Don Hook, as acting editor, with chief sub-editor Alan Tye. (© Radio Australia)

Supervisor Doug
Helleur (left) and staff
of the Japanese
service, which was
closed in 1990.
(© Radio Australia)

Indonesian
broadcaster Murtjono
checks a taped
program.
(© Radio Australia)

Broadcaster Nuim
Khaiyath reads one of
the first news updates
in Indonesian on
Australia Television.
(© Radio Australia)

Top: Foreign
correspondent Ian
Macintosh in East Timor
with the lawyer of
gaoled Fretilin leader
Xanana Gusmao.

more or less formal instructions' to avoid writing in any substantive ways about what might be called 'the trilogy of taboo topics': the position and business interests of the first family; the role of the armed forces; and anything which might inflame ethnic or religious tensions; particularly matters touching on the position of the small but economically powerful Chinese community.[64] He said, 'the threat of expulsion is such that the correspondents will, in most cases, apply a form of self-censorship so extensive that few officials could reasonably complain'. Jenkins described as 'sensible and to the point' the advice of former foreign minister Bill Hayden, that in writing articles likely to offend, 'journalists might want to consider their own self-interest and continued access to the country in question'.[65] Jenkins later commented, 'It's better to have three-quarters of the pineapple than no pineapple at all.' When he wrote the story,[66] the result was the prohibition of future visits by him and several other Australian journalists, as well as a rift in diplomatic relations between Australia and Indonesia.

During his two-year term, which ended in July 1993, Macintosh covered all of the 'trilogy of taboo topics', including the business interests of the Soeharto family and massacres in the staunchly Muslim province of Aceh as well as in East Timor.[67] Like Foreign Affairs, senior officers of Radio Australia were pleased with his performance. At the end of his term, Macintosh said he was not aware of having exercised self-censorship at any stage of his coverage of the Dili massacre and its aftermath. He said the return of the ABC to Indonesia had been unconditional, and his intention was simply 'to report accurately and as comprehensively as the circumstances and our resources permitted'.[68] This analysis of his coverage, and that of Radio Australia, during the fortnight following the Dili massacre, seems to show that, during that period, this goal was substantially accomplished.

11 | Voice of Australia

The ways in which Radio Australia has operated as an instrument of foreign policy, indeed of Australian propaganda, have not been limited to the pressures and influence of the Department of Foreign Affairs on its selection and treatment of news and current affairs. Many other forces have helped ensure that Radio Australia has operated as the voice of Australia. These forces have included the selection of staff, self-censorship, the selection of target priorities, English-teaching programs, and promotional programs.

Selection of staff

Governments and government departments have had considerable influence on the selection of those in positions of power. Since the ABC took permanent control of Radio Australia in 1950, those in positions of power have included successive chairmen, chief executives and members of the commission (since 1983, corporation). The selection of chief executives of the ABC has been to a greater or lesser degree political, none more so than the selection of David Hill, a former adviser to the Wran Labor government in New South Wales, as the second managing director of the Australian Broadcasting Corporation in July 1986.

Not surprisingly, it has been unusual for a government to appoint one of its ideological opponents as ABC chairman, although, according to the ABC's historian, the politics of Boyer, appointed by a Labor government in

1945, were 'those of the Australian Woolgrowers' Council'.[1] Some chairmen have played an important role in the policies of Radio Australia and, together with the commissioners (now the board of the corporation), in the selection of senior ABC executives, including those with a say in the choice of the senior executives of Radio Australia.

The chairman who, after Boyer, had most influence on Radio Australia was Darling. When he retired as headmaster of Geelong Grammar School, one suggestion was that he should stand for preselection to be a Liberal Party candidate for the Senate.[2] He declined, but his political sympathies remained conservative.[3] It must have been a serious disappointment for the Menzies government which appointed him that, while not ideologically opposed to it, he was a champion of the integrity and independence of the overseas service.

The position of chief executive of Radio Australia has been crucial not only because of the direct power of the person holding the position, but also because of the influence of the chief executive in appointing staff to positions at the next most senior levels. Executives tend to choose likeminded people as subordinates. Once appointed, the subordinates and the executives who have had most influence in their appointment tend to reinforce each other in their attitudes and approach.[4]

Some governments have played a direct part in the selection of the chief executive of Radio Australia; others have had a strong influence on the process. But not all the chief executives of the service have been the same political colour as the government of the day. The first director was, politically, an odd choice for a conservative government, the Menzies government of 1939-41. Macmahon Ball had lectured on Marxism during the 1930s, and his political sympathies were with the Labor Party. One of the students who attended those lectures was the man chosen to succeed him when he resigned in 1944. Geoffrey Sawer was a logical choice: in addition to his qualifications and experience, he was also sympathetic to the Labor government, and in fact he had known Evatt before the war, when he had been an active member of the Melbourne University Labor Club.[5]

After Sawer's dismissal, he was replaced by another supporter of the Labor Party, Thomas Hoey (whose wartime role as Victorian State Censor had been the antithesis of a positive role in communication). Hoey did not long survive the victory of Menzies in the 1949 election because, according to Robin Wood, who succeeded him, he was too closely associated with the Chifley government. Wood said that, after the defeat of Chifley, 'word went out' that a certain number of people in Radio Australia had to be dismissed because they were allied to the Department of Information under Calwell.

Wood, on secondment from the ABC to the Department of Information, had worked under Hoey as program manager. He was a friend of Hoey (they had married step-sisters), but was of a different political colour. He said later he thought it had been known that he was a Liberal voter when he was appointed as the ABC's first supervisor of programs, overseas. It was the beginning of the end for Hoey. After losing his job, he began drinking heavily. His pre-war employer, the *Argus*, would not give him a job, nor would the Melbourne *Herald*. As state publicity censor during the war, he had heavily censored both of them. He ended his journalistic career reporting bowls for the *Age*.[6]

One of the most remarkable episodes in the selection of Radio Australia's chief executives was the choice of an Englishman who had never worked in radio to succeed Wood. The fact that the appointee, Peter Homfray, was not an Australian and had been Liberal candidate for the Tasmanian Legislative Assembly brought criticism of his appointment by Calwell in parliament, as discussed below. In August 1956, Wood had been promoted to the position of director of programs for the ABC. Robert Horne, who had worked to him as talks editor, acted in Wood's position, director of programs, overseas, for nearly twelve months. But he was unable to apply for it because he could not pass the necessary medical examination for a permanent appointment.

The Department of External Affairs was concerned that the job should go to a man who suited its purposes. It feared that the ABC might appoint 'an ABC officer who is not readily adaptable to or interested in the special functions of Radio Australia'.[7] A senior officer of the department suggested to the minister, Casey, that he might wish to speak to Boyer and 'indicate a hope that the appointment will go to someone who will give to Radio Australia the same efficient and enthusiastic service as Mr Wood has given'. Casey obliged. In a personal letter beginning 'My Dear Dick' and signed simply 'Yours, Dick', he wrote: 'I venture to mention this subject in the hope and expectation that you will appoint a really good man, who will give to Radio Australia the same efficient and enthusiastic service as Robin Wood has done.'[8]

Peter Homfray had a colourful background. He joined the British army in 1940 and trained to be an officer in India. During his eight years in South Asia he was nothing if not versatile. He served in the Indian intelligence corps (where he worked to Major-General Walter Joseph (Bill) Cawthorne, later director of the Australian Secret Intelligence Service)[9] and as aide-de-camp to the Governor of Burma (whose daughter he married), and was appointed founder-director of the statistics office in Delhi. He got to know Casey during his time as Governor of Bengal from 1944 to 1946, an acquaintance which was to be renewed when Homfray was director of Radio Australia and Casey was Minister for External Affairs.

Although Homfray had broadcast 'fairly frequently' on All India Radio during his time as director of the statistics office, he said later that he regarded his main qualification to be head of Radio Australia as his flair for administration—for administering to the needs and requirements of a multi-lingual, multi-racial group of people.[10]

In September 1948, Homfray emigrated to Australia, where eventually he moved to Tasmania, returned to farming (he had been born on a farm in Kent), and became a local councillor and a member of the Liberal Party.[11] It was here that he acquired an influential patron, Dame Enid Lyons, the widow of a prime minister, and herself a former minister, who described herself as 'the mother figure of Australian public life'.[12] She was also a commissioner of the ABC. Lyons told Homfray it was about time he 'stopped farming and did something for the country of your adoption'.

She asked him if he would be interested in a role in Radio Australia, believing, said Homfray, that he might be 'an appropriate person to look after the destiny of Radio Australia'.[13] After Lyons spoke to ABC general manager Moses about Homfray, he was invited to go to Melbourne in February 1956 to meet the full commission. At this stage, Wood had not applied for promotion to a more senior position, but Moses apparently felt that it was only a matter of time before he did. (Wood said later that he had never felt under any pressure to relinquish his position as director.)[14]

After Wood had been promoted the following August, Moses encouraged Homfray to apply for his position. But it could be filled only from inside the ABC, so Homfray was made the ABC's supervisor of talks in Victoria 'as a means to an end'.[15] He then applied for the position, and the commission appointed him director of programs, overseas, with effect from 1 July 1957. Homfray later believed that Casey, remembering him from their days in South Asia, might have had a hand in his appointment, as well as Lyons.[16] But the evidence is that, far from supporting his appointment, Casey did his best to discourage it. Homfray had earlier applied to join the Department of External Affairs, but Casey felt that his outlook tended to be British rather than Australian, and the application was unsuccessful. Casey recalled later that when Homfray's appointment to head Radio Australia was first suggested, 'I did all I could to discourage Boyer from appointing him.' The minister added philosophically that 'in spite of this, he has been appointed—and so we have to make the best of it'.[17]

Soon after taking up his position, Homfray summarised his views about the service in a statement which was acknowledged enthusiastically by Moses. The department's Radio Australia liaison officer, Noel Goss, sent a copy to Canberra, with an accompanying note saying, in part,

Mr Homfray has had considerable experience in parts of Asia and to this extent his appointment as Director of Overseas Programmes is to be welcomed. He has not however been in Asia for some years and he appears convinced of his own competence and authority to determine the foreign policy of the country at least as far as Radio Australia is concerned.[18]

The secretary of the department, Arthur Tange, scrawled some caustic comments in the margin of Homfray's statement. Beside a reference to Australia's 'mission to help the Asian peoples towards a greater understanding of our way of life', Tange wrote: 'Why not just call it a political objective.' Beside an assertion that,'With more than half the world's population on Australia's doorstep, she cannot hope to stand alone or ally herself permanently with countries with no physical roots in Asia', Tange, a believer in the centrality of the American alliance, simply wrote: 'Oh dear.'[19] An officer of the department sent the statement to Casey with the note: 'Herewith a somewhat rhetorical note by Homfray ... I think that we shall have to bring him up here, explain just what we are doing, how we are doing it and what we hope to achieve through this medium.' After meeting Homfray in Canberra, Casey agreed that his statement was 'rather rhetorical and airy-fairy'. He added: 'Confidentially I can say that I think Homfray has got a good deal to learn—as indeed I think you and I agreed when his appointment was first suggested.'[20]

Calwell, who had a running battle with Moses over many years, raised an outcry in parliament over his latest senior appointment:

I want to protest as vigorously as I can against his policy of refusing to appoint Australians to important positions in the Commission, and his preference for Englishmen in high positions in the ABC service ... the worst feature of all the skulduggery which is operating in the Australian Broadcasting Commission was the appointment of a man named Homfrey—I think that is the way it is spelt—to take charge of Radio Australia over the heads of many members of the staff of the ABC who have had years and years of experience, and who are sickened and disheartened by the treatment they have received. Now this man Homfrey was a Liberal Party candidate in Tasmania ... He claimed to be an expert on Asian affairs, but I know the Department of External Affairs laughs at him and his pretensions ... Moses, in that sickening, slimy way he has ... waited until the Parliament closed down before he confirmed the appointment of Homfrey ... When I know that this man Homfrey was a Liberal Party candidate in Tasmania within the last two years, and has been appointed over the heads of many who had served with the Commission for years and years, I think there is a real cause for protest by the parliament ... Moses, who is an Englishman, whose place is really with the British Broadcasting Corporation, is attempting to prevent Australians from securing high positions in the ABC service.[21]

Homfray attributes his eventual fall from grace at Radio Australia to the hostility of Prime Minister Gough Whitlam in the early 1970s. When he met Margaret Whitlam at the opening of Papua New Guinea House in Canberra in 1973, she took him to meet her husband. Whitlam, unable to hear her introduction over the noise of the crowd, asked Homfray who he was. Homfray replied in his very pukka accent, 'Peter Homfray, Mr Whitlam, director of Radio Australia.' 'With a voice like that?' the Prime Minister responded, and turned on his heel.[22]

Homfray said that, from that time, Whitlam constantly criticised him and Radio Australia in messages which reached the ABC's general manager, Talbot Duckmanton. But, as recorded earlier (p. 132), records now made public for the first time show that Duckmanton had his own reasons for wanting to replace him.

When Homfray finally lost his job, his logical successor as director of overseas services was his editor, Philip Koch. Nothing remains in the archives to indicate the extent of support by the government or External Affairs for his appointment. But he had a number of good friends in the department, including Keith Shann, who had been ambassador in Jakarta when Koch was ABC correspondent there. In the years he had been editor of Radio Australia, his liaison with the department had been harmonious. Whether or not the department actively supported him for the position of director, it certainly did nothing to oppose his promotion.

Koch's successor as director, Peter Barnett, was strongly supported by the department. He had for several years been the ABC's correspondent in Washington, where he had ingratiated himself with President Lyndon Johnson and Lady Bird (whom it was reported he addressed as 'dear lady'). He had impressed Duckmanton by getting him a three-and-a-half-hour audience with the President in the Oval Office during one of the general manager's visits to Washington.[23] When in mid-1969 the ABC announced that Barnett was to be brought out of Washington to be news editor of Radio Australia, a draft submission to the minister, Freeth, said he was 'well and favourably known to officers of this Department'.[24]

The following year, the Australian Security Intelligence Organisation regarded Barnett as an exception to the rule that it could not give formal security clearances to journalists, 'even Radio Australia ones'. He was regarded as 'completely acceptable' to receive proposed confidential briefings from the department. A report on the proposal by the department's public information officer said:

Mr Barnett is well, and I believe favourably, known to the Secretary [Waller] and to Sir J. Plimsoll, among others. I know him well personally and have a high regard to him [*sic*]. His brother was in the embassy in Djakarta for some years. [This brother, Tudor Harvey Barnett, was in fact the station commander in Jakarta of the Australian Secret Intelligence Service and was to become director-general of ASIO in 1981.][25]

But the report pointed out that, if the department gave confidential briefings to Barnett, this would create a precedent for his successors. This 'could be awkward in certain circumstances', though such circumstances seemed unlikely to arise, since Radio Australia's senior officers were 'aware of the need for a sound relationship with the Department'. In a frank admission of the department's influence in the selection of the senior officers of Radio Australia, the report went on to say that the organisation 'would be unlikely to appoint someone to the News Editor's position who was unsatisfactory to the Department'.[26]

After two years as news editor, Barnett returned to Washington, where he found favour with some of Johnson's successors. (For years as director of Radio Australia he had on his desk an autographed photograph of Jimmy Carter with his hands on the shoulders of Barnett's only son.) When Duckmanton suggested that he apply to be director in 1979, the department had no doubts about his appreciation of the importance to Australia of the American alliance.

Perhaps the most surprising choice as chief executive of Radio Australia was Barnett's successor, appointed in late 1989, on the eve of the fiftieth anniversary of the service. After the long struggle for independence from the Department of Foreign Affairs, a senior officer of the department, Richard Broinowski (at one stage the department's Radio Australia liaison officer), was appointed as the first general manager of Radio Australia. When he applied for the position, Broinowski was Australia's ambassador to South Korea.

There were some who saw the appointment as setting a fox to guard the chickens. But the evidence so far available suggests that his appointment was due more to the determination of David Hill than to the influence of the department. Two members of the four-person selection committee, the ABC's assistant managing director, Stuart Revill, and its radio director, Malcolm Long (promoted in 1992 to be assistant managing director), are reported to have favoured an internal applicant for the position, Geoff Heriot, Radio Australia's controller of news and current affairs. A third member of the committee, Joan Spiller, a member of the corporation's board, reportedly had no strong views either way. But it is reported that Hill—a forceful man—was determined that the job should be offered to Broinowski, and pressured the committee into choosing him.

When he took up his new position on 17 January 1991, Broinowski was the first diplomat ever appointed chief executive of a service which for more than fifteen years had been administered by journalists. He reportedly said, 'I'm not a journalist, but I see some similarities between the profession of diplomat and journalist.' In an article in the *Age,* the author expressed the fear that the appointment could end Radio Australia's relative freedom from control by the Department of Foreign Affairs and Trade.[27] The article contended that, although he might come to the position with the best of intentions, it would be difficult, if not impossible, for him to turn his back on a lifetime of conditioning. 'Will a diplomat', it asked, 'be able to put his conditioning to one side when crucial decisions have to be made about what Radio Australia's news and current affairs programs should reveal and what, if anything, they should conceal?' Broinowski responded by asserting that he intended to be 'completely objective and reinforce the independence and objectivity of Radio Australia'.[28]

Broinowski said in late 1991,

I am still professionally a diplomat; I still feel an attachment to the Department of Foreign Affairs; I still have the option under the mobility provisions of the Public Service Act to rejoin the department if I wish. My options are all open, including staying with the ABC and moving beyond Radio Australia to other parts of the ABC. I just don't know what I am going to do yet.[29]

Broinowski did in fact return to the department after his replacement as director of Radio Australia the following year.

Time, and the release of documents now classified, will show the extent to which he carried out this promise. But the evidence available so far is that, right up to his sudden removal by Hill on 10 April 1992, he was careful to keep his department (of which he remained a substantive officer) at arm's length and not to give directions to Radio Australia's staff which could be seen as trying to make the service an overt instrument of foreign policy. On at least one occasion, as a former ambassador to South Korea, he wanted to go to air to comment on a Korean issue, but he was talked out of it. In fact, there were some reports that relations between Radio Australia and Foreign Affairs deteriorated during his two years in the job. Some of his shortcomings in the job resulted not from the fact that he was an officer of Foreign Affairs, but from his lack of experience in journalism or broadcasting, and his inexperience in budget management.

The new general manager, Derek White, was reportedly one of the many ABC executives who had fallen out with David Hill. Nevertheless, he had a reputation as a 'fixer', with skills in administration and budgeting, and was sent from Sydney to Melbourne to 'fix' Radio Australia. At the time of his appointment, Hill described him as 'one of the ABC's most experienced editorial executives'.[30] But his experience was largely in a series of managerial positions. White had never been a foreign correspondent in Asia or the Pacific, and there were gaps in his knowledge of Radio Australia's target areas. (He was puzzled by the use of the term, 'South Asia', to refer to the sub-continent, thinking that South Asia included Southeast Asia.[31] This was more than a little surprising, as the Revill report named South Asia as a major priority[32] and one of Radio Australia's executives was designated 'Manager South & South-East Asia Region'.[33])

In October 1993, Hill gave White an additional responsibility, as assistant director of ABC Radio, Victoria. This seemed to suggest that Hill did not regard Radio Australia as significant enough to claim the full attention of a chief executive, although White explained that in fact the job had been created to achieve closer relations between Radio Australia and ABC Radio.[34] He was loaded with even more responsibility in February 1994, when he was appointed to the new position of general manager of ABC international broadcasting, with responsibility for both Radio Australia and Australia Television.[35]

Some Radio Australia executives have worked in intelligence. William Petrie, the talks officer who for several years was responsible for the politically sensitive news commentaries, was an officer of the Joint Intelligence Bureau of the Department of Defence before joining Radio Australia.[36] Most of the linguists selected to supervise Radio Australia's foreign-language sections had 'a service background carrying with it an effective immunity to left wing propaganda',[37] a number of them having been intelligence officers. Most were graduates of the RAAF school of languages at Point Cook, Victoria, who are 'by far the most competent linguists in Australia'.[38] Point Cook provides language training to intelligence officers of all the armed services and of the security and intelligence services. John Dudley, who for eighteen years was Radio Australia's supervisor, Chinese, had previously served in the defence signals division of the Defence Department,[39] and after joining Radio Australia remained a commander in the naval reserve. In 1983, another five supervisors or assistant supervisors of foreign-language sections (Indonesian, Chinese, Japanese and Thai) were Point Cook graduates. In 1985, Dudley was promoted to the second most senior position in Radio Australia, controller of overseas programs.

The influence of the Department of Foreign Affairs in the selection of Radio Australia executives has extended to the choice of ABC foreign correspondents, who have also served as correspondents for Radio Australia. In May 1969, the ambassador in Jakarta, Gordon Jockel, said in a personal letter to a first assistant secretary of the department:

I wonder if the Minister and/or the Department are sinking their teeth into the ABC over the adventures of their youngsters in Djakarta or trying to define the relationship between the Government and Radio Australia? If it is 'all too difficult', I wonder if the Department could go for more mature representation by the ABC in Djakarta. This year there have been three relief persons [the author was one of them] in charge of the ABC/Radio Australia office and our best guess is that the present youth is to be relieved in July by Michael Carlton, who is about 24 years old and, when here previously, did not think it was part of his job to consult seriously with the Embassy.[40]

The recipient doubted whether Jockel's suggestion was practicable. Forwarding the letter to a subordinate, he jotted: 'How far is this in our power? But it wd be a possible approach.'

In a follow-up telegram to the department, Jockel said:

I SHOULD LIKE THE DEPARTMENT TO THINK ABOUT WORKING ON DUCKMAN-TON TO GET THE ABC STAFF POSITION IN DJAKARTA STABILIZED ... A MATURE AND EXPERIENCED PERSON IS VERY MUCH NEEDED IN THE INTERESTS OF BOTH THE GOVERNMENT AND THE ABC ITSELF. THE FOREIGN CORRESPONDENTS HERE ARE A VOLATILE GROUP, WITH A STRONG AUSTRALIAN ELEMENT, AND THERE IS A NATURAL TENDENCY FOR THE YOUTHFUL ABC STAFF TO BE OVER INFLUENCED BY THEM. THIS BEING SO I INTEND TO PROCEED CAUTIOUSLY ABOUT TAKING THE ABC STAFF INTO MY CONFIDENCE FOR DISCREET AND PRIVATE TALKS.[41]

A memo, prompted by Jockel's complaint, said, in part:

Throughout the ABC, extending to the very top of management and to the Commission itself, there is an inherent resistance to any formal suggestions coming from this Department as to how the ABC should do its job. It is possible, however, on an informal basis, to convey views—even on the subject of staffing.

The officer who wrote the memo also said he had already intended to suggest to James Plimsoll that in conversations he had from time to time with the general manager of the ABC he might mention 'the deterioration in the quality' of the ABC's diplomatic correspondent in Canberra (who worked largely to Radio Australia). He added: 'I propose therefore that the matter of the calibre of the ABC's representatives in Djakarta could be a second subject which the Secretary could raise informally with the General Manager of the ABC.'[42]

Laurence McIntyre, the department's acting secretary, told one of his officers that the matter might be raised informally with the ABC on an appropriate occasion 'which we ourselves might contrive'.[43] A fortnight later, McIntyre told Walter Hamilton about the unhappiness with the ABC's representation in Indonesia. He said that, 'Although we as a Department in Canberra, and our representatives abroad, were supposed in theory to treat all news-gathering agencies alike, we tended in practice to treat the ABC as slightly more equal than others, and we instinctively expected the ABC to be correspondingly responsive.' Hamilton agreed that the ABC's current representation in Jakarta was not as good as it should be. The ABC was hoping to put in a more experienced reporter as soon as they could.[44] At the beginning of the following year, the author was sent there for a two-year posting.

Self-censorship

A second force which ensures that Radio Australia is to an extent an instrument of foreign policy is self-censorship. Before proceeding to an examination of the effect of deliberate self-censorship, it should be acknowledged that Radio Australia has had a built-in bias because most of its journalists (including its foreign correspondents), and all except one of its chief executives, have been Australians who have seen the world from a particular perspective.

In addition to the unconscious biases of its journalists and broadcasters, self-censorship, by correspondents in the field and the reporters, sub-editors, producers, editors and directors of Radio Australia, has been a seldom-acknowledged but ever-present force in shaping its news and current affairs broadcasts. Journalists, obviously, have an incentive not only to make decisions which will not prejudice future promotion or even lead to job loss, but also to make decisions which will not incur the displeasure of supervisors.

Peter Homfray, the man who headed Radio Australia for eighteen years—far longer than any other executive—has questioned the extent to which Radio Australia really has a free hand in determining its policy in programming. He said the 'veneer of independence' remained only as long as the staff 'stick to the rules of international broadcasting'. The first rule, he said, was not to create a diplomatic rift between Australia and any country in which it had representation. Other rules, few of them written, 'depend on common sense, instinct, responsibility and natural courtesy more than anything else'.[45]

Self-censorship is sometimes justified on grounds of journalistic pragmatism. In early 1969 Radio Australia's news editor, Lachlan Shaw, told Broinowski, then a Radio Australia liaison officer, that his staff had 'voluntarily exercised a good deal of discretion over reporting on West Irian', and gave some examples of the care he had taken with reports. For example, he had voluntarily refrained from using any item about statements by West Irian rebels who were overseas[46] (a practice not always followed subsequently by Radio Australia in regard to East Timorese rebels overseas).

Another example of self-censorship came to the department's attention a few months later, over the story about the national union of Australian university students raising money to rebuild schools bombed in North Vietnam. The acting news editor told the liaison officer that he had 'realised and avoided the problems of using this item in news to South East Asia and had kept it from those services'.[47] Three years later, Radio Australia exercised self-censorship to avoid upsetting Singapore in its reports of proposed arrangements for the British forces broadcasting station there. An officer of the department who discussed the question with Radio Australia said, 'they already go to considerable lengths to ensure that Singaporean ire is not raised'.[48]

At times, foreign correspondents tried to press Radio Australia into self-censorship. Beutler's plea to the author to avoid reference to Indonesia's 'invasion' of East Timor (although he personally did not quarrel with the word) has been recorded earlier. Beutler's last major story from Indonesia, that of the petition by fifty prominent Indonesians criticising President Soeharto in 1980 (a story which may have contributed to the decision to expel him), was treated with great care. The author believed the duty chief sub-editor had erred on the side of caution in placing the story in eighth position, after five headline stories and two other stories. He considered that at least three of the headline stories and the two other stories were of less interest to listeners in Southeast Asia than the story about the petition.[49]

After living in Singapore for well over a decade, the ABC's manager, Asia, J. A. (Peter) Hollinshead, had become particularly sensitive to the need for self-censorship. Not unnaturally, he regarded the coverage of Singapore as his bailiwick. No doubt he also saw anything that would disrupt the ABC's friendly relations with the Singapore government as a threat to his own comfortable lifestyle. In early 1983, he sounded the alarm about Radio Australia's intention to prepare a program on Singapore incorporating a commentary from Kathryn Davies recently commissioned by the ABC's radio public affairs staff. The first warning Hollinshead received was a telephone call from Radio Australia asking correspondent Bob Wurth to do a report on 'democracy in Singapore'. Hollinshead suggested sarcastically that this could be 'the first in a series in which we pick off just about every country in Asia, the Middle East, Africa, etc., before we move into Latin America for good measure'.

Hollinshead told the ABC's assistant general manager, radio, Keith Mackriell, that, if radio public affairs was going to use contentious reports by Davies and feed them to Radio Australia,

you had better book your ticket and sharpen up the Sukarno soft shoe song and dance act [a reference to Mackriell's visit to Indonesia in 1980 to try to persuade Sukarno that the ABC should be readmitted] because it will be Jakarta all over again.

Now that we've had the Amateur Follies of '83 would it be too much to ask for a pennyweight of professionalism.

I truly do not want to deny you a visit to Singapore and half a dozen slashes of the rotan across your backside but you are not as young as you used to be.[50]

Hollinshead's persuasiveness, as usual, was effective. Although Radio Australia did broadcast the program on democracy in Singapore, it was the last time they used Davies. Mackriell told Hollinshead that, on investigation, Barnett believed the program 'was not handled as well as it might have been'. He added:

'Peter is aware of the situation and appreciates the delicacy with which it must be handled. Thank you for bringing it to my attention and for saving me from half a dozen of the best!'[51] Under Barnett's guidance, Radio Australia's sub-editors and current affairs reporters were learning that self-censorship was the *sine qua non* of a quiet life.

On 28 March 1985, the ABC's London office sent a story quoting the London-based Catholic Institute for International Relations as saying one-sixth of the population of East Timor had been killed since Indonesia's takeover. The story was used in the Indonesian news bulletins, but was not headlined and was relegated to fifth place. Preference (and headline treatment) was given to a 'ho-hum' story about a statement by Indonesia's Energy Minister welcoming China's support for efforts by OPEC to stabilise oil prices.[52]

When an Indonesian minister suddenly cancelled a visit to Australia in protest at David Jenkins's *Sydney Morning Herald* article about the Soeharto family's business interests, the story, incredibly, was not headlined in the first Indonesian bulletin in which it was run. Once again, the Energy Minister got priority, this time with headline treatment for a warning that oil prices could drop further unless production levels were 'disciplined'.[53] The sub-editors on duty the following morning headlined the story of the cancelled visit in the first two Indonesian bulletins, but then dropped it out of the headlines. As the protest over the Jenkins article continued, the Indonesian government gave Australian journalists a lesson in the need for self-censorship by placing an indefinite ban on their entry to the country.

Barnett assured the Joint Parliamentary Committee on Defence and Foreign Affairs in 1985 that the ABC's long-time correspondent in Malaysia, Wong Puan Wah, was 'very circumspect' in his coverage, and 'knew what issues not to cover'. Barnett was responding to a question by the committee's chairman, Senator Kerry Sibraa, during a visit to Radio Australia.[54]

Singapore's Prime Minister added his support to the need for self-censorship. On a visit to Australia, he told journalists that criticism of Third World leaders by the Australian media aroused intense resentment and antagonism. Sooner or later, he said, journalists would have to decide whether their highest duty was to the freedom of the press or to 'their obligations as citizens'.[55]

Target priorities

A direct influence by governments on Radio Australia has been that, as with the BBC World Service, the target priorities and the languages in which it broadcast were for many years prescribed by the government of the day. Events in Australia's region—Indonesia's perceived drift towards China in the early 1960s, Australia's increasing involvement in Vietnam in the 1960s, and the emergence of China from the cultural revolution in the late 1970s—certainly had their effect on the duration of broadcasts in particular languages and even on the languages in which Radio Australia broadcast, as was seen with the introduction of broadcasts in Vietnamese in 1962.

At times, initiatives for the introduction of broadcasts in foreign languages have come from executives of the ABC or Radio Australia, but until the past few years the final decision has rested with the government, as advised by its departments, particularly the Department of Foreign Affairs.

Boyer was keen that the initiative in proposing that new languages should come from the ABC rather than the Department of External Affairs. In 1950 and 1952, he pressed for the reintroduction of broadcasts in Chinese and Japanese, telling the Postmaster-General, H. L. (Larry) Anthony, he believed Japanese to be the more important. The ABC, he said, had been requesting some firm expression of policy on the introduction of new languages, as was necessary according to the terms under which it had been given control of Radio Australia.[56] He told Moses later that he thought the ABC, not the Department of External Affairs, should take the initiative in *any* suggested changes relating to programs.[57]

But despite the advocacy of influential officers of the Departments of External Affairs and Defence, of the commission and of Boyer, it took many years for Radio Australia to recommence broadcasting in Chinese and Japanese. Broadcasts began in Standard Chinese (Mandarin) in 1956, Japanese in 1960, Vietnamese in 1962 and Cantonese in 1964.

Many decisions on target priorities were made by the department in consultation with the ABC, with the department always having the final say. A meeting of the two bodies late in 1971 on the short- and long-term future of Radio Australia agreed that, over the next few years, the People's Republic of China would become increasingly important as a target area.[58] The Postmaster-General in 1971 initiated inter-departmental discussions on Radio Australia, involving the Department of Foreign Affairs, the PMG Department and the ABC. A working committee was appointed which assessed the order of priority of Radio Australia's target areas as: Indonesia; Malaysia and Singapore; Japan; China; South Pacific and Mid-Pacific; Thailand and the Philippines; Indo-China; Burma and the Indian sub-continent; North America and Europe; Africa; and Latin America.

The working committee's draft paper stated frankly: 'This order is based on political considerations.'[59] The resultant recommendation to the ministers raised the tone to: 'This order is based on national considerations'.[60] At this stage Radio Australia was broadcasting in major languages (including English) spoken in the first seven of these target areas, but not in Burmese or any of the major languages of the sub-continent. The department regarded these as the next priority, and in 1973 said that Burmese, Hindi and Bengali were to be introduced as soon as transmitters were available.[61] These developments never eventuated.

By the early 1970s, the department was also becoming increasingly aware of the importance of Papua New Guinea to Australia's long-term interests, and its standing as a target area of Radio Australia rose in consequence. At the meeting at the Department of the Media in August 1973, a Foreign Affairs representative said the department regarded Papua New Guinea as being of highest priority, with the Indonesian service and the upgrading of the general Southeast Asian service sharing second priority. He said the Chinese service was third in priority, with the Japanese service fourth.[62] He was obviously speaking without the sanction of the department, which officially still regarded Indonesia as the first priority, with Malaysia and Singapore second, but in general terms the shift in priorities which he foreshadowed was to come to pass more than a decade later.

A paper prepared by the Department of Foreign Affairs following the meeting of August 1973 suggested that Radio Australia should make the structure of its language services more consistent with the priorities outlined by the inter-departmental committee. In particular, the paper suggested, Radio Australia should immediately upgrade its Japanese and Chinese services at the expense of some existing English and French services.

Explaining the rationale for this conclusion, the Foreign Affairs paper said the time devoted to the various services:

> does not adequately reflect *Government foreign policy priorities* [emphasis added] or the priorities which the Interdepartmental Committee on Radio Australia agreed should be observed in respect of Radio Australia's future expansion ... A similar imbalance exists in respect of length of various services and listener response etc. In other words we feel better use could probably be made of the limited resources at Radio Australia's disposal. Probably the best illustration of this is a comparison between the Japanese service and the French service to Africa. Both are of one hour duration, yet the Japanese service receives a response of some 24,000 letters a year as opposed to the French service to Africa of about 100 letters per year.[63]

The Waller committee in 1975 recommended the promotion of Japan and Papua New Guinea in the list of prime target areas, but the downgrading of Malaysia and Singapore from their previous second position, and China from its previous fourth position. It listed the five prime targets as: Indonesia; Japan; Papua New Guinea; Malaysia, Singapore and Thailand; South Pacific and Mid-Pacific.[64] The Waller report demoted China from a prime target to a 'target of opportunity', because, it said, the 'listening audience' in such countries could not be accurately estimated.

As mentioned above, the initiative for changes in target priorities sometimes came from Radio Australia itself, although the department made the final decision. In March 1979, the author, as acting director, suggested to the assistant secretary in charge of the department's information branch, David Evans, that, in view of the huge and unprecedented flow of mail from China, the priority of Radio Australia's language services should be changed to raise Standard Chinese to fourth place, above Neo-Melanesian (Pidgin) and behind only English, Indonesian and Japanese. No new list of actual target areas was proposed, although the implication was that China as a target area should be raised above Papua New Guinea but remain below Indonesia and Japan.[65] Evans agreed by telephone to the suggested change.

A few months later, a further change was suggested: that 'in view of recent developments in our broadcasting to the People's Republic of China', the Chinese service should be raised one step further, above the Japanese, and second only to the Indonesian service.[66] The department agreed.

Radio Australia's suggestions, of course, would not have been approved by the department simply 'in view of recent developments in our broadcasting'. The elevation of China in the list of priorities was a direct consequence of Australia's changing foreign policy: it reflected an increasing conviction by the government of China's growing and potential importance to Australian interests.

In July 1980, the author suggested to the department that Indo-China should be elevated from a 'target area of opportunity' to a prime target area. The department accepted the suggestion, but rejected an associated proposal that it be placed above the South Pacific, deciding that it should be placed immediately below. Three senior officers stressed the increasing importance which the department was placing on the South Pacific as a vital target area for Radio Australia. The assistant secretary, media, C. R. (Kim) Jones, and the head of the South Pacific desk, Colin McDonald, both said Radio Australia's news and current affairs programs were essential listening for every well-informed Pacific Islander. They also said that because Radio Australia broadcast virtually no voice reports from the Pacific, there was a grave dearth of in-depth, analytical reporting from the area.

In 1983, the department and the ABC undertook a further review of target areas (as opposed to foreign-language services) 'to take into account contemporary changes in Australia's regions of interest'.[67] Keith Jennings, who had taken over a year earlier as general manager, told the secretary of the department, Peter Henderson, that 'with the advice of your Department ... our officers have prepared a new priority list of target areas'. The major changes were the elevation of Papua New Guinea and the rest of the Pacific to third and fourth position, below only Indonesia and China, and the free-fall of Japan from third place to eighth—a foretaste of the dropping of Japanese from Radio Australia's broadcast languages in 1990. Jennings told Henderson that a strategy plan based on these target priorities would be presented to the government for approval, and further Foreign Affairs involvement would be sought 'at the appropriate time'.[68]

The following month, in a renewed bid for the establishment of a transmitting station at Brandon, eighty kilometres southeast of Townsville (set aside by the government the previous year), Barnett sought the department's support. He pointed out that the station would serve Papua New Guinea and the Pacific, which had recently had their target priorities upgraded.[69] For the time being at least, the department's decisions on the priorities of Radio Australia's target areas continued to be a major way in which Radio Australia was used by government as an instrument of foreign policy.

In 1988, for the first time, the ABC board made the Southwest Pacific the major priority ahead of Southeast Asia.[70] According to Barnett, Radio Australia took the initiative in this change and, after getting the approval of the Department of Foreign Affairs and Trade, submitted it to the ABC board for ratification.[71] Concluding the following year that the recognition of the Central and Southwest Pacific as Radio Australia's top priority was appropriate, the *Radio Australia Review* (the Revill review) quoted the submission from the Department of Foreign Affairs and Trade: 'There are internal tensions (eg Fiji, New Caledonia and Vanuatu) and an increased external interest that, in some circumstances, could potentially destabilise the region in ways inimical to Australian interests.' Stressing the importance of the service in the Pacific, the department said, 'It has been reported from our posts that Radio Australia is regularly listened to by a cross section of people including those at Ministerial level. Cabinet meetings have been known to be interrupted in some South Pacific countries for Radio Australia news programs.'

Second to the Central and Southwest Pacific was Southeast Asia, followed by North Asia, and then South Asia. The Revill report said such regional priorities were influenced by their importance to Australia in terms of proximity and economic, political and cultural links; and the popularity and demand for Radio Australia's programming and the prevalence of listening to international shortwave services.[72]

Among the reasons that, up to this time, Indonesia had retained its place at the top of the list of target priorities were its size and importance to Australia's national interest and the size of the Indonesian audience, which almost certainly outnumbered the entire population of the Southwest Pacific. The Indonesian government also showed considerable sensitivity to Radio Australia's broadcasts. The Southwest Pacific, by contrast, appeared relatively insensitive to Radio Australia's broadcasts until the coups in Fiji and political instability in Papua New Guinea and Vanuatu alerted Radio Australia and the department to the importance of the region to the national interest.

By 1993, the department reportedly no longer had any say at all in choosing Radio Australia's target priorities. In 1991, Broinowski said the department could offer its thoughts on the subject, but Radio Australia made its own decisions. Asked in mid-1993 what say the department had in choosing the current target priorities, White replied bluntly, 'None. If they interfered I'd tell them to get stuffed!'[73]

Pointing out that shortwave listening was limited in Japan, the Revill report recommended that 'a change of role is appropriate for the Japanese section'.[74] Instead of broadcasting in Japanese, it recommended such alternatives as Japanese-language news on the 0055 Telecom dial service, taped services to hotel audio systems and on domestic and international airlines, and a dedicated radio outlet, with pre-tuned receivers.[75] Radio Australia acted on this recommendation, and in 1990 ended the daily two-hour Japanese broadcast. The following year, the Japanese service was supplying news, information and entertainment programs to six commercial radio stations in Japan. In Australia, Radio Australia was operating a recorded telephone service for Japanese visitors, and supplying the Japanese text for a news bulletin broadcast on television outlets in major hotels. But budget cuts hit the service hard, and brought an end to all these activities. After 1993, only one of the Japanese staff was retained, preparing promotional material for a satellite-linked cable radio network in Japan carrying parts of Radio Australia's English program and doing translation work for outside companies.

White said in mid-1993 that the department had not had any input in the decision to stop broadcasting in Japanese or the decision to halve the French service in 1991 to one hour a day, and then halve it again in 1992 to only half an hour a day. Nor had Foreign Affairs had any input into the decision to reduce the Indonesian transmission from nine hours to eight daily in 1986, and from eight to seven in 1992, or to reduce transmissions in Standard Chinese or Cantonese. These decisions, he said, had all been made because of budget cuts. As secretary of the department, Woolcott confirmed in early 1992 that it no longer had the final say in language priorities.[76]

The department presumably had an input into the decision to begin broadcasting in Khmer (half an hour a day, five days a week) in 1992. Nor was it recommended by the Revill review, which concluded, 'Khmer and Laotian are languages in an internationally volatile part of Southeast Asia, but ... the populations are rather too small to warrant the investment involved in starting a whole new language service', adding that 'The multiplication of small foreign-language operations heightens problems of quality control and organisational consistency.'[77] The idea of broadcasting in Khmer, originally Broinowski's, was taken up by Cambodian Premier Hun Sen during a visit to Radio Australia in 1991. Told about Radio Australia's budgetary problems, he saw Hill the next day in Sydney, and the managing director became enthused with the idea. So the service began at the initiative of Radio Australia and the ABC, not Foreign Affairs.

White thought in 1993 that Radio Australia should be looking at the possibility of services to Burma and Laos, and wondered aloud whether the service to Thailand should be continued. About Thailand, he said, 'I think we have to review the Thai service because that is now a society that has literally scores of radio stations and a very well developed television system.'[78] The Revill report in 1989 observed that shortwave listening was more limited in Thailand than in Vietnam, but said the use of Radio Australia material by domestic radio stations to some extent compensated for this. About Burma, it said there was a significant shortwave audience there, but Australia's links were relatively weak, and in current financial circumstances the committee did not consider the introduction of Burmese warranted. White's comments on Burma were,

I think we should be looking at a service to Burma because that would appear to be, at least in communications, a closed society which could use outside information. I know our signal gets in there very well. We have the capacity, as we have done with our Cambodian staff, to recruit personnel from ethnic communities within Australia who have high language skills.[79]

English teaching

A fourth contributor to Radio Australia's role as the voice of Australia has been English-teaching programs. Most major international broadcasters have programs to teach listeners the major language of the country they serve, the BBC's 'English by Radio' being one of the leaders. Usually there are subtle or not-so-subtle overtones in the content of the lessons. Before World War II, Italy's shortwave Italian lessons included exercises with dictation messages selected from Mussolini's speeches.[80]

Programs to teach English through Radio Australia have served four main purposes, all of them favourable to Australia's interests. First, Australia has earned the gratitude of millions of Asians by filling a widely felt need to learn the world's major international language.[81] Second, an increase in the number of Asians who speak some English facilitates intercourse between Australia and Asian countries in a number of spheres, including trade, aid, education and culture. Third, because the lessons teach English in an Australian context, with a story-line about Australians and their friendly intercourse with people of the target country, the programs promote understanding of Australian society and values and a feeling of friendship towards Australians. Fourth, many listeners attracted by the English-teaching programs stay tuned to other programs, and are thus exposed to other elements of Radio Australia's 'message'. A Radio Australia executive (later promoted to the second most senior position in the service) wrote of an English-teaching program in 1982, 'Our basic objective is via this programme to attract listeners to the information programmes of Radio Australia. Teaching English is merely a means to this end.'[82] A BBC survey in 1975 showed that the first two reasons given by Indonesians for wanting to listen to Radio Australia were: information and to learn English.[83] Foreign Affairs has shown its appreciation of the value of the English-teaching programs to Australia's interests by funding some of them, in full, through its cultural relations division or through AIDAB, the Australian International Development and Assistance Bureau.

In the early 1950s, when the cultural cringe to the motherland was very much alive in Australia, it was proposed that the ABC ask the BBC for transcription tapes of its English-language lessons, to be rebroadcast by Radio Australia. In April 1955, the commission decided to proceed with this proposal.[84] But during Wood's visit to Indonesia the following year, the director of the Jakarta studios of *Radio Republik Indonesia*, Jusuf Ronodipuro, suggested that Radio Australia should broadcast English lessons for Indonesians in its Indonesian-language program. Wood endorsed the proposal.[85] Casey supported the idea and the department's backing was assured.[86] Eventually, the ABC asked the Commonwealth Office of Education for its help in preparing the scripts,[87] and the program became a joint project between the two of them and the Department of External Affairs. The Treasury made a special grant to the Commonwealth office to cover the cost of distributing the booklets to accompany the lessons.

The series of 104 weekly lessons was launched on 6 October 1959 with a speech by Barwick (as acting Minister for External Affairs), who said, 'Our two countries have much in common and visits from one to the other are steadily increasing.'[88]

The popularity of the program exceeded expectations. Homfray had estimated that 35,000 booklets would be needed, but two months after the launch revised his estimate to at least 85,000. He told Casey that the reaction in Indonesia was 'heart warming'.[89] The lessons were 'sweeping the country', he said, and the Indonesian Department of Education was 'thrilled'.

Not all of the Indonesian authorities were as thrilled as their education department was reported to be. In 1962 the Indonesians refused an offer of transistor radios for school broadcasts, primarily for Radio Australia's English lessons. Tange said the reluctance to begin school broadcasts with a foreign program was understandable.[90] He also said there was not much doubt that for many years Indonesian officials had been less than happy with Radio Australia's position and probably also with Australian efforts to improve it further. But the series achieved its purposes: it was tremendously popular among Indonesians of many kinds, including government officials. By 1982, when it had been running twenty-three years, more than five million booklets had been distributed to listeners.[91] In 1988 Radio Australia estimated that at least two million Indonesians had learned English from the program.[92] Since 1984, when Foreign Affairs stopped funding the program, the booklets have been produced and sold by a Jakarta publisher.

English lessons began in Radio Australia's Thai service in May 1965, and in the Vietnamese service in October 1967. By mid-1968, 140,000 booklets had been distributed to Thai listeners and 180,000 to listeners in South Vietnam. The lessons in the Thai service were rebroadcast by the Thai army radio station and the Thai Department of Education station. Because Radio Australia's signal to Vietnam was weak, master tapes of the lessons in the Vietnamese service were sent to South Vietnam government stations for rebroadcast.[93] After the communist takeover in 1975, the story-line of the lessons became unsuitable, and in any case listening to Western radio was made illegal. The course was discontinued in October of that year,[94] but, funded by AIDAB, was reintroduced with a very different story-line in 1991. As well as Radio Australia, the lessons were also broadcast by the Voice of Vietnam. In 1993, Radio Australia negotiated a contract with AIDAB for an English teaching series to Cambodia, due to begin in 1994.

The avalanche of mail from China in 1979 gave a new lease of life to plans for an English-teaching program for the Standard Chinese transmission, first proposed in 1970. An inter-departmental committee met in Canberra in February 1979[95] to plan the program, to be introduced simultaneously with a morning transmission to China. The following year, cabinet approved an appropriation of $1.4 million for the program as a special project, reflecting the increasing emphasis the government was placing on relations with China.[96]

By the end of 1987, when the series of 104 weekly programs had been completed, well over three-quarters of a million sets of reading material had been distributed. Bearing in mind the fact that some listeners learn English in groups, that probably means that close to one million people in China had learned some English from Radio Australia. In 1993, the lessons were also being broadcast on two radio stations in China.

The government's increased emphasis on the South Pacific as a foreign-policy priority in the 1980s resulted in the region's increased prominence as a target area for Radio Australia, as mentioned earlier. It also led to pressure for an English-teaching program for Pacific islanders. The regional information and cultural relations conference, South Pacific, in Port Moresby in February 1982 recommended that 'consideration be given to ways in which Radio Australia could be used for the teaching of the English language in the Pacific'.[97] Radio Australia program staff immediately began working on this recommendation, seeking help from experts in the teaching of English as a second language. Though the project lapsed, it was given fresh impetus in 1989, when the Joint Parliamentary Committee on Foreign Affairs, Defence and Trade, in a report on Australia's relations with the South Pacific, recommended 'further extension of the service in the region through the development of an English-language instruction program'.[98] But up to 1994, these moves had come to nothing. Derek White explained that he was advised that, considering the diverse range of Pacific languages, a worthwhile English course would be 'very difficult if not impractical'.[99] He said that to suggest (as the author had done) that AIDAB would probably be happy to fund such a program was to reveal 'either experience different to the current financial environment or a lack of knowledge of the detailed consideration AIDAB gives to all such projects'.

Promotional programs

A fifth means by which Radio Australia has furthered Australia's interests is through promotional programs. In most such programs the stress has been on a positive image, with little or no attempt to provide the balance aimed at in news and current affairs programs. For much of Radio Australia's history, these promotional programs were not confined to its shortwave broadcasts. Many of them were also distributed to overseas radio stations through its transcription service.

The Department of Trade showed its appreciation of the value to Australia's interests of some of the promotional programs by subsidising them. In 1989 the Department of Foreign Affairs and Trade was paying half the cost of the programs 'Business Horizons' and 'Innovations'. Radio Australia has had a number of programs, in several languages, which have promoted Australian exports and business enterprise. The program, 'Pacific Sunrise', reporting business and export developments in the Southwest and Central Pacific, with obvious benefits to Australia, was subsidised by AIDAB, through the South Pacific Trade Commission, until March 1993, when the scarcity of funds brought an end to the subsidy. The program itself subsequently came to an end. (French and Tok Pisin—PNG Pidgin—versions of 'Pacific Sunrise' had been broadcast, as well as a taped version in Bislama, the language of Vanuatu.) In mid-1993, promotional programs in English included—as well as 'Pacific Sunrise' and 'Innovations'—'Business Weekly', 'Science File', 'Study in Australia' and 'This Australia'—a social history program.

Radio Australia has furthered Australia's commercial and other interests by broadcasting programs promoting not only exports, but also other business enterprises, tourism,[100] scientific, educational and artistic achievements, Australian culture, aid projects and immigration (selectively). A program called 'The Australian Inventor', which ran in the English service for ten years, resulted in the sale of some of the inventions covered.[101]

Virtually every international broadcaster has 'mailbag' programs, in which letters from listeners, or purporting to be from listeners, are answered by one or more broadcasters. These programs serve several purposes: they are a vehicle for imparting information and/or propaganda; they enable the establishment of a person-to-person relationship between (generally warm and friendly) broadcasters and their listeners, thus, by extension, engendering goodwill towards a country and people; and they encourage the flow of letters which are sometimes referred to as proof of a broadcasting service's effectiveness, or at least of the size of its audience.

Radio Australia has had mailbag programs in all of the nine languages in which it broadcasts except, so far, Khmer. In the first few years after the ABC took over the service, the answers to listeners' questions to the English-language mailbag were written by an officer of the Australian News and Information Bureau staff in Melbourne, with occasional reference to External Affairs when the questions touched on political matters. When the officer resigned in 1957, the ANIB suggested to the ABC that Goss, the External Affairs Radio Australia liaison officer, might be prepared to 'help out' until a new man could be assigned to the job by the ANIB.[102] The department told Casey that the proposal had received 'a very cool reception', and the ABC had decided to carry on unaided until the ANIB could fill the position. This never happened, and Radio Australia ran the program until it was suspended in the late 1980s. It was reintroduced in 1993.

For twenty-five years from 1956, the compere was Keith Glover, who regularly replied to about thirty letters a week. Glover said his perception of the program was that it was 'a public relations exercise in which I was relating to listeners on a one-to-one basis, and others were eavesdropping'.[103]

About 70 per cent of the questions were about Australia. In reply to these, he said, he tried to present an image that was 'positive but not untruthful'. 'If there were things that didn't make us sound too good,' he said, 'I wouldn't shy away from them.' For example, before its abolition, he spoke about the white Australia policy, though in an explanatory rather than derogatory way. He tried to explain that it was designed to protect the lifestyle of Australians, but that it might be changed in the future. Overall, he believed he gave the impression of a tolerant, liberal democracy in which immigrants were welcome, but in which there was some prejudice against other races, and there were quotas limiting their entry.

Overall, Radio Australia's promotional programs have almost certainly done more to foster goodwill towards Australia and Australians than the news and current affairs programs. But, despite their shortcomings and the sometimes successful attempts to manipulate them as government propaganda, those news and current affairs programs have established for Radio Australia a credibility without which the audience would undoubtedly be smaller, and the other programs would probably be more widely recognised for what most of them are in reality, soft-sell propaganda.

The emphasis of this book on the direct government control of the news and current affairs output during the war and immediate post-war years, when the service was closest to the American model of international broadcasting, and the attempts to move closer to the American model through influencing that output during subsequent years, should not be allowed to obscure the fact that the role of the service as an instrument of foreign policy has extended far beyond the area of news and current affairs.

12   A future for Radio Australia?

Now that Radio Australia, after half a century of struggle, has achieved a large measure of freedom from political interference and established its editorial integrity, what is its future? Among the options are its closure, an option without strong support in the 1990s; its takeover by a government department, also an option with little support; and its establishment as a separate statutory authority. If it survives, in whatever form, one possibility is that its budget will decline; as a result, its hours on air and the size of its audiences will continue to be eroded. This chapter will look at the options, and at the recent decline in some of its operations (though, thanks to the Department of Foreign Affairs and Trade and the Department of Transport and Communications, the decline in its transmissions has been arrested).

Closure

There was a time when many of the critics of Radio Australia simply proposed that it should be closed down. The deterioration of relations with Australia's nearest Asian neighbour, partly as a result of Radio Australia's reporting of issues and events over which the Soeharto government would have preferred to draw a veil, has done more than anything else to persuade some of the opponents of the (idealised) British model that Radio Australia may have outlived its usefulness. Among those who believed it probably should be closed down are three former senior diplomats, Arthur Tange (a former secretary not only of the Department of External Affairs but also of the Department of Defence), William Pritchett (another former secretary of the Defence Department) and Malcolm Booker (first assistant secretary of Foreign Affairs under Tange and his successor). Basically, they feel that Radio Australia, once a national asset, now does more harm than good.

Some of those who advocate the closure of Radio Australia ask what gives Australia the right to wash the dirty linen of others in public. The reply might well be that, in some countries, most notably Indonesia, most people would remain ignorant of the existence of the dirty linen were it not for Radio Australia. In Indonesia, it is never washed by government radio or television, or by private radio stations which want to remain open. And, as newspapers and magazines require government licences, it is a simple matter to close one that embarrasses the government, or publishes matter which could exacerbate the country's political, religious, ethnic, or regional tensions. The pragmatic justification for Radio Australia's broadcasting both good and bad news about Indonesia in the early 1960s was that it was in Australia's national interest to keep fully informed those likely to bring an end to the rule of Soekarno, and the adventurism of his foreign policies, in particular the Confrontation of Malaysia. Radio Australia, and Australia itself, inherited a legacy of goodwill from the leaders of Soeharto's New Order because of the role they had played in keeping them informed during the Soekarno era. But, with the survival of the Soeharto regime apparently in Australia's interest, some find it hard to see any immediate justification for reporting both bad and good news about Soeharto's Indonesia and consequently exacerbating relations between his government and that of Australia.

Tange remarked in 1988 that he was not sure there was any justification for the continued existence of Radio Australia in the circumstances of the 1980s and 1990s. He added:

I don't see any justification for the Australian taxpayer providing an entertainment and information service to people round the world. Why should we? The only justification could lie—I don't say it does lie, but it could lie—in the circumstances in which Australian official policy or the conduct of Australian diplomacy, the conduct of Australian defence relations, was impeded by ignorance abroad, in societies with whose governments we were dealing, of Australian motivations and Australia's intentions—was impeded by misunderstandings such as we had, to give an historical analogy, of Australia's white Australia policy: that certainly was an obstacle 20 to 30 years ago. I doubt today that we have those obstacles residing in the minds of countries with which we do official business. So the question arises: why do we need a Radio Australia?[1]

Tange said that, at this point in history, the only justification for Radio Australia could be, if Australia's interests were under real threat, to supplement the efforts of diplomats and trade negotiators with a service that 'dexterously tries to present Australia in a favourable light to voluntary listeners in other countries'. He firmly believed that the service should act in ways which did not conflict with 'the foreign policy of the government of the day, as superintended by the parliament of the day'. Tange said in 1993 that he stood by those beliefs, adding, 'That is my reaction to some of the proselytising about human rights when Malaysia decides to hang a drug trafficker.'[2]

Like Tange, his one-time superior, Booker felt strongly that Radio Australia was doing the national interest more harm than good. He wrote in 1988 that the conclusion of a series of reports that it was 'a good thing' had been reached 'on the basis of dubious reasoning, transferred successively from one report to another'.[3] Asking why the Australian taxpayer should contribute $24 million annually to provide such a service, Booker said, 'Many of those who monitor its programs find them biased and patronising. And in applying the principle of objectivity to its presentation of Australia, the overseas service adopts a "warts and all" approach—which to outsiders is absurd.'

In an interview four months later, Booker again raised the question of what the taxpayers were paying for. They were not getting their money's worth, he said, unless Radio Australia won the goodwill of governments (as well as ordinary people): 'You can't engender goodwill by exposing the deficiencies of your neighbours and their government. If you want to engender goodwill, it's a highly expert propaganda exercise.'[4] Elaborating on the theme of propaganda, he said:

There is conceivably a case for a shortwave propaganda service which is deliberately designed to combat anti-Australian material and deliberately designed to promote a favourable view of Australia, deliberately and professionally designed as a propaganda organisation. There's no good mincing words: that is what it would be. I really don't see that it is any value in its present form.[5]

Booker said in 1993 that these were still his views.[6]

William Pritchett was far more scathing about Radio Australia and its journalists, whom he regarded as a threat to Australia's national interest. In a letter in the *Sydney Morning Herald* in 1988, he said that, as a high commissioner in Singapore, and later as secretary of the Defence Department, he had found Radio Australia 'at best irrelevant to the management of our foreign relations, or at its more frequent worst, a source of damage', adding: 'I have long held that it should be closed down.'[7] Its supporters, he said, strongly defended what he called its 'comment' on the domestic affairs of other countries by invoking 'journalistic freedom'. They seemed to see Radio Australia as having a political role to play in the region, 'as though the sort of governments there preferred by journalists would necessarily be more supportive of our interests'. Echoing the views of other hard-liners among diplomats and, more particularly, former diplomats, he asked rhetorically: 'Why should broadcasts to foreign countries, paid for by the taxpayer, be controlled by a small, independent bureaucracy of journalists?' Pritchett ended his letter with the call, 'Abolish it and save the money, or at least ensure that it speaks for us and not just for itself.' Pritchett later admitted on television that his letter to the *Herald* had contained 'a bit of hyperbole', but he did question whether there was a need for Radio Australia.[8] He said the service was proud of its circumvention of censorship during the Fijian coups in 1987, but it did not sound very clever to have got Rabuka offside by doing so. Speaking in 1993, he repeated that his call for the closure of Radio Australia had contained some hyperbole. He said he did not know enough about Radio Australia's current operations to say whether it should be closed down. But, he said, foreign relations was a matter for the Minister for Foreign Affairs and Trade and his department, not for a few anonymous bureaucrats who were not answerable to the people.[9]

In 1988, the journalist Peter Hastings took up the cry of Booker and Pritchett. He said most of the senior officers of the Department of Foreign Affairs he had spoken to over more than thirty years in 'the region' and Australia regarded Radio Australia as at best an impediment to Australia's regional relations.[10] It is notable, that, although Tange, Booker, Pritchett and Hastings questioned whether Radio Australia was giving value for money, they left open the question of whether, run according to the American model, it might justify its cost.

To some, it seemed that a new danger to the continued existence of Radio Australia emerged with the threat by the leader of the Opposition, Dr John Hewson, in November 1991 that if the coalition were elected to power, it would cut the ABC's funding by $50 million, or 10 per cent of its annual budget. Some thought one option open to the ABC, if Hewson had carried out this threat, was to close Radio Australia. But internal documents drawn up by ABC executives show that Radio Australia would have had its budget cut by $1.5 million rather than being closed down altogether.[11] Richard Broinowski said in early 1992 that it was possible the ABC board might decide to close down Radio Australia if the ABC budget were drastically slashed, but that the government would have to leave it to the board to decide. 'The cynical comment made by some people, including a very senior shadow minister I travelled to Canberra with on Monday morning, is that there were no votes in Radio Australia. Therefore it's vulnerable—more than domestic services are, to being closed down.'[12] But Broinowski added that he was not so sure that there were not votes in Radio Australia. Speaking shortly afterwards, Richard Woolcott, as secretary of the department, said he did not know why Broinowski feared that Hewson would close Radio Australia down. He said Radio Australia's expenditure would be cut under a coalition government, but Hewson could not close it, or even privatise it.[13]

American model

The possibility of running Radio Australia once again according to the American model, under the direct control of a government department, has been considered on more than one occasion since the service was taken away from the Department of Information in 1950. As described earlier, Hasluck failed in his attempt to have it separated from the ABC, moved to Canberra, and operated under the supervision of his department. In April 1973, the Minister for the Media, Senator Douglas McClelland, proposed another variant of the American model. He suggested in a letter to Whitlam that Radio Australia be put directly within his ministerial responsibility and be attached to the Department of the Media. Whitlam was unresponsive. He replied that Radio Australia must be able to demonstrate 'its comparative freedom from direct Government control'.[14] This, he said, could be jeopardised by the incorporation of the service into McClelland's department.

The option of placing Radio Australia in the Department of the Media (though as a 'largely autonomous unit') was one of the lines of approach examined by the review of Radio Australia by the ABC and the Public Service Board in 1975. But the review concluded that this was open to the same administrative and cost objections as complete independence.[15] The possibility of incorporating the service in a government department was looked at again by the Dix committee in 1980, and again rejected.[16]

In his book *Breaking up the ABC*, in 1988, Dr Glyn Davis added his voice to the calls for Radio Australia to be separated from the ABC.[17] Showing his ignorance of the extent to which Radio Australia had become independent of Foreign Affairs, he suggested that the department 'should run Radio Australia itself, rather than cloak it within the folds of ABC independence'.[18] He explained in 1993 that, when he was researching his book, people had described Radio Australia in foreign policy terms, and 'What I meant was that if people saw it as serving interests of foreign-policy, why should it not be run by the Department of Foreign Affairs.'[19] The Revill review in 1989 concluded that there was 'no merit' in such a proposal, and noted that there was 'no voice in Australia today which seriously suggests that Radio Australia should become a direct arm of government'.[20]

Asked in 1993 for his comment on the possibility of the transfer of Radio Australia to the department, Derek White said, 'It would substan-tially change our reputation and standing as an independent source of information. Many of our listeners would recognise that we were a government-run broadcasting organisation like the Voice of America and Radio Moscow.'[21]

A possible advantage of the American model is that funding might well be more generous. Successive heads of Radio Australia have com-mented on the reluctance of the ABC to fund Radio Australia projects at the expense of domestic radio and television. Most new projects of the shortwave service have been either funded directly by Foreign Affairs (like the English-teaching programs) or have depended for funding on the department's support (like the construction of the Darwin station and the introduction of new languages). An officer of the department reported, prophetically, as early as 1955:

at the meeting between the Department and the ABC on 15th December last, Moses stated that the Commission felt it wrong to curtail the Home Service in order to spend additional money on the Overseas Service, but I doubt whether the reverse is the case, particularly with the advent of television.[22]

One disadvantage of the American model is the possibility, after a change of government, of major swings in policy which could seriously damage not only the service's credibility, but also its effectiveness as propa-ganda. The department's first Radio Australia liaison officer, Noel Goss, felt in 1988 that Radio Australia might have been more effective if run directly by External Affairs, but said that, at times, for example when Evatt was minister, it was 'very much under ministerial pressure', and this might have been disastrous if it had been translated directly into the broadcasts.[23] He conceded that direct control by the department would have led to a loss of credibility, and that the department's officers were 'not really equipped personally' to run a broadcasting service. Radio Australia's longest-serving director, Peter Homfray, also felt that the propensity of government departments to change alignment with a change of government was a persuasive argument against this model. He said that, if operated directly by a government department, Radio Australia could find itself 'in business one day and out of business the next'.[24] Even Booker, so hostile to the continuation of Radio Australia in its current form, when asked whether it should be transferred to the Department of Foreign Affairs and Trade, would say only that 'a case could be made'.[25]

Defenders of the operation of Radio Australia according to the BBC model say that a change to the American model would damage its credibility, and thus make it less helpful to the national interest. But the question arises whether it might be more useful to the national interest if it were run as a more overt instrument of propaganda which was at the same time, like the Voice of America, more careful not to offend the sensitivities of those whom the government is attempting to cultivate.

Statutory authority

One option examined by various reviews was a variant on the BBC model—the creation of a separate statutory authority to run Radio Australia. This was one of the possibilities looked at by External Affairs in 1964 and 1965, when Darling and others were frustrating Hasluck's desire to make it a more compliant instrument of government policy. A draft entitled 'Location of Radio Australia' by a senior officer of the department said it might 'take some time to achieve the desirable end of a separate institution'.[26] This, he said, would help Radio Australia to accept that there was a 'fundamental difference between the objectives of an internal and an external broadcasting service and that the considerations which govern the presentation of programmes of news on one are not necessarily valid for the other'. Read in the context of Hasluck's ambition to have Radio Australia controlled by his department, these words make it clear that, if a separate statutory authority had been established at that stage, the authority would probably have fallen under the power of External Affairs. What at first would have appeared to be a variant of the BBC model would in fact have become a variant of the American model.

Homfray, disgusted by what he saw as ABC parsimony, proposed the option of a separate statutory authority to McClelland in 1973. But the Foreign Affairs report on the meeting on 13 August of that year said his 'general performance at the meeting' had done little to enhance the prospect.[27] Homfray later changed to the view that, rather than becoming a separate entity, Radio Australia should join the Special Broadcasting

Service as its external broadcasting wing—another variant of the BBC model.[28] He said that realistically he could not see the government supporting three separate publicly funded public broadcasting organisations.

The Public Service Board–ABC inquiry into Radio Australia in 1975 found that the establishment of Radio Australia as a separate government entity would engender new problems, for example by eliminating wider career horizons for staff, or making it hard to recruit specialist staff. The inquiry regarded this as only a 'last resort' approach.[29]

The ABC's submission to the Waller inquiry in 1975, drafted by Philip Koch and approved, substantially without amendment, by Keith Mackriell (not surprisingly), rejected the option of a separate authority. It said that, although it would be an advantage to have a board of directors or commissioners devoted solely to Radio Australia, there would be considerable disadvantages, including 'exceedingly high' costs.[30]

The Dix committee in 1980 commented,

it has become part of the conventional wisdom in Australia that a service guaranteed independence from direct government control by statute is bound to have more credibility with its audience than one operated by a government department, as is the Voice of America. It is a wisdom which we share.[31]

Describing independence as 'the only institutional alternative deserving serious consideration',[32] the Revill review in 1989 said it was 'a high risk option', and concluded that there was 'no guarantee and little indication that the Government would favour Radio Australia with greater largesse if it were independent of the ABC'. Furthermore, there was no guarantee that an independent Radio Australia could achieve or maintain the same level of political independence it had as part of the ABC, enshrined as it was by legislation, and 'buffered by a strong tradition of jealously guarding that independence'. As a much smaller organisation, it would be in a weaker position to resist potential government pressures. The review also considered that 'the ABC standards of credibility in its news service enhance both Radio Australia's performance and reputation'. Furthermore, the ABC offered Radio Australia advantages of efficiency and quality in its programming, and a small, independent Radio Australia would face greater problems of organisational rigidity and stagnation.[33]

Budget erosion

Even though Hewson was not elected to power in 1993, Radio Australia's budget has been seriously eroded under the Labor government to the time of writing. Observing in 1986 that Radio Australia received 'a mere two per cent of the ABC's domestic budget', the former chairman of the ABC, Ken Myer, said, 'I strongly believe that until the Government assesses that RA is an important part of promoting Australia in the Pacific Basin and, until it is funded totally independently of the domestic budget of the ABC, it will continue to decline ... it will become a whisper in the 1990s.'[34]

Some of the consequences of the progressive attrition of the budget are detailed in the following examination of Radio Australia's current operation. An early attempt to reduce costs was the elimination in 1985 of the 'monitors' who were a safeguard against mistranslation (either inadvertent or deliberate). The monitors were given scripts and tapes chosen at random, and checked the accuracy of translation and delivery. Asked about the monitors in mid-1993, White said he had never heard of them.[35]

Budget problems have not only afflicted Radio Australia directly, but have also limited the amount which the Department of Transport and Communications is prepared to spend on maintaining the strength of its signal. Before 1994, the broadcasts were sent from three transmitters near Darwin, each of 250 kilowatts, three at Carnarvon, Western Australia, of 300, 250 and 100 kilowatts; six of 100 kilowatts at Shepparton, Victoria; and three of 10 kilowatts at Brandon, near Townsville, aimed at Papua New Guinea. Shepparton, which transmits more than half of Radio Australia's programming, is poorly sited, and its transmitters are underpowered for providing reception to most of the target areas. The Revill review concluded that 'failure to invest adequately in improved transmission capacities has seriously impaired its ability to compete even in its highest priority regions'.[36] The review concluded that Radio Australia's performance had already been adversely affected by the weakness of its transmitters, and that 'unless action is taken urgently, its position will continue to deteriorate'.[37] The report recommended federal government funding to provide two additional transmitters at Darwin. Fortunately for Radio Australia's continued visibility, Foreign Affairs joined the Department of Transport and Communications in support of this recommendation, and $11.6 million was being spent over three years to upgrade transmission facilities at Darwin and Shepparton. Two additional transmitters of 250–300 kilowatts were installed at Darwin, and went into operation in May 1994. A new aerial arrangement and switching system were installed at Shepparton to replace antiquated equipment.

One solution to transmission problems recommended by the Revill review was that the ABC board and the Australian government should allow Radio Australia to transmit from offshore, should allow other broadcasters to transmit from Australia under agreed conditions, and should allow Radio Australia to share or lease transmitter time. Only by transmitting from offshore, the review said, could Radio Australia get a satisfactory signal into northern China, including Beijing and Shanghai. The report noted that, according to the *World Radio TV Handbook*, 'Almost every month during 1988 signified the start of some relay exchange between two international broadcasters.' The handbook listed thirty-seven radio relay agreements between international broadcasters. The expenditure review committee of cabinet agreed in mid-1990 that the Ministers for Transport and Communications and for Foreign Affairs and Trade, in consultation with Radio Australia and the ABC, should develop options for offshore transmission facilities for further consideration 'if costs can be contained to reasonable levels'.[38] The ABC's corporate plan for 1991–94 proposed that Radio Australia 'Plan and develop an offshore facility to increase penetration of potential audiences in North and South Asia'.[39] The idea was endorsed in the ABC's priorities for 1992–95, which specified as a priority for Radio Australia, 'Acquire access to additional modern, reliable transmission facilities, including off-shore facilities'.[40] But, up to 1994, there had been no progress towards offshore transmission, and White was decidedly unenthusiastic about the proposal, drawing attention to the tremendous cost involved.

The budget cuts imposed by the government, and by the ABC, forced Radio Australia to cut its time on air by $3^{1}/_{2}$ hours daily between 1989 and 1993, from 49 hours to $45^{1}/_{2}$. Its transmission in English had remained at 24 hours daily, and durations were unchanged in Cantonese ($1^{1}/_{2}$ hours) and Thai (1 hour). There were even some increases. With the greater emphasis on Indo-China, there was the new half-hour program in Khmer, broadcast twice each weekday, and transmission in Vietnamese had increased from 1 hour to $1^{1}/_{2}$ hours daily with the introduction of English lessons in 1991. The daily transmission in Tok Pisin had increased from 2 hours to 3 hours, though at the expense of the 1 hour in 'Pacific English' (English spoken by Pacific islanders). But daily broadcasting had been cut from 8 hours to 7 in Indonesian, $6^{1}/_{2}$ hours to 6 in Standard Chinese, and 2 hours to $^{1}/_{2}$ hour in French. The Japanese transmission of 2 hours daily had been eliminated altogether. Even in 1989, Australia had ranked thirteenth among international broadcasters in hours on air, well behind the leader, the USA (337 hours).

Audience size

The total of nine languages broadcast by Radio Australia compared with forty-nine by the Voice of America and thirty-eight by the BBC. In terms of audiences, the Voice of America and the BBC claimed to have weekly audiences of more than 120 million. Radio Australia's audience can only be guessed at, because of the impossibility of conducting quantitative audience research in China, where it probably has a huge audience, but an educated guess suggests that its *weekly* audience there may be fewer than 10 million. The 1992–93 ABC annual report claimed that Radio Australia had a total audience (that is, the number of adults who listened less often than once a week) of 50 million,[41] but this figure is almost certainly highly inflated. The previous annual report claimed that a mid-1991 survey estimated that the Indonesian service alone reached 18 million people.[42] But this figure appears to have been calculated by multiplying the percentage claiming to have listened (9.6 per cent in Indonesian and 2.7 per cent in English, almost certainly with a big overlap) by Indonesia's total population of more than 180 million. As the latest Indonesian census shows that about 80 million are under the age of fifteen, the number of adult listeners is probably closer to 10 million than 18 million. Radio Australia's 'regular' audience (adults listening at least once a week) in any language in Indonesia is around 3 per cent, or 3 million. The survey, conducted by the BBC, showed that the BBC's audience was slightly larger than Radio Australia's, though Radio Australia shaded the BBC in eastern Indonesia. Probably more significant was that a higher percentage of Indonesians with post-secondary education listened to Radio Australia than to the BBC. Also significant is that almost a quarter of those who listened to Radio Australia in Indonesian or English said that, as a result, they now had a more favourable attitude towards Australia.

Surveys in New Caledonia in 1989 and Papua New Guinea in 1989–90 showed the strength of Radio Australia's audience in both countries. In New Caledonia, it shared market leadership with Radio France Internationale. In Papua New Guinea, 28 per cent of respondents said they listened to Radio Australia each week. This audience was almost equal to that of major local stations, and ahead of other international broadcasters.

In its submission to the Revill review, the Department of Foreign Affairs and Trade said that 'although difficult to ascertain accurate figures, it is believed that tens of millions listen to Radio Australia each day'.[43] This figure is questionable, but it is hard to argue with the department's conclusion that 'No other instrument of Australian society reaches more people in our neighbouring region than Radio Australia.'

The mail from listeners, once a source of pride and satisfaction to Radio Australia, has fallen steadily, both because the organisation cannot afford to respond adequately, and also no doubt because of falling audiences. Radio Australia began actively discouraging listeners from writing after the peak year of 1979–80, when they sent a staggering 566,000 letters and cards. Of these, 183,000 flooded in from China, where, after the end of the Cultural Revolution, people were permitted, even encouraged, to listen to foreign radio. But in recent years Radio Australia's mail, especially that from China, has fallen steeply, and mail totals are no longer reported with pride in Radio Australia's section of ABC annual reports. The overall total has fallen every year since 1987-88, dropping by more than half from 207,000 in 1987-88 to less than 79,000 in 1992–93. The number received by the Indonesian section also dropped by more than half over the same period, from 75,600 to less than 35,000. The number of letters in Chinese fell to less than one-sixth of its 1987–88 level, from 91,600 to only 14,500. The only bright spot was the Vietnamese mail, which rose steadily over four years, reaching more than 7000 in 1992–93.

The audiences in the Pacific for some of the English and French programs is increased by relays and rebroadcasts. Many local stations relay live the news and/or the current affairs program, 'International Report'. In 1993 the national broadcasting organisation in Papua New Guinea and one station in Fiji transcribed these programs for translation and later broadcast, and Radio Kiribati translated three news bulletins for later broadcast. More than twenty stations in the Pacific rebroadcast programs provided on cassette by Radio Australia's English-language transcription service. The French-language news and current affairs program, '*Pacifique Info*', was relayed locally in Vanuatu, New Caledonia and Tahiti.

Recent changes in the organisation of Radio Australia and in the nature of its programming have been driven as much by fresh ideas as by budget constraints. Program sections have been organised into three broad groupings, the Pacific, Southeast and South Asia, and North Asia, each headed by a regional manager (the regional manager for the Pacific also being responsible for English-language programs). The intention, in the words of the Revill review, was 'to enhance sensitivity to particular audiences, to make organisational structures better support program outputs, and to encourage more fruitful collaboration between individual language sections'.[44] A side effect—or, for those who believe in conspiracy theories, an ulterior motive—was the replacement of the generally conservative, largely military-trained supervisors of the language sections. All foreign-language sections, except Khmer, are now headed by executive producers who are natives of the target areas at which their programs are aimed (or, in the case of the French section, a native of metropolitan France). At least one of the displaced language supervisors believes that he and his colleagues, who spoke the languages and were in direct contact with their staffs, were seen as a stumbling block in the way of control by the broader ABC and by ambitious executives within Radio Australia.

The Revill review, which approved of 'regionalisation', also recommended internal restructuring to break down 'the isolation and reactive nature of the news desk' and the alleged insensitivity of the journalists. This had already been achieved in part by the appointment of information program coordinators (IPCs) from each language section to work with the sub-editors in the preparation of news bulletins. The IPCs have a role in selecting stories (from an approved 'queue') for bulletins in their languages, deciding on the order of stories and preparing the headlines. This development led to a lengthy industrial dispute about demarcation, but a compromise was eventually reached on condition that the duty editor was given the final say on editorial decisions, including the right to nominate 'must take' stories. One senior journalist says the newsroom has impressed on the IPCs that they must use human rights stories, regardless of sensitivity in their target areas. But increasingly, according to another informant, the heavy demands on the understaffed news desk mean that the choices made by the IPCs sometimes go unchecked. Another measure to reduce the alleged insensitivity of the journalists, or at least some of them, has been an increase in the number who have university degrees and who speak Asian languages.

Whatever the future of Radio Australia, it seems that it will never return to the days when, in the view of some of its critics, it was in effect 'nine separate radio stations', served by a single news and current affairs staff, but in other respects with little communication between them.

Survival of shortwave

There are some who doubt whether shortwave radio, depending on a technology developed in the 1930s, has much of a future in a world where listeners are increasingly familiar with television, frequency modulation radio broadcasting and digital sound. But the Revill review concluded that shortwave radio would remain a relevant medium of international communication, particularly in the Asia–Pacific region, 'in the foreseeable future'.[45] The committee which conducted the review noted that studies undertaken by the BBC and the Voice of America had concluded that continued transmission by shortwave was their best strategy. After reviewing the possibilities and problems associated with direct broadcasting by satellite of an audio signal, directed to individual receivers, the BBC External

Services concluded that its application 'appears to be limited and it is not being pursued by the BBC at the present time'.[46] In the three years to mid-1993, the BBC increased its shortwave transmission hours by about 6 per cent.[47] The Revill review concluded that direct broadcasting by satellite was unlikely to become a widespread or feasible alternative to international shortwave broadcasting, especially in Radio Australia's target regions, 'for at least some decades to come'.[48] The committee pointed out that, over the previous five years, the BBC had spent about $120 million and the Voice of America roughly $490 million on their shortwave transmitters and related equipment. Radio Australia's controller of resources and distribution believed in 1993 that shortwave broadcasting would continue to be, for at least ten years, the cheapest means to reach a distant mass audience. He said it was still cheaper than launching a satellite, and the potential audience was larger because there were so many shortwave receivers in use around the globe.[49]

In any case, the eventual replacement of shortwave technology by alternative methods need not mean the end of Radio Australia. International audio broadcasting will continue well into the twenty-first century by alternative means, including transmission via satellite as well as direct broadcasting by satellite. Satellites are now the primary program delivery vehicle of the Voice of America. On a typical day, Intelsat and Eurosat circuits carry some 300 hours of Voice of America programs in thirty-eight languages. The Voice of America has sixteen overseas relay transmitters as well as three in the continental United States.

Already Radio Australia's English program is being transmitted twenty-four hours a day via Indonesia's Palapa B2P satellite, which has a footprint extending as far as southern China, so that those in more than fifteen countries with access to satellite dishes can listen to that program with much better quality than is available from the shortwave band. Parts of the English program are also carried through Japan by a satellite-linked cable radio network. Eventually, satellite delivery may immeasurably improve the quality of the signal available for programs in other languages, including Standard Chinese and Indonesian.

The proliferation of international television will not necessarily bring an end to international radio. Audiences who can listen to international radio, with satellite quality, while engaged in other activities will not necessarily want to sit in front of a screen looking at international television.

13 The new wave: international television, 1985–1994

Though international radio broadcasting will probably survive well into the twenty-first century, international satellite television will no doubt supplant it as the principal means of international mass communication. And Australian international television, without Radio Australia's long tradition of fighting for integrity and credibility, could provide new opportunities for news and current affairs programs to be softened to avoid offending neighbouring countries. Even before the launch of Australia Television (initially called Australia Television International, or ATVI) in February 1993, such attempts, by the Department of Foreign Affairs and Trade and by nervous members of the ABC's staff, had already begun. Furthermore, the service had been on air for only eighteen months when it gave seven hours of its transmission every day to American news and current affairs programs.

The idea of international satellite television was well established by the 1980s. In a speech to the Los Angeles Council for World Affairs in February 1984, the BBC's managing director, external broadcasting, Douglas Muggeridge, referred to the idea of a world news service by television. The following April, a news release by the BBC External Services remarked that, although shortwave broadcasting would continue to be important at least until the end of the century, it was likely to become less competitive in parts of the world where cable and satellite brought a greatly increased choice of services to audiences. The External Services, it said, believed that if the BBC's reputation in the field of international broadcasting were to be maintained in the future, in the face of increasing competition, it was time to give serious consideration to planning for the development of a world news service in television.[1]

It seemed to many in Australia that, if Radio Australia were to survive for long into the new century, it would have to progressively metamorphose into Television Australia. In June 1985, the ABC's director of sales and marketing asked the director of Radio Australia to prepare a submission on the subject. The author drafted a reply for the director saying that for some years Radio Australia had been aware of the potential benefits to Australia of 'Television Australia', and its corporate plan steering committee had referred to this as a desirable future development. The draft said, in part,

We would envisage 'Television Australia' broadcasting suitable programs (including many from the ABC's Home Service Television) via satellite to whichever national broadcasting organizations or island communities (or even individuals) are interested in erecting a dish and receiving such programs, either in toto or on a selective basis.[2]

The draft (assuming that such an enterprise would begin in the Pacific) added that Radio Australia had laid the groundwork for such an enterprise by developing an extensive network of news correspondents throughout the Pacific and broadcasting ten daily bulletins of world and Pacific news in three languages. These had established Radio Australia as the major disseminator of news about the Pacific to the Pacific. It went on to mention that twelve Pacific radio broadcasting organisations relayed or rebroadcast some of Radio Australia's news bulletins, current affairs programs and even general programs. The credibility of Radio Australia, and the resultant respect for and even affection for the organisation, the draft said, would predispose many nations, communities and individuals in the Pacific to a favourable response to 'Television Australia'. Referring to a rival proposal by Australia's Nine Network, the draft said programs produced by 'Television Australia' would certainly be far more suited to the Pacific. The author said that on a recent visit to the Pacific, several national leaders and senior broadcasters had expressed concern to him about the possible social effects of some American television shows which would be relayed by the Nine Network. The draft reply suggested that all major English-speaking Pacific countries should be approached, except for those that were virtually part of the USA. The draft apparently languished in the director's office. It appears from Radio Australia's files that no reply was sent to the ABC's director of sales and marketing. In January 1986, a proposed ABC television service to the South Pacific (not necessarily an enterprise of Radio Australia) was put to the government, but not acted on.[3]

In 1989, the Revill report concluded that the ABC could not undertake regular international television programming without a major infusion of funds.[4] The report did observe, however, that the ABC had high-quality capacities, especially in the production of television news, current affairs and documentaries, had the most developed network of correspondents in Asia and the Pacific, and had 'years of experience through Radio Australia in the sensitivities of transmitting to international audiences'.[5] Recommending that if international television services were to be provided to the South Pacific, the ABC should be involved, the report suggested that 'such services should pay due attention to the wishes and sensitivities of the governments and peoples involved'.[6] That suggestion was to have echoes when Australia Television began broadcasting to Asia in 1993.

Broinowski, as general manager of Radio Australia, said in early 1992 that the service would 'play a very important role in the provision of suitable audio-visual material for broadcast overseas'.[7] But the ABC's managing director, David Hill, was reported to be adamant that Radio Australia should not handle international television. Perhaps the ABC thought a clean break from Radio Australia would avoid some of the problems ABC executives (and possibly Foreign Affairs) had had with the international radio broadcaster, and that it should set up an entirely new division. Whether or not this had been true, after Australia Television had been broadcasting for almost a year, the ABC's overseas television and radio operations were both put under the control of the general manager of Radio Australia, Derek White. Hill appointed him general manager of ABC international broadcasting.[8]

In March 1992, the assistant managing director, Malcolm Long, had announced that the ABC was planning a Southeast Asia–Pacific satellite television service which would beam the best of Australian television production into the region in much the same fashion as Radio Australia did with the spoken word. It had not yet been decided how it would be funded and delivered, but he thought it might be possible to launch an initial version of the service by the end of 1992. Long, who was coordinating television, radio and Radio Australia input into the venture, ruled out any kind of 'propaganda' service.[9]

Two months later, Hill told the Senate estimates committee that the annual cost of a Southeast Asian television service could range from $2 million for a recycled domestic menu with a 'rip and read' news service to $20 million for a more tailored service. He said the service would probably be redistributed by 'host broadcasters' in each country, rather than beamed directly into homes. 'I think it does require a bit of sensitivity on the ABC's part', he said.[10]

By this time, the American CNN news and current affairs channel was already broadcasting around the world; Rupert Murdoch's commercial Star TV, complete with commercials and the BBC's international television news (since dropped), was beaming into Asia from Hong Kong; and the United States Information Service's TV Worldnet was broadcasting to 125 countries.

The ABC decided to distribute its satellite television service via Indonesia's Palapa B2P satellite. This would enable it to reach all or part of more than fifteen countries. The satellite's primary area, where a dish of 2 to 3.6 metres diameter was required, covered all of Papua New Guinea, Indonesia, Singapore, Malaysia, Brunei, the Philippines, Taiwan, Hong Kong, Macau, Vietnam, Laos, Cambodia, Thailand and Burma. The primary area also included the southern provinces of China, the easternmost part of India and most of Bangladesh. In the satellite's secondary area, a dish of 3.6 to 7 metres was needed; it extended to the central provinces of China, more of eastern India, eastern Nepal and all of Bhutan.[11] From about August 1994, Australia Television intended to beam off the Chinese Apstar 1 satellite, increasing its reach to virtually the whole of China, Japan, Mongolia, the two Koreas and more of northern India. But the Chinese had problems with the satellite, and by mid-August 1994 Australia Television had decided not to use it. The Australians had felt that access to the huge Chinese audience would be a tremendous gain. Although in 1994 the Chinese government was clamping down on privately owned satellite dishes, there were estimates that some 40,000 were already in private hands and that this figure could grow tenfold in the following three years.[12] Despite the failure of the plan to beam off Apstar 1, Australia Television plans a huge extension of its reach in 1995 by beaming off China's Apstar 2. As well as the area that would have been reached by Apstar 1, the footprint of Apstar 2 (for viewers with dishes a little less than four metres in diameter) will include most of the former Soviet Union, eastern, central and southern Europe (including the Dalmatian coast and the heel and toe of Italy), the Middle East, northeastern Africa and the whole of India and Pakistan (as well as Australia itself).[13]

Sponsorship

In September 1992 the ABC asked cabinet for $5 million to trial the service. Cabinet deferred a decision on the bid, and asked the ABC to consider using advertising and commercial sponsorship to help fund the project.[14] The ABC agreed, on condition that Parliament approve the necessary amendment to the ABC Act.[15] Hill estimated that the enterprise would need start-up capital of about $5–6 million.[16]

Cabinet approved an allocation of $5.4 million to enable the ABC to begin the broadcasts, screening up to ten hours of news, current affairs and other programs each day. The Opposition spokesman on communications, Warwick Smith, described the move to accept corporate sponsorship for the television service as 'realistic', adding, 'perhaps it should now be considered for Radio Australia'. ABC staff, including staff-elected board director Quentin Dempster, immediately opposed the move, saying it would make commercial control of program content a fact of life.[17] In fact, the television service eventually accepted both sponsorship and advertising, but with strict guidelines. There was to be no sponsorship of news and current affairs programs; other programs were not to be interrupted by advertising or sponsorship announcements; and there was to be no hard-sell advertising. Australia Television had been broadcasting barely a year, though, when the ABC announced that a one-minute block of what it euphemistically described as 'announcements' was to be inserted in the main news bulletin.[18] No doubt the fact that some television stations in Asia were relaying only the news from Australia Television, and not the rest of its programs, was a factor in this decision. (The 'announcements' do not interrupt the news proper, but are inserted in 'natural breaks', for example, between the news and the weather.)

Curiously, an ABC background paper released in April 1993 says the prohibition of advertising enables ABC domestic radio and television and Radio Australia

> to remain free from commercial pressures to maximise audiences that a reliance on advertising may bring. This allows the ABC to provide audiences within Australia and Radio Australia listeners with a range of services and innovative programs that do not depend on the number of listeners or viewers they can deliver to advertisers.
>
> It is crucial to the public credibility of the ABC that it is not seen to be influenced by, or dependent on, commercial interests.[19]

But apparently the same criterion did not apply to Australia Television. Later, the same background paper goes on to say: 'Sponsorship of the Australia Television service has allowed the ABC to initiate the service without diverting funds from domestic television and radio production.'

The new service was launched in Darwin on 17 February 1993 by Prime Minister Paul Keating. The program included news and current affairs at 11.30 every night, Australian Eastern Time, with periodic news updates during the day and night.[20] Later, the service broadcast 'Lateline', 'Foreign Correspondent' and editions of 'Four Corners' compiled by ABC staff (reports on 'Four Corners' produced by overseas organisations like the BBC being subject to international copyright). Most of the news and current affairs items came from ABC domestic television, though some items believed to be of particular interest to Asian audiences were broadcast at greater length than the edited versions seen on the home service. Australia Television had access to all material from the ABC's overseas offices, of which there were ten in the target area. It received the unedited Visnews news agency, and ran some Visnews items not used at all on the home service. It also ran Reuters 'Asian Report' and Reuters 'American Report'. Its criterion for which news and current affairs stories to use, and at what length, was said to be whether they were likely to interest its viewers. But there was a hidden agenda: whether the stories might offend the 'cultural sensitivities' of the audiences and their governments. It is true that the service does handle some thorny issues. In May 1994 Australia Television broadcast a 'Four Corners' program about the devastation of forests in Papua New Guinea by Malaysian timber interests at the risk of displeasing the Malaysian Government. Nevertheless, there have been instances of editorial interference with its news programs, as shown later in this chapter.

Most of the journalists working for Australia Television were drawn from the ABC's domestic television news. They were chosen partly for their knowledge of Asia and their sensitivity to Asian values. But none of them had had experience in any of the ABC's bureaus in Asia.

When the service opened, an advertisement for 'sponsorship opportunities' said the audience would include English-speaking people throughout the region, among them decision-makers and professional and business leaders, and also tourists with access in their hotel rooms to direct-by-satellite broadcasts. The sponsorship guidelines specified that the service would 'retain editorial control and independence in all programming and shall not enter into any sponsorship arrangement which is likely adversely to affect the real and/or apparent independence and integrity of the Service or ATVI's reputation as a socially responsible broadcaster'.[21] An information sheet issued by the corporation in 1994 said there were no significant restrictions on satellite dishes in Indonesia, Brunei, the Philippines, Thailand, Hong Kong and Taiwan, but dishes were regulated in Papua New Guinea, Vietnam, Laos and China and prohibited without consent in Malaysia and Singapore. No regulatory system had yet been developed in Burma, Bangladesh or Cambodia.[22]

An astonishing development in a service purporting to be an international voice of Australia was that, from August 1994, with benefit to its ailing finances, it began broadcasting an overnight block of seven hours of uninterrupted news and current affairs from the American NBC network. The intrusion of American material enabled Australia Television to boast that it was on air 24 hours a day, but many viewers tuning to the overnight transmission must assume that they are watching an American station. And those who are aware that the signal is being carried by the Australian service must wonder about its national identity and its journalistic integrity. Australia Television's willingness to broadcast hour after hour of foreign news and current affairs is in stark contrast to the stance of Radio Australia, which for fifty-five years refused even to consider carrying American material.

Australia Television has tremendous potential. In mid-1994, it could be received by satellite receiving dishes serving an estimated one million homes and hotel rooms, giving it a potential audience of more than four million people, with thousands of additional satellite dishes expected to be erected in the near future. Australia's Foreign Minister, Senator Gareth Evans, had said in 1992 that the service represented Australia's most important means of communicating about itself to Asia.[23]

Australia Television was seeking to have all or part of its service carried on more than thirty free-to-air or cable services in the region. Before it began broadcasting, it entered an agreement for its complete service to be carried on a new channel on the Philippine cable system, giving access to a potential additional audience of 100,000. In June 1993, Singapore cable television, a subsidiary of the Singapore Broadcasting Corporation, began taking Australia Television's news service. This was an important breakthrough in a country where private receiving dishes were prohibited. A cable channel in Bangkok was the next to carry the Australia Television news, and Channel 21 Metro in Manila added the news to its terrestrial service. In mid-1994 negotiations for rebroadcasting agreements were under way with Indonesia, Malaysia, India, China, Vietnam, Cambodia and Laos. Australia Television is carried on 140 cable channels in the Philippines, with a potential audience of hundreds of thousands.

In 1993 the acting general manager of Australia Television, Bruce Donald, said it was hoped eventually to expand the service into foreign languages, the priorities being Indonesian, Standard Chinese, Cantonese and Thai, but the cost was a problem. From October 1993, however, a camera in Radio Australia's newsroom in Melbourne enabled Radio Australia staff to read some of the two-minute news updates on Australia Television in

Indonesian, Standard Chinese and Cantonese (one per weeknight in each language), with English subtitles.

The ABC described Australia Television as 'the only satellite service in the region that is tailored for the region', and said programming 'emphasises news and current affairs about Asia and the Pacific'.[24] To an extent, this seems to be true. John Ritchie[25] has reviewed the weekday news in the three weeks from 22 March to 9 April 1993, when Australia Television was broadcasting one hour of news each night (not counting read-only news updates). He found that 313 stories were broadcast, of which seventy-five, or 23.5 per cent, were from the target area in Asia and the Pacific. In the weekday news in the nine weeks from 12 April to 11 June 1993, when the news had been cut to half an hour a night, Australia Television increased the percentage of stories from the target area to 32.3 per cent (231 stories out of a total of 724).

Ritchie's figures appear to show that Australia Television did not shy away from contentious stories about human rights. In the three weeks in March and April, he classified five of the stories from the target area as about human rights—three from Indonesia, two of these concerning East Timor. In the nine weeks from April to June, he classified twenty-four stories from the target area as about human rights, including six from China (three of them concerning Tibet), four from Indonesia (two of them concerning East Timor), four from Burma, two each from Papua New Guinea, the Philippines, Thailand and Vietnam and one each from Bangladesh and Singapore.

Ritchie is critical of the fact that a high proportion of the stories in the period he surveyed was from Australia (118, or 37.7 per cent, in the three-week period and 227, or 31.4 per cent, in the nine-week period). But it should be remembered that, apart from Reuter's TV 'Asian Report' and 'American Report' (also received by ABC domestic television), from which it can select and edit items for itself, Australia Television is heavily dependent on video from ABC newsrooms throughout Australia and from ABC correspondents overseas. It is only to be expected that, with these limitations, it would have a high proportion of video from Australia. In any case, an ABC background paper on Australia Television says its programming is 'designed to increase regional awareness of Australia and the activities of Australians'.[26]

But stories showing involvement with the region sometimes reflect Australia in a very poor light. For instance, on 18 May 1994, the news included a story about allegations in Papua New Guinea that the BHP Ok Tedi copper mine had caused an environmental catastrophe. It was followed by a story even more damaging to the image of Australians. It said laws aimed at ending decades of Australian sexual exploitation of children overseas had run into legal problems. A child abuse campaigner said on camera that it was 'a brave move by the government to publicly and internationally admit that Australians are some of the worst sexual offenders overseas'.[27]

Ritchie claims that Australia Television news may be accused of favouring popularity and acceptance over objectivity. He says that if it attempts to legitimise itself by restricting itself to representations that are popular by communicating a 'reverse orientalist' perspective where Australia is posited as part of the Asian 'them', 'it ceases to function as "news", and operates primarily, albeit covertly … to construct an image of Australia appropriate to the goals of the Australian Government.'[28]

But there is clear evidence that there has been interference in the kind of stories about the target area selected by Australia Television, and the treatment of those stories. Before Australia Television began broadcasting, its executive producer, Prakash Mirchandani, in consultation with Bruce Donald, asked Foreign Affairs to send a team to Darwin to brief its staff. Donald wrote later, 'This was in the normal course of providing journalists broadcasting to a new and sensitive region with as much detailed background on Australia's Foreign Policy and current knowledge from those who had worked in the region.'[29] The four officers of the department who made the visit, including the assistant secretary in charge of its Southeast Asian branch, Judith Pead, are reported to have pointed out where in the region Australia's interests lay. At an informal dinner which followed the formal briefing session, Pead is reported to have been particularly dogmatic about stories that would be sensitive in Indonesia. According to one of those present, she said Australia Television should not run stories about the issue of East Timor, or about the rebel leader, Xanana Gusmao. She had been backed up in this by another of the Foreign Affairs officers. Her friends in Asia, Pead had said, were not interested in East Timor. What's more, Indonesian viewers with access to satellite dishes would be watching Indonesian television beamed off the Palapa satellite, not Australia Television.

Pead later denied this account of what had taken place, saying it was 'not an accurate reflection of the views that were put forward, by myself or anyone else'.[30] But she refused to say specifically what aspects of the report she was denying. Asked to confirm or deny particular details, she became defensive and secretive. She refused to reveal, for example, whether she had actually mentioned Gusmao. She denied that she and her colleagues had tried to influence the Australia Television journalists, and maintained this denial even when it was pointed out that 'trying to influence' did not necessarily connote impropriety. Asked by the author whether she had served in the Australian embassy in Jakarta, Pead replied that she had served one term, but refused to say when, or in what capacity. (In fact, she served two terms in Jakarta, the first as third secretary from 1977 to 1979, and the second as counsellor from 1990 to 1992, immediately before her appointment to head the Southeast Asia branch in Canberra.)

The ABC, for its part, gave an assurance before the service began that journalists working for Australia Television would have the same editorial independence as other ABC journalists. The ABC Board had promulgated guidelines for all ABC international services which said, in part:

> Occasionally, reports may create difficulties in Australia's foreign relations with another country. This problem is the price of a genuinely independent overseas service and is recognised and accepted by the ABC and the Australian Government ... ATVI ... will follow and build on Radio Australia's position as an authoritative, independent and impartial provider of international news and information.[31]

But the guidelines went on to say that this did not mean that ATVI and Radio Australia should not be mindful of the concept of 'cultural intrusion', and to add that 'television may represent a more potent cultural challenge than radio'.[32]

The guidelines gave some examples of cultural sensitivity:

> Most Asian societies ... do not easily accept direct comment or innuendo disparaging the authority, pride and self-respect of leaders and countries within the region.
>
> There may be a reluctance to reflect or have portrayed racial, ethnic or religious differences or conflicts which may impinge on or threaten the national identity or sense of community.
>
> Media in some countries may be reluctant to have depicted or reported events, even in other and distant countries or societies, which may be seen as likely to provoke agitation or communal tension (e.g. demonstrations or conflict for political, economic or religious motives).

The media in some countries certainly are reluctant to report events seen as likely to promote communal tension. But does this mean that Australian international radio or television should not report them?

On the other hand the guidelines went on to affirm that 'the overseas services will *not* distort or censor program material, particularly information programs, in order to avoid the possibility of offence', and to assert that awareness of areas of sensitivity ... will not mean that ATVI or Radio Australia will be restrained in any way from the full and accurate reporting and reflection of events in the region, in the tradition of independence, authority and integrity developed over sixty years [*sic*] by Radio Australia's news and information services.

'The ABC', the guidelines said, 'will stand by the authority, integrity and independence of the news, current affairs and information services provided by ATVI and Radio Australia based on the accuracy and balance of their reportage.' With slight amendments (including the correction of the claim that Radio Australia's experience went back sixty years), the guidelines were incorporated into a new handbook of ABC editorial policies issued in June 1993.

Donald told the *Sydney Morning Herald* in May 1993 that the motto of Australia Television news was 'sensitivity, not censorship'. As an example of a potentially sensitive story, he quoted a news item used the previous month: 'An item about a United Nations-sponsored conference on racism noted that Indonesia had come in for specific criticisms: it then pointed out that Australia had likewise been cited for its treatment of Aborigines.'[33]

Television wars?

There were problems later in May, just over three months after Australia Television began broadcasting. ABC broadcaster Geraldine Doogue had done a television interview with the wife of Xanana Gusmao, the Timorese rebel leader who had just been sentenced to life imprisonment by an Indonesian court. The interview was run on 'The 7.30 Report' at a length of about eight minutes. Mirchandani, who was visiting Sydney, sent an e-mail message to Darwin asking the presenter who was writing the word stories for the Australia Television news updates, 'Should we be putting this to air?' He later sent another message asking whether Australia Television should be seeking 'balancing material'. Mirchandani is reported to have written, 'Don't upset the Indonesians'.[34] (He later denied having said this on that occasion,[35] although the senior producer in Darwin said he had heard him use the words, 'We don't want to upset the Indonesians', on at least one previous occasion.)[36]

The senior producer, a journalist on secondment from Radio Australia, later told Mirchandani there was no way of 'balancing' the story, as it was well known that the Indonesians had a policy of not responding to such interviews. The producer said later that he regarded the instruction as a 'deliberate and blatant attempt' to slant the news.[37]

Two days later, when a one-hour news and current affairs program provided scope for the interview itself, it was broadcast. The senior producer cut the interview from its original length to just under five and a half minutes.

In the same week as the Gusmao issue, there was another clash over news judgment. In a telephone call from Sydney, Mirchandani told the senior producer that 'those above us' were upset about the failure the previous night of an attempt to send by satellite to Hanoi video showing the arrival in Australia of the Vietnamese Prime Minister, Vo Van Kiet. Mirchandani reportedly said he wanted that night's news bulletin to lead with video of a parliamentary reception in Canberra to welcome Kiet (a reception to be attended, incidentally, by David Hill).[38] The producer responded that the story would have to be judged on its news value. When Mirchandani asked him what he *was* going to lead the bulletin with, the producer replied that he would not know until that night, when he saw what stories were available. He pointed out that Kiet did not speak English, and suggested that his speech, delivered through an interpreter, would hardly be compelling viewing. The producer reported the incident to the chairperson of the house committee of the Australian Journalists' Association section of the Media, Arts and Entertainment Alliance.

The reason that 'those above us' were upset at the failure the previous night to deliver to Hanoi the video of the official welcome to Kiet was that Hill had personally undertaken that this would be done. He had given the undertaking at a meeting with the Vietnamese ambassador in Canberra some weeks previously to discuss his planned visit to Vietnam to arrange for the opening of an ABC office in Hanoi (the first office established there by a Western broadcaster since the Vietnam War). Hill told the ambassador that the ABC camera operator to be stationed in Hanoi would use the Palapa satellite to send his video to Australia. The ambassador responded by saying that Kiet was to visit Australia in late May, and it would help if the ABC could use the satellite to send Vietnam same-day video of the official welcome in Canberra. Hill enthusiastically agreed to have the video sent to Vietnam on the same day via the Palapa satellite before Australia Television began its evening broadcast. (Some said the ABC was also trying to win favour with Hanoi because it was hoping to get a lucrative contract, funded by the Australian International Development Assistance Bureau, to train radio and television broadcasters in Vietnam.) The promised video of the welcome to Kiet on 28 May went out from Canberra to Darwin, and was sent via the satellite, but, for some reason, was not used by Vietnamese television (though it was recorded—and the sound replayed—by Vietnamese radio). The ABC was clearly not to blame, but Hill was embarrassed and angry. Telephoning the ABC's manager in Canberra, Philip Koch (a former head of Radio Australia), the managing director, who had a reputation for shooting from the hip, reportedly told him he was sacked. Koch says he responded that he would take Hill and the ABC to court over the matter. Apparently after the managing director realised that he did not have the power unilaterally to sack Koch, he told ABC radio that the Canberra manager knew he could not be summarily dismissed. Koch released a statement which said that, given the words spoken to him by Hill, he had no choice but to accept that he was purporting to exercise a power of summary dismissal.[39]

(Koch said two months after the incident that Hill was not speaking to him, but was sending messages telling him his position was untenable, and he should resign.[40] He and the managing director remained on non-speaking terms until the deadlock was broken by a handshake at the ABC Board's Christmas party in December 1993.[41])

Concerned about Mirchandani's 'suggestion', the journalists of ABC radio and television in Darwin (domestic as well as international) called a stopwork meeting (on 28 May 1993) at which the following resolution was carried unanimously:

This meeting of the Media, Arts and Entertainment Alliance house committee in Darwin condemns what appears to be editorial pressure placed on Australian Television news staff to give prominence to a specified story. We believe the direction to be a flagrant breach of the ABC charter of editorial practice and are dismayed and alarmed that the incident occurred, given management's assurances of the editorial independence during the leadup to the establishment of the service. We believe ATVI journalists should be covered by the ABC charter of editorial practice which states that journalists will not allow their professional judgment to be influenced by pressures from political, commercial or other sectional interests. If there is to be a separate charter of editorial independence for Australia Television International it should be drafted as a matter of urgency after consultation with Australia Television journalists and the Media Alliance.[42]

The resolution was transmitted to ABC newsrooms throughout Australia. Mirchandani phoned the chairperson of the house committee from Sydney to ask why the journalists were taking industrial action. After a telephone conference the following day to discuss the dispute, Mirchandani gave an assurance in writing that ATVI news was conforming to ABC editorial practices. The senior producer did use Kiet's speech in that night's news bulletin, but in third place, not at the top of the news.

Mirchandani said later that there had been no pressure on Australia Television from Foreign Affairs about what should be covered in its news and current affairs programs, or how. He said, though, that in 1993, when passing through Darwin at the end of his posting as ambassador in

Indonesia, Philip Flood had told him of his reservations about its coverage of Indonesia.[43]

A remarkable appointment was announced by the ABC on 29 May 1994. The Australian ambassador to Laos, Michael Mann, had been chosen to be chief executive of Australia Television, replacing the acting general manager. The appointment to such a sensitive position of an officer of the department with which Radio Australia had had to fight a long battle for independence was reminiscent of the choice of Richard Broinowski to be general manager of Radio Australia in 1990, when he was ambassador to South Korea.

With Australia Television certain to expand its target area and increase its audiences as more satellites are launched, and eventually to broadcast in the major languages of the Asia–Pacific region, including Standard Chinese and Indonesian, international television seems likely eventually to supplant international radio as the major medium for Australia to communicate with mass audiences beyond its shores.

The ABC's annual report for 1992–93 says:

For 50 years the ABC, through Radio Australia, has built a valuable reputation throughout Asia and the Pacific for independent, quality broadcasting based on editorial integrity. Australia Television builds on that tradition.[44]

Whether it has built on Radio Australia's tradition, or distorted it, is in dispute. Perhaps, like their predecessors in Radio Australia, the journalists of Australia Television will have to fight a war of independence against those who want its news and current affairs programs tailored to take account of 'sensitivities' in the region. Such a struggle may be necessary if this medium which 'may represent a more potent cultural challenge than radio' is to establish a reputation for credibility and integrity to match that won over half a century by Radio Australia.

Notes

INTRODUCTION

1 *Radio Australia, Independent Inquiry Report* (*Waller report*), December 1975 (Parliamentary Paper No. 97/1977), p. 2.

2 Submission 7303, attachment B—future arrangements for Radio Australia; Cabinet minute no. 14006 (ER), expenses review committee, Canberra, 23 July 1990.

3 Graham Mytton and Carol Forrester, 'Audiences for International Radio Broadcasts', *European Journal of Communication* (Vol. 3, no. 4, 1988).

4 *ibid.*, p. 458.

5 Recorded interview with A. H. Tange, Canberra, 27 December 1988.

6 J. A. C. Mackie, letter to author, 2 November 1993.

7 Julian Hale, *Radio Power: Propaganda and International Broadcasting* (London: Paul Elek, 1975), p. 4.

8 *ibid.*

9 *ibid.*, p. x.

10 R. J. F. Boyer, 'Overseas Shortwave Service', report by ABC chairman to the commission, 20 October 1950, p. 16 (DFATA 570/1/2 part 6A).

11 C. J. A. Moses to commission, 2 February 1956 (ABCDA).

12 Recorded interview with M. R. Booker, Canberra, 20 March 1989.

13 Recorded interview with Tange, *op. cit.*

14 Charles Curran, *A Seamless Robe: Broadcasting—Philosophy and Practice* (London: Collins, 1979), p. 75.

15 These programs, in all foreign languages in which Radio Australia has broadcast, have, at least since the war, originated in English and been under the control of the Anglophone news and current affairs staff.

16 These long-term residents have included British, French, Japanese, Thai and Vietnamese nationals.

CHAPTER 1

1   Transcript of recording of opening broadcast, 20 December 1939 (RAA).
2   Interview with G. J. Smith, 1 November 1989.
3   *International Who's Who, 1988–9* (London: Europa, 1988), *s.v.*
4   *The Constant Voice: Radio Australia: 30th Anniversary 1939–1969* (Melbourne: Radio Australia, 1969), p. 30.
5   W. M. Ball to G. Williams, 26 July 1941 (AA MP272/2 31/12/3).
6   Recorded interview by Stan Correy with Ball, 20 May 1981 (ABC sound archives).
7   John Robertson and John McCarthy, *Australian War Strategy 1939–1945* (St Lucia: University of Queensland Press, 1985), p. 267.
8   Gavin Long, *The Six Years War: A Concise History of Australia in the 1939–45 War* (Canberra: Australian War Memorial and AGPS, 1973), pp. 164–5.
9   *Age*, 9 June 1988, p. 13.
10 *Bulletin*, 18 February 1992, p. 36.
11 *Age*, 3 November 1988, p. 14.
12 'The Truth of It Is …', 8 January 1943 (AA MP727/3 Series File 'The Truth of it Is').
13 *Age*, 9 June 1988, p. 13.
14 Long, *op. cit.*, p. 193.
15 Recorded interview with G. S. Sawer, Guerilla Bay, NSW, 3 May 1988.
16 Censorship was of course partly responsible for Radio Australia's reticence, despite Ball's belief in airing bad news and controversy as a matter of principle.
17 Comprehensive accounts may be found in John Hammond Moore, *Over-Sexed, Over-Paid and Over Here: Americans in Australia, 1941–45* (St Lucia: University of Queensland Press, 1981), and E. Daniel Potts and Annette Potts, *Yanks Down Under, 1941–45: The American Impact on Australia* (Melbourne: Oxford University Press, 1985).
18 Recorded interview with Sawer, *op. cit.*
19 Ball to M. Stiver (United States representative on Allied Political Warfare Committee), 9 October 1942 (AA MP 272/3 I-1A).
20 Script of program 'Australian Wings Over the World', 17 October 1942 (AA MP272/1 part 3).
21 Potts and Potts, *op. cit.*, p. 303.
22 Moore, *op. cit.*, pp. 220–1.
23 Recorded interview with Sawer, *op. cit.*
24 L. D. Meo, *Japan's Radio War on Australia 1941–1945* (Melbourne: Melbourne University Press, 1968), p. 58.
25 Secret draft directive from Ball to staff responsible for Mandarin transmissions, 11 January 1943 (ABCDA).
26 Confidential 'off the record' information, F. P. Jost (Canberra) to Ball, 25 November 1943 (AA MP272/3 (1939–45), 115).
27 C. L. Burns to Ball, 8 July 1942 (AA MP272/3 C3).
28 Burns to Ball, 11 August 1942 (*loc. cit.*).
29 T. P. Hoey to Ball, 4 October 1943 (*loc. cit.*).
30 'Report submitted on the overseas short wave broadcasts by Messrs Molesworth, Kirke and Smith', January(?) 1940 (ABCDA).
31 'Topical Talks', Ball to T. Mathew, 22 May 1941 (AA MP272/5 item 9).

32   H. A. Stokes to Ball, 24 November 1943 (AA MP272/3 I-1A)

33   Sawer, action report no. 29, 15 November 1944 (AA MP272/3 action reports).

34   W. R. Hodgson to Ball, 4 March 1943 (AA MP272/2 31/12/3).

35   Hodgson to Ball, 7 March 1943 (*loc. cit.*).

36   Secret message from American legation, 9 March 1943 (*loc. cit.*).

37   Sawer to Ball, 10 September 1943 (AA MP272/3 I-5C).

38   Harry Gordon, *Die Like the Carp!: The Story of the Greatest Prison Escape Ever* (Moorebank, NSW: Corgi Books, 1978).

39   J. Curtin to B. Penton (editor, Sydney *Daily Telegraph*), 19 August 1944, quoted in Colm Kiernan, 'Arthur A. Calwell's Clashes with the Australian Press, 1943–45', *Historical Journal* (University of Wollongong Historical Society), 2, no. 1 (March 1976), p. 91.

40   Recorded interview with Sawer, *op. cit.*

41   Confidential message from DEA to H. A. Graves (British adviser to Minister for External Affairs), 24 January 1944 (AA MP272/3 I–5A).

42   Emergency directive, Washington combined emergencies propaganda committee, 25 January 1944 (*loc. cit.*).

43   Special directive concerning handling of Japanese atrocity stories, H. V. Evatt to DEA, 30 January 1944 (*loc. cit.*).

44   Censorship instruction, 3 March 1944 (AA MP272/3 C3).

45   Edwards states that arguments over the control of propaganda between the ABC and the Departments of External Affairs, Defence, Army, Navy, Air and Information were so frequent that there was an unintended irony in the title of the inter-departmental committee created to coordinate their work—the political warfare committee: (P. G. Edwards, *Prime Ministers and Diplomats: The Making of Australian Foreign Policy 1901–1949* (Melbourne: Oxford University Press, 1983), p. 176.

46   Political warfare (Japan) committee, overseas planning committee, Far East sub-committee: guidance for action on aim 1 of the British and American plan for political warfare against Japan, (undated) (AA MP272/3 I/5A).

47   'Political Warfare Agencies', author unknown, 30 July 1942 (AA MP272/3 I-1A).

48   Script, 'The Truth of It Is ...' 19 March 1943 (AA MP727/3 series file).

49   *ibid.*, 30 July 1943 (*loc. cit.*).

50   *ibid.*, 24 December 1943 (*loc. cit.*).

51   Ball to Sawer (undated) (AA MP272/3 I-5A).

52   Draft memorandum Ball to staff, 18 January 1943 (ABCDA).

53   E. R. Dickover to Ball, 2 March 1943 (AA MP272/3 I-5A). Dickover would presumably have approved of Drake's satire.

54   G. Williams to Ball, 3 March 1943 (ABCDA).

55   Script of commentary by P. McGuire, 8 March 1943 (*loc. cit.*).

56   S. Woodburn-Kirby, *The War Against Japan*, vol. 2 (London: Her Majesty's Stationery Office, 1958), p. 376.

57   Long, *op. cit.*, p. 256.

58   Curtin to D. MacArthur, 12 July 1989 (AA MP 272/3 1-5B).

59   MacArthur to Curtin, 23 July 1943 (*loc. cit.*).

60   Holmes to W. Ashley, 18 December 1941 (ABCDA).

61   Ball to W. Bearup (acting general manager, ABC), 2 November 1942 (*loc. cit.*).

62   Ball to Moses (general manager, ABC), 24 March 1943 (*loc. cit.*).

63   Ball to Stokes, 26 February 1943 (AA MP272/3 secret files I-1A).
64   D. Potts and A. Potts, 'Australian Wartime Propaganda and Censorship', *Historical Studies*, vol. 21, no. 85, October 1985, p. 572.
65   Ball to Stokes, 12 March 1943 (ABCDA).
66   Dispatch by G. Williams, 8 March 1943 (ABCDA).
67   Ball to Stokes, 21 July 1943 (AA MP272/3 I-1A).
68   John Hilvert, *Blue Pencil Warriors: Censorship and Propaganda in World War II* (St Lucia: University of Queensland Press, 1984), p. 134.
69   'The Weekly Review', 1941–42, undated report by shortwave division (AA MP272/3 A2 part 3).
70   Hodgson to W. J. Cleary, 24 August 1942 (AA MP272/3 A2 part 4).
71   Recorded interview with Sawer, *op. cit.*
72   Ball to Stokes, 7 September 1942 (*loc. cit.*).
73   Ball to Hodgson, 23 October 1942 (AA MP272/3 I-1A).
74   Secret and confidential letter Ball to Moses, 8 November 1943 (ABCDA).
75   *ibid.*
76   Curtin to Ashley, 26 November 1943 (*loc. cit.*).
77   Ball to Moses, 2 December 1943 (*loc. cit.*).
78   Hilvert, *op. cit.*, p. 161; *The Constant Voice: Radio Australia: 25th Anniversary 1939–1964* (Melbourne: Radio Australia, 1964), p. 10.
79   Ball to Curtin, 20 March 1944 (ABCDA).
80   Recorded interview with Sawer, *op. cit.*
81   Hilvert, *op. cit.*, p. 156.
82   W. M. Ball, foreword to Meo, *op. cit.*, p. vii.
83   *ibid.*, pp. vii–viii.
84   *ABC Annual Reports*, 1945 (Sydney: ABC), pp. 5–6.
85   Quoted in 'Department Relations with Shortwave and Listening Post', report to P. C. Spender, 24 January 1950 (AA CRS 570/1/2 part 3A).
86   Quoted in R. J. Greet to A. P. Renouf, 14 March 1958 (DFATA 570/1/2, part 5).
87   Quoted in Booker to J. W. Burton, 23 January 1950 (*loc. cit.*).
88   Spender to R. G. Menzies, 3 February 1950 (AA CRS A1838 570/1/2 part 5A).
89   Spender to Menzies, *op. cit.* Burton to E. G. Bonney, 5 October 1948 (AA CRS A1838 570/1/2 part 1A).
90   Burton to Bonney, 5 October 1948 (*loc. cit.*).
91   T. H. E. Heyes (secretary, Department of Immigration) to K. Murphy, 29 August 1949 (AA SP306/3 SG47). The director-general of the Department of Information, Kevin Murphy, referred to these transmissions as 'our immigration broadcasts': Murphy to Hoey, 12 November 1948 (*loc. cit.*).
92   J. A. Camilleri, *An Introduction to Australian Foreign Policy*, 4th edn (Brisbane: Jacaranda Press, 1979), p. 11.
93   H. Buggy to Burton, 8 February 1949 (*loc. cit.*).
94   H. I. London, *Non-White Immigration and the 'White Australia' Policy* (Sydney: Sydney University Press 1970), pp. 16–17.
95   Buggy to Burton, 10 February 1949 (*loc. cit.*).
96   Quoted in Burton to Boyer, 2 March 1949 (*loc. cit.*).
97   Burton to P. Shaw, 29 April 1949 (*loc. cit.*).
98   Boyer to Burton, 11 May 1949 (*loc. cit.*).
99   Secret memorandum from DEA to Asian and Pacific posts, 16 March 1949 (*loc. cit.*).

100 Extract from draft article on broadcasting for *Australian Encyclopaedia*, 1951, p. 4. (ABCDA).
101 'Radio Australia and Programmes', undated report by Hoey(?) (AA CRS A1838 570/1/2 part 2A).
102 Recorded interview with R. I. Horne, Melbourne, 15 May 1988.
103 *Commonwealth Parliamentary Debates*, vol. 192, p. 3213 (30 May 1947).
104 G. C. Bolton, *Dick Boyer: An Australian Humanist* (Canberra: ANU Press, 1967), pp. 164–5.
105 *Commonwealth Parliamentary Debates*, vol. 207, p. 2182 (3 May 1950).

CHAPTER 2

  1 See also Ann Curthoys and John Merritt (eds), *Better Dead Than Red*, vols 1–2 (Sydney: Allen and Unwin, 1986), and Nicholas Whitlam and John Stubbs, *Nest of Traitors: The Petrov Affair* (Brisbane: Jacaranda Press, 1974).
  2 Camilleri, *op. cit.*, 3rd edn (Brisbane: Jacaranda Press, 1976), p. 27.
  3 *Sydney Morning Herald*, 29 July 1989, p. 1.
  4 Alan Renouf, *The Champagne Trail: Experiences of a Diplomat* (Melbourne: Sun Books, 1980), p. 44.
  5 *Commonwealth Parliamentary Debates*, vol. 217, p. 872 (27 May 1952).
  6 Renouf, *loc. cit.*
  7 Casey to L. R. McIntyre, 21 April 1952 (AA CRS A1838 570/1/2 part 1).
  8 *Sydney Morning Herald*, 8 August 1992, p. 7.
  9 David Bowman, 'Can the ASIO Revolution Last?', *Australian Society*, November 1989, p. 23.
 10 Harvey Barnett, *op. cit.*, p. 44.
 11 *Age*, 21 November 1981, quoted in Rodney Tiffen, *News and Power* (Sydney: Allen and Unwin, 1989), p. 1.
 12 Recorded interview with Tange, *op. cit.*
 13 W. J. Hudson, *Casey* (Melbourne: Oxford University Press, 1986), p. 236.
 14 *ibid.*, pp. 249–50.
 15 *ibid.*, p. 251.
 16 *ibid.*, p. 252.
 17 *ibid.*, p. 255.
 18 *ibid.*, p. 242.
 19 *ibid.*, p. 243.
 20 *ibid.*, pp. 243–4.
 21 *ibid.*, p. 229.
 22 Recorded interview with Tange, *op. cit.*
 23 Toohey and Pinwill say that in the late 1950s Tange, who had drafted the ASIS directive which put the secretary of the DEA 'firmly on top', emerged as 'the wielder of most influence in the intelligence arena': Brian Toohey and William Pinwill, *Oyster: The Story of the Australian Secret Intelligence Service* (Melbourne: Heinemann, 1989), p. 78.
 24 Tange to Australian embassy, Washington, 1 May 1959 (DFATA 570/1/2, part 7).
 25 Recorded interview with Tange, *op. cit.*
 26 Paul Hasluck, *Mucking About* (Melbourne: Melbourne University Press, 1977), p. 26.
 27 *ibid.*, p. 27.

28 P. M. C. Hasluck, letter to author, 28 July 1989.
29 *ibid.*
30 Renouf, *op. cit.*, p. 99.
31 Recorded interview with R. A. Woolcott, Canberra, 24 January 1992.
32 *Who's Who in Australia.*
33 Bolton, *op. cit.*, p. 5.
34 *ibid.*, pp. 8–10.
35 *ibid.*, p. 21.
36 *ibid.*, p. 182.
37 Personal and secret letter O. L. Davis to J. C. G. Kevin, 29 July 1958 (DFATA 570/1/2 part 5).
38 N. F. Goss to O. L. Davis, 10 March 1954 (AA CRS A1838 570/1/2 part 2).
39 Goss's notes of meeting, 14 February 1955 (AA CRS A1838 570/1/3 part 3).
40 Kevin to O. L. Davis, 18 June 1958 (DFATA, *loc. cit.*).
41 W. J. Dixon (first secretary, information, British High Commission, Canberra), letter to author, 11 January 1989.
42 Personal and secret letter O. L. Davis to Kevin, 29 July 1958 *(loc. cit.)*.
43 *ibid.*
44 Boyer to Tange, 12 November 1958 (ABCDA).
45 James Darling, *Richly Rewarding* (Melbourne: Hill of Content, 1978), p. 234.
46 *ibid.*
47 K. S. Inglis, *This is the ABC: The Australian Broadcasting Commission 1932–1983* (Melbourne: Melbourne University Press, 1983), p. 268.
48 Confidential memo W. S. F. Hamilton to A. N. Finlay, 2 May 1950 (ABCDA).
49 Transcript of Public Service Arbitrator, determination 11/1959: evidence of Hamilton, 23 July 1958.
50 W. S. F. Hamilton, 'The People and the Media', from transcript of seminar on 'The Australian News Media—Problems and Prospects', Adelaide, 3 March 1972.
51 *loc. cit.*
52 Booker to Burton, 10 January 1950 (AA CRS A1838 570/1/2 part 3A).
53 A. S. Brown to Burton, 31 January 1950 (AA CRS A1838 570/1/2 part 5A). The Department of Information was abolished a few weeks later. The ABC took over Radio Australia on 6 April 1950.
54 Spender to Menzies, 3 February 1950 *(loc. cit.)*.
55 Spender to Cabinet Committee on the Department of Information, 27 April 1950 (ABCDA).
56 W. E. Dunk (chairman, Public Service Board) to Burton, 16 March 1950 (*loc. cit.*).
57 Burton to Boyer, 18 April 1950 (*loc. cit.*).
58 Goss to secretary, 12 April 1950 (DFATA 570/1/2 part 4A).
59 The ABC subsequently decided to retain only 34 of the 97 staff: 'Overseas Shortwave Service', statement by Boyer to H. L. Anthony, 1 May 1950 (AA CRS A1838 570/1/2 part 5A).
60 Bolton, *op. cit.*, pp. 182–3.
61 W. S. F. Hamilton to assistant general manager, 21 March 1950 (ABCDA).
62 Boyer to commissioners, 29 March 1950 (*loc. cit.*).
63 Recorded interview with Goss, Melbourne, 3 May 1988.
64 Boyer to Anthony, 31 March 1950 (*loc. cit.*).

65   Boyer to commissioners, 3 April 1950 (*loc. cit.*).
66   Burton to Dunk, 6 April 1950 (*loc. cit.*).
67   Burton to secretary, Department of Defence, 6 April 1950 (DFATA 570/1/2 part 4A).
68   Goss to Burton, 16 April 1950 (*loc. cit.*).
69   Goss to Burton, April 1950 (*loc. cit.*).
70   Joint Intelligence Committee, report no. 8/1950, 17 April 1950 (ABCDA).
71   Spender to Menzies, 20 April 1950 (DFATA 570/1/2 part 4A).
72   Burton to Spender, 24 April 1950 (AA CRS A1838 570/1/2 part 3A).
73   Spender to cabinet committee, 27 April 1950 (DFATA 570/1/2 part 4A).
74   Anthony to Boyer, 20 April 1950 (*loc. cit.*).
75   Spender to Boyer, 27 April 1950 (*loc. cit.*).
76   Boyer to Spender, 2 May 1950 (AA CRS A1838 570/1/2 part 5A).
77   'Overseas Shortwave Service', statement by Boyer to Anthony, 1 May 1950 (*loc. cit.*).
78   Bolton, *op. cit.*, pp. 186–7.
79   *ibid.* He of course ignored the fact that these 'difficulties' had occurred when Australia was fighting in a world war, and the shortwave service was being used for political warfare.
80   Bolton, *op. cit.*, p. 187.
81   Spender to Boyer, 9 May 1950 (AA CRS A1838 570/1/2 part 5A).
82   Boyer to Spender, 24 May 1950 (*loc. cit.*).
83   A. S. Watt to Spender, 25 May 1950 (*loc. cit.*).
84   Minutes of meeting, cabinet committee on Department of Information, 31 May 1950 (AA CRS A1838 570/1/2 part 5A).
85   Confidential memo W. S. F. Hamilton to Finlay, 2 May 1950 (ABCDA).
86   Confidential memo Finlay to W. S. F. Hamilton, 5 May 1950 (*loc. cit.*).
87   Goss to Watt, 14 June 1950 (AA CRS A1838 570/1/2 part 5A).
88   Goss to Watt, 16 June 1950 (*loc. cit.*).
89   Spender to P. A. M. McBride, September 1950 (AA CRS A1838 570/1/2 part 5A).
90   C. R. Wood to Finlay, 15 September 1950 (ABCDA).
91   Finlay to Moses, 17 October 1950 (*loc. cit.*).
92   Chairman's report to the commission, 20 October 1950 (DFATA 570/1/2 part 6A).
93   Minutes of commission meeting, 30–31 October 1950 (ABCDA).
94   Boyer to Anthony, 17 November 1950 (*loc. cit.*).
95   Draft report by Goss to DEA, 15 November 1950 (AA CRS A1838 570/1/2 part 1).
96   Quoted in Goss to Watt, 11 September 1951 (DFATA 570/1/2 part 8A).
97   Quoted in Goss to S. Jamieson, 31 August 1951 (DFATA 570/1/2 part 8A).
98   *ibid.*
99   Wood to Moses, 30 August 1951 (ABCDA).
100   Recorded interview with Wood, Sydney, 6 July 1988.
101   'Radio Australia', report by Green to Renouf, 14 March 1958 (DFATA 571/1/2 part 5).
102   Goss to Watt, 30 September 1952 (*loc. cit.*).
103   Mission to UN to Goss, 12 December 1952 (DFATA 570/1/2 part 4A).
104   Wood to Barry, 23 December 1952; Wood to Barry, 29 January 1953 (RAA).
105   Script of broadcast, 22 September 1953 (*loc. cit.*).

106   Personal letter R. G. Casey to Boyer, 16 July 1952 (AA CRS A1838 570/1/2 part 1).
107   T. B. Millar, ed., *The Diaries of R. G. Casey 1951–60* (London: Collins, 1972), p. 85 (1 August 1952).
108   Casey to Boyer, *op. cit.*
109   Casey to D. G. Acheson, 7 August 1952 (AA CRS A1838 570/1/2 part 1).
110   Casey to Kevin, 13 August 1952 (*loc. cit.*).
111   Watt to embassy, 25 November 1952 (*loc. cit.*).
112   These commentaries, the cause of the greatest friction between the department and Radio Australia, are examined in some detail in chapter 5.
113   Minutes of meeting with ABC and RA officers in Sydney, 10 June 1954 (DFATA 570/1/2 part 2).
114   F. J. Blakeney to Casey, 12 May 1953 (AA CRS A1838 570/1/2 part 1).
115   Confidential note for use of Australian planning team for item on psychological warfare, 8 June 1953 (AA CRS A1838 570/1/2 part 2).

CHAPTER 3

1   Greet to Renouf, 14 March 1958 (DFATA 570/1/2 part 5), quoting letter Blakeney to Moses, 13 October 1953.
2   Quoted in confidential memo T. W. Cutts, head, information branch, to Goss, 5 June 1958 (DFATA 570/1/2 part 5).
3   Boyer to Casey, 9 February 1954 (ABCDA).
4   Casey to Boyer, 9 March 1954 (AA CRS A1838 570/1/2 part 2).
5   C. O. G. Buttrose to Moses, 3 August 1973 (ABCDA).
6   W. S. F. Hamilton to Moses, 19 March 1954 (*loc. cit.*).
7   J. Plimsoll to Boyer, 12 April 1954 (AA CRS A1838 570/1/2 part 2).
8   'Radio Australia', DEA document, 9 June 1954 (*loc. cit.*).
9   Barry to Moses, 30 July 1954 (ABCDA).
10   'Record of Conversation' prepared by O. L. Davis, 2 August 1954 (AA CRS A1838 570/1/2 part 2).
11   Casey to McBride, 3 November 1954 (DFATA 570/1/2 part 2).
12   Minutes of commission meeting 19–20 August 1954 (ABCDA).
13   Goss to W. S. F. Hamilton, 13 August 1954 (ABCDA).
14   Moses to W. S. F. Hamilton, 30 August 1954 (*loc. cit.*).
15   Casey, unpublished diaries (National Library, Canberra), 12 October 1954. (Some of Casey's diary material was published.)
16   *ibid.* Whether such material was ever passed to Radio Australia by External Affairs is not clear.
17   *ibid.*, 30 September 1956. It is unclear what form such cooperation would have taken, and whether it ever eventuated. Toohey and Pinwill state that Casey 'tried to sell Dulles' on US financing of the booster station (*op. cit.*, p. 46.)
18   Top secret submission by Casey to cabinet, 5 January 1955 (AA CRS A4906/XM1 vol. 9).
19   Cabinet minute, decision no. 262, 7 January 1955 (*loc. cit.*).
20   'Summary of Talks—Overseas Service', submission by Wood to Joint Parliamentary Committee on Foreign Affairs, 4 February 1955 (ABCDA).
21   Wood to Moses, 15 February 1955 (*loc. cit.*).
22   B. H. Molesworth and W. S. F. Hamilton to Moses, 11 February 1955 (*loc. cit.*).

23 Boyer to Anthony, 16 February 1955 (AA CRS A1838 570/1/2 part 1).
24 B. G. Dexter to O. L. Davis, 1 April 1955 (AA CRS A1838 570/1/2 part 3).
25 Goss to Dexter, 4 May 1955 (*loc. cit.*).
26 J. D. L. Hood to Casey, 6 May 1955 (*loc. cit.*).
27 'Anti-Communist Planning in South and South-East Asia', cabinet submission by Casey, 10 May 1955 (AA CRS A1838 570/1/2 part 3).
28 Cabinet minute, South-East Asia committee, decision no. 411 (HOC), 10 May 1955 (DFATA 570/1/2 part 3).
29 Hood to secretary, 18 May 1955 (AA CRS A1838 570/1/2 part 3).
30 Notes of meeting between representatives of ABC and DEA, 20 May 1955 (AA CRS A1838 570/1/2 part 3).
31 Tange to Moses, 4 May 1959 (ABCDA).
32 Cabinet submission by Casey, 10 May 1955, *op. cit.*
33 T. S. Duckmanton to commission, 10 June 1965 (ABCDA).
34 Marginal note in secret memo Hood to Tange, 18 May 1955 (AA CRS A1838 570/1/2 part 3).
35 Greet to Renouf, 14 March 1958, *op. cit.*
36 Casey to Hood, 27 May 1955 (AA CRS A1838 570/1/2 part 3).
37 C. W. Semmler, letter to author (undated) April 1989.
38 *ibid.*
39 Casey, unpublished diaries, 28 July 1955.
40 Confidential report on meeting, 14 September 1955 (DFATA 570/1/2 part 3).
41 Plimsoll to Moses, 20 December 1955 (AA CRS A1838 570/1/2 part 3).
42 Dexter to Tange, 16 January 1956 (*loc. cit.*).
43 Dexter to Tange, 19 December 1955 (*loc. cit.*).
44 Wood to O. L. Davis, 22 August 1956 (ABCDA).
45 'Australian–Asian Relationships—Overseas Service', statement by P. W. R. Homfray, August 1957 (DFATA 570/1/2 part 7).
46 Casey to Kevin, 23 August 1957 (*loc. cit.*).
47 Goss to L. J. Arnott, 22 August 1957 (*loc. cit.*).
48 Draft letter Boyer to C. W. Davidson, 6 June 1958, with marginal comments by Tange (DFATA 570/1/2 part 5).
49 Tange to Boyer, 11 June 1958 (*loc. cit.*).
50 Boyer to Davidson, 12 June 1956 (ABCDA).
51 Draft letter, Casey to Davidson, June 1958 (DFATA 570/1/2 part 5).
52 Boyer to Tange, 12 November 1958 (ABCDA).
53 Tange to Boyer, 14 November 1958 (DFATA 570/1/2 part 5).
54 *ibid.*
55 Moses to Tange, 12 November 1958 (DFATA 570/1/2 part 5).
56 Casey to Davidson, 5 February 1959 (ABCDA).
57 *ibid.* In mid-1959, Casey told Boyer he had decided, for the time being, to let the matter of Hindi rest: Casey to Boyer, 8 June 1959, *loc. cit.*
58 Casey to Davidson, 5 February 1959, *op. cit.*
59 *ibid.*
60 Boyer to Casey, 18 March 1959 (DFATA 570/1/2 part 6).
61 Tange to Moses, 1 May 1959 (*loc. cit.*).
62 J. M. McMillan to Tange, 21 May 1959 (DFATA 570/1/2 part 7).

63   Minutes of commission meeting, 28–29 May 1959 (ABCDA).
64   'Radio Australia Service, 1955/56 to 1961/62' (undated) (ABCDA).
65   File note by McMillan, 7 September 1959 (DFATA 570/1/2/1).
66   Script of RA news item, 22 July 1959 (*loc. cit.*).
67   *ibid.*
68   McMillan to L. R. McIntyre, 24 September 1959 (DFATA 570/1/2 part 7).
69   McMillan to Tange, 14 October 1959 (*loc. cit.*).
70   Minutes of ABC–DEA–PMG's Department meeting, 8 December 1959 (RAA).
71   Minutes of commission meeting, 10–11 November 1960 (ABCDA).
72   Quoted in P. R. Heydon to Tange, 23 November 1960 (DFATA 570/3/1 part 2).
73   'Liaison between Radio Australia and the Department of External Affairs' (undated) 1961 (DFATA 570/1/2 part 7).
74   'Radio Australia Review', DEA, 12 November 1973 (DFATA 570/1/6 part 2).
75   Darling had used the title Doctor from the time he was headmaster of Geelong Grammar School, although both his doctorates were honorary: recorded interview with J. R. Darling, Melbourne, 13 December 1988.
76   Davidson to Darling, 6 July 1961 (ABCDA). As usual, External Affairs was given no defined power, and it was never made clear how far it could go in providing 'effective guidance'. Someone (probably Darling) underlined the word 'guidance' in Davidson's letter.
77   Confidential memo L. H. Border to Tange, 17 March 1959 (DFATA 570/1/2 part 6).
78   Confidential memo Tange to Australian embassy, Washington, 1 May 1959 (*loc. cit.*).
79   'Australian Contribution to Cold War Activities', undated secret DEA draft (1962?) (DFATA, 570/1/2, part 7).
80   Casey to McMillan, 19 May 1959 (DFATA 570/1/2 part 6).
81   *Commonwealth Parliamentary Debates*, Senate, vol. 21, p. 1036 (2 May 1962).
82   P. F. Peters to H. Gilchrist, 3 May 1962 (*loc. cit.*).
83   Toohey and Pinwill, *op. cit.*, p. 57.
84   R. L. Harry to Moses, 1 November 1962 (DFATA 570/1/2 part 7).
85   Script of RA news item, 13 February 1963 (*loc. cit.*).
86   P. Shaw to Harry, 27 February 1963 (*loc. cit.*).
87   P. Shaw to Tange, 27 February 1963 (*loc. cit.*).
88   Confidential memo, J. H. A. Hall to J. G. Oakley, 18 March 1963 (RAA).
89   Homfray to Semmler, 18 March 1963 (ABCDA).
90   P. Shaw to Tange, 20 March 1963; marginal notes by Tange, 27 March 1963 (DFATA 570/1/2 part 7).
91   H. N. Truscott to Tange, 18 April 1963; margin notes by Tange (undated) (*loc. cit.*).
92   Record of conversation, Moses and Tange, 23 April 1963 (*loc. cit.*)
93   *ibid.*
94   Record of conversation, Moses, W. S. F. Hamilton, Tange and Harry, 14 May 1953 (*loc. cit.*).
95   Secret memo Harry to G. E. J. Barwick, 12 June 1963 (DFATA 570/1/2 part 7).
96   Darling to Barwick, 6 September 1963 (*loc. cit.*).
97   G. A. Jockel to Truscott, 17 October 1963 (DFATA 570/3/1 part 2).

CHAPTER 4

1   Recorded interview with Woolcott, *op. cit.*
2   Draft memo by Harry, 14 January 1965 (DFATA 570/1/2 part 8).
3   C. T. Moodie to A. H. Body, 29 March 1965 *(loc. cit.)*.
4   Draft by K. McDonald for Truscott, 21 January 1965 *(loc. cit.)*.
5   Body to Moodie, 6 April 1965 *(loc. cit.)*.
6   Future of Radio Australia: Basic Documents (undated) 1965 (DFATA 570/1/2 part 11).
7   Hasluck to A. S. Hulme (undated) March–April 1965 *(loc. cit.)*.
8   P. Shaw to Hasluck, 12 April 1965 *(loc. cit.)*.
9   Woolcott to Hall, 9 March 1965 (DFATA 570/1/2 part 8).
10 Hall to Woolcott, 18 March 1965 *(loc. cit.)*.
11 Woolcott to W. S. F. Hamilton, 9 April 1965 *(loc. cit.)*.
12 W. S. F. Hamilton to Woolcott, 22 March 1965 (DFATA 570/1/2 part 8).
13 Woolcott to W. S. F. Hamilton, 24 March 1965 *(loc. cit.)*.
14 H. L. Bickel to Oakley (undated), (ABCDA).
15 Oakley to Duckmanton, 24 March 1965 *(loc. cit.)*.
16 Handwritten draft by Darling (undated) *(loc. cit.)*.
17 Recorded interview with Darling, *op. cit.*
18 Darling to Hulme, 3 May 1965 (ABCDA).
19 *ibid.*
20 Draft summary, meeting of DEA, 5 May 1965 (DFATA 570/1/2 part 8).
21 Truscott to D. O. Hay, 11 May 1965 *(loc. cit.)*.
22 Hasluck to Plimsoll, 11, 12 May 1965 *(loc. cit.)*.
23 Hay to Plimsoll, 13 May 1965 *(loc. cit.)*.
24 Report by Plimsoll, 17 May 1965 *(loc. cit.)*.
25 Duckmanton to commission, 10 June 1965 (ABCDA).
26 DEA file note, 26 May 1965 (DFATA 570/1/2 part 8).
27 C. R. Jones to M. L. Johnston, 1 July 1968 (DFATA 570/1/2 part 9).
28 Report by Duckmanton, 20 July 1965 (ABCDA).
29 Hay to Plimsoll, 22 June 1965 (DFATA 570/1/2, part 8).
30 W. S. F. Hamilton to Duckmanton, 10 August 1965 (ABCDA).
31 Telephone interview with Homfray, 19 November 1989.
32 Woolcott to Hay, 9 August 1965 (DFATA 570/1/2 part 9).
33 Woolcott to Hay, 19 October 1965 *(loc. cit.)*.
34 Hasluck to Menzies, October(?) 1965 *(loc. cit.)*.
35 Note by Hay, 19 November 1965 (DFATA 570/1/2 part 9).
36 'List of points for discussion with Radio Australia', 21 December 1965 (ABCDA).
37 Hasluck to Hulme, 21 December 1965 (DFATA 570/1/2 part 9).
38 Darling to Hulme, 17 January 1966 *(loc. cit.)*.
39 Hasluck to Hulme, 22 February 1966 (ABCDA).
40 Duckmanton to commissioners, 13 May 1966 *(loc. cit.)*.
41 Handwritten comment on chairman's copy of general manager's memo, 13 May 1966 *(loc. cit.)*.
42 Hasluck, letter to author, 28 July 1989.
43 Recorded interview with Woolcott, *op. cit.*

44 F. K. Crowley, *Modern Australia in Documents: vol. 2, 1939–1970* (Melbourne: Wren, 1973), p. 545.
45 Tange to Plimsoll, 17 November 1967 (DFATA 570/3/1 part 3).
46 P. N. B. Hutton to J. R. Rowland, 15 May 1969 (DFATA 570/1/2 part 9).
47 Cable to high commission, 19 May 1969 (DFATA 570/3/1 part 4).
48 Cable from Australian High Commission, Kuala Lumpur, 22 July 1969 *(loc. cit.)*.
49 McDonald to R. P. Broinowski, 12 June 1969 *(loc. cit.)*.
50 Broinowski to McDonald, 25 June 1969 *(loc. cit.)*.
51 Confidential draft submission from Plimsoll to G. Freeth, July 1969 *(loc. cit.)*.
52 Freeth to Hulme, 28 July 1969 (DFATA 570/3/1 part 4).
53 Handwritten notes on cable dated 10 February 1970 (DFATA 570/3/1 part 5).
54 Handwritten notes on news release dated 20 March 1970 *(loc. cit.)*.
55 *Current Notes*, vol. 40, no. 9 (September 1969) p. 525.
56 *ibid.*, vol. 41, no. 3 (March 1970) p. 96.
57 *ibid.*, vol. 42, no. 5 (May 1971) p. 267.
58 W. G. Miller to J. K. Waller, 13 October 1971 (DFATA 570/1/2 part 11).
59 J. D. McCredie to K. C. O. Shann, 10 December 1971 (DFATA 570/1/2 part 12).
60 Marginal note by Shann, report by McCredie, *op. cit.*, 14 December 1971.

CHAPTER 5

1   Goss to Waller, 11 October 1950 (DFATA 570/1/2 part 6A).
2   Minute by Waller, 11 October 1950 *(loc. cit.)*.
3   Recorded interview with Waller, Canberra, 28 February 1989.
4   Goss to Jamieson, 19 June 1951 (DFATA 570/1/2 part 6A).
5   Jamieson to Radio Australia, 20 July 1951 *(loc. cit.)*.
6   Confidential memo Goss to secretary, 8 November 1951 (DFATA 570/1/2 part 8A).
7   'Development of Asian Language Transmissions: Background', paper prepared by Goss, early 1952(?) *(loc. cit.)*.
8   Goss to Jamieson, 21 November 1951 *(loc. cit.)*.
9   Handwritten comment on memo, Goss to secretary, 27 August 1952 (AA CRS A1838 570/1/2 part 1).
10 Confidential file note by Goss on discussion with Wood, January 1953 *(loc. cit.)*.
11 Confidential memo Wood to Goss, 9 April 1953 (AA CRS A1838 570/1/2 part 2).
12 G. C. Bolton, *Dick Boyer* (Canberra: ANU Press, 1976), p. 141.
13 Recorded interview with R. W. Neal, Melbourne, 7 February 1988.
14 Goss to secretary, DEA, 25 July 1951 (DFATA 570/1/2 part 6A).
15 'Radio Australia—Weekly Commentary', file note by Blakeney, 30 April 1953 (AA CRS A1838 570/1/2 part 4).
16 'Radio Australia and the Department of External Affairs', confidential report by public information section, DEA, December 1968 (DFATA 570/1/2 part 9).
17 'Radio Australia', confidential report to secretary by Miller (public information officer), 13 October 1971 (DFATA 570/1/2 part 11).
18 Note for Australian planning team for item on psychological warfare at five-power planning conference, Pearl Harbor, 8 June 1953 (AA CRS A1838 570/1/2 part 2).
19 Recorded interview with H. D. Black, Sydney, 29 August 1988.
20 *Scan* (ABC, Sydney), October 1986, p. 5.

21 Recorded interview with Black, *op. cit.*

22 Script (as amended) of news commentary by Black, 2 September 1953 (AA CRS A1838 570/1/2 part 2).

23 Black to B. H. Molesworth, 3 September 1953 (*loc. cit.*).

24 Goss to Blakeney, 2 September 1953 (*loc. cit.*).

25 'Questions asked by Black in his letter to Molesworth of 3–9–1953; and External Affairs answers'—undated and unsigned, but submitted by Davis (who was to become Blakeney's successor as head of the department's information branch) and obviously drafted by Goss himself, to the extent of reproducing word for word his handwritten statement 'He is primarily an explainer of important issues and of the Australian point of view thereon. If this does not commend itself to him, he should not be employed' (*loc. cit.*).

26 Blakeney to Moses, 13 October 1953 (*loc. cit.*).

27 Report by Blakeney, 30 October 1953, on meeting with Moses, 23 October 1953 (*loc. cit.*).

28 Blakeney to O. L. Davis, 5 November 1953 (*loc. cit*).

29 Molesworth to Wood, 4 December 1953 (ABCDA).

30 Moses to O. L. Davis, 30 December 1953 (AA CRS A1838 570/1/2 part 2).

31 Casey to Hood, 21 April 1955 (AA CRS A1838 570/1/3 part 3).

32 Secret cabinet submission, 10 May 1955 (AA CRS A1838 570/1/2 part 2).

33 Dexter to O. L. Davis, 1 April 1955 (AA CRS A1838 570/1/3 part 3).

34 Recorded interview with Neal, *op. cit.*

35 Confidential memo Booker to Tange, 23 August 1955 (DFATA 570/2/1 part 2).

36 Confidential report by Booker to Tange, 8 November 1955 (AA CRS A1838 570/1/3 part 3).

37 I. Hamilton to Tange, 8 October 1955 (DFATA 570/2/1 part 2).

38 Bangkok legation to DEA, 6 October 1955 (*loc. cit.*).

39 Confidential letter Tange to Moses, 25 January 1956 (ABCDA).

40 A. H. Carmichael to Moses, 1 February 1956 (*loc. cit.*).

41 Horne to Moses, 1 February 1956 (*loc. cit.*).

42 Marginal note in *ibid.*

43 Minutes of commission meeting, 2–3 February 1956 (*loc. cit*).

44 Confidential letter Moses to Tange, 15 February 1956, and undated draft by Carmichael (AA CRS A1838 570/1/2 part 5).

45 Secret letter Tange to Moses, 14 March 1956 (*loc. cit.*).

46 Booker to Tange (undated) (*loc. cit.*).

47 Carmichael to Moses, 24 February 1956 (ABCDA).

48 Wood to Carmichael, 8 March 1956 (*loc. cit.*).

49 Tange to Cowen, 28 March 1956 (AA CRS A1838 570/1/2 part 4).

50 Confidential memo Wood to Moses, 2 September 1955 (ABCDA).

51 Wood to Moses, 2 September 1955 (*loc. cit.*).

52 Script of news commentary, 1 September 1955 (*loc. cit.*).

53 Wood to Moses, *op. cit.*

54 Barry to Moses, 12 September 1955, submitted to commission meeting 13–14 September 1955 (*loc. cit.*).

55 Minutes of commission meeting, 13–14 September 1955 (*loc. cit.*).

56 Moses to Barry, 26 September 1955 (*loc. cit.*).

57 Casey to Tange, 11 November 1955 (DFATA 570/1/2 part 4).
58 Recorded interview with Burns, Melbourne, 19 February 1988.
59 Draft script of Burns's news commentary, 17 May 1956 (AA CRS A1838 570/1/2 part 4).
60 O. L. Davis to Tange, 18 May 1956 (*loc. cit.*).
61 File note by O. L. Davis, 11 June 1956, on meeting in Sydney, 8 June 1956 (*loc. cit.*).
62 Barry to Moses, 18 June 1956 (ABCDA).
63 Burns to Wood, 22 August 1956 (*loc. cit.*).
64 Minutes of interim commission meeting, 6 June 1958 (*loc. cit.*).
65 Telephone interview with Wood, 1 January 1989.
66 Recorded interview with Burns, *op. cit.*
67 Recorded interviews with Neal, *op. cit.*, and with E. S. Sayers, Melbourne, 18 April 1988.
68 Bolton, *op. cit.*, p. 219.
69 Telephone interview with Homfray, 5 March 1988.
70 Recorded interview with Z. Cowen, Melbourne, 17 August 1988.
71 Quoted in O. L. Davis to Tange, 29 November 1956 (DFATA 570/1/2 part 9).
72 W. Macmahon Ball, 'Why Australia Should Object', in *Australia's Neighbours,* December 1956 (Melbourne: Australian Institute of International Affairs).
73 B. L. Cook to Moses, 6 February 1957 (ABCDA).
74 Recorded interview with D. Wilkie, Melbourne, 27 November 1988.
75 Boyer to Davidson, 6 June 1958 (ABCDA).
76 Tange to Boyer, 11 June 1958 (*loc. cit.*).
77 Quoted in Gilchrist to W. A. Vawdrey, 1 September 1961 (DFATA 570/1/2 part 7).
78 Harry to Tange, 13 April 1962 (DFATA 570/3/1 part 2).
79 Recorded interview with Sayers, *op. cit..*
80 Recorded interview with M. E. Teichmann, Melbourne, 11 April 1988.
81 Recorded interview with W. Pinwill, Sydney, 9 May, 1989.
82 Truscott to Plimsoll, 6 July 1965 (DFATA 570/1/2 part 9).
83 Recorded interview with Pinwill, *op. cit.*
84 Woolcott to Hay, 22 March 1966 (DFATA, 570/2/1 part 2).
85 'Radio Australia and the Department of External Affairs', confidential paper prepared by public information section, DEA, December 1968 (DFATA 570/1/2 part 9).
86 Duckmanton to Waller, 9 June 1972 (ABCDA).

CHAPTER 6

1 Wood, confidential report to secretary, DEA, on visit to Southeast Asia (undated) 1956 (DFATA 570/1/2 part 5).
2 Script of RA news item, 22 November 1960 (DFATA 570/3/1 part 2).
3 DEA file note, 22 November 1960 (*loc. cit.*).
4 Confidential letter Tange to Moses, 28 November 1960 (ABCDA).
5 Oakley to Moses, 2 December 1960 (*loc. cit.*).
6 Moses to Tange, 6 December 1960 (DFATA 570/3/1 part 2).
7 Script of RA news item, 9 January 1961 (*loc. cit.*).

8   Gilchrist to Peters, 27 January 1961 (*loc. cit.*).
9   Wood, confidential report on visit to Southeast Asia, *op. cit.*
10 Tange to Moses, 31 January 1962 (RAA).
11 Moses to Tange, 10 April 1962 (*loc. cit.*).
12 H. E. Holt to Davidson, 31 May 1962 (*loc. cit.*).
13 Moses to Darling, 11 October 1962 (*loc. cit.*).
14 H. D. Anderson to Duckmanton, 31 December 1964 (DFATA 570/1/2 part 8).
15 Woolcott to Hall, 9 March 1965 (*loc. cit.*).
16 Hall to Woolcott, 18 March 1965 (*loc. cit.*).
17 W. S. F. Hamilton to Woolcott, 22 March 1965 (*loc. cit.*).
18 Woolcott to Hay, 21 July 1965 (DFATA 570/1/2 part 9).
19 Hasluck to J. Plimsoll, 11 May 1965 (DFATA 570/3/1 part 3).
20 Hay to Hasluck (undated) May(?) 1965 (DFATA 570/1/2 part 9).
21 DEA, 'List of points for discussion with Radio Australia', 21 December 1965 (ABCDA).
22 Report no. 76, Homfray to Duckmanton for commission, 27 May 1966 (*loc. cit.*).
23 Report no. 83, Homfray to Duckmanton for commission, 23 January 1967 (*loc. cit.*).
24 During the Paris peace talks in 1968, allied troops captured a secret directive warning Viet Cong field commanders not to let their men listen to BBC or other Western news broadcasts for fear that news of the talks would weaken their will to fight: *Times*, 4 July 1968.
25 Submission by Homfray to Joint Parliamentary Committee on Foreign Affairs, 2 May 1968 (ABCDA).
26 R. B. Madgwick to Semmler, 21 May 1968 (*loc. cit.*).
27 Draft agreement between Madgwick and Plimsoll (undated) (DFATA 570/3/1 part 3).
28 W. S. F. Hamilton to Semmler, 22 May 1968 (ABCDA).
29 W. S. F. Hamilton to L. C. Shaw, 21 May 1968 (*loc. cit.*).
30 Minutes of commission meeting, 23–24 May 1968 (*loc. cit.*).
31 Embassy to DEA, 3 July 1969 (DFATA 570/3/1 part 4).
32 Secret telex Broinowski to embassy, 4 July 1969 (*loc.cit.*).
33 Quoted in Broinowski to Hutton, 26 August 1969 (DFATA 570/3/1 part 4).
34 Marginal note Broinowski to Hutton, *op. cit.*
35 Broinowski to Hutton, *op. cit.*
36 *ibid.*
37 Broinowski, letter to author, 25 January 1990.
38 Telephone interview with Homfray, 3 March 1990.
39 M. G. D. Williams to Plimsoll, 10 September 1969 (*loc. cit.*).
40 Embassy to DEA, 5 December 1969 (*loc. cit.*).
41 Embassy to DEA, 18 April 1970 (DFATA 570/3/1 part 5).
42 DEA to embassy, 20 April 1970 (*loc. cit.*).
43 'Radio Australia—Departmental meeting of 19th August', J. D. McCredie to J. W. C. Cumes (undated) (DFATA 570/1/2 part 10).
44 Shann to McCredie, 5 November 1971 (DFATA 570/3/1 part 6).
45 Embassy to DFA, 14 November 1972 (*loc. cit.*).
46 Waller to Duckmanton, 6 February 1973 (*loc. cit.*).

CHAPTER 7

1   J. McG. Trotter to Cumes, 4 August 1970 (DFATA 570/1/2 part 10).
2   Draft paper for proposed departmental meeting on Radio Australia (undated) August 1970 (*loc. cit.*).
3   *ibid.*
4   Script of RA news item, 21 June 1972 (DFATA 570/3/1 part 5).
5   R. D. Harris (director, ANIB, London) to I. Hamilton, director, ANIB, 21 June 1972 (*loc. cit.*).
6   Woolcott to P. B. Koch, 30 June 1972 (*loc. cit.*).
7   Waller to Woolcott, 30 June 1972 (*loc. cit.*).
8   Woolcott to Waller, 30 June 1972 (*loc. cit.*).
9   *ABC Annual Report,* 1972–73, p. 21.
10 Quoted in Koch to Duckmanton, 18 June 1975 (ABCDA).
11 Report by Homfray, 20 August 1974 (*loc. cit.*).
12 *ibid.*
13 D. McClelland to E. G. Whitlam, 26 April 1973 (DFATA 570/1/6 part 2).
14 Whitlam to McClelland, 22 May 1973 (*loc. cit.*).
15 Recorded interview with Homfray, Melbourne, 27 February 1988.
16 Position paper by DFA for meeting on 13 August 1973 (DFATA 570/1/6 part 2).
17 The department's acting secretary had the germ of an idea which, in a different form, was to emerge later as a recommendation of an independent inquiry into Radio Australia. He wondered if it were possible for the secretary of Foreign Affairs to be an ex-officio member of the Australian Broadcasting Commission. In this way, he said, the department's views on Radio Australia could be made known at the senior policy-making level: P. C. J. Curtis to W. Mayne-Wilson, 6 February 1974 (DFATA 570/1/6 part 2).
18 Foreign Affairs report on Radio Australia, April 1974, *loc. cit.*
19 *ibid.*
20 Review of Radio Australia, February 1975 (ABCDA).
21 ABC Staff Association comments on review of Radio Australia, August 1975 (*loc. cit.*).
22 *Radio Australia: independent inquiry report, December 1975,* parliamentary paper no. 97/1977 (Canberra: Commonwealth Government Printer, 1978), hereinafter referred to as the *Waller report,* pp. 21, 22.
23 Homfray to Waller inquiry, June 1975 (ABCDA).
24 Draft statement of basic objectives, 28 July 1975 (*loc. cit.*).
25 Summary of comments from overseas posts, undated submission to Waller inquiry, 1975 (*loc. cit.*).
26 Report of inter-departmental committee to consider the future of Radio Australia, 1977 (RAA).
27 Woolcott to DFA, 28 August 1975 (ABCDA).
28 ABC draft discussion paper on program policies, 28 July 1975 (*loc. cit.*).
29 *Waller report,* p. 10.
30 ABC draft discussion paper, *op. cit.*
31 Program policies approved by Waller, 11 August 1975 (*loc. cit.*).
32 A draft guideline referring specifically to coverage of 'the policies of both the Government and Opposition parties' was not included in the final four, but the reason may well have been that it would have been redundant.

33 Program policies approved by Waller, *op. cit.*

34 Koch to Duckmanton, 18 June 1975 (ABCDA).

35 'Role of Radio Australia', draft prepared by Koch, 18 June 1975 (*loc. cit.*).

36 H. C. Mott to Renouf, 29 July 1975 (DFATA 570/3/1 part 6).

37 Koch to Mott, 13 August 1975 (*loc. cit.*).

38 Semmler to Mott, 30 September 1975 (*loc. cit.*).

39 Duckmanton to N. W. Swancott (federal secretary, Australian Journalists' Association), 3 June 1981 (*loc. cit.*).

40 Koch to Shann, 9 September 1975 (ABCDA).

41 *Waller report*, p. 3; quoted by W. E. R. Hackett (acting chairman, ABC) to Robinson, 17 February 1976 (*loc. cit.*).

42 *Waller report*, p. 17.

43 Press release by Robinson, 28 January 1977 (*loc. cit.*).

44 Postal and Telecommunications Department *Australian Broadcasting: a report on the structure of the Australian broadcasting system and associated matters* (F. J. Green, secretary, September 1976) (Canberra: AGPS, 1976), p. 135.

45 Koch to Semmler, 29 October 1976 (ABCDA).

46 Minutes of inter-departmental meeting, 5 December 1976 (*loc. cit.*).

47 Press release by Robinson, *op. cit.*

48 *Commonwealth Parliamentary Debates*, H. of R., vol. 102, p. 3027 (1 December 1976).

49 Cabinet decision no. 2978, May 1977 (*loc. cit.*).

50 P. I. McCready to T. D. Wilson, 12 August 1977 (DFATA 570/3/1 part 7).

51 D. W. Evans to McCready *et al.*, 19 June 1978 (*loc. cit.*).

52 McCready to D. W. Evans, 26 June 1978 (*loc. cit.*).

53 Minutes of Radio Australia board of management, 8 February 1978 (ABCDA).

54 Quoted in Koch to Duckmanton, 21 January 1978 (*loc. cit.*).

55 A. S. Peacock to A. A. Staley, 20 February 1978 (*loc. cit.*).

56 A. S. Peacock to J. W. Howard, 3 May 1978 (*loc. cit.*).

57 *Australia and the Third World: Report of Committee on Australia's Relations with the Third World* (Canberra: AGPS, 1979) p. 182.

58 Report to commission by assistant general manager (radio), 11 May 1979 (ABCDA).

59 'Radio Australia', confidential paper by DFA, April 1974 (DFATA 570/1/2, part 2), p. 12.

60 *Age Green Guide*, 13 March 1980, p. 1.

61 DFA, submission to Committee of Review of the Australian Broadcasting Commission (hereinafter, Dix committee), April 1980 (RAA).

62 Dix committee, *The ABC in Review: National Broadcasting in the 1980s* (Canberra: AGPS, 1981), p. 421.

63 *ibid.*, pp. 431–2.

64 See chapter 3.

65 *Radio Australia Review* (Sydney: ABC, 1989) (hereinafter, *Revill review*), p. 8.

66 Quoted in P. L. Barnett to K. C. Mackriell, 25 February 1981 (ABCDA).

67 Minutes of commission meeting, 13 February 1981 (*loc. cit.*).

68 *Age*, 1 April 1981, p. 1.

69 *Herald*, 1 April 1981, p. 15.

70 *Sun News-Pictorial*, 2 April 1981, p. 25.

71   *ibid.*
72   R. E. Hodge to P. L. Barnett, 20 November 1981 (RAA).
73   Hodge to staff, 13 August 1983 (*loc. cit.*).
74   Hodge to P. L. Barnett, 13 August 1983 (*loc. cit.*).
75   *Commonwealth statutes supplement 1974–1985* (Sydney: Law Book Company, 1986), p. 132.
76   *Revill review*, p. 8.
77   Telephone interview with J. B. Campbell, 13 July 1993.
78   DFAT, submission to *Revill review*, pp. 2–3.
79   *ibid.*, p. 3.
80   *ibid.*, p. 7.
81   Gareth Evans and Bruce Grant, *Australia's Foreign Relations in the World of the 1990s* (Melbourne: Melbourne University Press, 1991), p. 69.
82   Recorded interview with Broinowski, Melbourne, 31 October 1991.
83   David Hill, 'AM', 22 January 1991.
84   *Australian*, 24 January 1991, p. 1.
85   *Age*, 12 January 1991, p. 5.
86   *ibid.*
87   Recorded interview with G. W. Heriot, Melbourne, 11 November 1991.
88   Bruce Donald, 'Legal restrictions and government pressures on reporting the Gulf war', paper delivered to Media and Communications Law Interest Group, University of Melbourne Law School, 21 March 1991.
89   Recorded interview with Broinowski, *op. cit.*
90   *ibid.*
91   *ibid.*
92   Recorded interview with Heriot, *op. cit.*
93   Donald, *op. cit.*

CHAPTER 8

1   Literally 'the Indonesian language'. The word *bahasa* alone means simply 'language'.
2   Stokes to Ball, 18 October 1943 (AA MP271 W494).
3   A. W. Dibley to deputy-director of security services, 30 August 1944; reply to Dibley, 20 September 1944 (AA MP272/3 C1).
4   Dibley to deputy-director of security, 14 February 1945; reply to Dibley, 7 March 1945 (*loc. cit.*).
5   Script prepared by Ball, 7 March 1942 (AA MP272/3 31/9/9).
6   Script prepared in Dutch, 11 March 1942 (*loc. cit.*).
7   Report by J. E. van Hoogstraten, 23 March 1942 (*loc. cit.*).
8   Ball to H. V. Quispel, 11 September 1942 (AA MP272/3 I-1A).
9   Recorded interview with Horne, *op. cit.*
10   Draft political warfare regional directive, most secret report from J. de La Valette, Allied Political Warfare Committee, Canberra, to E. T. Nash, British Overseas Press Service, New York, 19 November 1942 (AA MP272/3 I-9).
11   Most secret memo Dibley to A. Lodewyckx, 20 January 1943 (AA MP272/3 I-1A NEI—PW).
12   Quoted in Stokes to Ball, 6 August 1943 (AA MP272/3 I-1A).
13   Ball to Hood, 10 August 1943 (*loc. cit.*).

14 Hood to Ball, 12 August 1943 (*loc. cit.*).

15 Ball to Hood, 13 August 1943 (*loc. cit.*).

16 Action report no. 55, 16 May 1945 (*loc. cit.*).

17 Action report no. 56, 23 May 1945 (*loc. cit.*).

18 P. G. Edwards, *Prime Ministers and Diplomats: The Making of Australian Foreign Policy, 1901–49* (Melbourne: Oxford University Press, 1983), p. 182.

19 Recorded interview with Sawer, *op. cit.*

20 *Argus*, 16 November 1945, p. 1.

21 *Sun News-Pictorial*, 16 November 1945, p. 6.

22 *ibid.*, p. 4.

23 Recorded interview with Sawer, *op. cit.*

24 A. A. Calwell, *Be just and fear not* (Melbourne: Lloyd O'Neill, 1972), p. 117.

25 Submission by Koch to Waller inquiry (ABCDA).

26 Herbert Feith, *The Decline of Constitutional Democracy in Indonesia* (Ithaca, NY: Cornell University Press, 1962), p. 12.

27 *ibid.*, p. 176.

28 Recorded interview with Wood, *op. cit.*

29 See, e.g., Charles A. Fisher, *South-East Asia: A Social, Economic and Political Geography* (London: Methuen, 1964), p. 394; J. R. Verrier, 'Australia, Papua New Guinea and the West New Guinea Question 1949–1969', unpublished Ph.D. Thesis, department of politics, Monash University, 1976, p. 3.

30 R.T.D. [initials only on memo] to Goss, 17 December 1958 (DFATA 570/3/1 part 1).

31 Casey to Davidson, 19 November 1957 (*loc. cit.*).

32 E. R. Dawes to Davidson, 6 December 1957 (*loc. cit.*).

33 Quoted by Hutton, 2 January 1958 (DFATA 570/3/1 part 4).

34 Finlay to Tange, 15 January 1958 (ABCDA).

35 Confidential letter C. V. J. Mason to Moses, 31 March 1958 (*loc. cit.*).

36 *ibid.*

37 W. S. F. Hamilton to Moses, 10 April 1958 (*loc. cit.*).

38 K. L. Barry to Moses, 9 April 1958 (*loc. cit.*).

39 Moses to commission, 14 May 1958 (*loc. cit.*).

40 *ABC Annual Report*, 1957–58 (Sydney: ABC, 1958), p. 7.

41 'Indonesian Attitude to Radio Australia', secret report by Tange, 5 July 1962 (DFATA 570/3/1 part 2).

42 ABC representative, Singapore to Moses, 5 February 1962 (ABCDA).

43 *ibid.*

44 'Indonesian Attitude to Radio Australia', *op. cit.*

45 Record of conversation between Moses and Tange, 6 June 1962 (DFATA 570/1/2 part 7).

46 Six years later it was reported that he received fan mail of about 10,000 letters a year: 'Radio Australia's Broadcasts and Impact' (RAA), p. 10.

47 R. J. Percival (first secretary, Australian embassy, The Hague) to Tange, 5 July 1962 (ABCDA).

48 John M. Echols and Hassan Shadily, *An Indonesian–English Dictionary* (Ithaca, NY: Cornell University Press, 1961), *s.v.*

49 Moses to Davidson, 23 July 1962 (ABCDA).

50   Press statement by Davidson, 10 August 1962 (*loc. cit.*).

51   The JIB was a liaison section in the Defence Department that was supposed to coordinate intelligence from the armed services: Toohey and Pinwill, *op. cit.*, p. 81.

52   Moses to assistant general manager, programmes, 30 July 1962 (ABCDA).

53   Moses to Davidson, 5 July 1962 (*loc. cit.*).

54   The pre-recording of the Indonesian transmissions was discontinued in June 1967, on the recommendation of Radio Australia's then assistant director, John Hall: W. S. F. Hamilton to Homfray, 7 June 1967, RAA.

55   Dawes to Davidson, 16 July 1962 (ABCDA).

56   'Indonesian Attitude to Radio Australia', *op. cit.*

57   Hall, report on tour of Asia, 11 July 1962 (DFATA 570/3/1 part 2).

58   Report by P. L. Barnett to ABC, 22 November 1962 (ABCDA).

59   Report by Hall, 24 May 1963 (*loc. cit.*).

60   *ibid.*, 22 May 1963 (*loc. cit.*).

61   File note by Hall, 22 May 1963 (ABCDA).

62   Script of RA news item, 28 May 1963 (*loc. cit.*).

63   Report by Hall, 28 May 1963 (*loc. cit.*).

64   File note by Hall, 28 May 1963 (*loc. cit.*).

65   A. G. Morris, confidential report on trip to Indonesia, 7–22 March 1987, 24 March 1987.

66   Jockel, record of conversation with Hall, 29 May 1963 (DFATA 570/3/1 part 2).

67   A. A. Cane, report on tour of duty Indonesia, (undated) 1964 (RAA).

68   Shann to DEA, 5 October 1963 (DFATA 570/3/1 part 2).

69   DEA to Shann, 8 October 1963 (*loc. cit.*).

70   Truscott to Tange, 18 May 1964 (DFATA 570/1/2 part 8).

71   He said in 1989 that he had been associated with ASIS within a few months of his appointment to head Radio Australia, through his friendship with Major-General Walter Joseph (Bill) Cawthorne, the third head of the service, to whom he had worked as an intelligence officer in India during the war. Homfray said he had also been associated with Cawthorne 'professionally' from time to time while director of Radio Australia. But he said this 'professional' association had involved reporting on information gathered on his overseas visits, and had not affected the programs broadcast by Radio Australia: Recorded interview with Homfray, 19 November 1989, *op. cit.*

72   Telephone interview with Homfray, 19 November, 1989, *op. cit.*

73   Waller to Duckmanton, 6 February 1973 (DFATA 570/3/1 part 6).

74   Oakley to Hall, 5 October 1965 (ABCDA).

75   Quoted in W. S. F. Hamilton to Semmler, 8 October 1965 (*loc. cit.*).

76   Report by Hall, 20 October 1965 (*loc. cit.*).

77   Woolcott to Jockel, 12 October 1965 (*loc. cit.*).

78   Report by Hay (first assistant secretary, division 3), 19 November 1965 (DFATA 570/1/2 part 9).

79   'List of points for discussion with Radio Australia', 21 December 1965 (ABCDA).

80   Script of RA news item, 7 May 1969 (DFATA 570/3/1 part 4).

81   Jockel to DEA, 8 May 1969 (*loc. cit.*).

82   Rowland to Freeth, (undated) May 1969, (*loc. cit.*).

83   DEA to Jockel, 9 May 1969 (*loc. cit.*).
84   Handwritten note on letter Duckmanton to Hulme, 17 June 1969 (*loc. cit.*).
85   Confidential draft submission from Plimsoll to Freeth, (undated) July 1969 (*loc. cit.*).
86   L. R. McIntyre to Plimsoll, 23 July 1969 (*loc. cit.*).
87   Rowland to Tange, 15 May 1969 (*loc. cit.*).
88   His replacement was the author, who, whether or not he was 'a mature and experienced person', was more than ten years older.
89   Embassy to DEA, 9 January 1970; Trotter to Homfray, 27 January 1970 (*loc. cit.*).
90   Radio Australia liaison officer to Homfray, 19 December 1974 (RAA).

CHAPTER 9

 1   Recorded interview with Koch, Canberra, 27 April, 1988.
 2   Jack Waterford, *Documents on Australian Defence and Foreign Policy 1968–1975* (Hong Kong, J. R. Walsh and G. J. Munster, 1980) (withdrawn), p. 191.
 3   *ibid.*, p. 200.
 4   Evans and Grant, *op. cit.*, p. 188.
 5   *ibid.*, p. 217.
 6   Draft letter Mott to Woolcott (undated), 23–28 September 1975 (DFATA 570/3/1 part 6).
 7   *ibid.*
 8   Renouf to minister, 16 October 1975.
 9   Recorded interview with Koch, *op. cit.*
10   James Dunn, *Timor: A People Betrayed* (Brisbane: Jacaranda, 1983), p. 235.
11   M. P. F. Smith (director, parliamentary liaison and FOI sub-section, DFAT) to author, 29 March 1989. The department later told the commonwealth ombudsman that their disclosure would, or could reasonably be expected to, damage relations between Indonesia and Australia: C. B. Blesing, acting senior assistant ombudsman, to author, 6 July 1989.
12   Secret message from Renouf (secretary of DFA) to Minister for Foreign Affairs, 16 October 1975.
13   Koch to Woolcott, 13 April 1977 (RAA).
14   Koch, 'Report to Radio Australia board of advice on visit to Indonesia, 14 June to 1 July 1977' (*loc. cit.*).
15   Hodge to W. J. Beutler, 28 December 1978 (ABCDA).
16   Koch, 'Report to Radio Australia board of advice', *op. cit.*
17   Camilleri, *op. cit.*, 3rd edn. (Brisbane: Jacaranda Press, 1976) p. 97.
18   Koch, 'Report to Radio Australia board of advice', *op. cit.*
19   *ibid.*
20   Referred to in Woolcott to Koch, 12 August 1977 (RAA).
21   Woolcott to Koch, 12 August 1977, *op. cit.*
22   *Indonesian Observer*, 23 January 1978.
23   J. A. Hollinshead to R. G. Handley (ABC controller of news), 25 January 1978 (RAA).
24   J. P. Coman, 'Reporting Indonesia: an Australian Perspective', in Paul Tickell, ed., *The Indonesian Press: Its Past, Its People, Its Problems* (Melbourne: Monash University, 1987).

25 D. J. Hook (acting assistant director, news and public affairs, Radio Australia) to D. W. Evans, 21 August 1978 (DFATA 570/3/1 part 7).
26 Script of Beutler's report, 8 September 1978 (RAA).
27 Embassy to DFA, 14 November 1978 (*loc. cit*).
28 'Radio Australia and Relations with Indonesia', confidential report by D. W. Evans, (undated) May 1979(?) (DFATA 570/3/1 part 7).
29 Beutler to Hodge, 22 January 1979, *op. cit.*
30 T. K. Critchley to DFA, 5 April 1979 (DFATA 570/3/1 part 7).
31 Critchley to DFA, 10 April 1979 (*loc. cit*).
32 'Radio Australia', confidential report D. W. Evans to Critchley, 11 May 1979 (*loc. cit*).
33 Nuim Khaiyath, *The ABC, Radio Australia and Indonesia*, Radio Australia submission to foreign affairs sub-committee of the Joint Parliamentary Committee on Foreign Affairs, Defence and Trade, June 1992, p. 4.
34 Coman, *op. cit.*, p. 54.
35 D. W. Evans, 'Radio Australia and Relations with Indonesia', *op. cit.*
36 Draft memo Michael Thorley to Critchley, 21 May 1979—possibly not sent (DFATA 570/3/1 part 7).
37 Critchley to M. E. Lyon, 8 June 1979 (*loc. cit.*).
38 Script of Beutler's report, 17 April 1980 (RAA).
39 Beutler to Hollinshead, 5 May 1980 (*loc. cit.*).
40 'Analysis of the Indonesian Government's list of complaints against Radio Australia', Beutler to Hollinshead, 5 May 1980 (*loc. cit.*).
41 Draft replies for minister on RA and Indonesia, (undated) October (?), 1981 (*loc. cit.*).
42 *Commonwealth Parliamentary Debates*, H. of R., vol. 126, p. 119 (16 February 1982).
43 Hodge to sub-editors, 7 May 1980 (RAA).
44 Morris to G. J. Ward, 13 May 1980 (*loc. cit.*).
45 Ward to Mackriell, 15 May 1980 (*loc. cit.*).
46 *Far Eastern Economic Review*, 8 August 1980, p. 30.
47 Coman, *op. cit.*, p. 56.
48 J. D. Norgard to B. Millane, 23 September 1980 (RAA).
49 Script of ABC news item, 25 June 1980 (*loc. cit.*).
50 *Age*, 5 July 1980, p. 22.
51 DFA translation of editorial in *Suara Karya* of 15 July 1980 (RAA).
52 P. L. Barnett to Mackriell, 31 July 1980, *op. cit.*
53 *Far Eastern Economic Review*, 8 August 1980, pp. 31, 32.
54 Millane to P. L. Barnett, 4 August 1980 (RAA).
55 Millane to Norgard, 18 August 1980; Millane to I. McC. Sinclair, 25 May 1981 (*loc. cit.*).
56 Norgard to Millane, 23 September 1980 (*loc. cit.*).
57 Sinclair to Millane (undated), July 1981 (*loc. cit.*).
58 *Sydney Morning Herald*, 3 November 1980.
59 Australian Associated Press report, 9 September 1980.
60 Duckmanton to R. B. Lansdown (secretary, Department of Communications), 2 January 1981 (ABCDA).

61 Confidential note by P. G. F. Henderson, 27 November 1980 (*loc. cit.*).

62 Lansdown to Duckmanton, 16 December 1980 (*loc. cit.*).

63 Duckmanton to Lansdown, 2 January 1981 (*loc. cit.*).

64 Peter Henderson, 'Foreign affairs and the role of the media', *Australian Journalism Review*, vol. 9, nos 1 & 2, 1987, p. 51.

65 Minutes of commission meeting, 13 February 1981 (ABCDA).

66 Norgard to Sinclair, 20 February 1981 (RAA).

67 *Age*, 2 April 1981, p. 13.

68 Mackriell to commission, 24 January 1981 (ABCDA).

69 Transcript of report, 30 June 1981 (DFATA 570/3/1 part 8).

70 F. R. Dalrymple to DFA, 16 July 1981, *op. cit.*

71 Embassy to DFA (undated), October 1982 (RAA).

72 Hodge to P. L. Barnett, 16 November 1982 (*loc. cit.*).

73 Confidential report by I. H. Hutchens (assistant secretary, public affairs branch, DFAT), 18 March 1987 (DFATA 3034/10/5/5).

74 Morris, confidential report on Hill's visit to Indonesia, 11–12 March 1987, p. 3.

75 *ibid.*, p. 4.

76 Record of conversation prepared by Hutchens, 19 March 1987 (*loc. cit.*).

77 W. G. Hayden to S. F. Harris, 25 March 1987 (*loc. cit.*).

78 *Age*, 9 August 1988.

79 Submission by DFA to Dix committee, April 1980 (RAA).

CHAPTER 10

1 Recorded interview with Broinowski, Melbourne, 31 October 1991, *op. cit.*

2 Quoted in Khaiyath, *op. cit.*, p. 24.

3 Interview with Broinowski, 31 October 1991, *op. cit.*

4 Ian Macintosh, script for 'International Report', 11 November 1991.

5 Macintosh, voice report for 'International Report', 11 November 1991.

6 AAP report, 17 March 1994.

7 *Death of a Nation: The Timor Conspiracy*, a film by John Pilger and David Munro, 1994.

8 Herbert Feith, paper presented to the conference of the Asian Peace Research Association, Christchurch, New Zealand, 30 January–4 February 1992.

9 Interview with I. R. Macintosh, Jakarta, 10 September 1992.

10 Macintosh, fax to author, 15 July 1993.

11 *Inside Indonesia*, December 1991, p. 4.

12 *ibid.*, p. 5.

13 *ibid.*

14 Khaiyath, *op. cit.*, pp. 27–9.

15 Echols and Shadily, *op. cit.*, p. 374.

16 Script of RA news item in Indonesian, 15 November 1991.

17 *The ABC, Radio Australia and Indonesia*, p. 13.

18 Macintosh, fax to author, *op. cit.*

19 Macintosh, script of RA news item, 12 November 1991.

20 Evan Williams, script of RA news item, 13 November 1991.

21 Macintosh, voice report for 'International Report', 13 November 1991.

22 Script of RA news item, 13 November 1991.

23   AFP report, 13 November 1991.
24   *Inside Indonesia, op. cit.*, p. 3.
25   Macintosh, transcript of interview with Felicity Biggins, 14 November 1991.
26   Shirley Shackleton, transcript of interview with David Burgess, Melbourne, 14 November 1991.
27   José Ramos Horta, transcript of interview with Agnes Warren, London, 14 November 1991.
28   Macintosh, voice report from Dili, 14 November 1991.
29   Macintosh, voice report, 'International Report', 15 November 1991.
30   Script of RA news item, 15 November 1991.
31   Voice report by Matt Peacock, Washington, 15 November 1991.
32   Script of RA news item, 17 November 1991.
33   *ibid.*
34   *ibid.*, 17 November 1991.
35   Macintosh, voice report, 'International Report', 18 November 1991.
36   *ibid.*
37   Script of ABC radio news item, 18 November 1991.
38   *ibid.*
39   Script of RA news item, 18 November 1991.
40   *ibid.*, 19 November 1991.
41   Macintosh, fax to author, *op. cit.*
42   AAP report, 19 November 1991.
43   AFP report, 22 November 1991.
44   Macintosh, voice report, 'International Report', 20 November 1991.
45   Script of RA news item, 20 November 1991.
46   Macintosh, voice report, 'International Report', 21 November 1991.
47   Tony Hastings, Canberra, voice report, 'International Report', 22 November 1991.
48   Script of RA news item, 26 November 1991.
49   Matt Peacock, New York, voice report, 'International Report', 25 November 1991.
50   Macintosh, voice report, 'International Report', 28 November 1991.
51   Script of RA news item, 26 December 1993.
52   Macintosh, fax to author, 16 July 1993.
53   *ibid.*
54   Telephone interview with Macintosh, Jakarta, 10 September 1992.
55   Macintosh, fax to author, *op. cit.*
56   *Inside Indonesia*, June 1992, p. 9.
57   *Age*, 31 December 1991, p. 6.
58   Nuim Khaiyath, *op. cit.*, p. 25.
59   Telephone interview with Macintosh, 15 December 1993.
60   Recorded interview with Broinowski, Melbourne, 19 February 1992.
61   Tiffen, 'New Order Regime Style and the Australian Media—the Cultural Contributions to Political Conflict', revised version of paper presented to Asian Studies Association of Australia conference, Griffith University, 3 July 1990.
62   Quoted from Clifford Geertz, 'The Politics of Meaning', in Claire Holt (ed.), *Culture and Politics in Indonesia* (Ithaca: Cornell University Press, 1972), p. 331.
63   Jenkins says this was 'something which, I must admit, I had steered around for 17 years': David Jenkins, 'Indonesia: government attitudes towards the domestic and foreign media', *Australian Outlook*, vol. 40 no. 3, December 1986, p. 153.

64 *ibid.*, p. 159.
65 *ibid.*, p. 160.
66 He finally wrote the story when foreign editor of the *Sydney Morning Herald*, not during either of his two terms (1969–70 and 1976–80) as a correspondent in Jakarta.
67 Telephone interview with Macintosh, 10 November 1993.
68 Macintosh, fax to author, 15 July 1993.

CHAPTER 11

1 Inglis, *op. cit.*, p. 109.
2 Darling, *op. cit.*, p. 221.
3 Recorded interview with Darling, 13 December 1988, *op. cit.*
4 M. W. Richards (ABC radio news editor, Victoria), recorded statement at seminar, The Australian Media: Directions and Dilemmas, Melbourne, 9 August 1989.
5 Recorded interview with Sawer, 3 May 1988, *op. cit.*
6 Recorded interview with Wood, *op. cit.*
7 Kevin to Casey, 6 September 1956 (AA A1838 570/1/2, part 5).
8 Casey to Boyer, 10 September 1956 (ABCDA).
9 Toohey and Pinwill, *op. cit.*, p. 79.
10 Recorded interview with Homfray, Melbourne, 29 March 1989.
11 Recorded interview with Homfray, 27 February 1988, *op. cit.*
12 Inglis, *op. cit.*, p. 134.
13 Recorded interview with Homfray, 27 February 1988, *op. cit.*
14 Recorded interview with Wood, *op. cit.*
15 Recorded interview with Homfray, 27 February 1988, *op. cit.*
16 *ibid.*
17 Confidential memo Casey to Kevin, 23 August 1957 (DFATA 570/1/2 part 7).
18 Goss to Arnott, 20 August 1957 (DFATA 570/1/2 part 7).
19 Kevin to Casey, 21 August 1957 (*loc. cit.*).
20 Casey to Kevin, 23 August 1957 (*loc. cit.*).
21 Estimates, 1957–58, House of Representatives, 24 October 1957, pp. 1726–7.
22 Telephone interview with Homfray, 14 February 1992.
23 Brian Furlonger, *Then and Now: ABC Correspondents Abroad* (Sydney: ABC, 1981), p. 41.
24 'Radio Australia and the Department of Foreign Affairs', draft submission for Plimsoll (undated), July 1969 (DFATA 570/3/1 part 4).
25 Toohey and Pinwill, *op. cit.*, p. 106.
26 Miller to Moodie, 2 September 1970 (DFATA 570/1/2 part 10).
27 *Age*, 19 January 1990, p. 13.
28 *ibid.*
29 Recorded interview with Broinowski, 31 October 1991, *op. cit.*
30 David Hill, media release, 9 April 1992.
31 Telephone interview with D. S. White, 7 July 1993.
32 *Revill review*, p. 13.
33 *ABC Annual Report*, 1991–92, p. 19.
34 Telephone interview with White, 22 October 1993.
35 ABC media release, 7 February 1994.
36 W. H. King, director, JIB, to Homfray, 26 June 1959 (RAA).

37   A. McAdam, *Defence 2000*, vol. 1, issue 9, 13 December 1985, p. 4.
38   Coman to Ward (acting controller Radio Australia), (undated) June 1981 (RAA).
39   Memo from Homfray to E. A. Whiteley (ABC manager, Victoria) 29 October 196(?) (ABCDA).
40   Jockel to Rowland, 14(?) May 1969 (DFATA 570/3/1 part 4).
41   Jockel to DEA, 14 May 1969 (*loc. cit.*).
42   Hutton to Rowland, 15 May 1969 (*loc. cit.*).
43   Quoted in Cumes to Hutton, 21 May 1969 (*loc. cit.*).
44   L. R. McIntyre to Plimsoll, 5 June 1969 (*loc. cit.*).
45   Homfray, submission to *Revill review*, (undated) 1988.
46   Quoted in Broinowski to Cumes, 8 January 1969 (DFATA 570/3/1 part 4).
47   Quoted in Broinowski to Hutton, 26 August 1969 (*loc. cit.*).
48   B. D. Hawkins to defence projects section, 30 October 1972 (DFATA 570/1/2 part 12).
49   Quoted in P. L. Barnett to Mackriell (undated), 1980 (RAA).
50   Hollinshead to Mackriell, 2 February 1983 *(loc. cit.)*.
51   Mackriell to Hollinshead, 16 February 1983 *(loc. cit.)*.
52   Script of RA news bulletins, 29 March 1985.
53   *ibid.*, 12, 13, 20 April 1986.
54   P. L. Barnett to S. L. Revill, May 1985 (RAA).
55   Script of RA news bulletin, 17 April 1986.
56   Boyer to Anthony, 6 June 1952 (AA CRS A1838 570/1/2 part 1).
57   Boyer to Moses, 3 July 1956, *loc. cit.*
58   Hawkins to Percival, 12 November 1971 (DFATA 570/1/2 part 12).
59   Working committee draft paper (undated), 1971 *(loc. cit.)*.
60   Report and recommendations to ministers, May 1972 (ABCDA).
61   Homfray to P. M. Smith (second secretary, Australian embassy, Rangoon), 12 June 1973 (RAA).
62   Notes of meeting, 13 August 1973 (DFATA 570/1/6 part 2).
63   'Radio Australia', DFA paper, 5 April 1974 (ABCDA).
64   *Waller report*, pp. 8–9.
65   Hodge to D. W. Evans, 6 April 1979 (RAA).
66   Hodge to D. W. Evans, 2 January 1980 *(loc. cit.)*.
67   K. L. Jennings to Henderson, 17 March 1983 (*loc. cit.*).
68   Jennings to Henderson, 17 March 1983 (*loc. cit.*).
69   The station at Brandon was subsequently built, and began operating in December 1989.
70   *Revill review*, p. 13.
71   Recorded interview with P. L. Barnett, Melbourne, 10 July 1989.
72   *Revill review, loc. cit.*
73   Interview with White, Melbourne, 13 April 1993.
74   *Revill review, op. cit.*, p. 15.
75   *ibid.*, p. 30.
76   Recorded interview with Woolcott, *op. cit.*
77   *ibid.*, p. 16.
78   Australian Broadcasting Corporation, *Fanfare*, March 1993, p. 21.
79   *ibid.*

80 Bernard Bumpus, 'International Broadcasting' (UNESCO: International Commission for the Study of Communication Problems, 1980), p. 13.

81 The Indonesian series, originally called 'English for You', was more pointedly renamed 'English from Australia' when the second series began in 1980.

82 J. B. Dudley to P. L. Barnett, 12 May 1982 (RAA).

83 Koch to Radio Australia board of advice, July 1977 (*loc. cit.*).

84 Minutes of commission meeting, 13–14 April 1955 (ABCDA).

85 Wood, confidential report on visit to Southeast Asia, *op. cit.*

86 Casey to Plimsoll, 15 May 1956 (AA A1838 570/1/2, part 5); K. L. Barry to Moses, 18 June 1956 (ABCDA).

87 Moses to acting director, Commonwealth Office of Education, 7 January 1958 (RAA).

88 Inaugural speech by Barwick, 6 October 1959 (*loc. cit.*).

89 Casey, record of conversation with Homfray, 1 December 1959 (DFATA 570/1/2 part 7).

90 'Indonesian attitude to Radio Australia', report by Tange, 5 July 1962. (DFATA 570/3/1 part 2).

91 'Radio Australia Indonesian Service: English from Australia', 2 September 1982 (ABCDA).

92 Recorded interview with Coman, Melbourne, 30 May 1988.

93 'Figures on English Language Lessons', 1 July 1968 (ABCDA).

94 N.-H. Hung to Hodge (undated), 1986. The story-line was about an Australian film team visiting South Vietnam which became mixed up with drug traffickers. (Telephone interview with Hung, 19 June 1989.)

95 Koch to Mackriell, 2 March 1979 (RAA).

96 The program was launched by the prime minister, R. J. L. Hawke, on 4 March 1985, the day after the introduction of a new two-hour morning program in Standard Chinese: *ABC Annual Report*, 1984–85.

97 P. L. Barnett to T. Ross, DFA, 23 November 1982 (*loc. cit.*).

98 *Revill review*, p. 14.

99 White, fax to author, 29 July 1993.

100 In 1979–80, a program called 'Holiday Australia' attracted many inquiries from listeners in Asia, the Pacific and other parts of the world interested in holiday packages sampled by Radio Australia broadcasters: Radio Australia report to commission, 14 December 1979 (ABCDA).

101 A program about an Australian who developed a prefabricated solar-serviced house costing a million dollars resulted in the sale of two of them to buyers in the Middle East. An interview about another Australian invention, non-metallic brake blocks for railway rolling stock, resulted in a sale worth more than one million dollars to the Indian government's rail authority: K. Smith, letter to author (undated), 1986.

102 DEA to Casey, 22 July 1957 (DFATA 570/1/2 part 5).

103 Recorded interview with K. N. Glover, Melbourne, 15 February 1989.

CHAPTER 12

1 Recorded interview with Tange, *op. cit.*

2 Telephone interview with Tange, 13 July 1993.

3   'Malcolm Booker's weekly review of international affairs', *Canberra Times*, 22 November 1988.

4   Recorded interview with Booker, Canberra, 20 March 1989.

5   *ibid.*

6   Telephone interview with Booker, 12 July 1993.

7   W. B. Pritchett, letter to the editor, *Sydney Morning Herald*, 13 August 1988.

8   Pritchett, Channel 28, Melbourne, 19 September 1988.

9   Telephone interview with Pritchett, 12 July 1993.

10 Peter Hastings, *Sydney Morning Herald*, 15 August 1988, p. 12.

11 *Sydney Morning Herald*, 20 March 1993, p. 43.

12 Recorded interview with Broinowski, Melbourne, 23 January 1992.

13 Recorded interview with Woolcott, *op. cit.*

14 Shann to Acting Foreign Affairs Minister, 6 August 1973 (DFATA 570/1/6 part 2).

15 *Public Service Board/ABC Review of Radio Australia*, February 1975, p. 4.

16 Dix committee, *op. cit.*, p. 423.

17 Glyn Davis, *Breaking up the ABC* (Sydney: Allen and Unwin, 1988), p. 132.

18 *ibid.*, p. 138.

19 Interview with G.C. Davis, Brisbane, 27 October 1993.

20 *Revill review*, p. 34. The review committee was either not aware of the suggestion of Glyn Davis about Radio Australia in his 1988 book, *Breaking up the ABC*, or did not believe it was serious.

21 Telephone interview with White, 5 July 1993.

22 Dexter to Hood, 29 June 1955 (AA A1838 570/1/3, part 3).

23 Recorded interview with Goss, 3 May, 1988, *op.cit.*

24 Recorded interview with Homfray, 27 February 1988, *op. cit.*

25 Recorded interview with Booker, *op. cit.*

26 Draft by McDonald for Truscott, 21 January 1965 (DFATA 570/1/2 part 8).

27 Report of Meeting on Status of Radio Australia, *op. cit.*

28 Homfray, submission to *Revill review*, 21 March 1988, p.3.

29 Management Consultancy Division, Public Service Board, *Review of Radio Australia*, February 1975, p. 4.

30 ABC submission to Waller inquiry, 28 July 1975 (*loc. cit.*).

31 Dix committee, *op. cit.* p. 423.

32 *Revill review, op. cit.*, p. 35.

33 *ibid.*, pp. 35–6.

34 *Age, Saturday Extra*, 6 December 1986, p. 3.

35 Telephone interview with White, 7 July 1993.

36 *Revill review*, p. 25.

37 *ibid.*, p. 28.

38 Khaiyath, *op. cit.*, p. 7.

39 *ABC Corporate Plan, 1991–94*, p. 18.

40 *ABC Annual Report*, 1991–92 p. 3.

41 *ibid.*, 1992–93, p. 50.

42 *ibid.*, 1991–92, p. 51.

43 DFAT, submission to *Revill review*, May 1989, p. 2.

44 *Revill review*, p. 39.

45 *ibid.*, p. 1.

46 *Review of the BBC External Services* (London: BBC, 1984), p. 82.
47 Fax from Neil Deer, Controller Resources and Distribution, Radio Australia, 14 July 1993.
48 *Revill review,* p. 29.
49 Deer, *op. cit.*

CHAPTER 13

1   BBC news release, 4 April 1984.
2   Draft memo for director of Radio Australia, prepared by controller of news and current affairs, June 1985.
3   *Proposed ABC Television Service to the South Pacific,* Australian Broadcasting Corporation, January 1986.
4   *Revill review,* p. 32.
5   *ibid.,* pp. 32–3.
6   *ibid.,* p. 33.
7   Recorded interview with Broinowski, 19 February 1992, *op. cit.*
8   *ABC International Broadcasting,* ABC media release, 7 February 1994.
9   *Australian,* 31 March 1992, p. 1.
10 *Modern Times,* May 1992.
11 *Australia Television Satellite Coverage* (ABC handout, undated, 1993).
12 *The Australian* 'Business Asia', 9–22 March 1994, p. 12.
13 *ibid.*
14 *Sydney Morning Herald,* 15 September 1992.
15 *ibid,* 16 September 1992.
16 *Australian Financial Review,* 16 September 1992.
17 *ibid.,* 22 September 1992.
18 ABC Radio News, 4QR Brisbane, 3 May 1994, 7.45 a.m.
19 *External Funding, Advertising and Sponsorship,* ABC background paper, April 1993.
20 *ATVI,* typical weekly schedule, ABC, February 1993.
21 *ATVI Sponsorship Guidelines,* ABC, November 1992.
22 *ATVI* information sheet, February 1993.
23 Gareth Evans, 'Foreign Policy and Media', paper delivered at conference, Media Images of Asia/Australia: Cross Cultural Relations, University of Canberra, 27 November 1992.
24 *Programs for an Asian-Pacific audience,* undated ABC release.
25 John Ritchie, 'Editorial independence and the ABC's international satellite news service', unpublished Master of Business thesis, QUT.
26 Australia Television International, ABC background paper, April 1993.
27 Australia Television news bulletin, 18 May 1994.
28 John Ritchie, 'The ABC's Regional International News Service, AusTV News: An Impartial Provider of International News?', paper delivered to seminar, School of Media and Journalism, QUT, 15 October 1993.
29 Bruce Donald, letter to author, 5 July 1991.
30 Telephone interview with J. P. Pead, 18 June 1993.
31 *ABC Editorial Policies* (International Services) Australian Broadcasting Corporation, October 1992, p. 25.
32 *ibid.*

33 'The Guide', *The Sydney Morning Herald*, 17 May 1993, p. 5s.
34 Recorded interview with B. J. Abbott, 31 May 1993.
35 Telephone interview with P. Mirchandani, 26 June 1993.
36 Recorded telephone interview with Abbott, *op. cit.*
37 *ibid.*
38 *ibid.*
39 *Weekend Australian*, 19–20 June 1993, p. 24.
40 Telephone interview with Koch, 28 July 1993.
41 *ibid.*, 14 March 1994.
42 Recorded telephone interview with Abbott, *op. cit.*
43 Telephone interview with Mirchandani, 26 June 1993.
44 *ABC Annual Report*, 1992–93, p. 33.

Bibliography of Works Cited

ORAL SOURCES

Recorded Interviews
P. L. Barnett, Melbourne, 10 July 1989
H. D. Black, Sydney, 29 August 1988
M. R. Booker, Canberra, 20 March 1989
R. P. Broinowski, Melbourne, 21 October 1991, 23 January 1992, 19 February 1992
C. L. Burns, Melbourne, 19 February 1988
J. P. Coman, Melbourne, 30 May 1988
Z. Cowen, Melbourne, 17 August 1988
J. R. Darling, Melbourne, 13 December 1988
K. N. Glover, Melbourne, 15 February 1989
N. F. Goss, Melbourne, 3 May 1988
G. W. Heriot, Melbourne, 11 November 1991
P. W. R. Homfray, Melbourne, 27 February 1988, 29 March 1989
R. I. Horne, Melbourne, 15 May 1988
R. W. Neal, Melbourne, 7 February 1988
W. Pinwill, Sydney, 9 May 1989
G. S. Sawer, Guerilla Bay, NSW, 3 May 1988
G. I. Smith, Melbourne, 1 November 1989
A. H. Tange, Canberra, 27 December 1988
M. E. Teichmann, Melbourne, 11 April 1988
J. K. Waller, Canberra, 28 February 1989
D. Wilkie, Melbourne, 27 November 1988
C. R. Wood, Sydney, 6 July 1988
R. A. Woolcott, Canberra, 24 January 1992

Telephone Interviews
B. Abbott, 31 May 1993
M. R. Booker, 12 July 1993
J. B. Campbell, 13 July 1993

G. C. Davis, Brisbane, 27 October 1993
P. W. R. Homfray, 5 March 1988, 19 November 1989, 3 March 1990, 14 February 1992
N.-H. Hung, 19 June 1989
P. B. Koch, 28 July 1993, 7 October 1993, 14 March 1994
I. Macintosh (Jakarta), 10 September 1992
P. Mirchandani, 26 June 1993
J. Pead, 18 June 1993
W. B. Pritchett, 12 July 1993
A. H. Tange, 13 July 1993
D. S. White, 5 July 1993, 7 July 1993, 22 October 1993, 30 May 1994
C. R. Wood, 1 January 1989

Other Interviews
D. S. White, Melbourne, 13 April 1993

ARCHIVAL SOURCES

ABC Documentary Archives (ABCDA)

ABC Sound Archives

Australian Archives (AA)
AA A1838 570/1/2, parts 2, 3 & 5
AA CRS 570/1/2 part 3A
AA CRS A1838 570/1/2 parts 1, I-1A, I-5B, I-A NEI—PW, 2, 2A, 3, 3A, 4, 5, 5A
AA CRS A4906/XM1 vol. 9
AA MP 271 W494
AA MP 272/2 31/12/3
AA MP 272/3 (1939–1945)
AA MP 272/3 I-5A, I-5B, I-5C, 1-9, C1, C3
AA MP 272/3 31/9/9; AA MP 272/3 A2 parts 3, 4
AA MP 272/3 action reports
AA MP 272/3 secret files I-1A
AA MP 272/5 item 9
AA MP 727/3 series file 'The Truth of it Is'
AA SP 306/3 SG47

Department of Foreign Affairs and Trade Archives (DFATA)
3034/10/5/5; 570/1/2 part 9
570/1/2/1; 570/1/2 parts 1, 2, 3, 4, 4A, 5, 6, 6A, 7, 8, 8A, 9, 10, 11, 12
570/1/6 part 2
570/2/1 part 2
570/3/1 parts 1, 2, 3, 4, 5, 6, 7, 8

Radio Australia Archives (RAA)

OFFICIAL SOURCES

The ABC in Review: National Broadcasting in the 1980s, report by the committee of review of the Australian Broadcasting Commission (Dix committee), May 1981 (Canberra: AGPS, 1981)
Australia and the Third World: Report of Committee on Australia's Relations with the Third World (Canberra: AGPS, 1979)

Commonwealth Parliamentary Debates
Commonwealth statutes supplement 1974–1985 (Sydney: Law Book Company, 1986)
Dix committee, see *The ABC in Review*
Estimates, 1957–58, House of Representatives, 24 October 1957
Khaiyath, Nuim, *The ABC, Radio Australia and Indonesia*, Radio Australia submission to foreign affairs sub-comittee of the Joint Parliamentary Committee on Foreign Affairs, Defence and Trade, June 1992
Postal and Telecommunications Department, *Australian Broadcasting: a report on the structure of the Australian broadcasting system and associated matters* (F. J. Green, secretary), September 1976 (Canberra: AGPS, 1976)
Public Service Board/ABC Review of Radio Australia, February 1975
Radio Australia, Independent Inquiry Report (*Waller report*), December 1975, Parliamentary Paper No. 97/1977 (Canberra: Commonwealth Government Printer, 1978)
Review of the BBC External Services (London: BBC, 1984)
Revill review, see *Radio Australia Review* under 'ABC Publications'
Submission 7303, attachment B—future arrangements for Radio Australia; Cabinet minute no. 14006 (ER), expenses review committee, Canberra, 23 July 1990
Transcript of Public Service Arbitrator, determination 11/1959: evidence of W. S. F. Hamilton, 23 July 1958
Waller report, see *Radio Australia, Independent Inquiry Report*

ABC PUBLICATIONS

ABC Annual Reports, 1945–1993 (Sydney: ABC)
ABC Corporate Plan, 1991–94
ABC Editorial Policies (ABC, June 1993)
ABC Editorial Policies (International Services) ABC, October 1992
ABC, media releases
ATVI, typical weekly schedule, ABC, February 1993
ATVI, information sheets
ATVI Sponsorship Guidelines, ABC, November 1992
Australia Television, media kit, 1994
Australia Television International, media kit, 1993
Australia Television International, ABC background paper, April 1993
Australia Television program guide, May 1994
The Constant Voice: Radio Australia: 25th Anniversary 1939–1964 (Melbourne: Radio Australia, 1964)
The Constant Voice: Radio Australia: 30th Anniversary 1939–1969 (Melbourne: Radio Australia, 1969)
External Funding, Advertising and Sponsorship, ABC background paper, April 1993
Fanfare (ABC, Sydney)
'International Services Editorial Guidelines' (ABC, October 1992)
Proposed ABC Television Service to the South Pacific, ABC, January 1986
Radio Australia Review (*Revill review*) (Sydney: ABC, 1989)

PRINTED SOURCES

Books
Barnett, Harvey *Tale of the Scorpion* (Sydney: Allen & Unwin, 1988)
Bolton, G. C. *Dick Boyer: An Australian Humanist* (Canberra: ANU Press, 1967)

Calwell, A. A. *Be just and fear not* (Melbourne: Lloyd O'Neill, 1972)

Camilleri, J. A. *An Introduction to Australian Foreign Policy*, 3rd and 4th edns (Brisbane: Jacaranda Press, 1976, 1979)

Crowley, F. K. *Modern Australia in Documents: vol. 2, 1939–1970* (Melbourne: Wren, 1973)

Curran, Charles. *A Seamless Robe: Broadcasting—Philosophy and Practice* (London: Collins, 1979)

Curthoys, Ann and Merritt, John eds. *Better Dead Than Red*, 2 vols (Sydney: Allen and Unwin, 1986)

Darling, James. *Richly Rewarding* (Melbourne: Hill of Content, 1978)

Davis, Glyn. *Breaking up the ABC* (Sydney: Allen and Unwin, 1988)

Dunn, James. *Timor: A People Betrayed* (Brisbane: Jacaranda Press, 1983)

Echols, John M. and Shadily, Hassan. *An Indonesian-English Dictionary* (Ithaca, NY: Cornell University Press, 1961)

Edwards, P. G. *Prime Minister and Diplomats: The Making of Australian Foreign Policy, 1901–1949* (Melbourne, Oxford University Press, 1983)

Evans, Gareth, and Grant, Bruce. *Australia's Foreign Relations in the World of the 1990s* (Melbourne: Melbourne University Press, 1991)

Feith, Herbert. *The Decline of Constitutional Democracy in Indonesia* (Ithaca, NY: Cornell University Press, 1962)

Fisher, Charles A. *South-East Asia: A Social, Economic and Political Geography* (London: Methuen, 1964)

Furlonger, Brian. *Then and Now: ABC Correspondents Abroad* (Sydney: ABC, 1981)

Gordon, Harry. *Die Like the Carp! The Story of the Greatest Prison Escape Ever* (Moorebank, NSW: Corgi Books, 1978)

Hale, Julian. *Radio Power: Propaganda and International Broadcasting*, (London: Paul Elek, 1975)

Hasluck, Paul. *Mucking About* (Melbourne: Melbourne University Press, 1977)

Hilvert, John. *Blue Pencil Warriors: Censorship and Propaganda in World War II* (St Lucia: University of Queensland Press, 1984)

Hudson, W. J. *Casey* (Melbourne: Oxford University Press, 1986)

Inglis, K. S. *This is the ABC: The Australian Broadcasting Commission 1932–1983* (Melbourne: Melbourne University Press, 1983)

London, H. I. *Non-White Immigration and the 'White Australia' Policy* (Sydney: Sydney University Press 1970)

Long, Gavin. *The Six Years War: A Concise History of Australia in the 1939–45 War* (Canberra: Australian War Memorial and AGPS, 1973)

Meo, L. D. *Japan's Radio War on Australia, 1941–45* (Melbourne: Melbourne University Press, 1968)

Millar, T. B., ed. *The Diaries of R. G. Casey 1951–60* (London: Collins, 1972)

Moore, John Hammond. *Over-Sexed, Over-Paid and Over Here: Americans in Australia, 1941–45* (St Lucia: University of Queensland Press, 1981)

Potts, Daniel and Annette. *Yanks Down Under, 1941–45: The American Impact on Australia*, (Melbourne: Oxford University Press, 1985)

Renouf, Alan. *The Champagne Trail: Experiences of a Diplomat* (Melbourne: Sun Books, 1980)

Robertson, John, and McCarthy, John. *Australian War Strategy 1939–1945* (St Lucia: University of Queensland Press 1985)

Tickell, Paul, ed. *The Indonesian Press: Its Past, Its People, Its Problems* (Melbourne: Monash University, 1987)

Tiffen, Rodney. *News and Power* (Sydney: Allen and Unwin, 1989)

Toohey, Brian, and Pinwill, William. *Oyster: The Story of the Australian Secret Intelligence Service* (Melbourne: Heinemann, 1989)

Waterford, Jack. *Documents on Australian Defence and Foreign Policy 1968–1975* (Hong Kong: J. R. Walsh and G. J. Munster, 1980) (withdrawn)

Whitlam, Nicholas, and Stubbs, John. *Nest of Traitors: The Petrov Affair* (Brisbane: Jacaranda Press, 1974)

Who's Who in Australia, 1974–1992 (Melbourne: Herald and Weekly Times and Information Australia)

Woodburn-Kirby, S. *The War Against Japan, vol. 2* (London: Her Majesty's Stationery Office, 1958)

ARTICLES AND UNPUBLISHED PAPERS

Ball, W. Macmahon. 'Why Australia Should Object', in *Australia's Neighbours*, December 1956 (Melbourne: Australian Institute of International Affairs)

David Bowman. 'Can the ASIO Revolution Last?', *Australian Society*, November 1989

Bumpus, Bernard. 'International Broadcasting', (UNESCO: International Commission for the Study of Communication Problems, 1980)

Casey, R. G., Baron, unpublished diaries (National Library, Canberra), 12 October 1954.

Donald, Bruce. 'Legal restrictions and government pressures on reporting the Gulf war', paper delivered to Media and Communications Law Interest Group, University of Melbourne Law School, 21 March 1991

Evans, Gareth. 'Foreign Policy and Media', paper delivered at seminar, 'Media Images of Asia/Australia: Cross Cultural Relations',University of Canberra, 27 November 1992

Feith, Herbert. paper presented to the conference of the Asian Peace Research Association, Christchurch, New Zealand, 30 January–4 February 1992

Hamilton, W. S. F. 'The People and the Media', from transcript of seminar on 'The Australian News Media—Problems and Prospects', Adelaide, 3 March 1972

Henderson, Peter. 'Foreign affairs and the role of the media', *Australian Journalism Review*, vol. 9 nos 1 & 2, 1987

Jenkins, David. 'Indonesia: government attitudes towards the domestic and foreign media', *Australian Outlook*, vol. 40 no. 3, December 1986)

Kiernan, Colm 'Arthur A. Calwell's Clashes with the Australian Press, 1943–45', *Historical Journal* (University of Wollongong Historical Society), 2, no. 1 (March 1976)

Mytton, Graham, and Forrester, Carol. 'Audiences for International Radio Broadcasts', *European Journal of Communication* (vol. 3, no. 4, 1988)

Potts, Daniel and Annette. 'Australian Wartime Propaganda and Censorship', *Historical Studies*, vol. 21, no. 85 (October 1985)

Richards, M. W. (ABC radio news editor, Victoria), recorded statement at seminar 'the Australian Media: Directions and Dilemmas', Melbourne, 9 August 1989

Ritchie, John. 'The ABC's Regional International News Service, AusTV News: An Impartial Provider of International News?', Seminar, School of Media and Journalism, QUT, 15 October 1993

Ritchie, John. 'Editorial independence and the ABC's international satellite news service', unpublished Master of Business thesis, QUT

Tiffen, Rodney. 'New Order Regime Style and the Australian Media—the Cultural Contributions to Political Conflict', revised version of paper presented to Asian Studies Association of Australia conference, Griffith University, 3 July 1990

Verrier, J. R. 'Australia, Papua New Guinea and the West New Guinea Question 1949–1969', unpublished PhD Thesis, department of politics, Monash University, 1976

JOURNALS AND NEWS SOURCES

ABC radio news
ABC radio news and current affairs scripts
Age
Argus
Australia Television news bulletins (videotaped)
Australia Television media releases
Australian
Australian Financial Review
BBC news releases
Bulletin
Canberra Times
Current Notes
Defence 2000
Far Eastern Economic Review
Herald
Indonesian Observer
Inside Indonesia
Modern Times
Radio Australia news and current affairs scripts
SBS Television, Sydney
Scan (ABC, Sydney)
Sun News-Pictorial
Sydney Morning Herald
Times
Weekend Australian

Letters and faxes

Blesing, C. B., 6 July 1989
Deer, N., 14 July 1993
Dixon, W. J., 11 January 1989
Donald, B., 5 July 1993
Hasluck, P. M. C., 28 July 1989
Macintosh, I. R., 15 July 1993, 16 July 1993
Mackie, J. A. C., 2 November 1993
Smith, K., 1986
Smith, M. P. F., 29 March 1989
Stone, D. J. C., 8 August 1994
White, D. S., 29 July 1993

Index